White
with the Red Hair

SORATA AKIDUKI

9

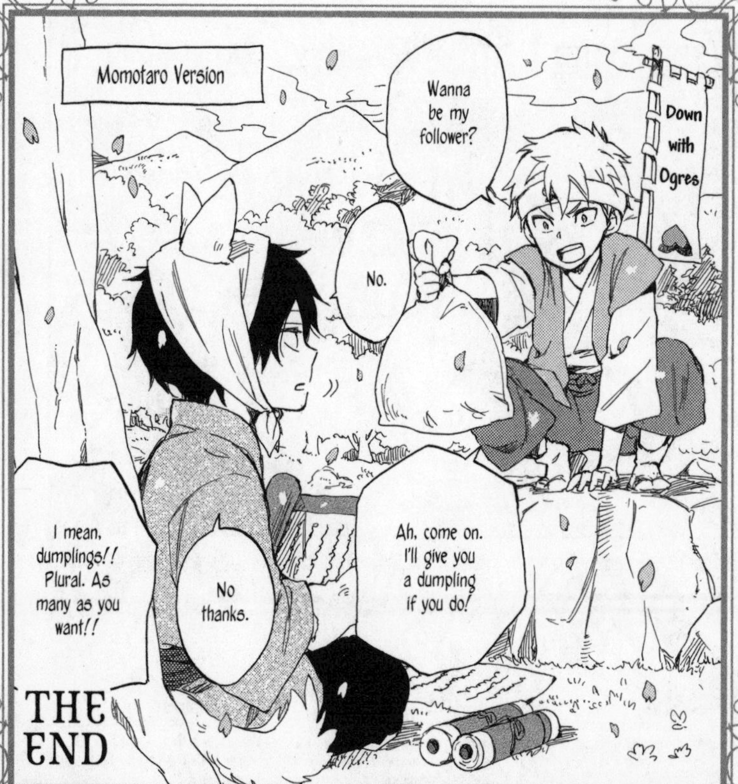
Momotaro Version
Down with Ogres
Wanna be my follower?
No.
Ah, come on. I'll give you a dumpling if you do!
No thanks.
I mean, dumplings!! Plural. As many as you want!!
THE END

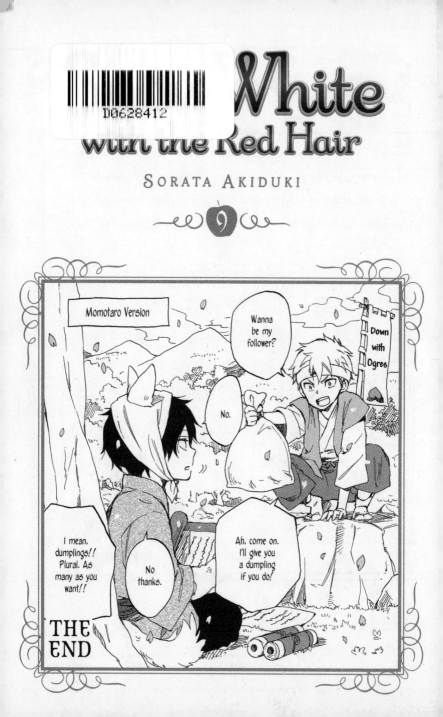

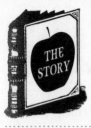

THE STORY

Shirayuki was born with beautiful hair as red as apples, but when her rare hair earns her unwanted attention from the notorious prince Raj, she's forced to flee her home. A young man named Zen helps her in the forest of the neighboring kingdom, Clarines, and it turns out he is that kingdom's second prince! Shirayuki decides to accompany Zen back to Wistal, the capital city of Clarines.

Shirayuki has met all manner of people since becoming a court herbalist, and her relationship with Zen continues to grow, as the two have finally made their feelings known to each other.

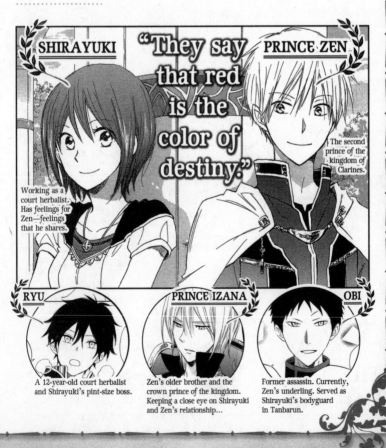

PRINCE ZEN
The second prince of the kingdom of Clarines.
"They say that red is the color of destiny."
SHIRAYUKI
Working as a court herbalist. Has feelings for Zen—feelings that he shares.
OBI
Former assassin. Currently, Zen's underling. Served as Shirayuki's bodyguard in Tanbarun.
PRINCE IZANA
Zen's older brother and the crown prince of the kingdom. Keeping a close eye on Shirayuki and Zen's relationship...
RYU
A 12-year-old court herbalist and Shirayuki's pint-size boss.

When the snowy checkpoint city of Lilias stops sending herbalism reports, Shirayuki and her boss, Ryu, are sent up north to investigate.

In the City of Academics, they meet a pair of herbalists named Shidan and Suzu, as well as a plant collector named Yuzuri. These prove to be exciting encounters for Shirayuki and Ryu.

But Shirayuki and Ryu soon discover it was actually the crown prince, Izana, who summoned them to Lilias! He's staying in the city too, though he remains incognito when out and about with Shirayuki and Ryu.

When a young boy suddenly collapses before their eyes, it's up to Shirayuki and Ryu to save him. Meanwhile, Zen and his aides are also heading north!

REALLY TAKES YOUR BREATH AWAY.
MHM.

IS THERE SOMETHING YOU NEED?
FROM THE HUMBLE HERBALIST ASSISTANT LOUEN?
!

PLEASE.
YOU GOTTA HELP HIM.

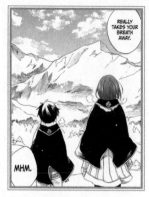

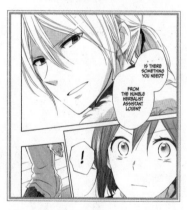

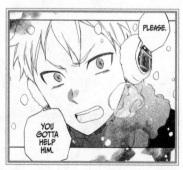

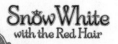

Snow White with the Red Hair

VOLUME 9
TABLE *of* CONTENTS

Snow White with the Red Hair

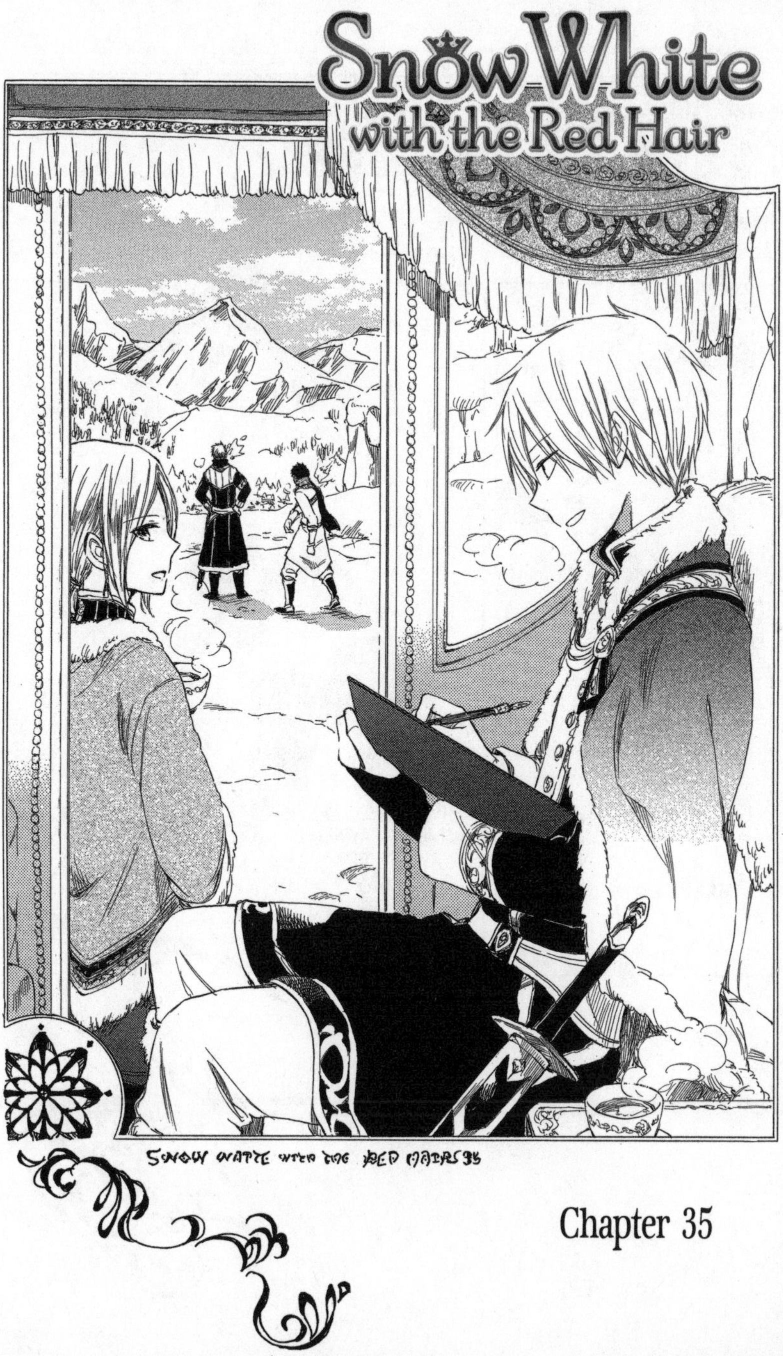

SNOW WHITE WITH THE RED HAIR 35

Chapter 35

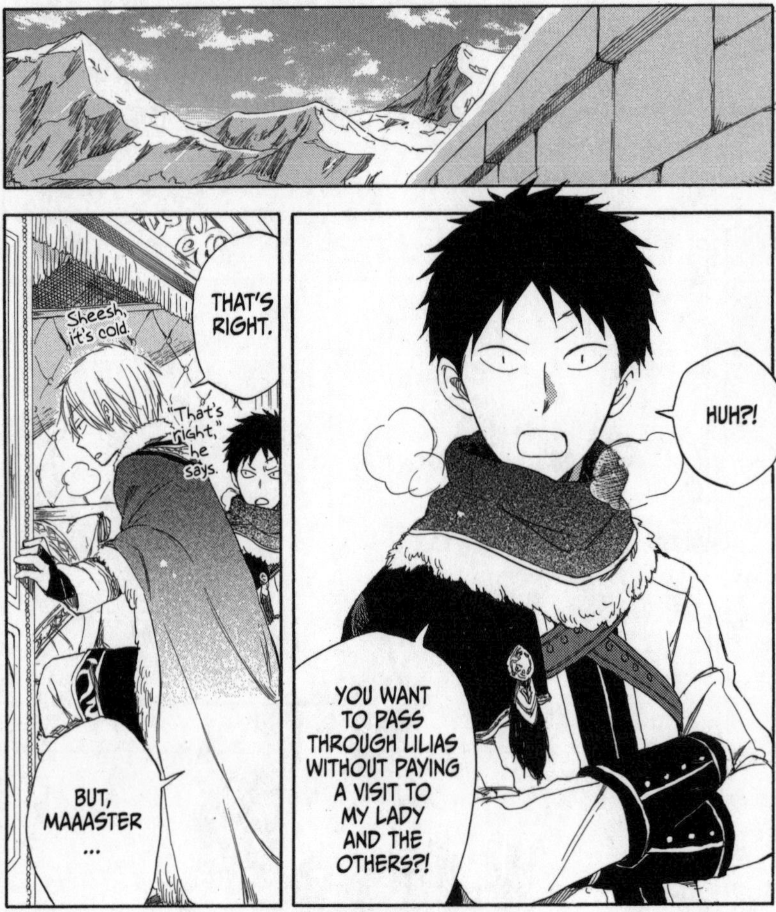
HUH?!
YOU WANT TO PASS THROUGH LILIAS WITHOUT PAYING A VISIT TO MY LADY AND THE OTHERS?!
THAT'S RIGHT.
Sheesh, it's cold.
"That's right," he says.
BUT, MAAASTER...

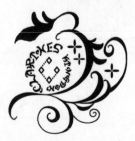

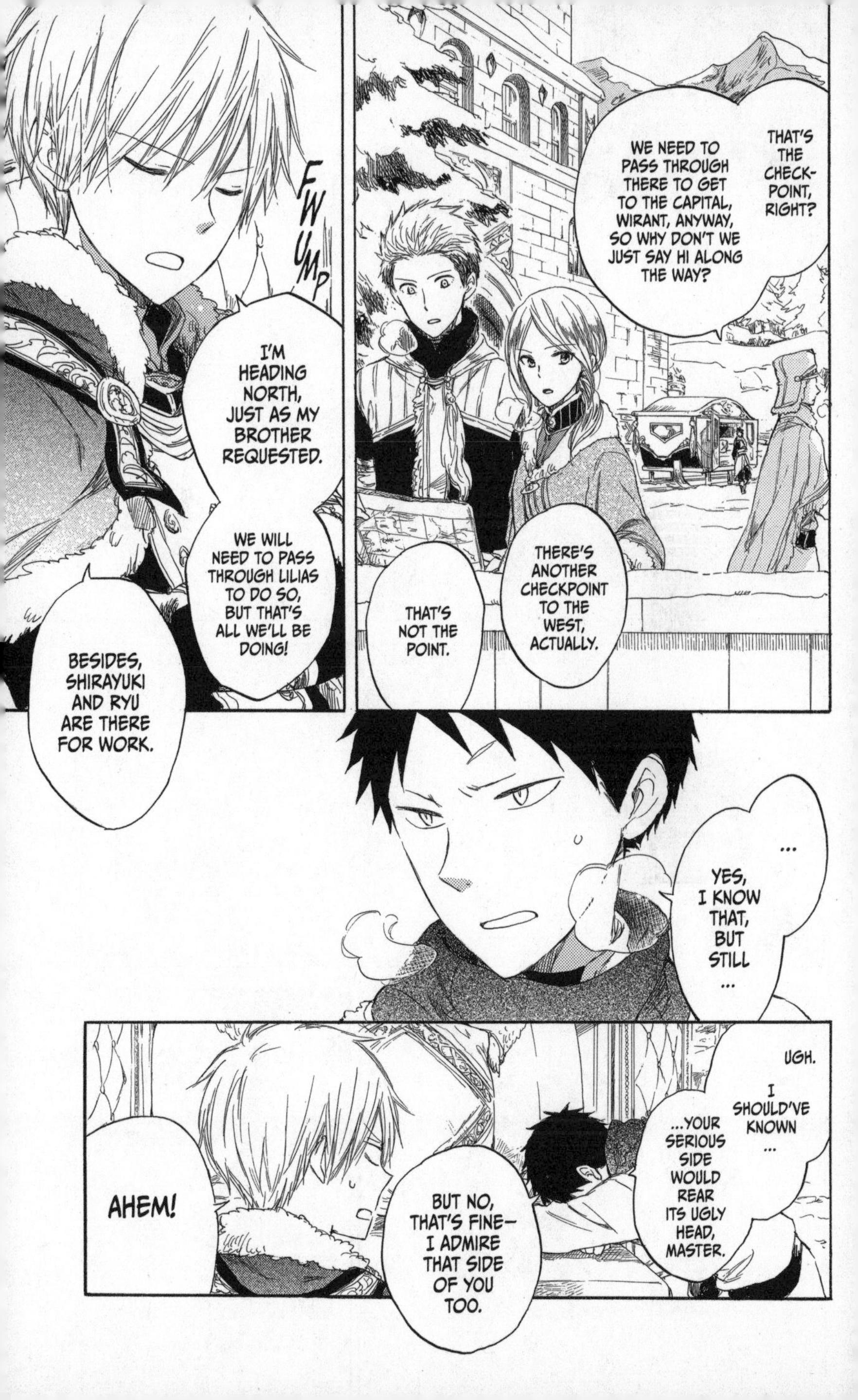
THAT'S THE CHECK-POINT, RIGHT?
WE NEED TO PASS THROUGH THERE TO GET TO THE CAPITAL, WIRANT, ANYWAY, SO WHY DON'T WE JUST SAY HI ALONG THE WAY?
THERE'S ANOTHER CHECKPOINT TO THE WEST, ACTUALLY.
THAT'S NOT THE POINT.
FWUMP
I'M HEADING NORTH, JUST AS MY BROTHER REQUESTED.
WE WILL NEED TO PASS THROUGH LILIAS TO DO SO, BUT THAT'S ALL WE'LL BE DOING!
BESIDES, SHIRAYUKI AND RYU ARE THERE FOR WORK.
... YES, I KNOW THAT, BUT STILL ...
UGH.
I SHOULD'VE KNOWN ...
...YOUR SERIOUS SIDE WOULD REAR ITS UGLY HEAD, MASTER.
BUT NO, THAT'S FINE— I ADMIRE THAT SIDE OF YOU TOO.
AHEM!

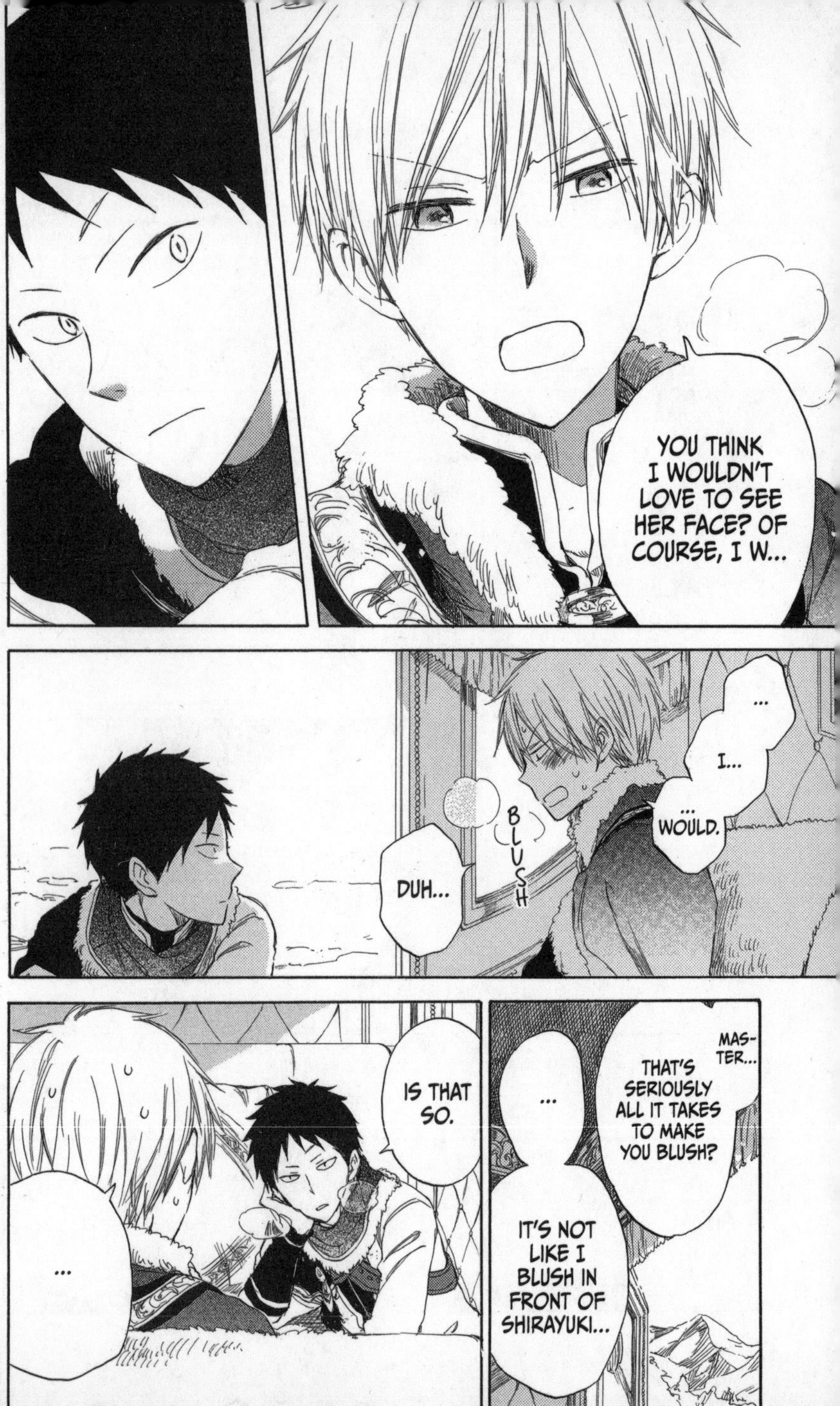
YOU THINK I WOULDN'T LOVE TO SEE HER FACE? OF COURSE, I W...
...
I...
... WOULD.
BLUSH
DUH...
MAS-TER...
THAT'S SERIOUSLY ALL IT TAKES TO MAKE YOU BLUSH?
...
IT'S NOT LIKE I BLUSH IN FRONT OF SHIRAYUKI...
IS THAT SO.
...

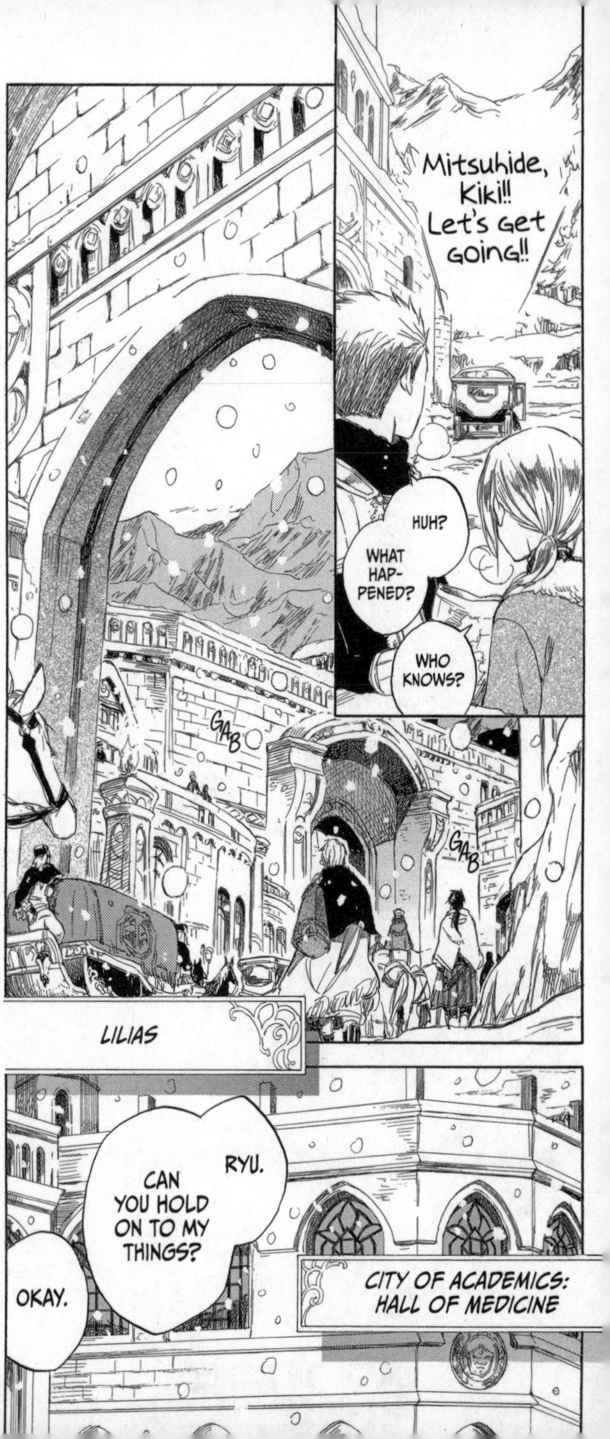
Mitsuhide, Kiki!! Let's get going!!
HUH?
WHAT HAPPENED?
WHO KNOWS?
GAB
GAB
LILIAS
CITY OF ACADEMICS: HALL OF MEDICINE
RYU.
CAN YOU HOLD ON TO MY THINGS?
OKAY.

GREETINGS

Hello! Thank you for purchasing volume 9 of Snow White with the Red Hair!

I'm Sorata Akiduki.

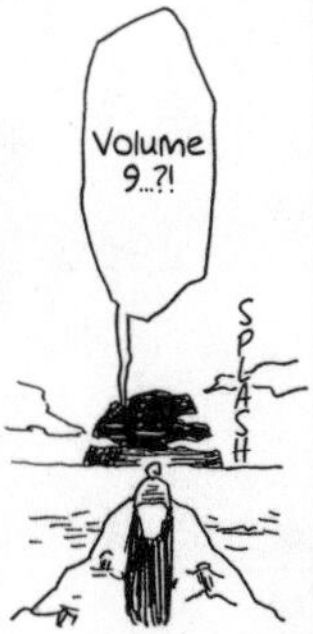
Volume 9...?!
SPLASH

I'm so grateful to all of you!

Now, let's jump right into volume 9.

BABAM

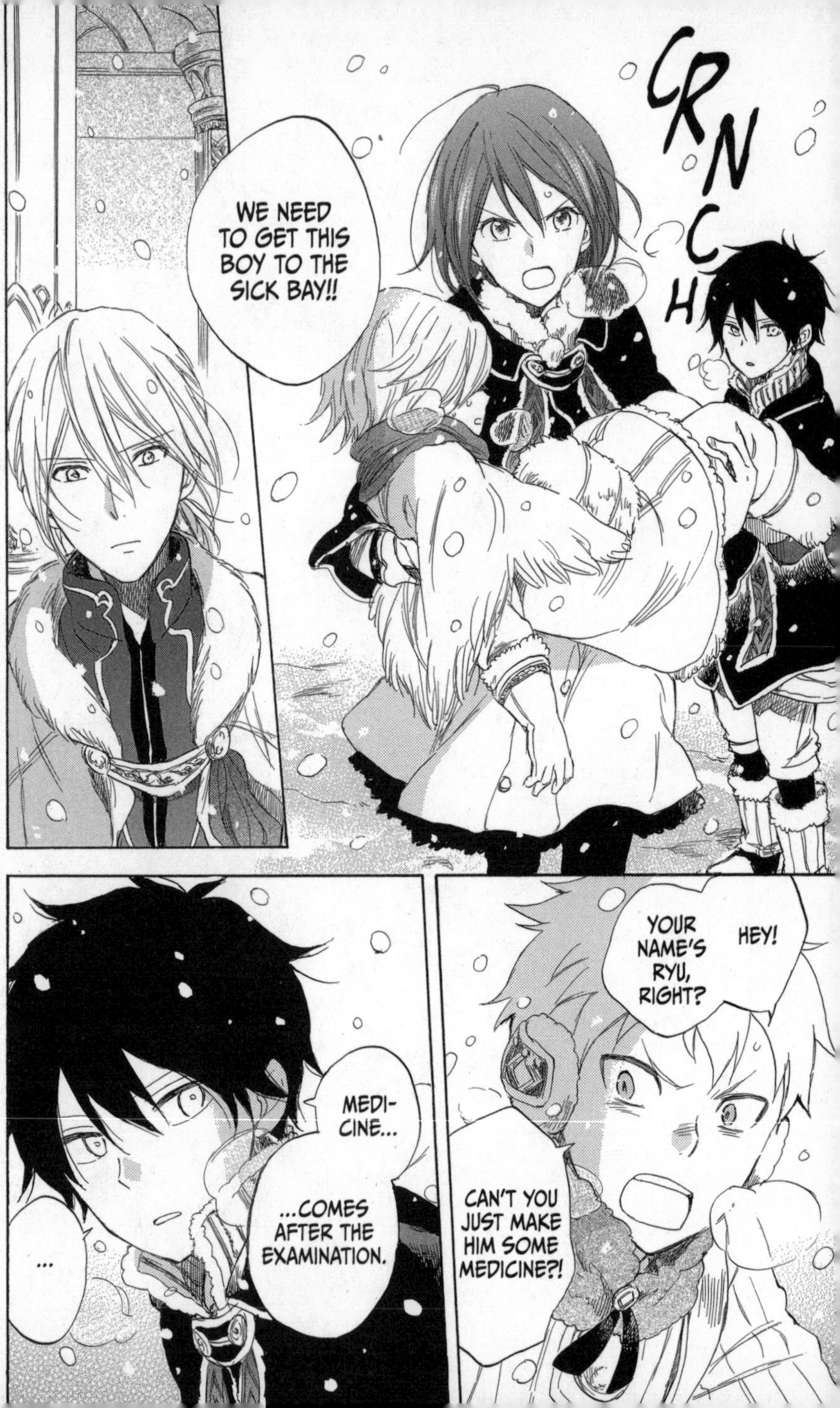
CRNCH
WE NEED TO GET THIS BOY TO THE SICK BAY!!
HEY!
YOUR NAME'S RYU, RIGHT?
CAN'T YOU JUST MAKE HIM SOME MEDICINE?!
MEDI-CINE...
...COMES AFTER THE EXAMINATION.
...

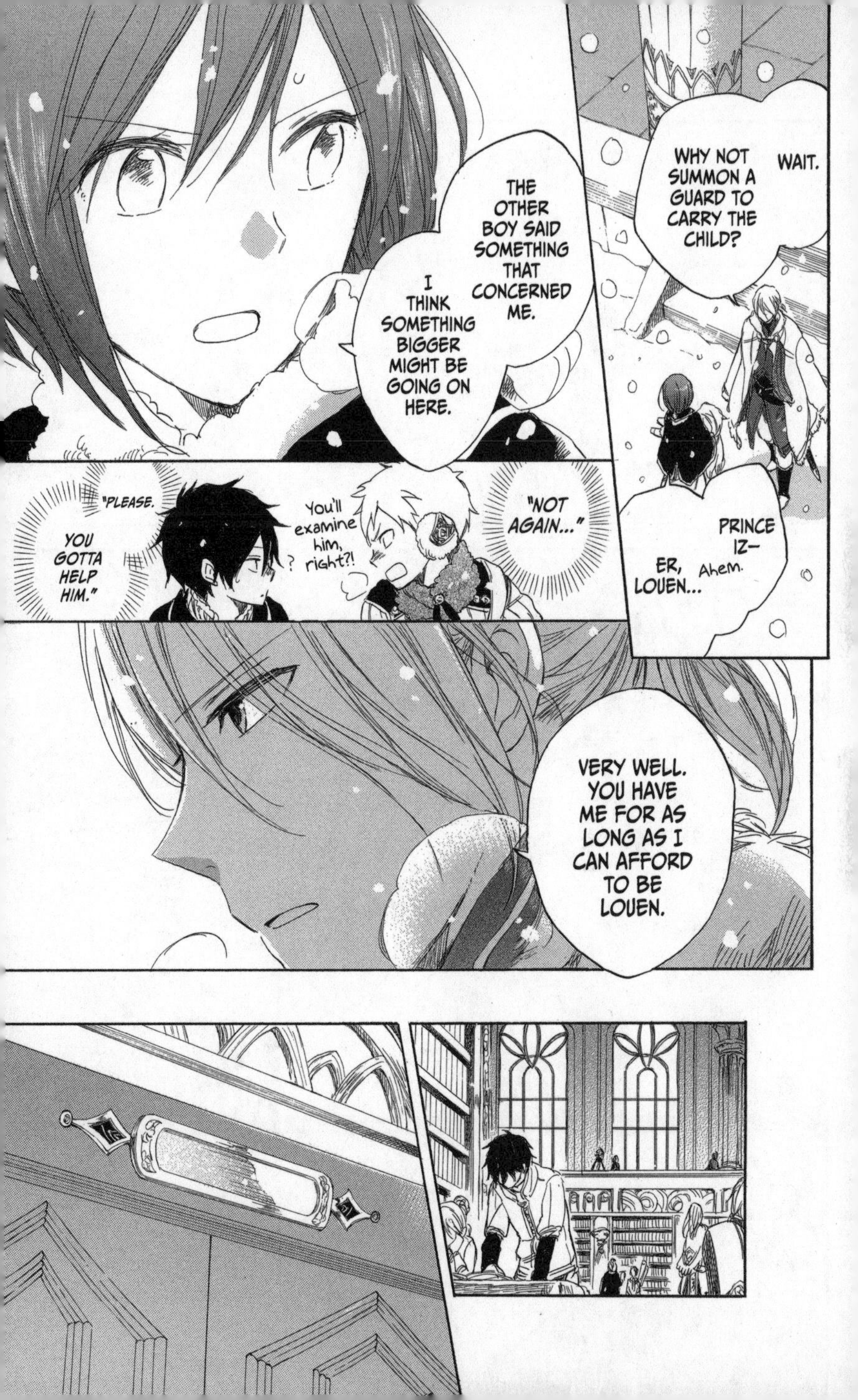
WAIT.
WHY NOT SUMMON A GUARD TO CARRY THE CHILD?
PRINCE IZ— ER, LOUEN...
Ahem.
THE OTHER BOY SAID SOMETHING THAT CONCERNED ME.
I THINK SOMETHING BIGGER MIGHT BE GOING ON HERE.
"NOT AGAIN..."
You'll examine him, right?!
"PLEASE. YOU GOTTA HELP HIM."
VERY WELL. YOU HAVE ME FOR AS LONG AS I CAN AFFORD TO BE LOUEN.

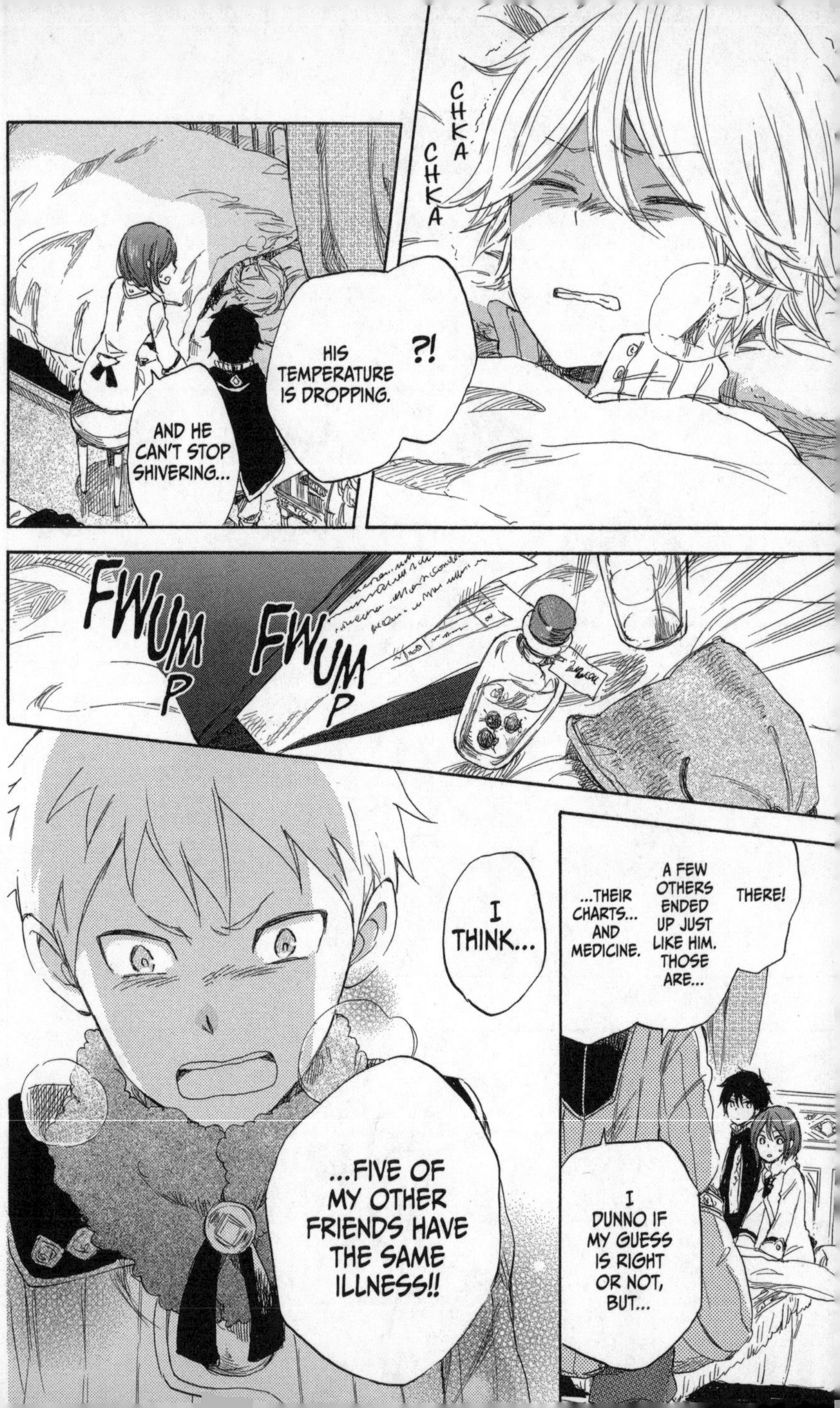
CHKA CHKA
CHKA CHKA
?!
HIS TEMPERATURE IS DROPPING.
AND HE CAN'T STOP SHIVERING...
FWUMP
FWUMP
THERE!
A FEW OTHERS ENDED UP JUST LIKE HIM. THOSE ARE...
...THEIR CHARTS... AND MEDICINE.
I DUNNO IF MY GUESS IS RIGHT OR NOT, BUT...
I THINK...
...FIVE OF MY OTHER FRIENDS HAVE THE SAME ILLNESS!!

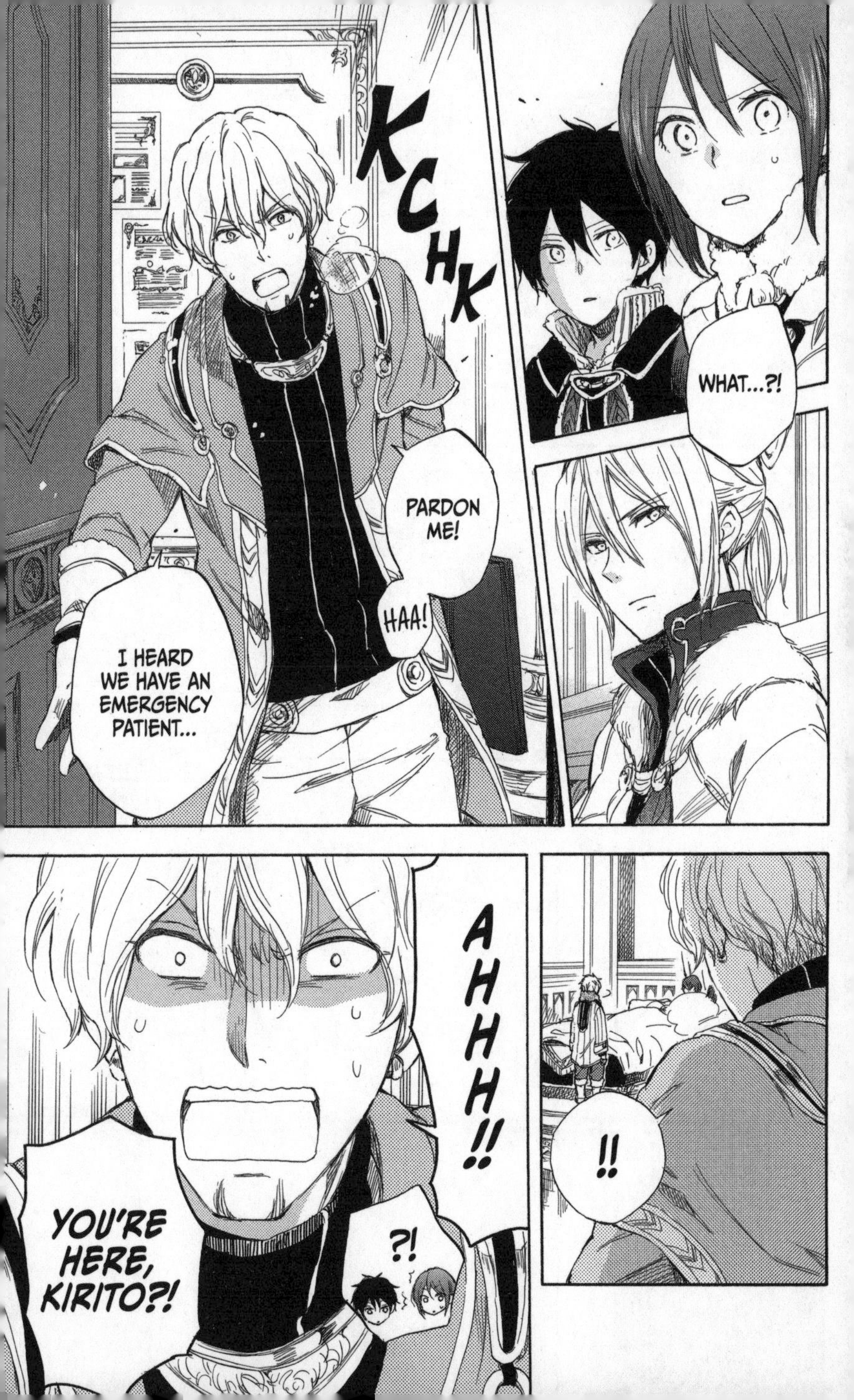
WHAT...?!
KCHK
PARDON ME!
HAA!
I HEARD WE HAVE AN EMERGENCY PATIENT...
!!
AHHHH!!
YOU'RE HERE, KIRITO?!
?!

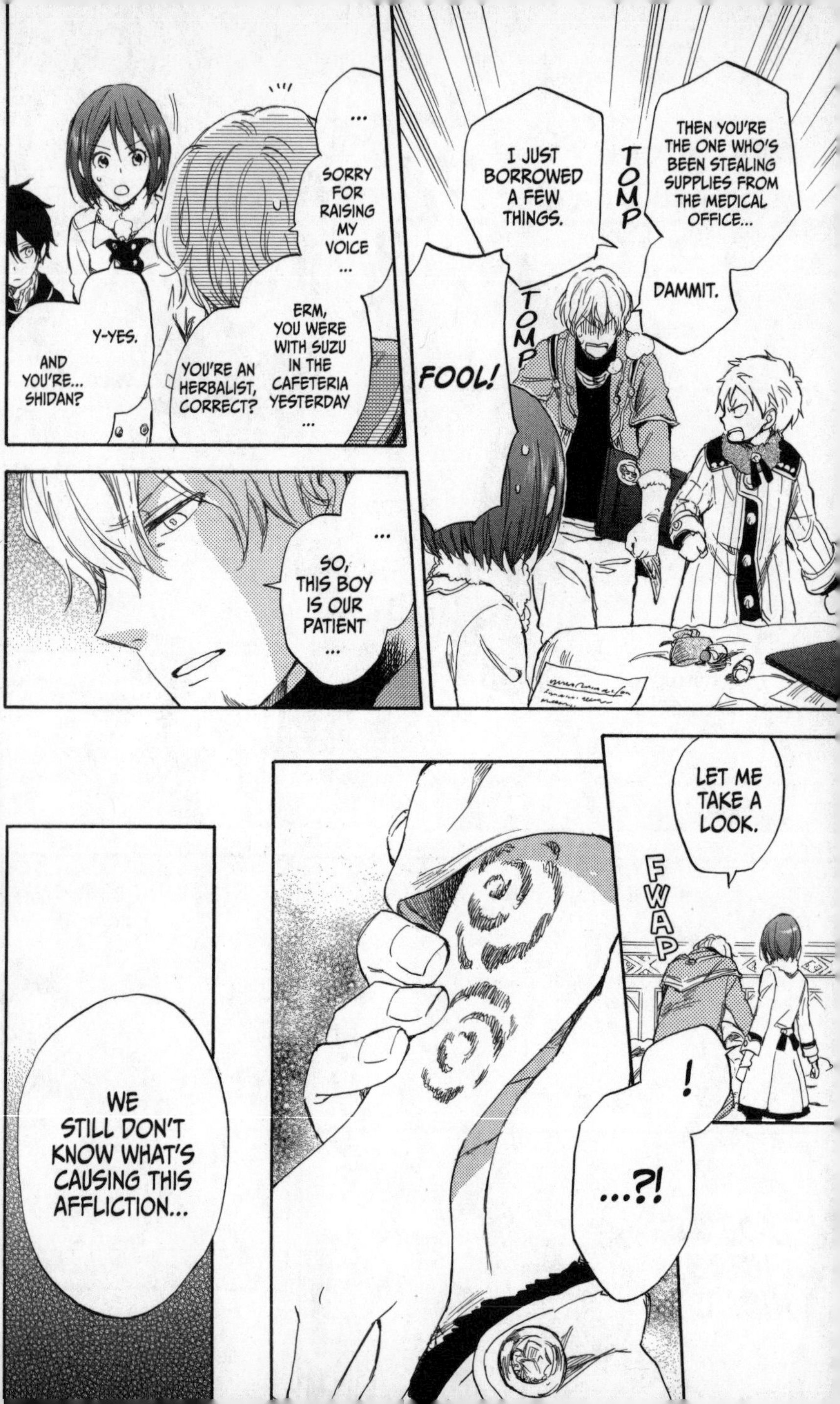

THEN YOU'RE THE ONE WHO'S BEEN STEALING SUPPLIES FROM THE MEDICAL OFFICE...
TOMP
I JUST BORROWED A FEW THINGS.
DAMMIT.
TOMP
FOOL!
...
SORRY FOR RAISING MY VOICE ...
ERM, YOU WERE WITH SUZU IN THE CAFETERIA YESTERDAY ...
YOU'RE AN HERBALIST, CORRECT?
Y-YES.
AND YOU'RE... SHIDAN?
...
SO, THIS BOY IS OUR PATIENT ...
LET ME TAKE A LOOK.
FWAP
!
...?!
WE STILL DON'T KNOW WHAT'S CAUSING THIS AFFLICTION...

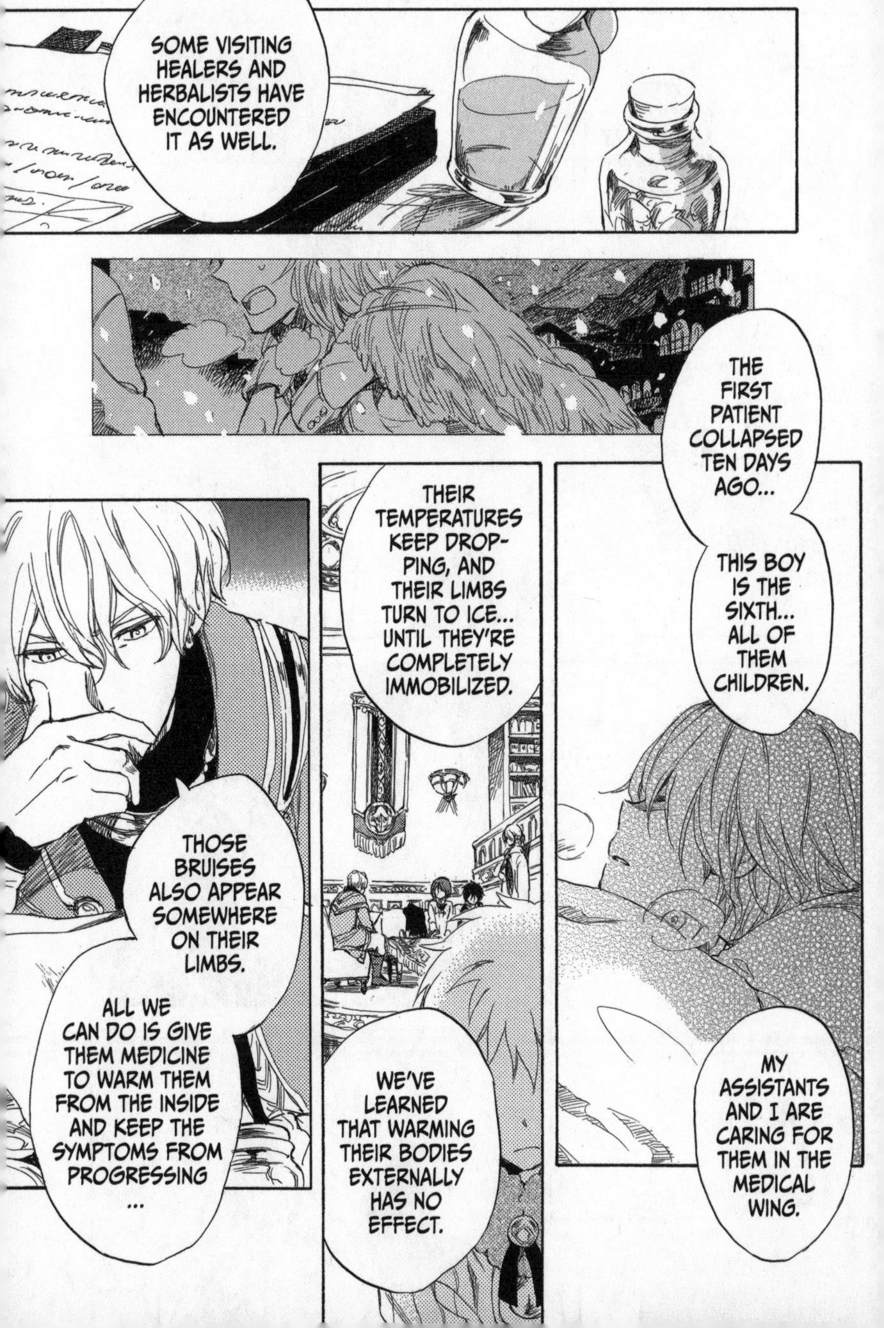
SOME VISITING HEALERS AND HERBALISTS HAVE ENCOUNTERED IT AS WELL.
THE FIRST PATIENT COLLAPSED TEN DAYS AGO...
THIS BOY IS THE SIXTH... ALL OF THEM CHILDREN.
MY ASSISTANTS AND I ARE CARING FOR THEM IN THE MEDICAL WING.
THEIR TEMPERATURES KEEP DROP-PING, AND THEIR LIMBS TURN TO ICE... UNTIL THEY'RE COMPLETELY IMMOBILIZED.
WE'VE LEARNED THAT WARMING THEIR BODIES EXTERNALLY HAS NO EFFECT.
THOSE BRUISES ALSO APPEAR SOMEWHERE ON THEIR LIMBS.
ALL WE CAN DO IS GIVE THEM MEDICINE TO WARM THEM FROM THE INSIDE AND KEEP THE SYMPTOMS FROM PROGRESSING...

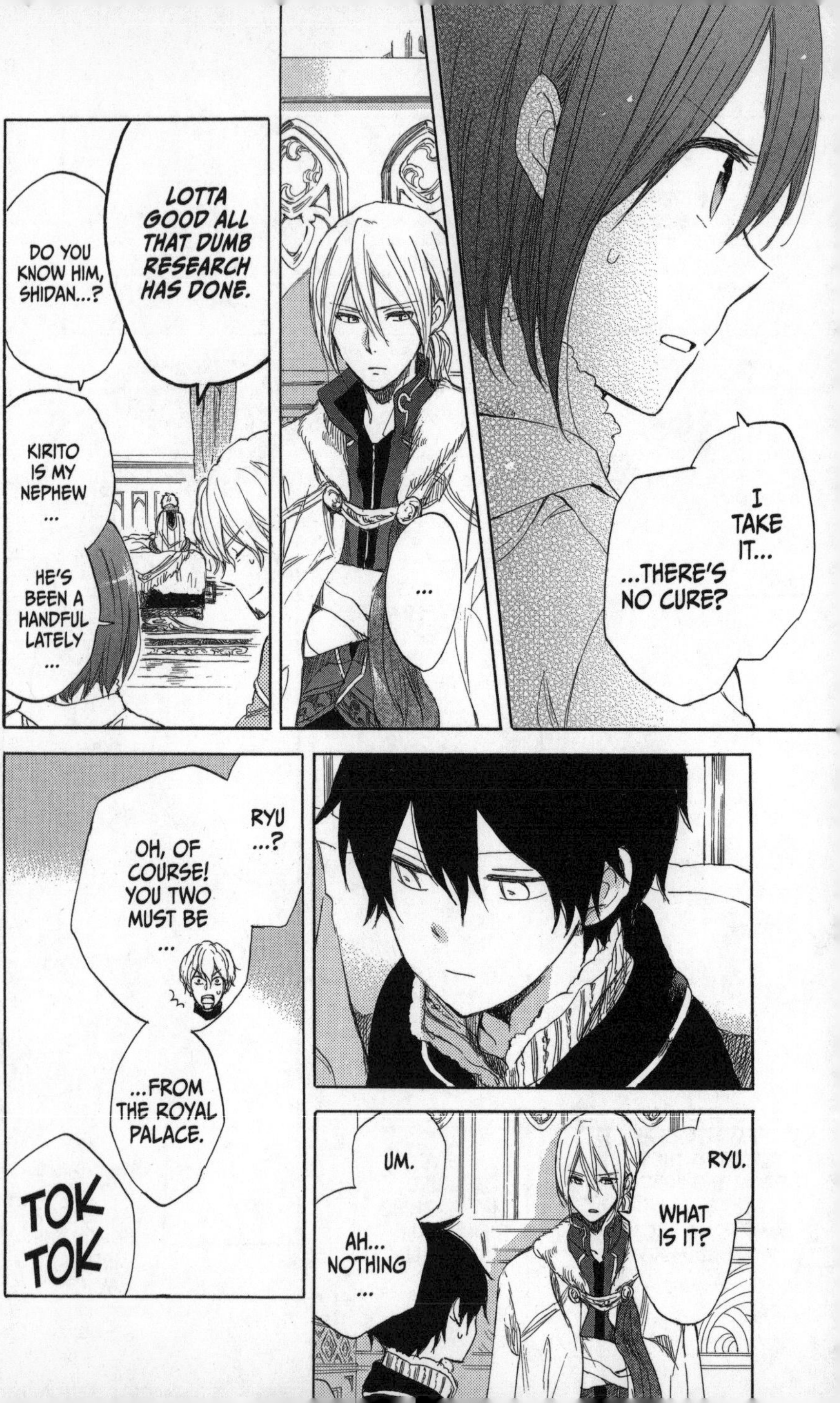
I TAKE IT...
...THERE'S NO CURE?
...
LOTTA GOOD ALL THAT DUMB RESEARCH HAS DONE.
DO YOU KNOW HIM, SHIDAN...?
KIRITO IS MY NEPHEW ...
HE'S BEEN A HANDFUL LATELY ...
RYU.
WHAT IS IT?
UM.
AH... NOTHING ...
RYU ...?
OH, OF COURSE! YOU TWO MUST BE ...
...FROM THE ROYAL PALACE.
TOK TOK

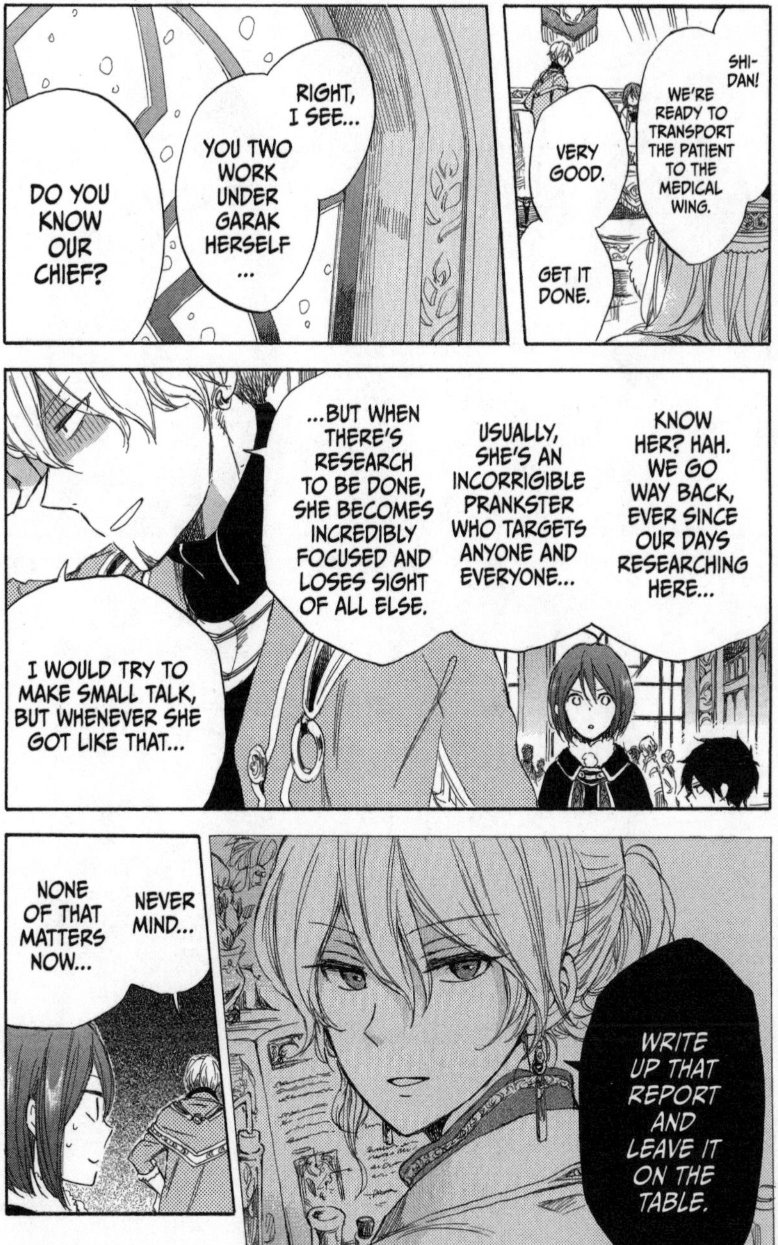
SHI-DAN!
WE'RE READY TO TRANSPORT THE PATIENT TO THE MEDICAL WING.
VERY GOOD.
GET IT DONE.
RIGHT, I SEE... YOU TWO WORK UNDER GARAK HERSELF...
DO YOU KNOW OUR CHIEF?
KNOW HER? HAH. WE GO WAY BACK, EVER SINCE OUR DAYS RESEARCHING HERE...
USUALLY, SHE'S AN INCORRIGIBLE PRANKSTER WHO TARGETS ANYONE AND EVERYONE...
...BUT WHEN THERE'S RESEARCH TO BE DONE, SHE BECOMES INCREDIBLY FOCUSED AND LOSES SIGHT OF ALL ELSE.
I WOULD TRY TO MAKE SMALL TALK, BUT WHENEVER SHE GOT LIKE THAT...
WRITE UP THAT REPORT AND LEAVE IT ON THE TABLE.
NEVER MIND...
NONE OF THAT MATTERS NOW...

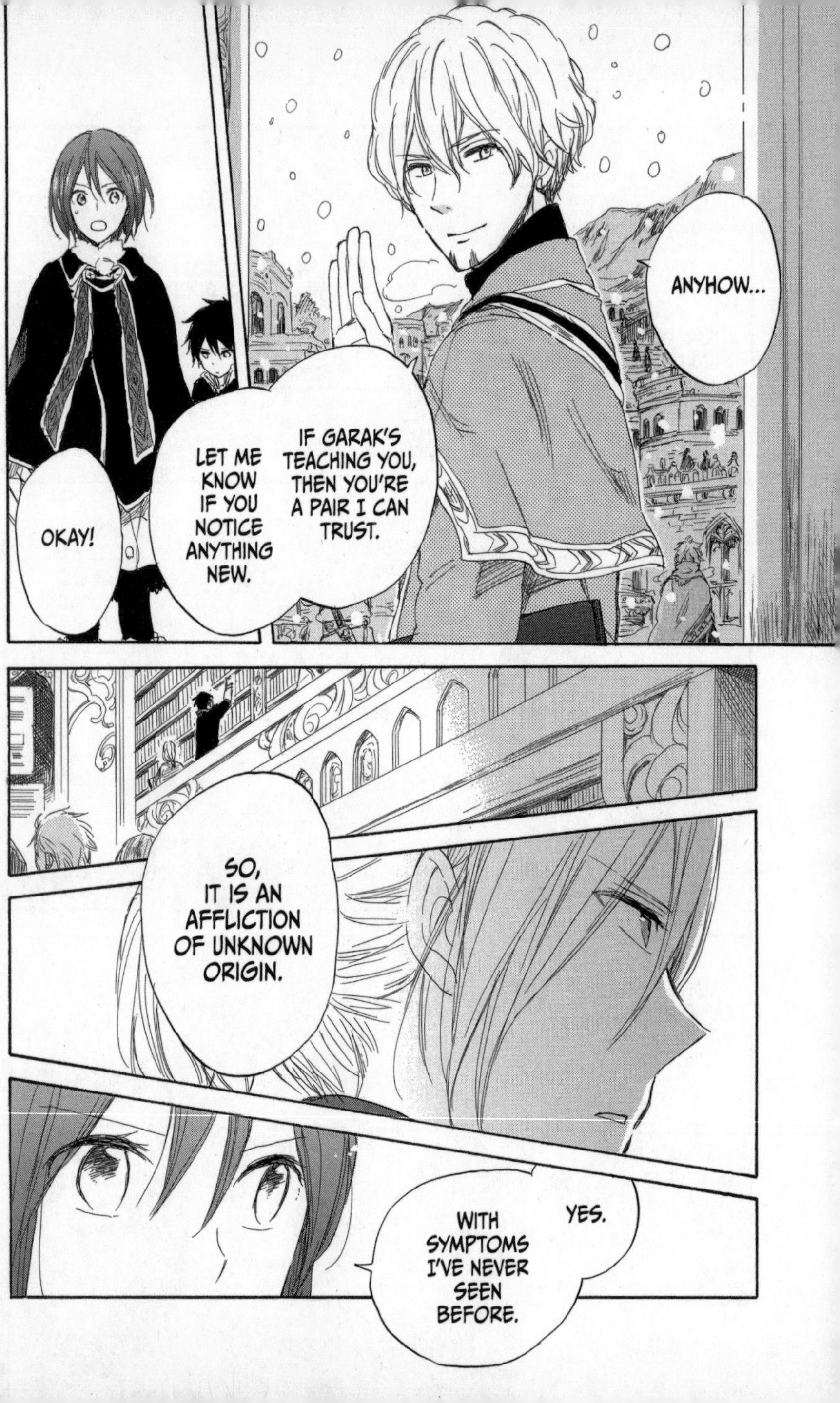
ANYHOW...
IF GARAK'S TEACHING YOU, THEN YOU'RE A PAIR I CAN TRUST.
LET ME KNOW IF YOU NOTICE ANYTHING NEW.
OKAY!
SO, IT IS AN AFFLICTION OF UNKNOWN ORIGIN.
YES.
WITH SYMPTOMS I'VE NEVER SEEN BEFORE.

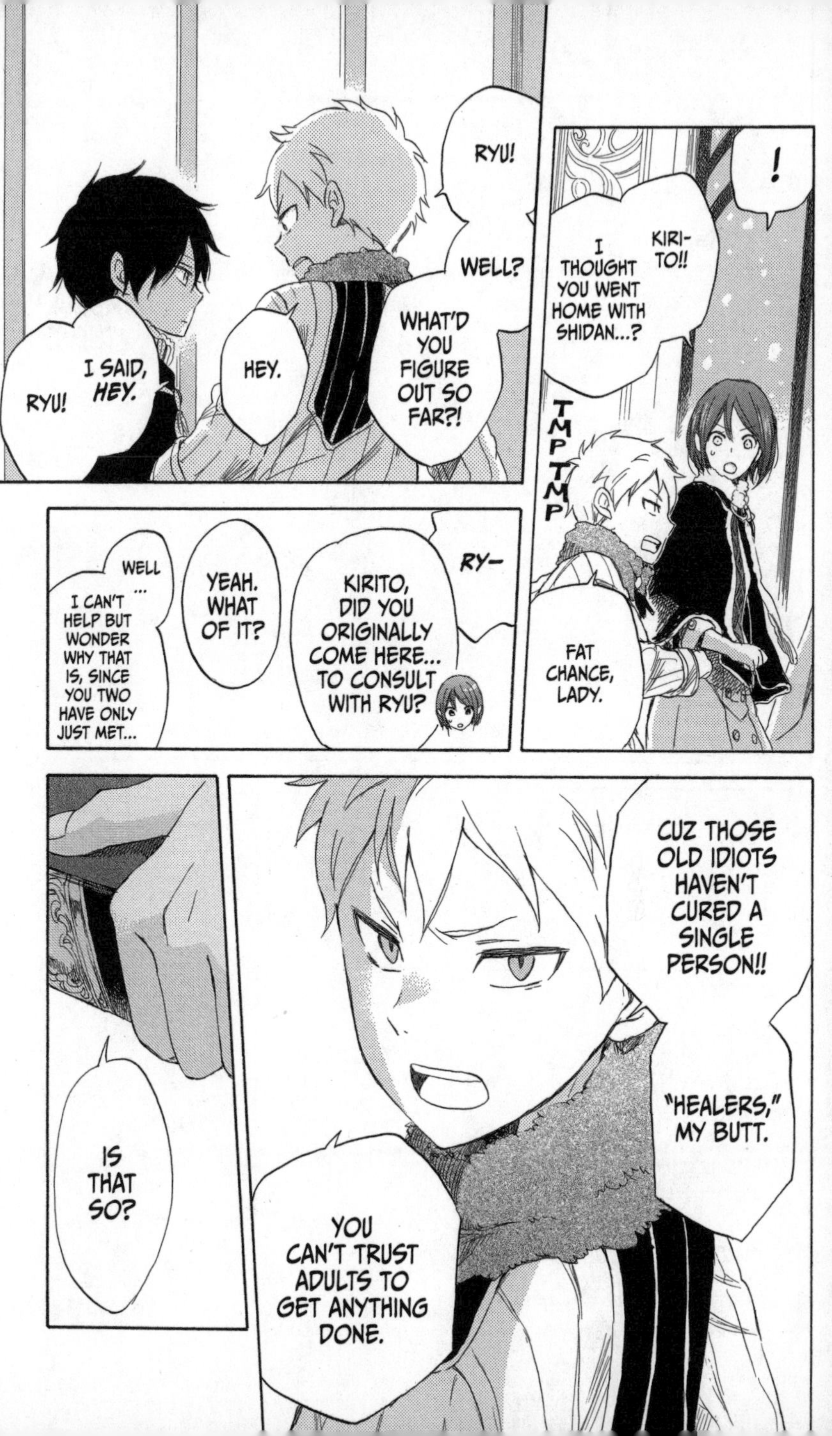
!
KIRI-TO!!
I THOUGHT YOU WENT HOME WITH SHIDAN...?
TMP TMP
FAT CHANCE, LADY.
RYU!
WELL?
WHAT'D YOU FIGURE OUT SO FAR?!
HEY.
I SAID, HEY.
RYU!
RY—
KIRITO, DID YOU ORIGINALLY COME HERE... TO CONSULT WITH RYU?
YEAH. WHAT OF IT?
WELL... I CAN'T HELP BUT WONDER WHY THAT IS, SINCE YOU TWO HAVE ONLY JUST MET...
CUZ THOSE OLD IDIOTS HAVEN'T CURED A SINGLE PERSON!!
"HEALERS," MY BUTT.
YOU CAN'T TRUST ADULTS TO GET ANYTHING DONE.
IS THAT SO?

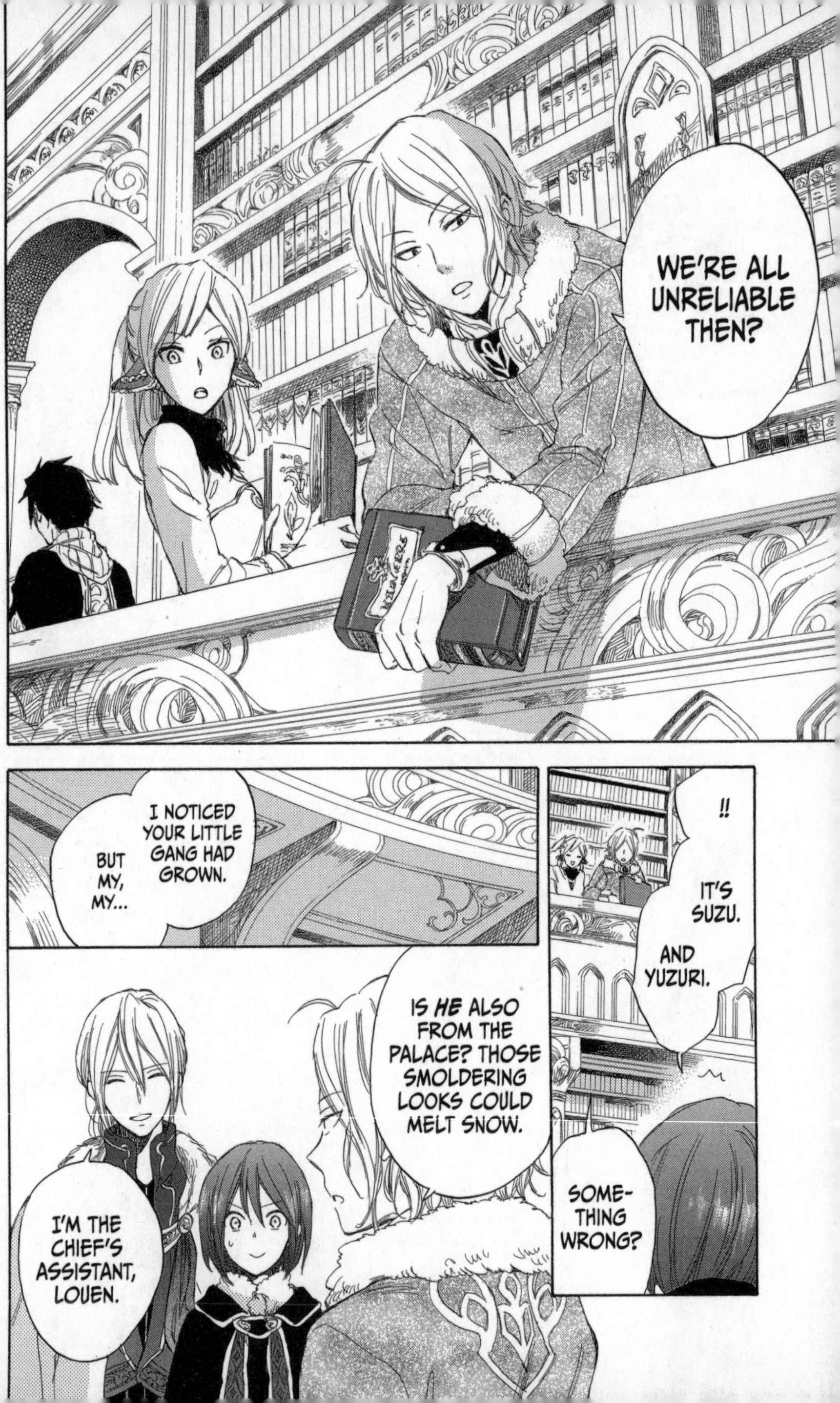
WE'RE ALL UNRELIABLE THEN?
!!
IT'S SUZU.
AND YUZURI.
I NOTICED YOUR LITTLE GANG HAD GROWN.
BUT MY, MY...
SOME-THING WRONG?
IS *HE* ALSO FROM THE PALACE? THOSE SMOLDERING LOOKS COULD MELT SNOW.
I'M THE CHIEF'S ASSISTANT, LOUEN.

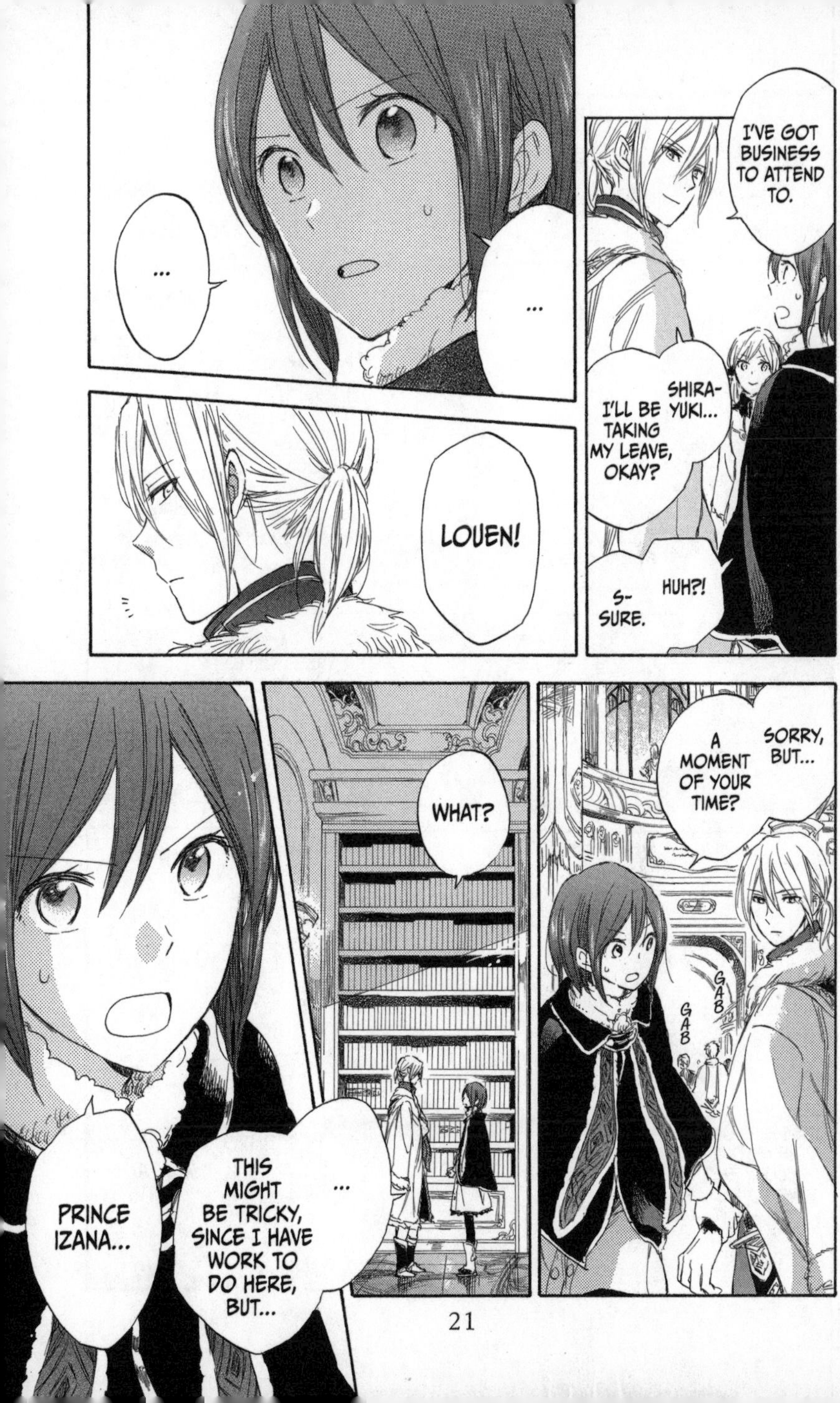
I'VE GOT BUSINESS TO ATTEND TO.
SHIRA-YUKI... I'LL BE TAKING MY LEAVE, OKAY?
HUH?!
S-SURE.
...
...
LOUEN!
SORRY, BUT... A MOMENT OF YOUR TIME?
GAB
GAB
WHAT?
...
THIS MIGHT BE TRICKY, SINCE I HAVE WORK TO DO HERE, BUT...
PRINCE IZANA...

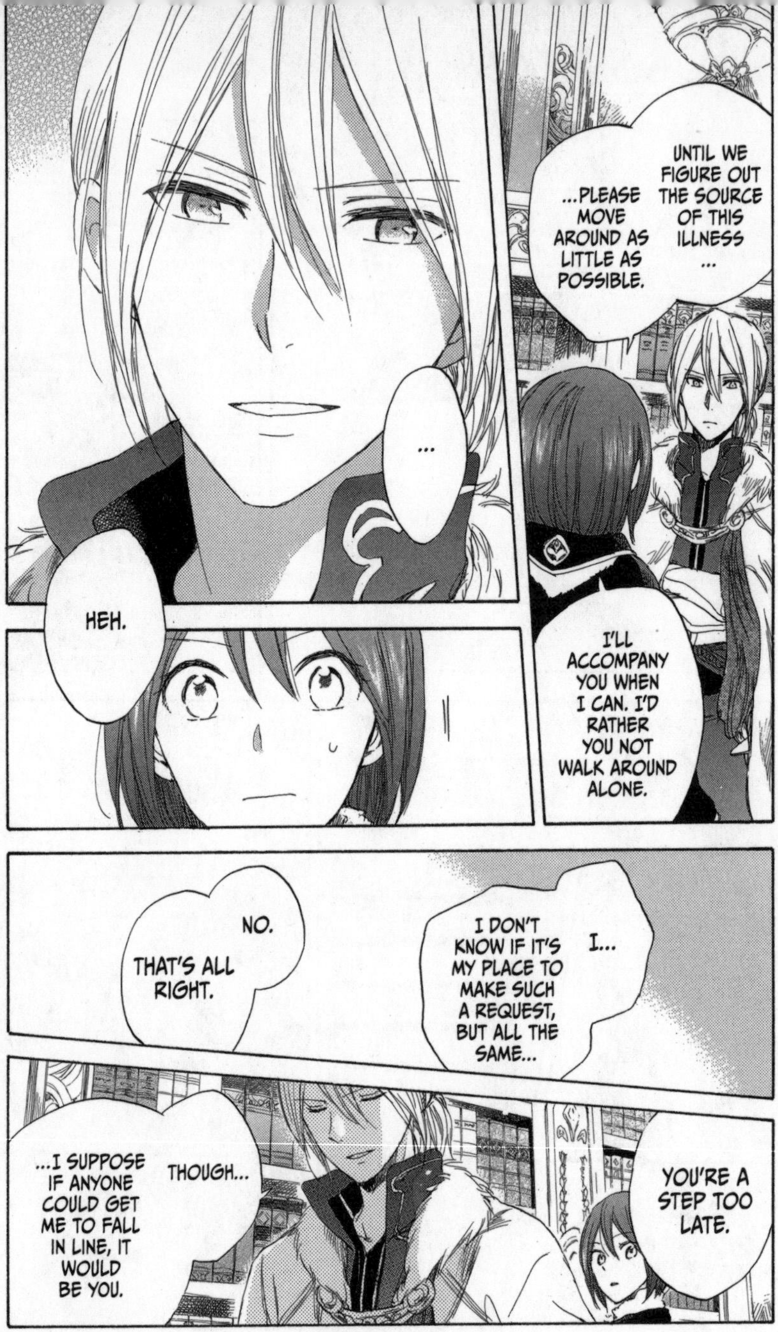
UNTIL WE FIGURE OUT THE SOURCE OF THIS ILLNESS ...
...PLEASE MOVE AROUND AS LITTLE AS POSSIBLE.
I'LL ACCOMPANY YOU WHEN I CAN. I'D RATHER YOU NOT WALK AROUND ALONE.
...
HEH.
I...
I DON'T KNOW IF IT'S MY PLACE TO MAKE SUCH A REQUEST, BUT ALL THE SAME...
NO.
THAT'S ALL RIGHT.
YOU'RE A STEP TOO LATE.
THOUGH...
...I SUPPOSE IF ANYONE COULD GET ME TO FALL IN LINE, IT WOULD BE YOU.

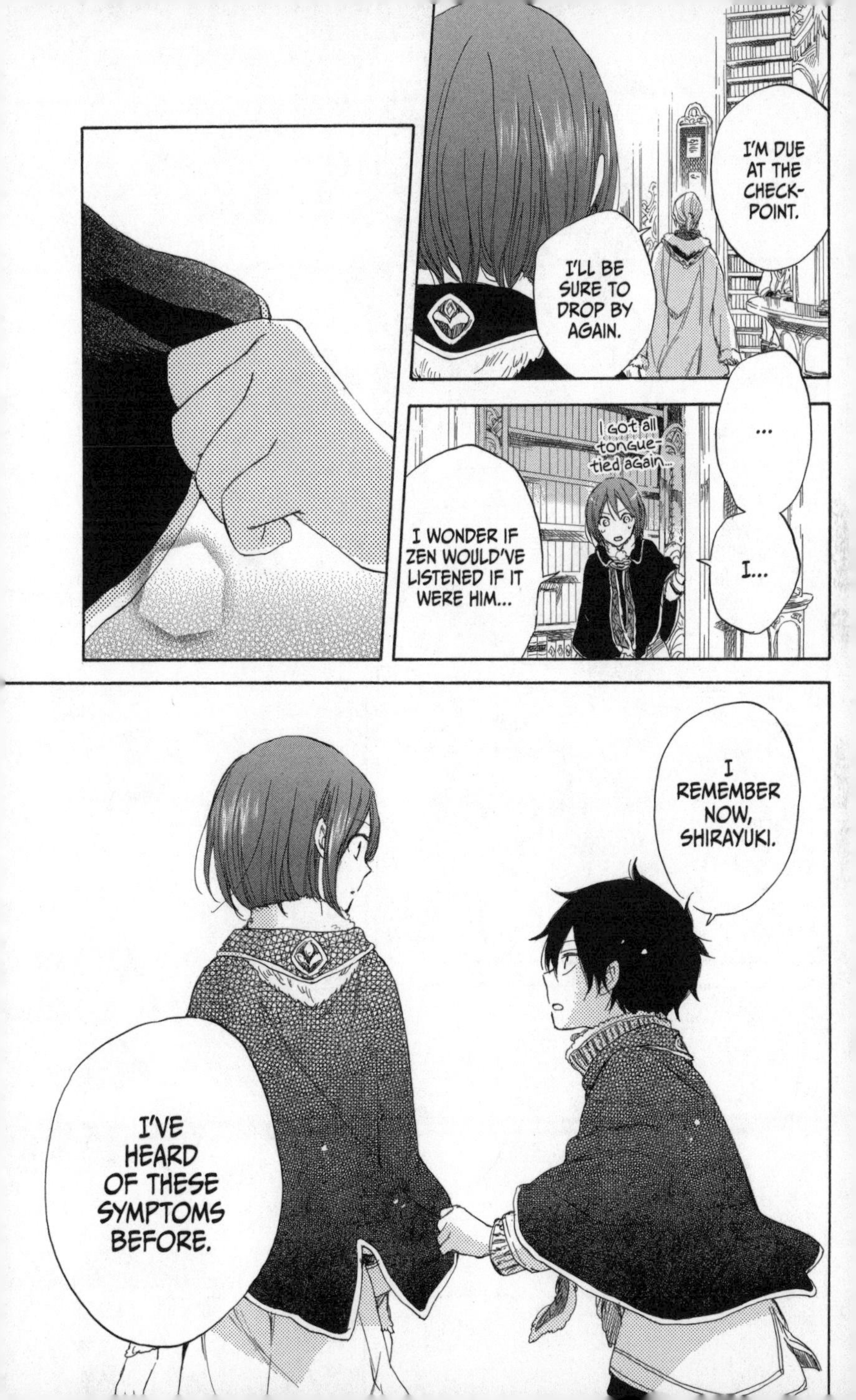
I'M DUE AT THE CHECK-POINT.
I'LL BE SURE TO DROP BY AGAIN.
...
I...
I got all tongue-tied again...
I WONDER IF ZEN WOULD'VE LISTENED IF IT WERE HIM...
I REMEMBER NOW, SHIRAYUKI.
I'VE HEARD OF THESE SYMPTOMS BEFORE.

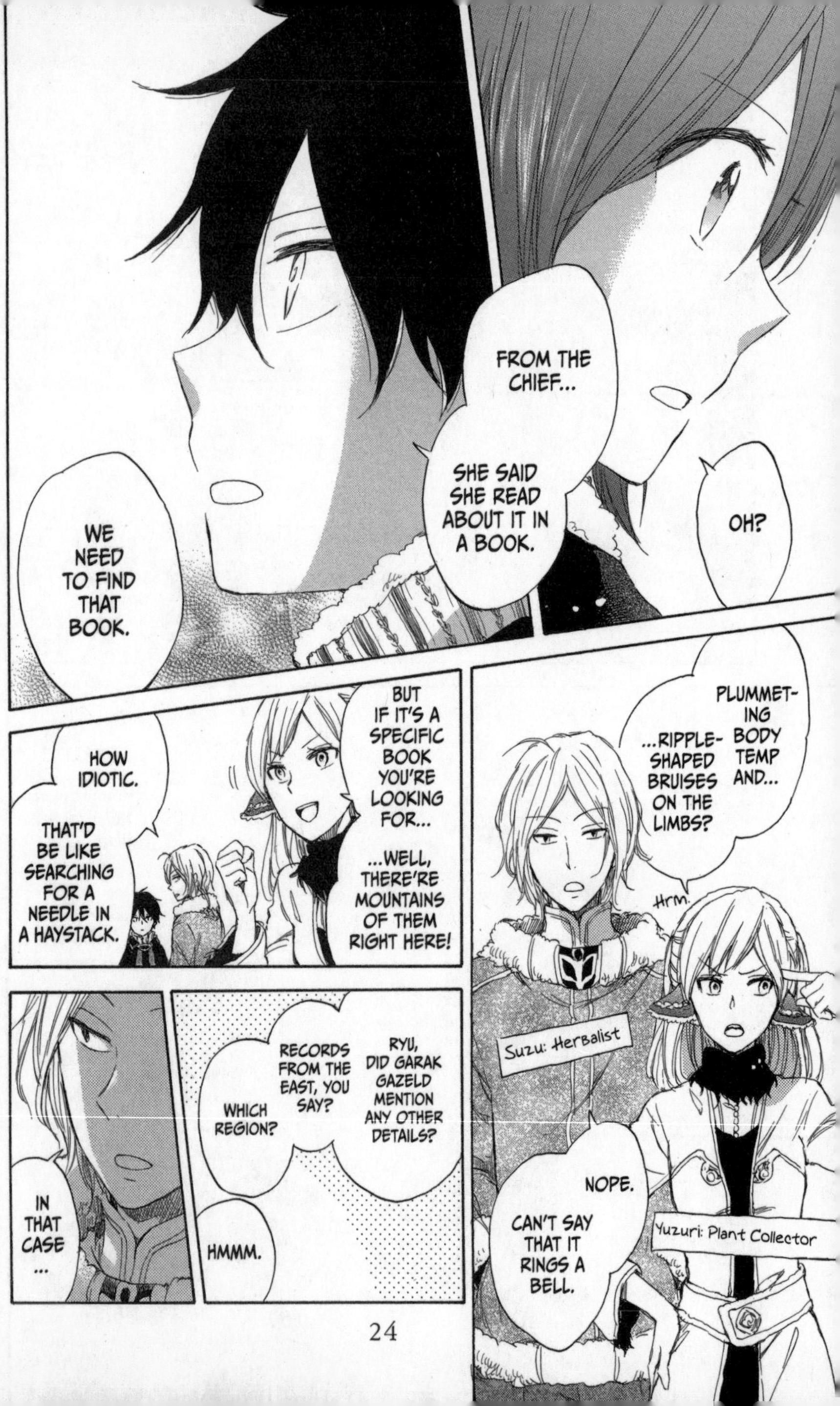
FROM THE CHIEF...
SHE SAID SHE READ ABOUT IT IN A BOOK.
OH?
WE NEED TO FIND THAT BOOK.
PLUMMETING BODY TEMP AND...
...RIPPLE-SHAPED BRUISES ON THE LIMBS?
Hrm.
Suzu: Herbalist
Yuzuri: Plant Collector
NOPE.
CAN'T SAY THAT IT RINGS A BELL.
BUT IF IT'S A SPECIFIC BOOK YOU'RE LOOKING FOR...
...WELL, THERE'RE MOUNTAINS OF THEM RIGHT HERE!
HOW IDIOTIC.
THAT'D BE LIKE SEARCHING FOR A NEEDLE IN A HAYSTACK.
RYU, DID GARAK GAZELD MENTION ANY OTHER DETAILS?
RECORDS FROM THE EAST, YOU SAY?
WHICH REGION?
HMMM.
IN THAT CASE ...

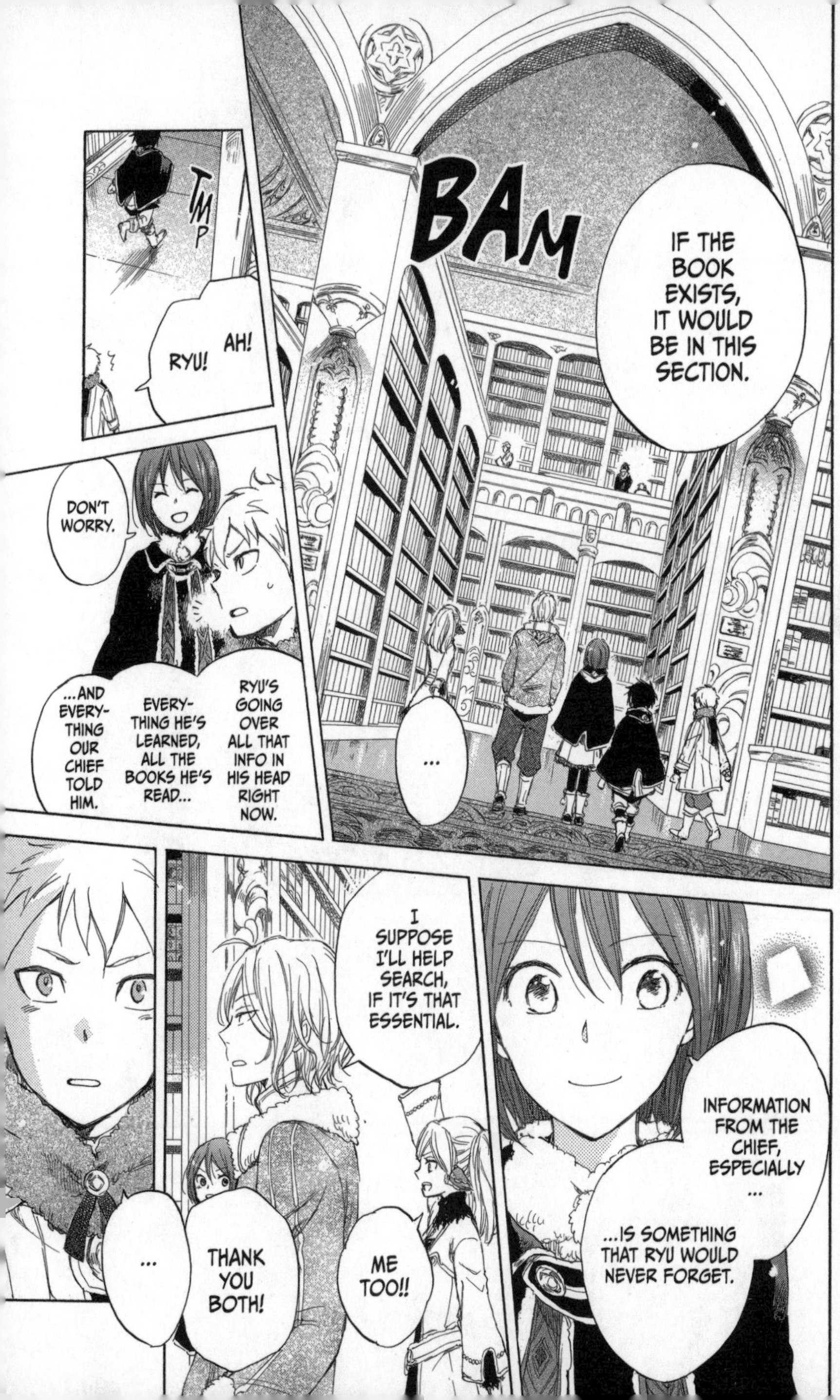
BAM
IF THE BOOK EXISTS, IT WOULD BE IN THIS SECTION.
...
TMP
AH!
RYU!
DON'T WORRY.
RYU'S GOING OVER ALL THAT INFO IN HIS HEAD RIGHT NOW.
EVERY-THING HE'S LEARNED, ALL THE BOOKS HE'S READ...
...AND EVERY-THING OUR CHIEF TOLD HIM.
INFORMATION FROM THE CHIEF, ESPECIALLY ...
...IS SOMETHING THAT RYU WOULD NEVER FORGET.
I SUPPOSE I'LL HELP SEARCH, IF IT'S THAT ESSENTIAL.
ME TOO!!
THANK YOU BOTH!
...

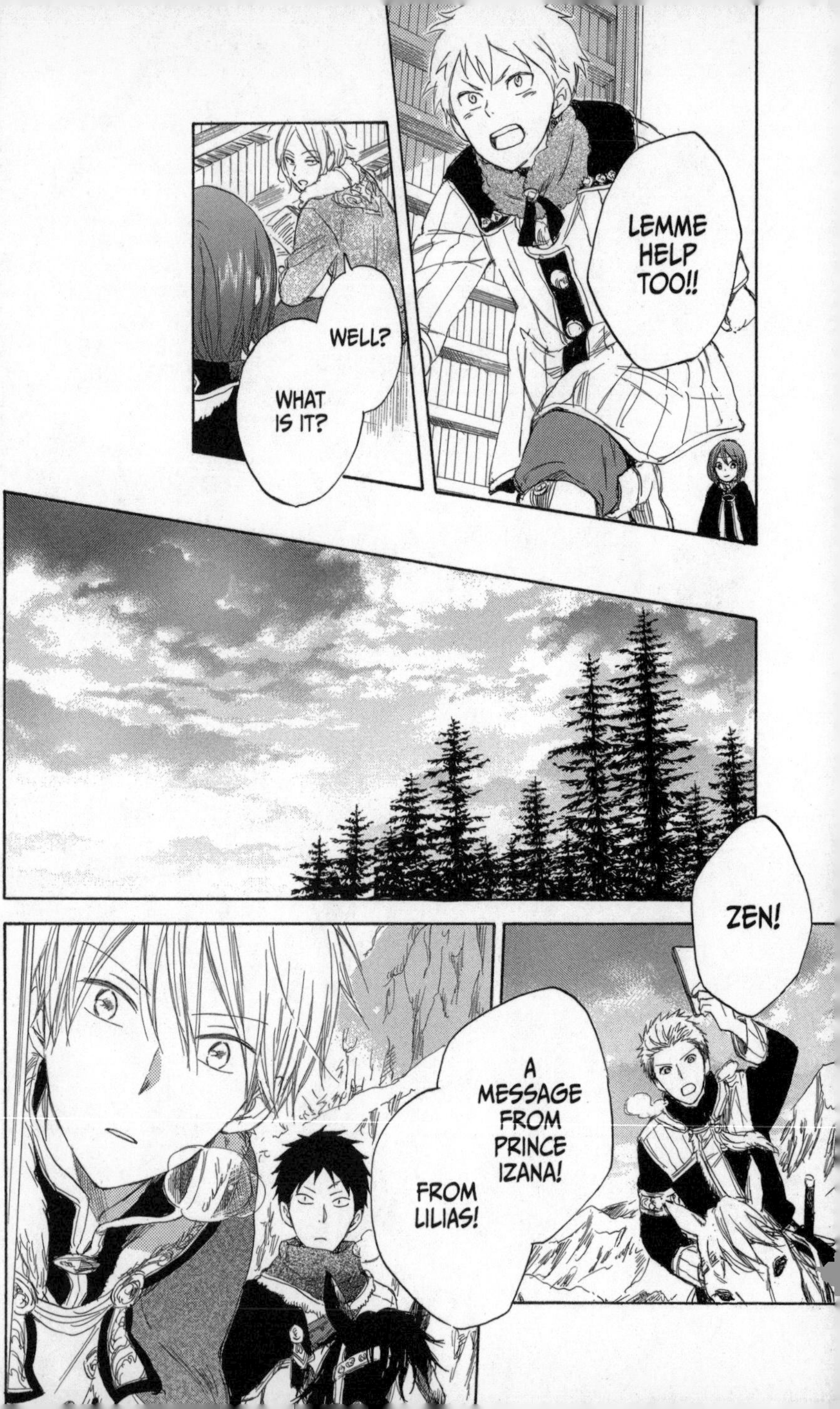
LEMME HELP TOO!!
WELL?
WHAT IS IT?
ZEN!
A MESSAGE FROM PRINCE IZANA!
FROM LILIAS!

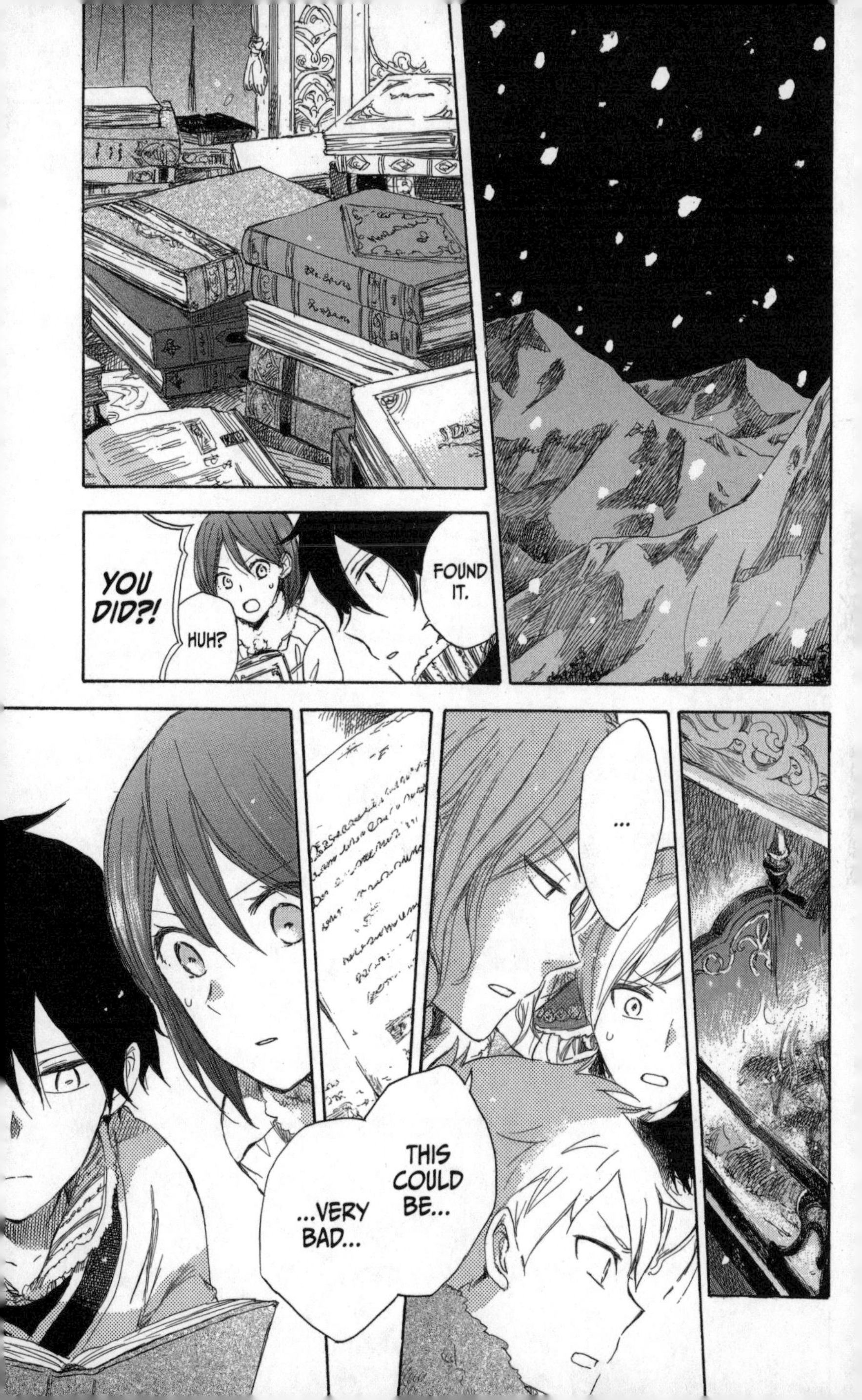
FOUND IT.
HUH?
YOU DID?!
...
THIS COULD BE...
...VERY BAD...

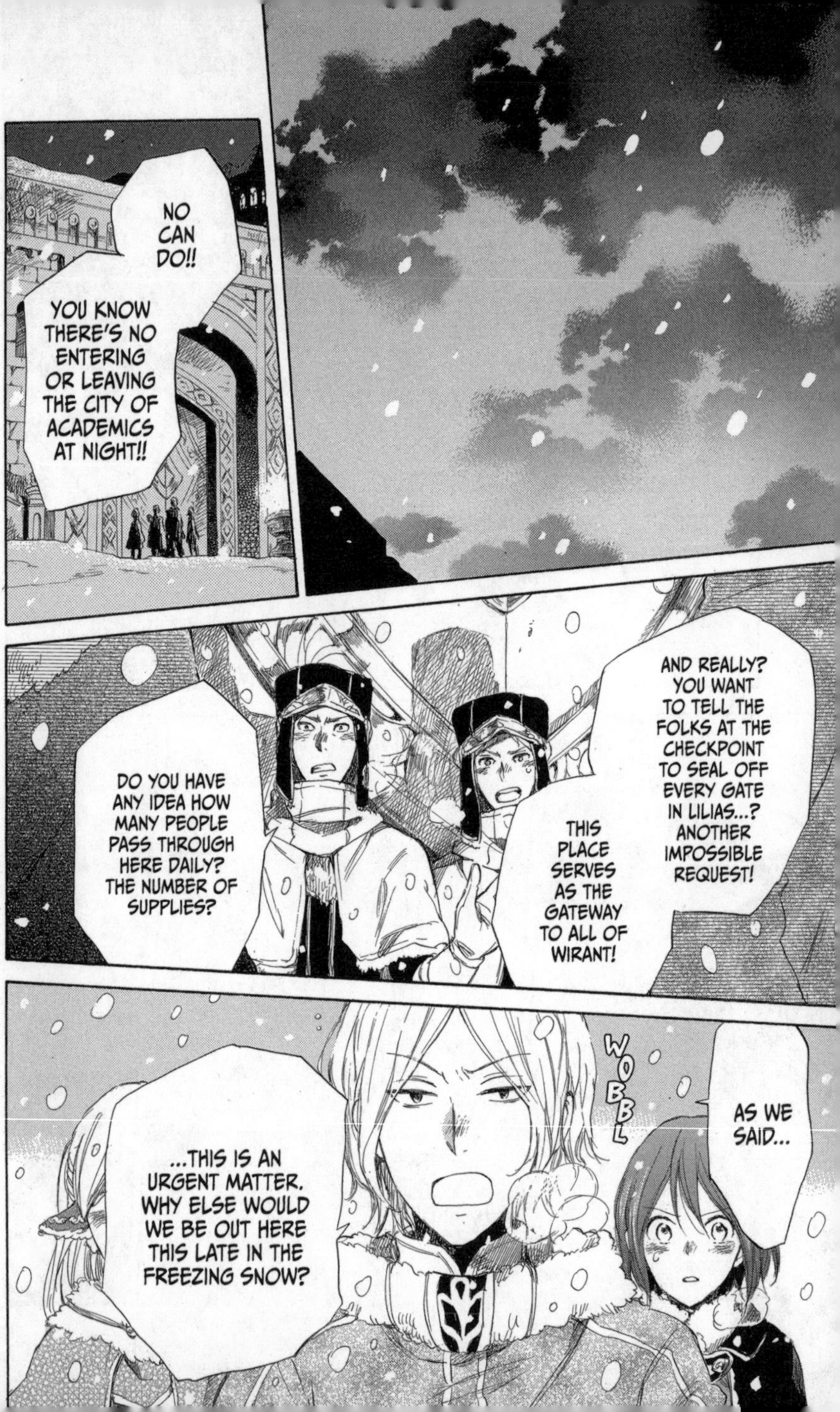
NO CAN DO!!
YOU KNOW THERE'S NO ENTERING OR LEAVING THE CITY OF ACADEMICS AT NIGHT!!
AND REALLY? YOU WANT TO TELL THE FOLKS AT THE CHECKPOINT TO SEAL OFF EVERY GATE IN LILIAS...? ANOTHER IMPOSSIBLE REQUEST!
THIS PLACE SERVES AS THE GATEWAY TO ALL OF WIRANT!
DO YOU HAVE ANY IDEA HOW MANY PEOPLE PASS THROUGH HERE DAILY? THE NUMBER OF SUPPLIES?
AS WE SAID...
WOBBL
...THIS IS AN URGENT MATTER. WHY ELSE WOULD WE BE OUT HERE THIS LATE IN THE FREEZING SNOW?

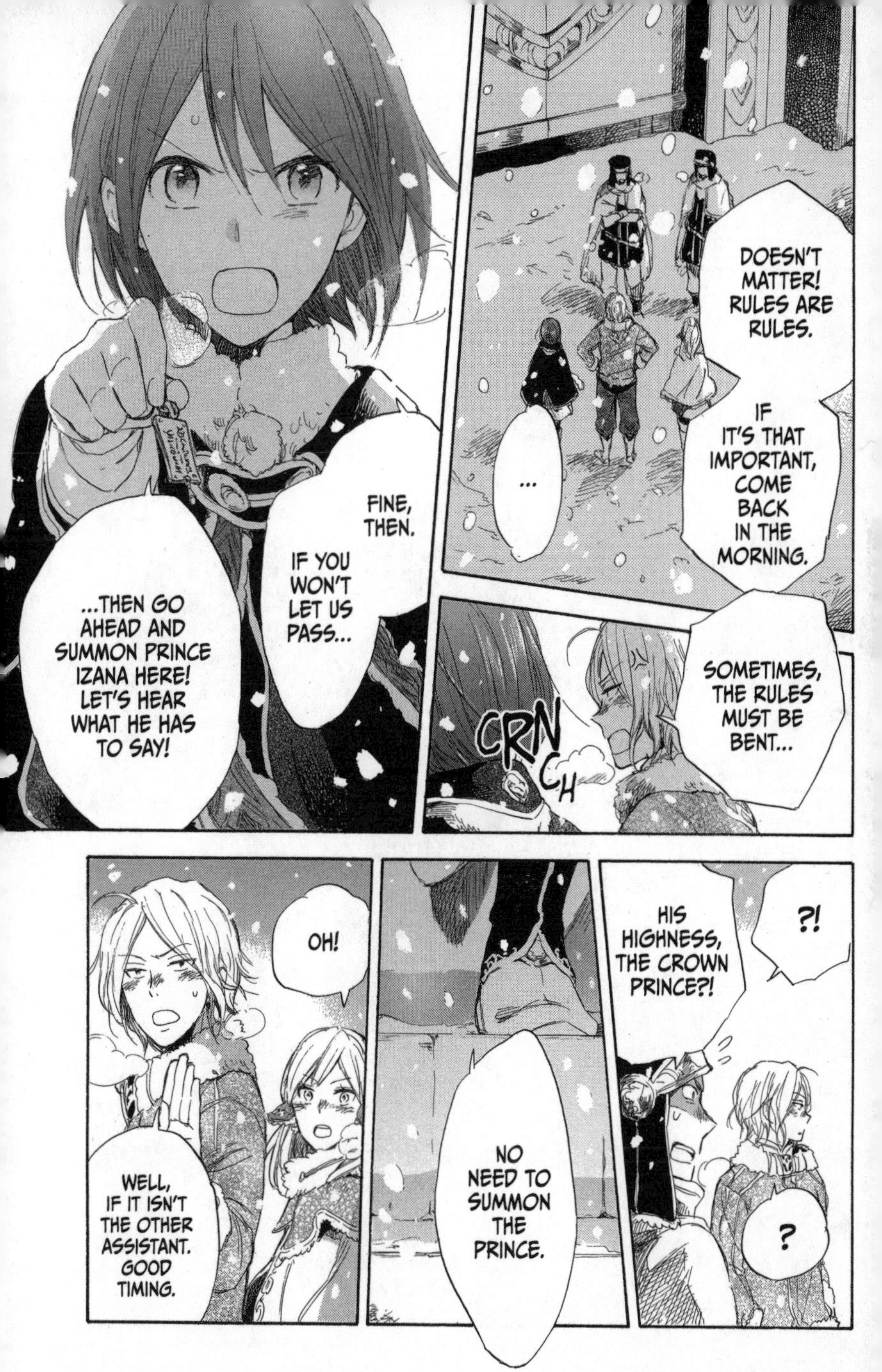
DOESN'T MATTER! RULES ARE RULES.
IF IT'S THAT IMPORTANT, COME BACK IN THE MORNING.
...
SOMETIMES, THE RULES MUST BE BENT...
CRNCH
FINE, THEN.
IF YOU WON'T LET US PASS...
...THEN GO AHEAD AND SUMMON PRINCE IZANA HERE! LET'S HEAR WHAT HE HAS TO SAY!
?!
HIS HIGHNESS, THE CROWN PRINCE?!
?
NO NEED TO SUMMON THE PRINCE.
OH!
WELL, IF IT ISN'T THE OTHER ASSISTANT. GOOD TIMING.

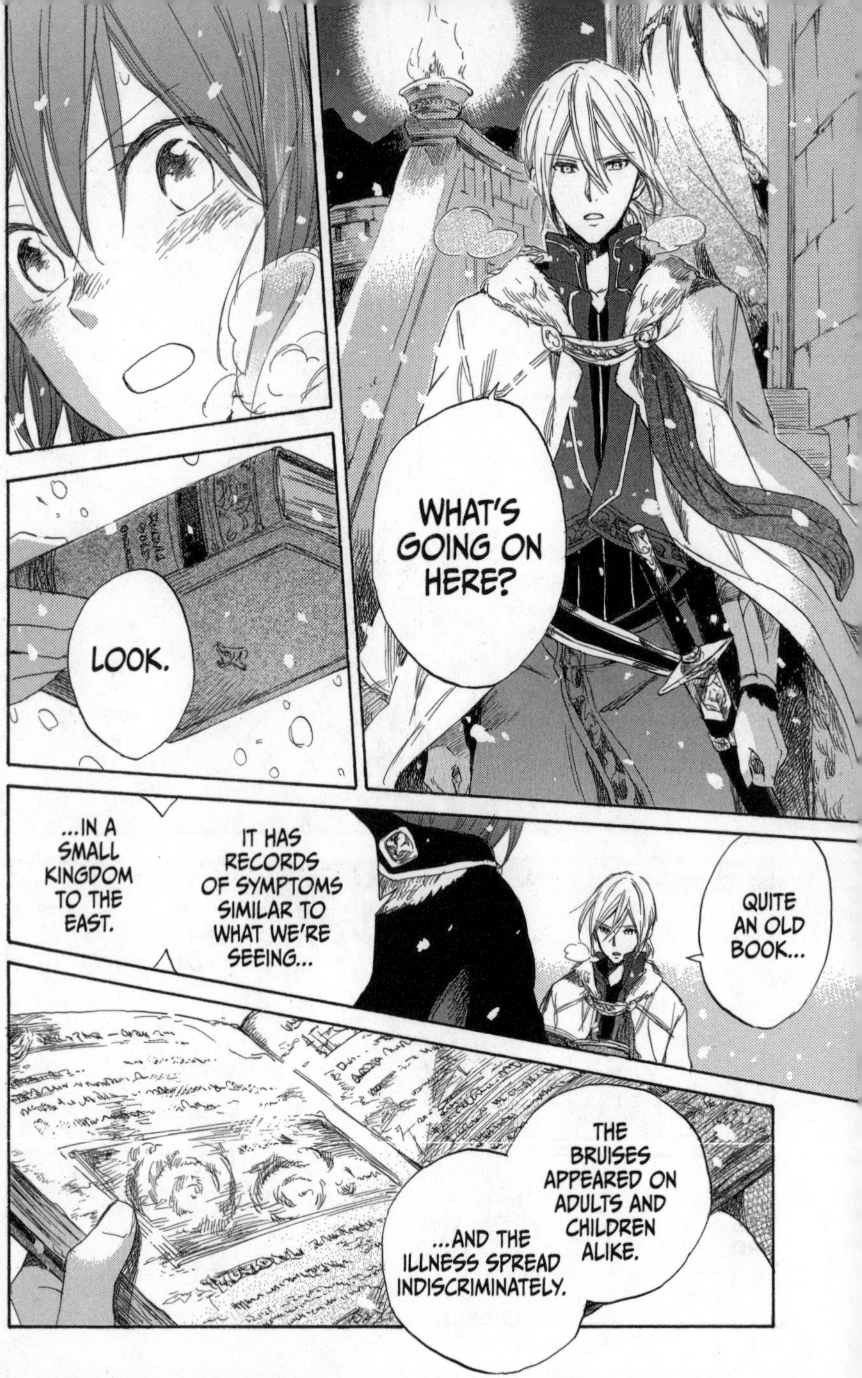
WHAT'S GOING ON HERE?
LOOK.
QUITE AN OLD BOOK...
IT HAS RECORDS OF SYMPTOMS SIMILAR TO WHAT WE'RE SEEING...
...IN A SMALL KINGDOM TO THE EAST.
THE BRUISES APPEARED ON ADULTS AND CHILDREN ALIKE.
...AND THE ILLNESS SPREAD INDISCRIMINATELY.

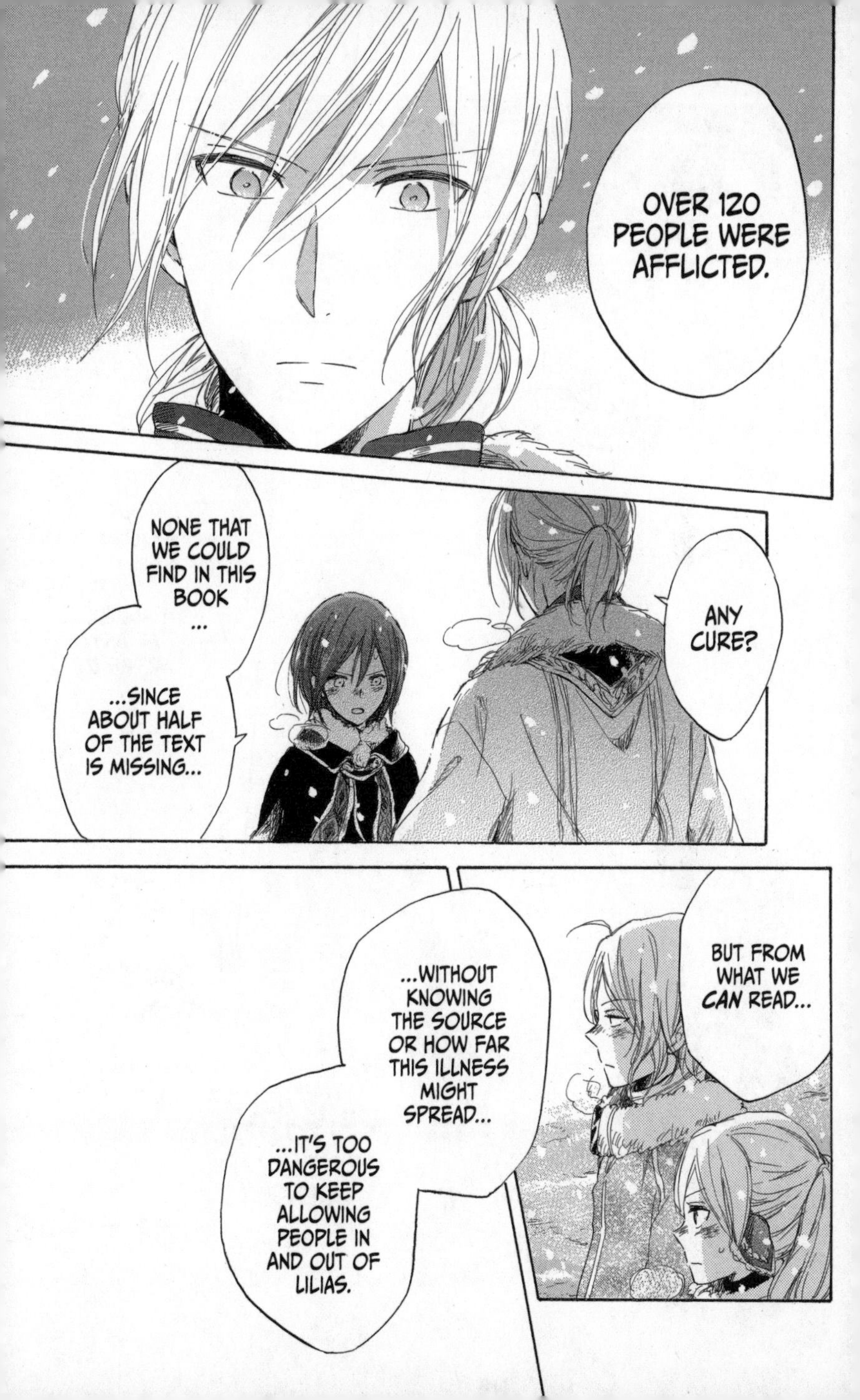
OVER 120 PEOPLE WERE AFFLICTED.
ANY CURE?
NONE THAT WE COULD FIND IN THIS BOOK ...
...SINCE ABOUT HALF OF THE TEXT IS MISSING...
BUT FROM WHAT WE CAN READ...
...WITHOUT KNOWING THE SOURCE OR HOW FAR THIS ILLNESS MIGHT SPREAD...
...IT'S TOO DANGEROUS TO KEEP ALLOWING PEOPLE IN AND OUT OF LILIAS.

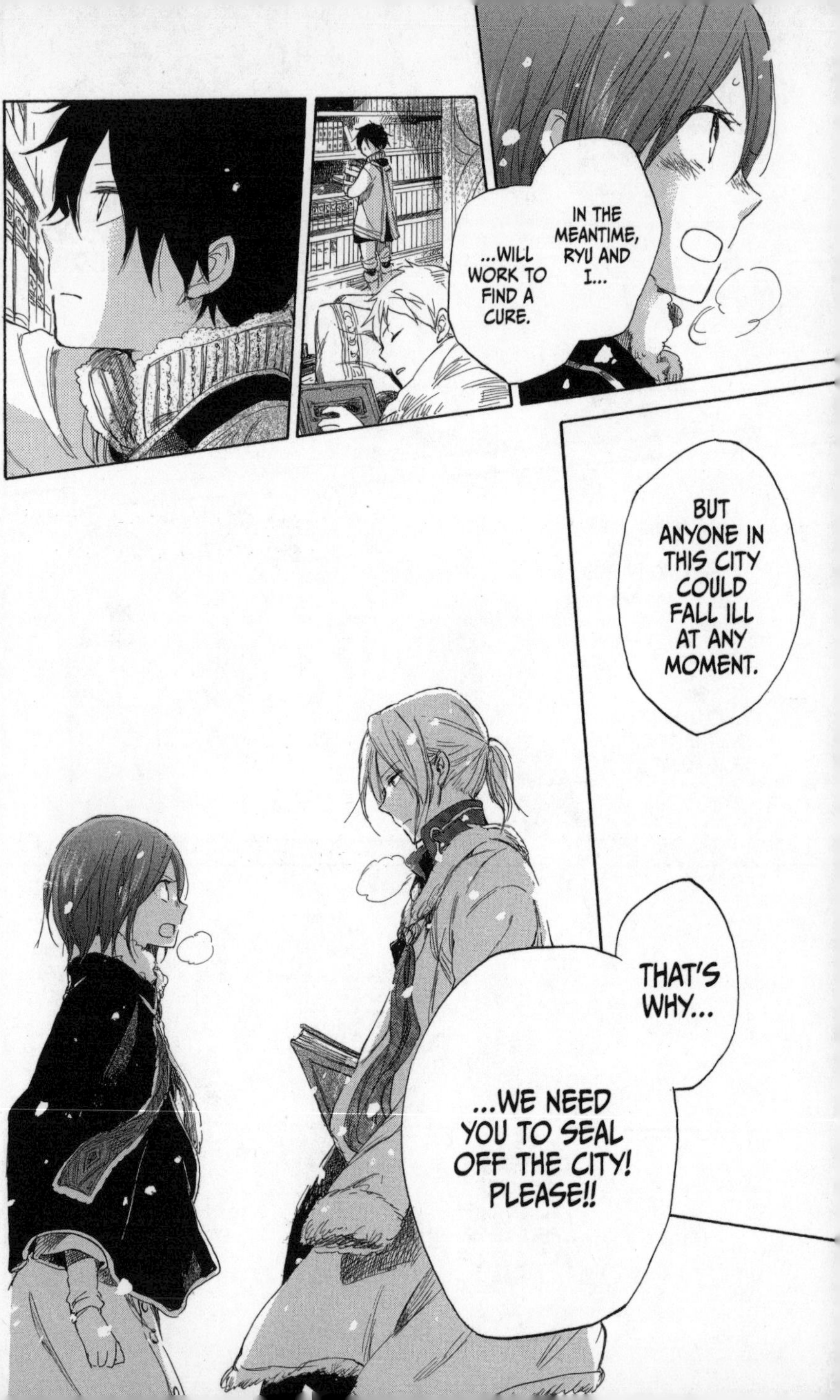
IN THE MEANTIME, RYU AND I...
...WILL WORK TO FIND A CURE.
BUT ANYONE IN THIS CITY COULD FALL ILL AT ANY MOMENT.
THAT'S WHY...
...WE NEED YOU TO SEAL OFF THE CITY! PLEASE!!

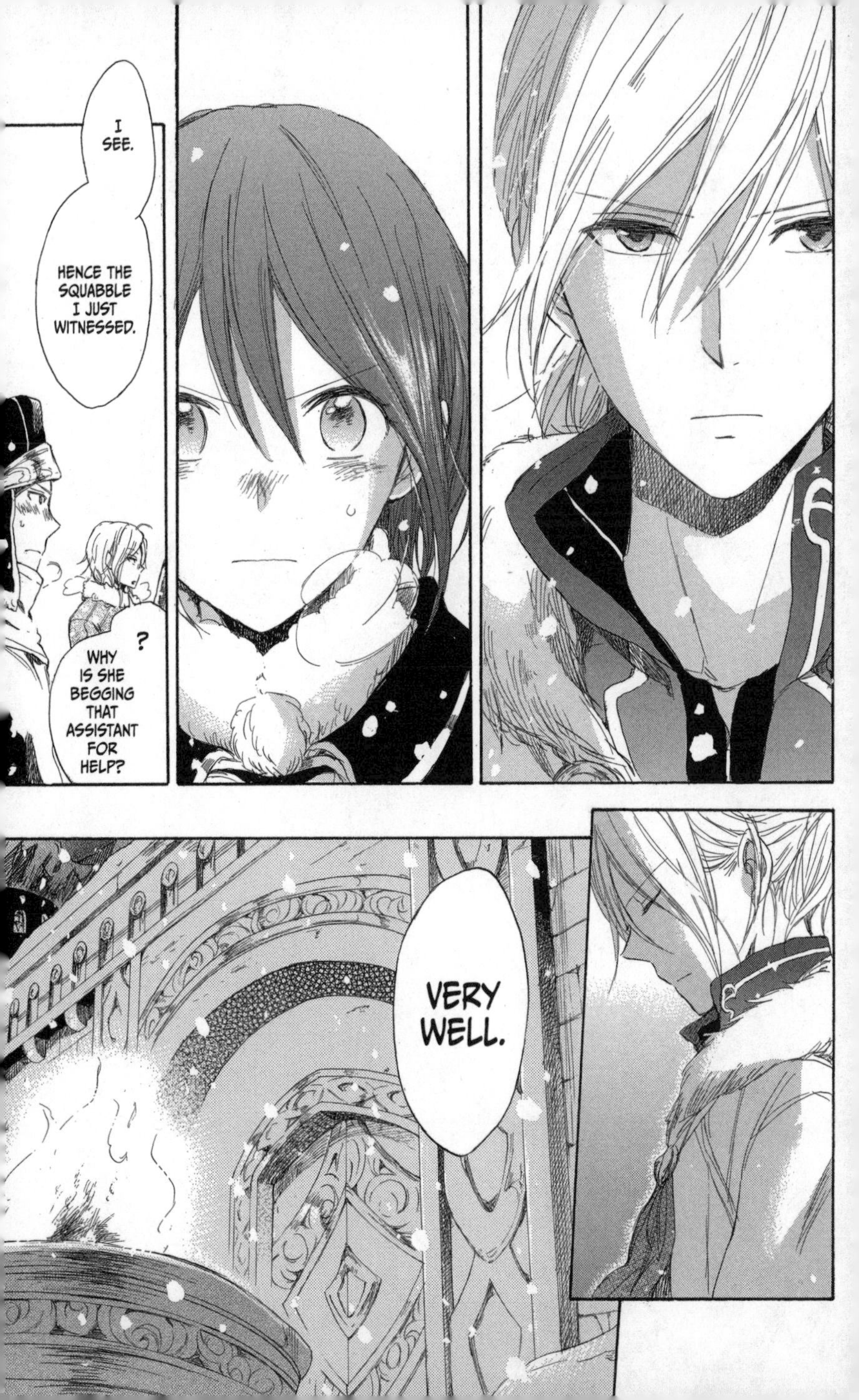
I SEE.
HENCE THE SQUABBLE I JUST WITNESSED.
?
WHY IS SHE BEGGING THAT ASSISTANT FOR HELP?
VERY WELL.

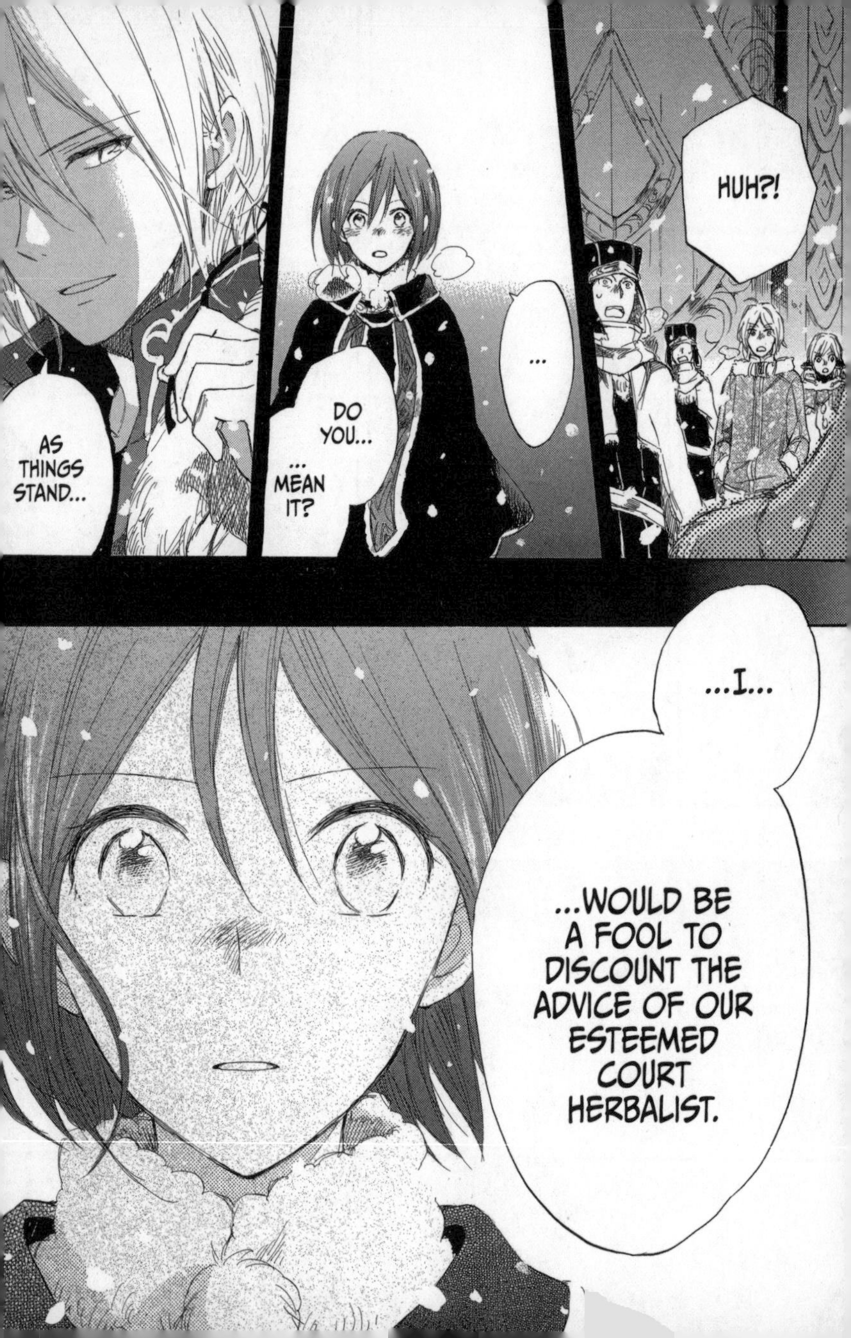
HUH?!
...
DO YOU...
... MEAN IT?
AS THINGS STAND...
...I...
...WOULD BE A FOOL TO DISCOUNT THE ADVICE OF OUR ESTEEMED COURT HERBALIST.

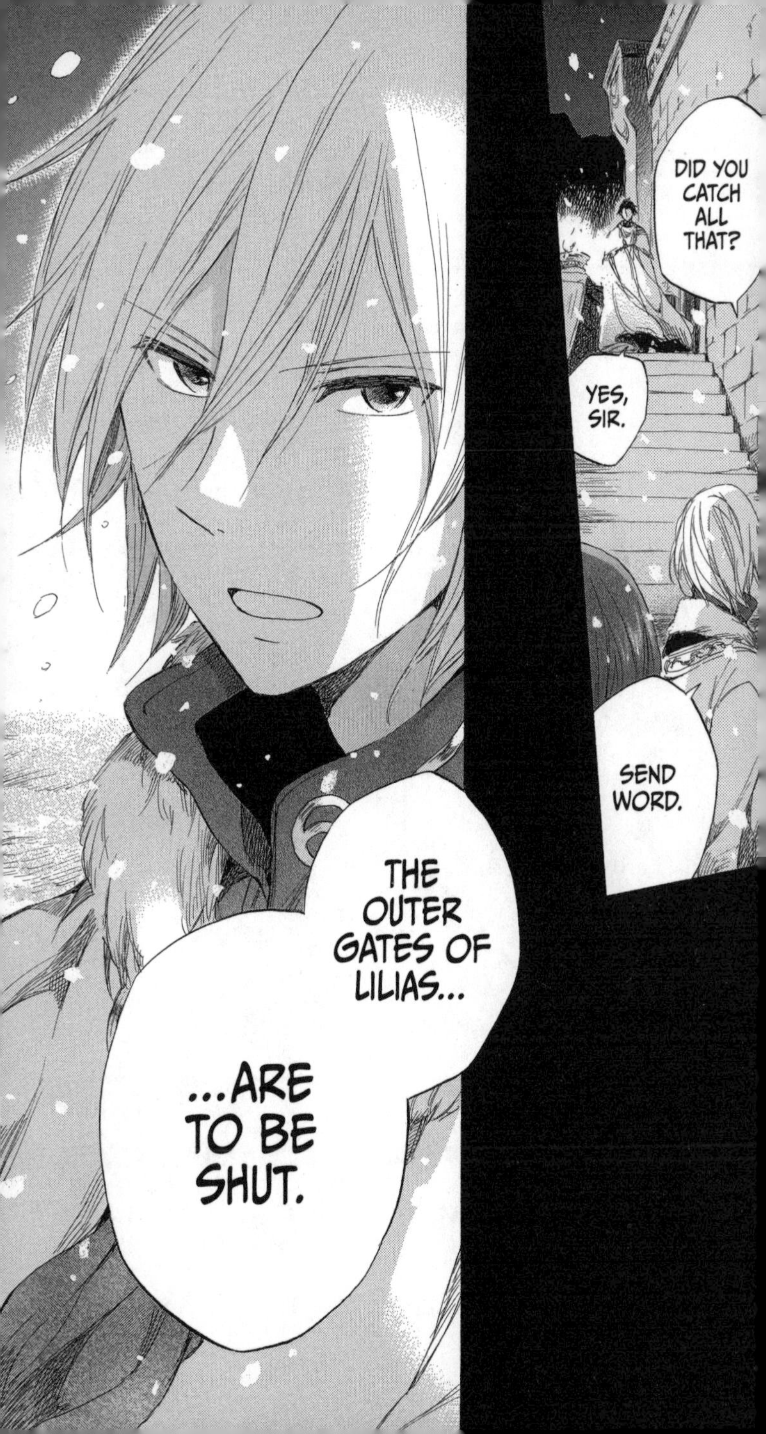
DID YOU CATCH ALL THAT?
YES, SIR.
SEND WORD.
THE OUTER GATES OF LILIAS...
...ARE TO BE SHUT.

The First Night (1)

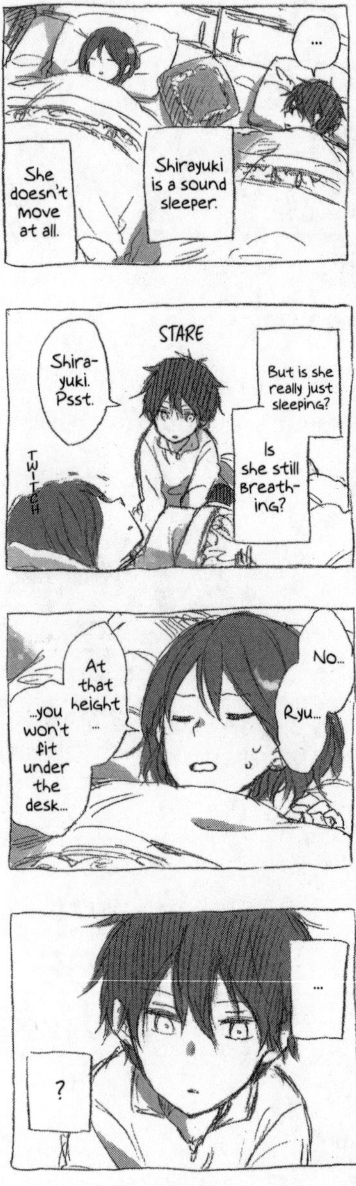
...
Shirayuki is a sound sleeper.
She doesn't move at all.
But is she really just sleeping?
Is she still breathing?
STARE
Shira-yuki. Psst.
TWITCH
No... Ryu...
At that height...
...you won't fit under the desk...
...
?

The First Night (2)

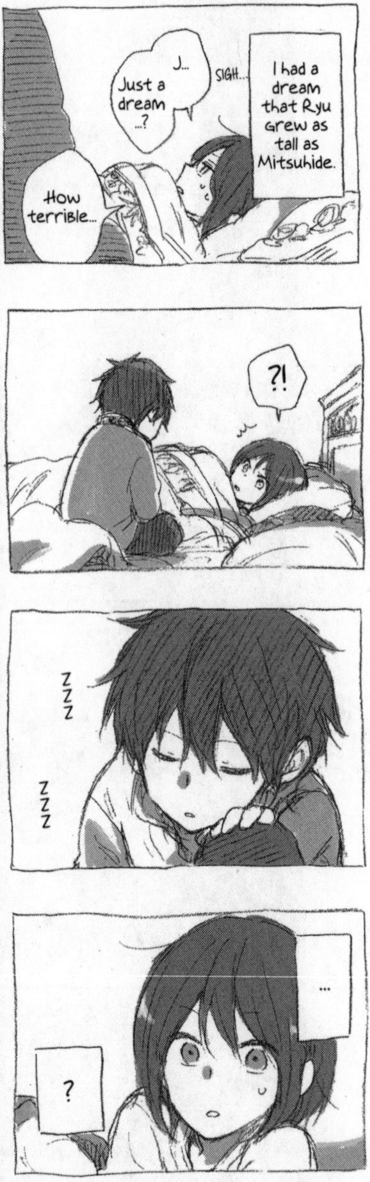
I had a dream that Ryu grew as tall as Mitsuhide.
SIGH...
J... Just a dream...?
How terrible...
?!
ZZZ
ZZZ
...
?

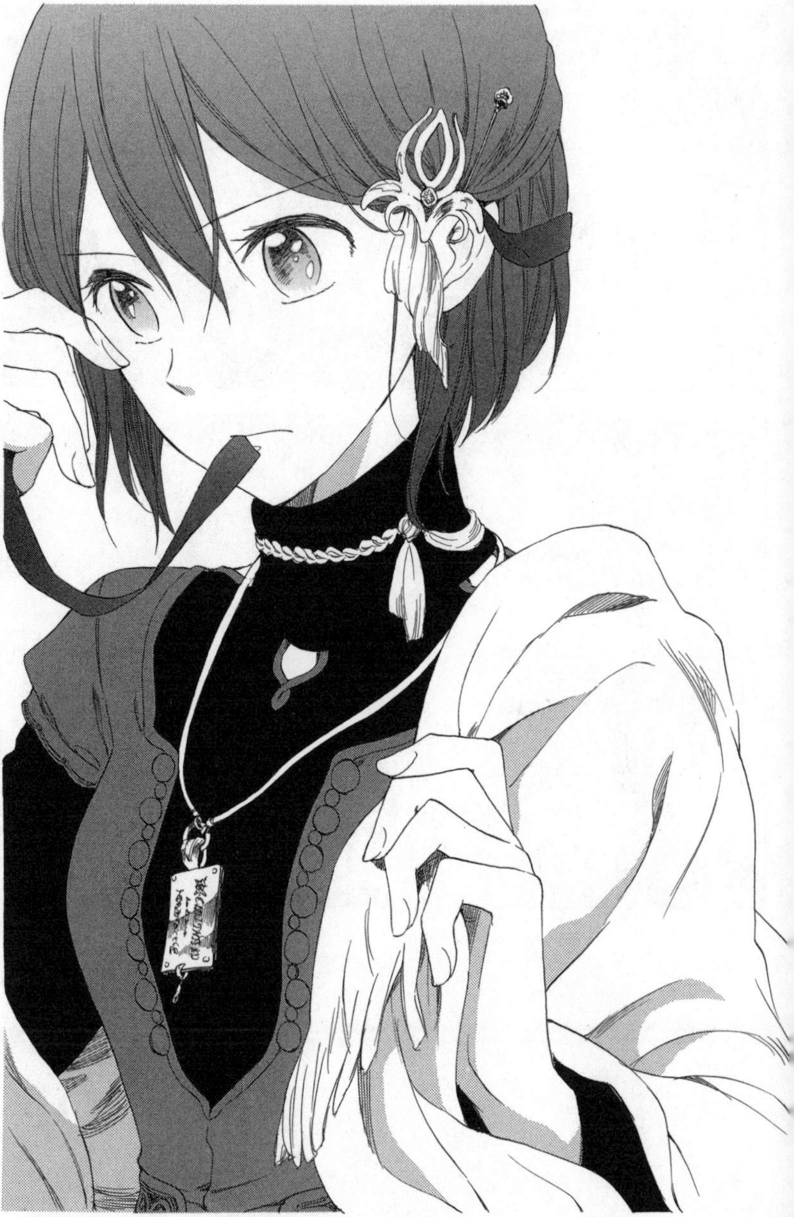

Chapter 36

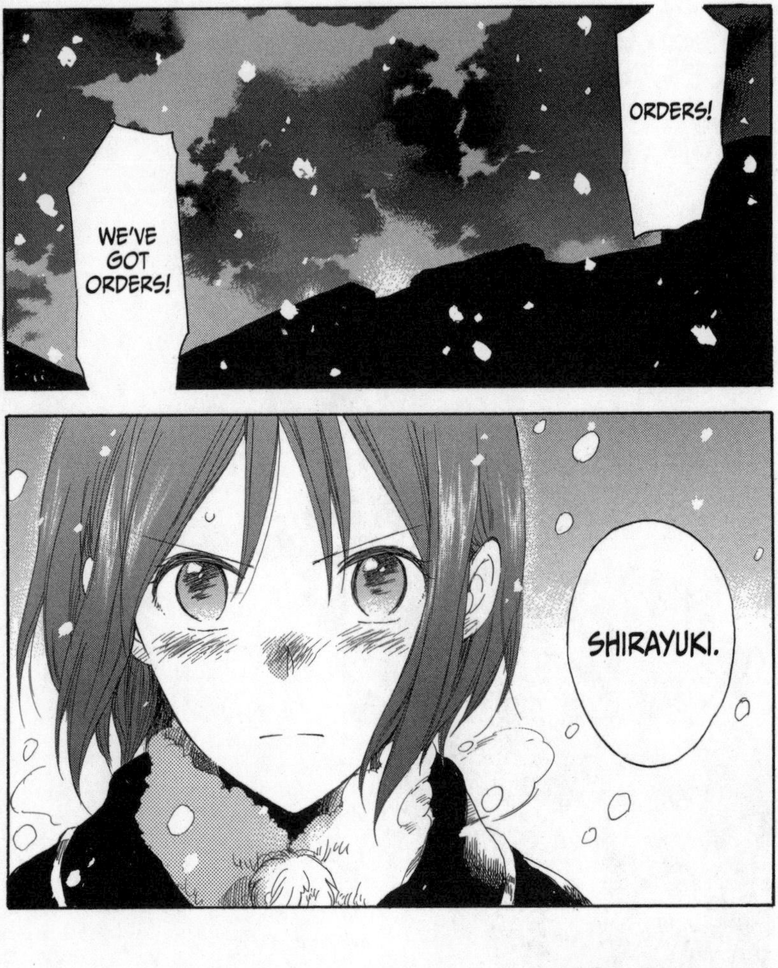
ORDERS!
WE'VE GOT ORDERS!
SHIRAYUKI.

CLARINES KINGDOM

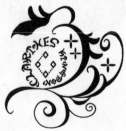

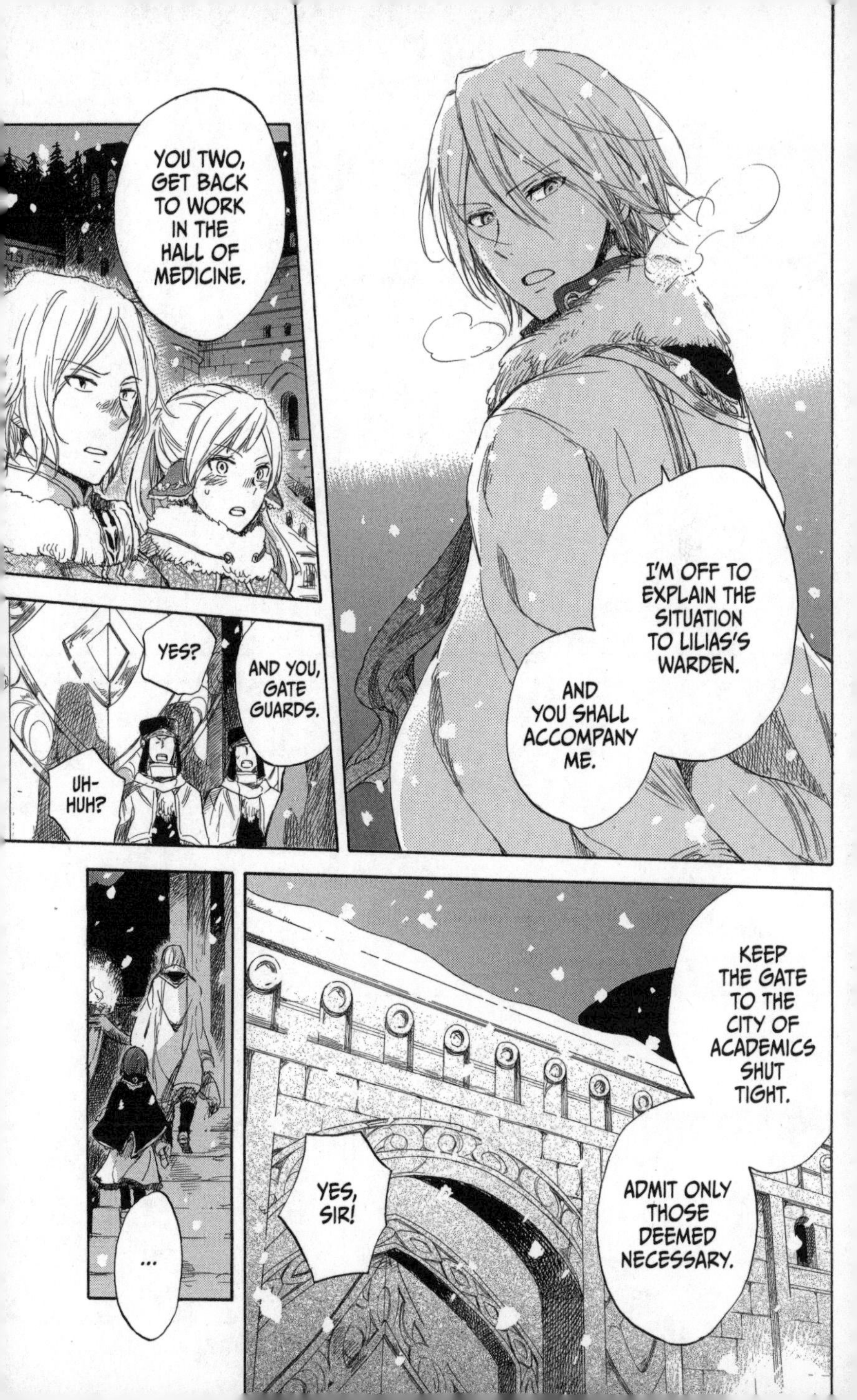
I'M OFF TO EXPLAIN THE SITUATION TO LILIAS'S WARDEN.
AND YOU SHALL ACCOMPANY ME.
YOU TWO, GET BACK TO WORK IN THE HALL OF MEDICINE.
AND YOU, GATE GUARDS.
YES?
UH-HUH?
KEEP THE GATE TO THE CITY OF ACADEMICS SHUT TIGHT.
ADMIT ONLY THOSE DEEMED NECESSARY.
YES, SIR!
...

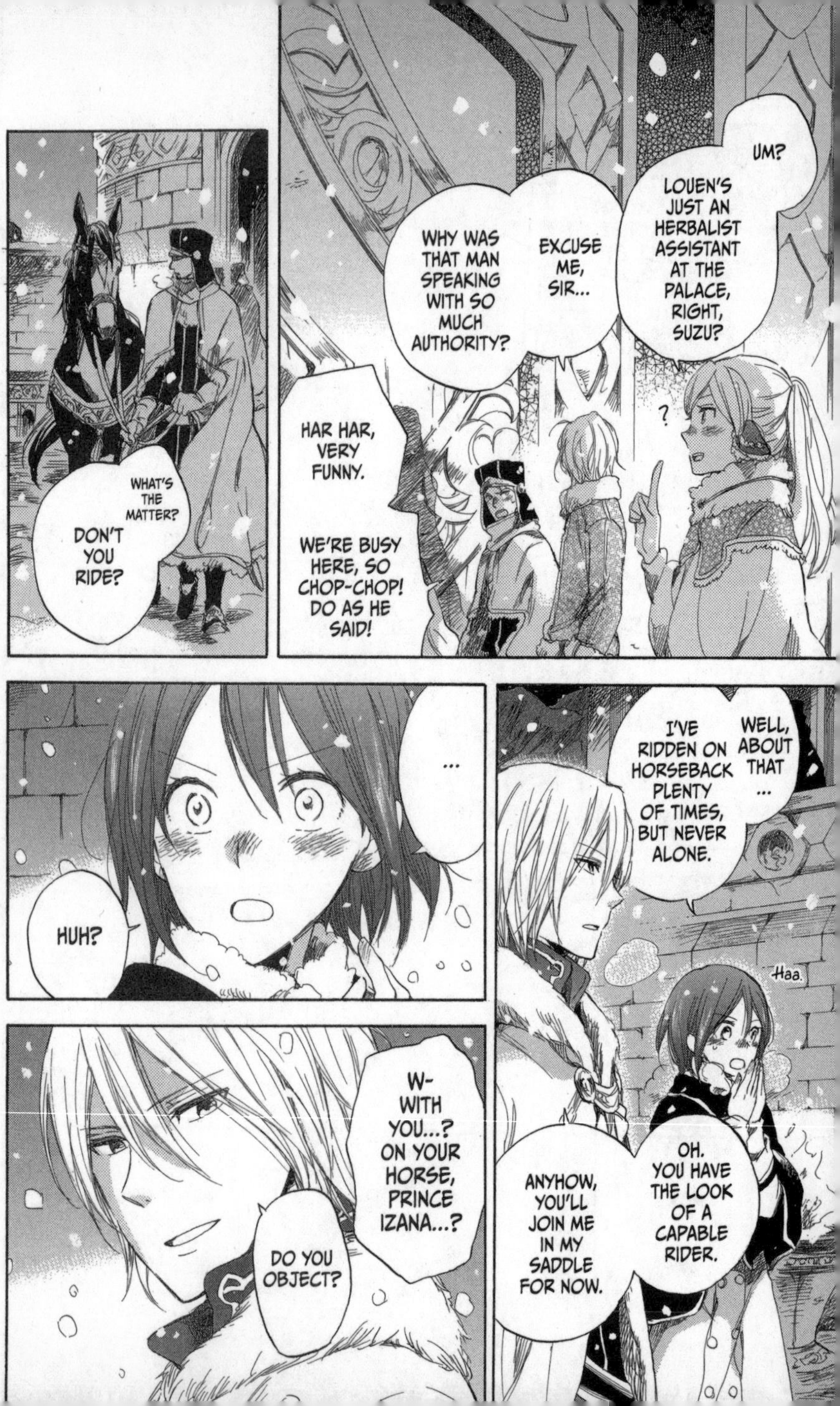
UM?
LOUEN'S JUST AN HERBALIST ASSISTANT AT THE PALACE, RIGHT, SUZU?
EXCUSE ME, SIR...
WHY WAS THAT MAN SPEAKING WITH SO MUCH AUTHORITY?
?
HAR HAR, VERY FUNNY.
WE'RE BUSY HERE, SO CHOP-CHOP! DO AS HE SAID!
WHAT'S THE MATTER?
DON'T YOU RIDE?
WELL, ABOUT THAT ...
I'VE RIDDEN ON HORSEBACK PLENTY OF TIMES, BUT NEVER ALONE.
Haa.
OH. YOU HAVE THE LOOK OF A CAPABLE RIDER.
ANYHOW, YOU'LL JOIN ME IN MY SADDLE FOR NOW.
...
HUH?
W- WITH YOU...? ON YOUR HORSE, PRINCE IZANA...?
DO YOU OBJECT?

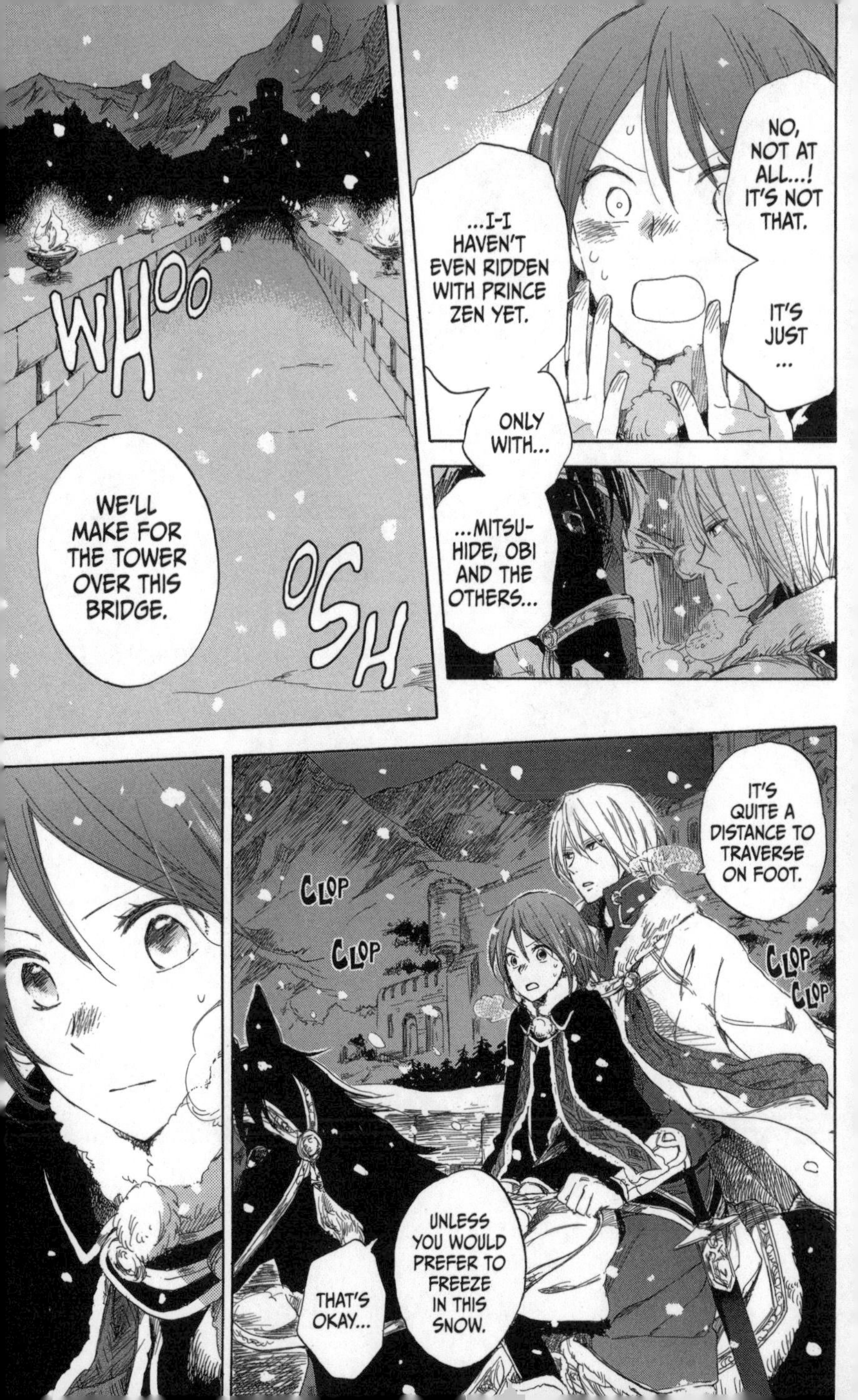
NO, NOT AT ALL...! IT'S NOT THAT.
IT'S JUST ...
...I-I HAVEN'T EVEN RIDDEN WITH PRINCE ZEN YET.
ONLY WITH...
...MITSU-HIDE, OBI AND THE OTHERS...
WHOOOSH
WE'LL MAKE FOR THE TOWER OVER THIS BRIDGE.
IT'S QUITE A DISTANCE TO TRAVERSE ON FOOT.
CLOP CLOP
CLOP
CLOP
UNLESS YOU WOULD PREFER TO FREEZE IN THIS SNOW.
THAT'S OKAY...

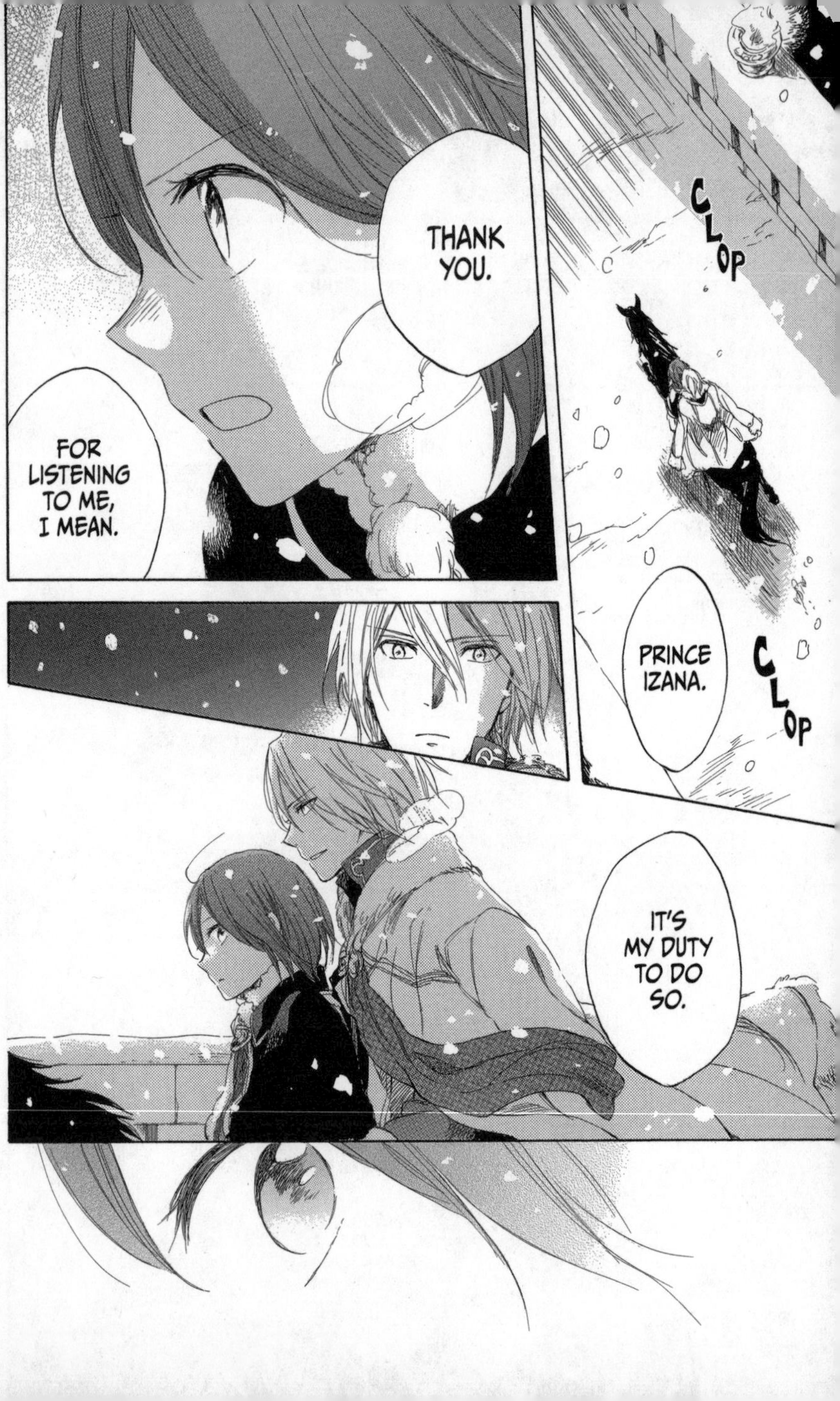

CLOP
PRINCE IZANA.
CLOP
THANK YOU.
FOR LISTENING TO ME, I MEAN.
IT'S MY DUTY TO DO SO.

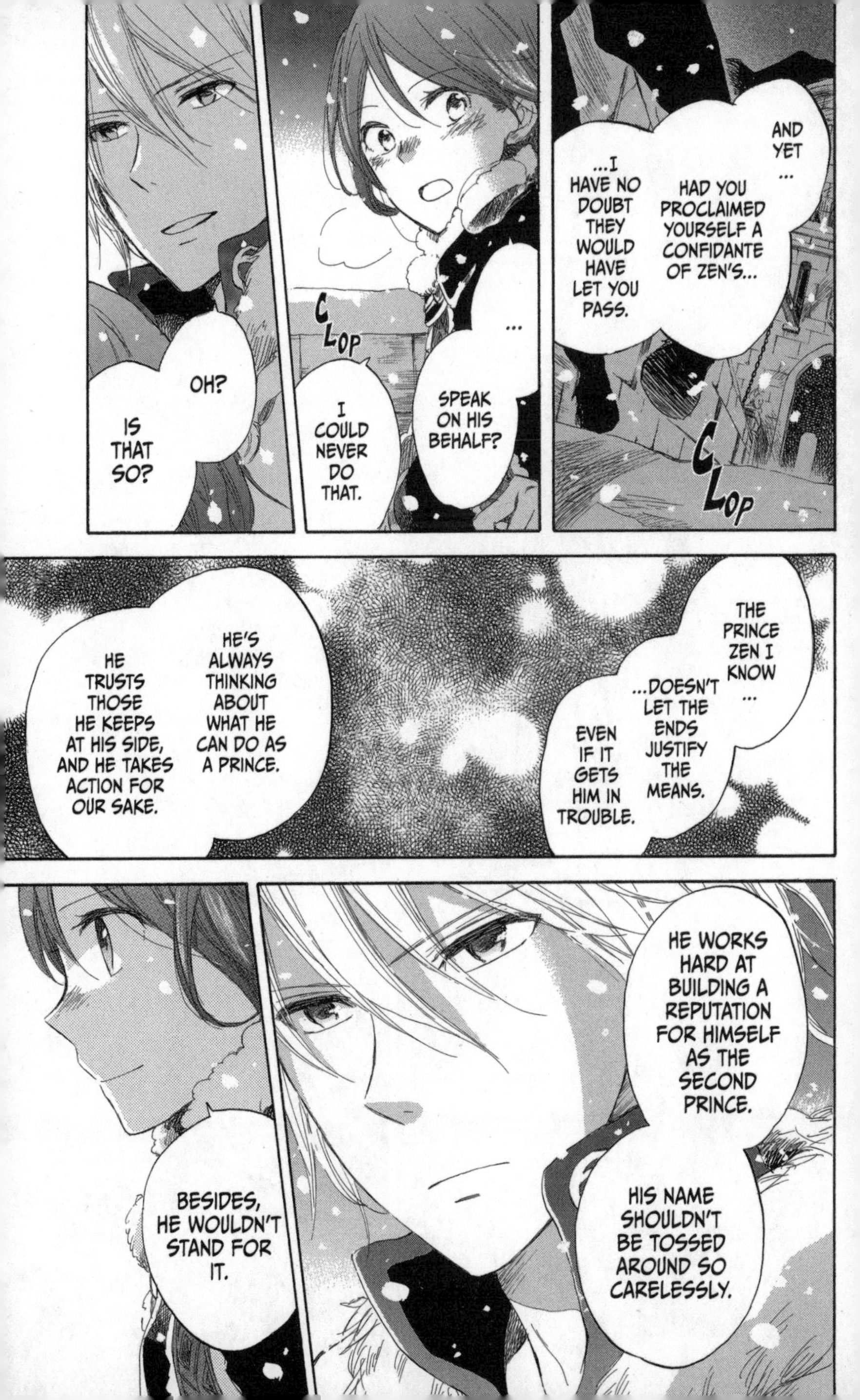
AND YET ...
HAD YOU PROCLAIMED YOURSELF A CONFIDANTE OF ZEN'S...
...I HAVE NO DOUBT THEY WOULD HAVE LET YOU PASS.
CLOP
...
SPEAK ON HIS BEHALF?
I COULD NEVER DO THAT.
CLOP
OH?
IS THAT SO?
THE PRINCE ZEN I KNOW ...
...DOESN'T LET THE ENDS JUSTIFY THE MEANS.
EVEN IF IT GETS HIM IN TROUBLE.
HE'S ALWAYS THINKING ABOUT WHAT HE CAN DO AS A PRINCE.
HE TRUSTS THOSE HE KEEPS AT HIS SIDE, AND HE TAKES ACTION FOR OUR SAKE.
HE WORKS HARD AT BUILDING A REPUTATION FOR HIMSELF AS THE SECOND PRINCE.
HIS NAME SHOULDN'T BE TOSSED AROUND SO CARELESSLY.
BESIDES, HE WOULDN'T STAND FOR IT.

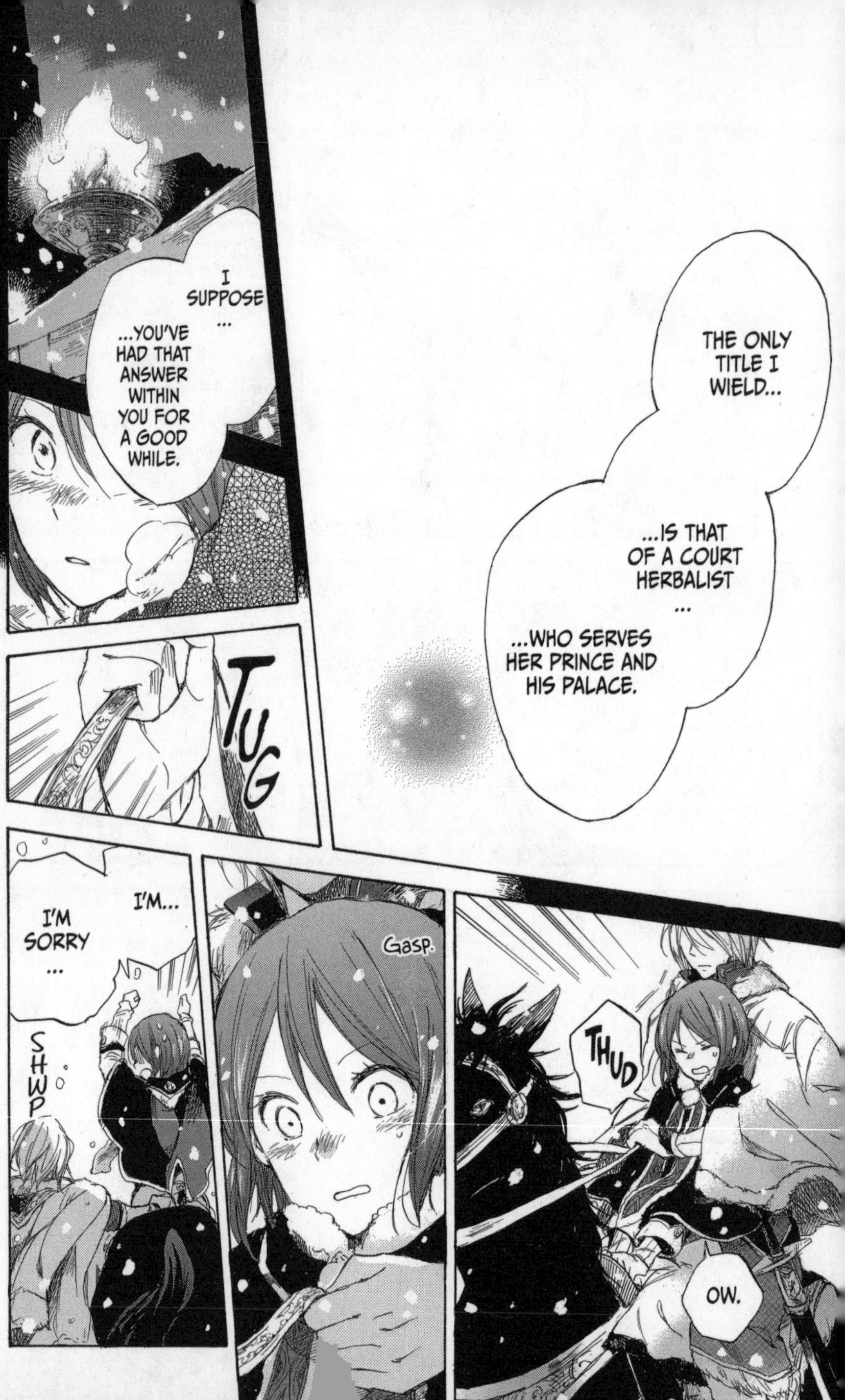
THE ONLY TITLE I WIELD...
...IS THAT OF A COURT HERBALIST ...
...WHO SERVES HER PRINCE AND HIS PALACE.
I SUPPOSE ...
...YOU'VE HAD THAT ANSWER WITHIN YOU FOR A GOOD WHILE.
TUG
THUD
OW.
Gasp.
I'M...
I'M SORRY ...
SHWP

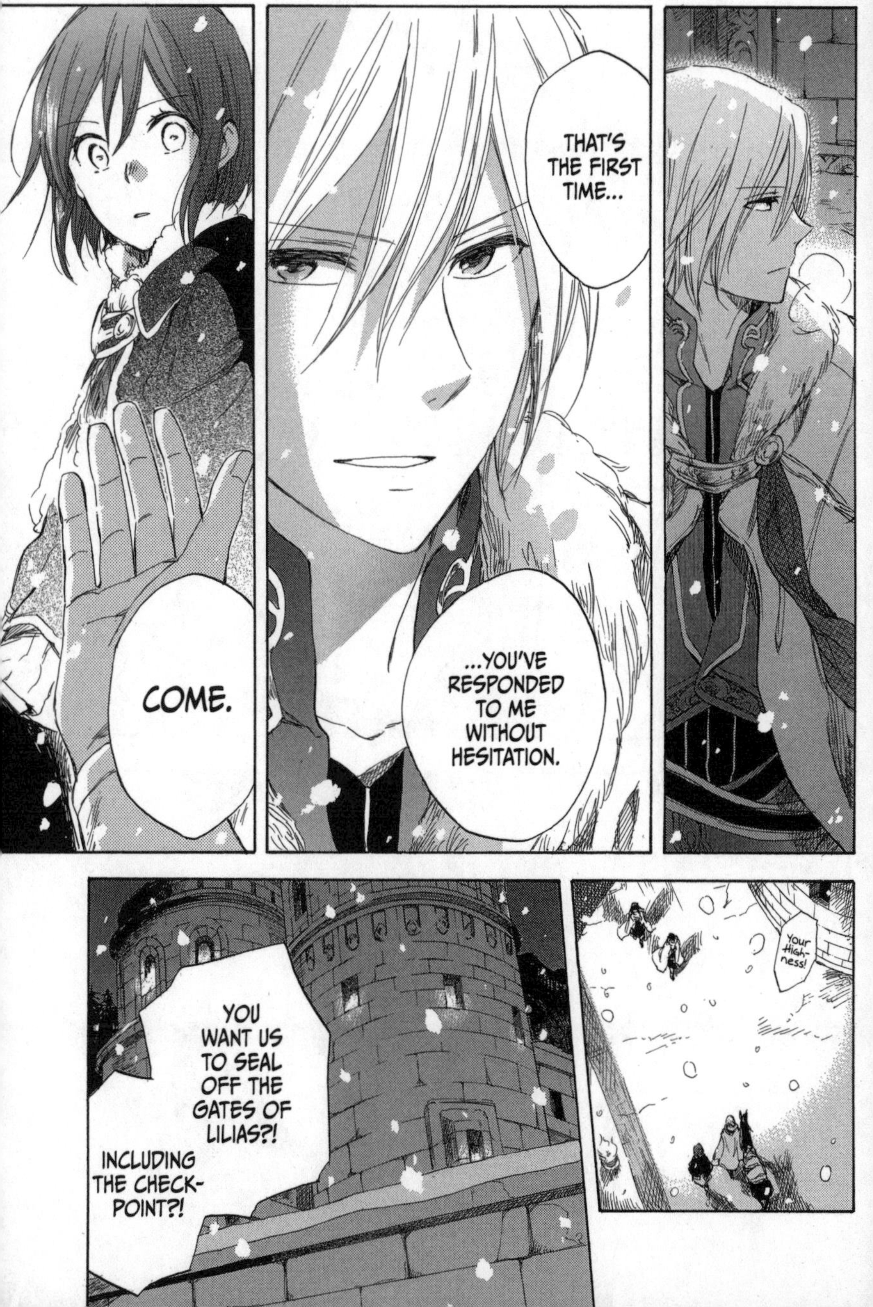
THAT'S THE FIRST TIME...
...YOU'VE RESPONDED TO ME WITHOUT HESITATION.
COME.
Your High-ness!
YOU WANT US TO SEAL OFF THE GATES OF LILIAS?!
INCLUDING THE CHECK-POINT?!

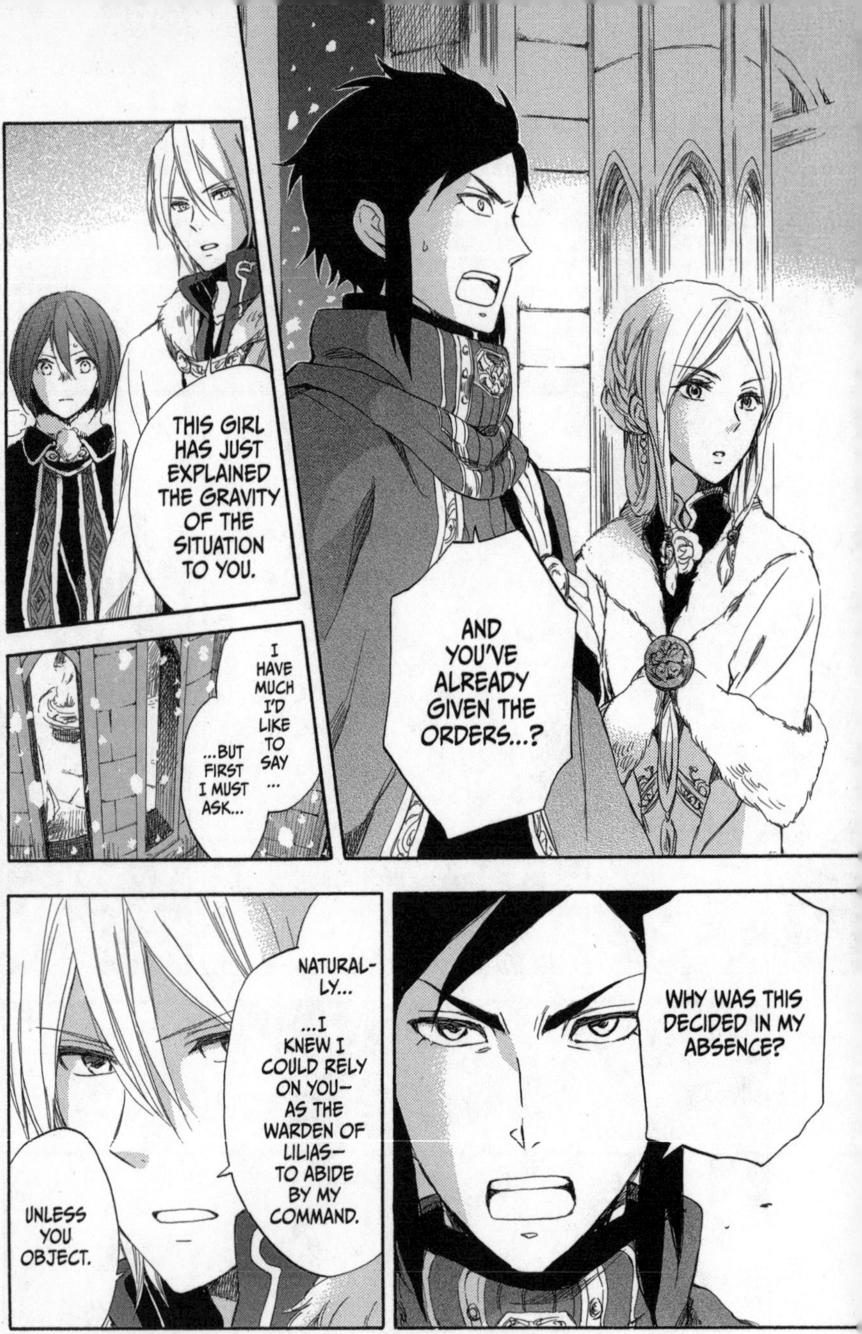
THIS GIRL HAS JUST EXPLAINED THE GRAVITY OF THE SITUATION TO YOU.
AND YOU'VE ALREADY GIVEN THE ORDERS...?
I HAVE MUCH I'D LIKE TO SAY ...
...BUT FIRST I MUST ASK...
WHY WAS THIS DECIDED IN MY ABSENCE?
NATURAL-LY...
...I KNEW I COULD RELY ON YOU— AS THE WARDEN OF LILIAS— TO ABIDE BY MY COMMAND.
UNLESS YOU OBJECT.

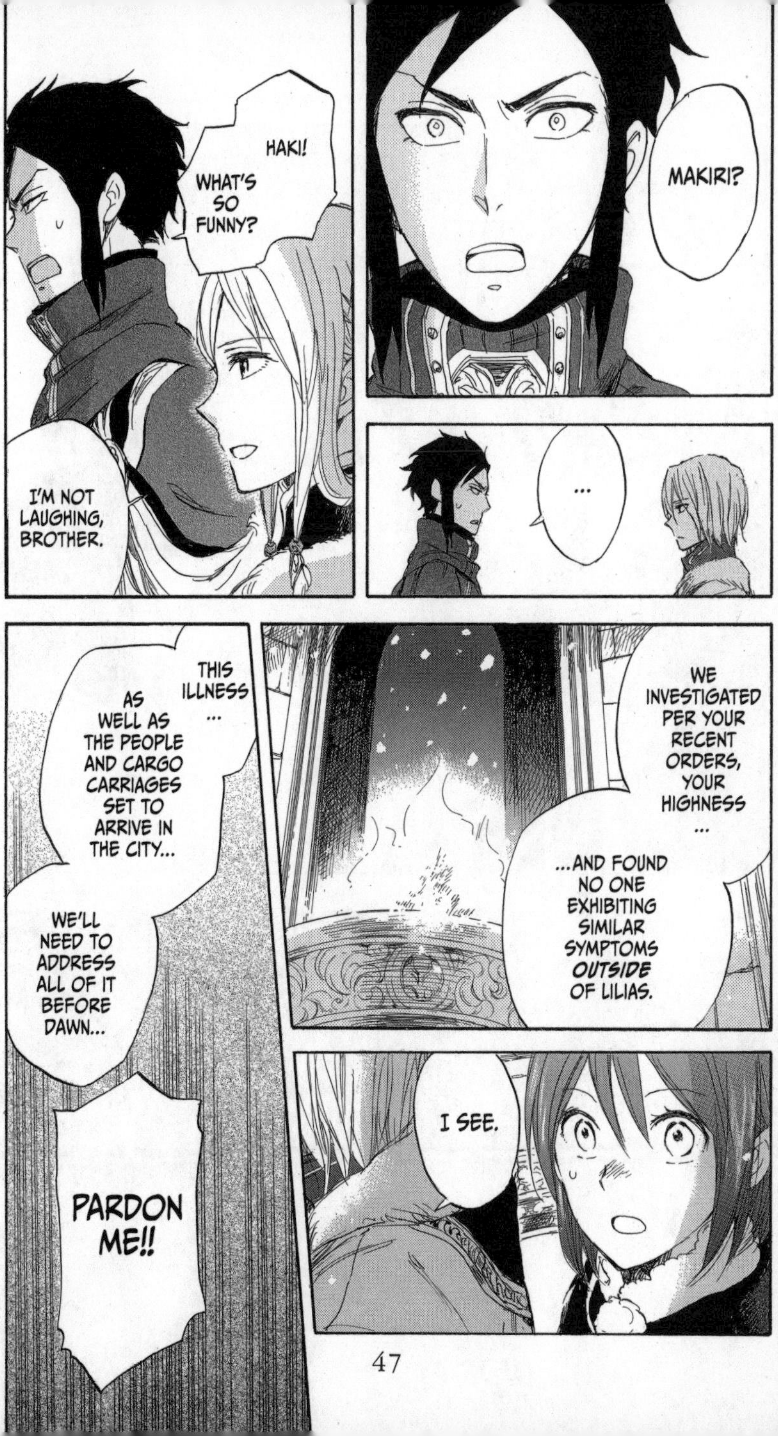
MAKIRI?
...
HAKI!
WHAT'S SO FUNNY?
I'M NOT LAUGHING, BROTHER.
WE INVESTIGATED PER YOUR RECENT ORDERS, YOUR HIGHNESS...
...AND FOUND NO ONE EXHIBITING SIMILAR SYMPTOMS *OUTSIDE* OF LILIAS.
I SEE.
THIS ILLNESS...
AS WELL AS THE PEOPLE AND CARGO CARRIAGES SET TO ARRIVE IN THE CITY...
WE'LL NEED TO ADDRESS ALL OF IT BEFORE DAWN...
PARDON ME!!

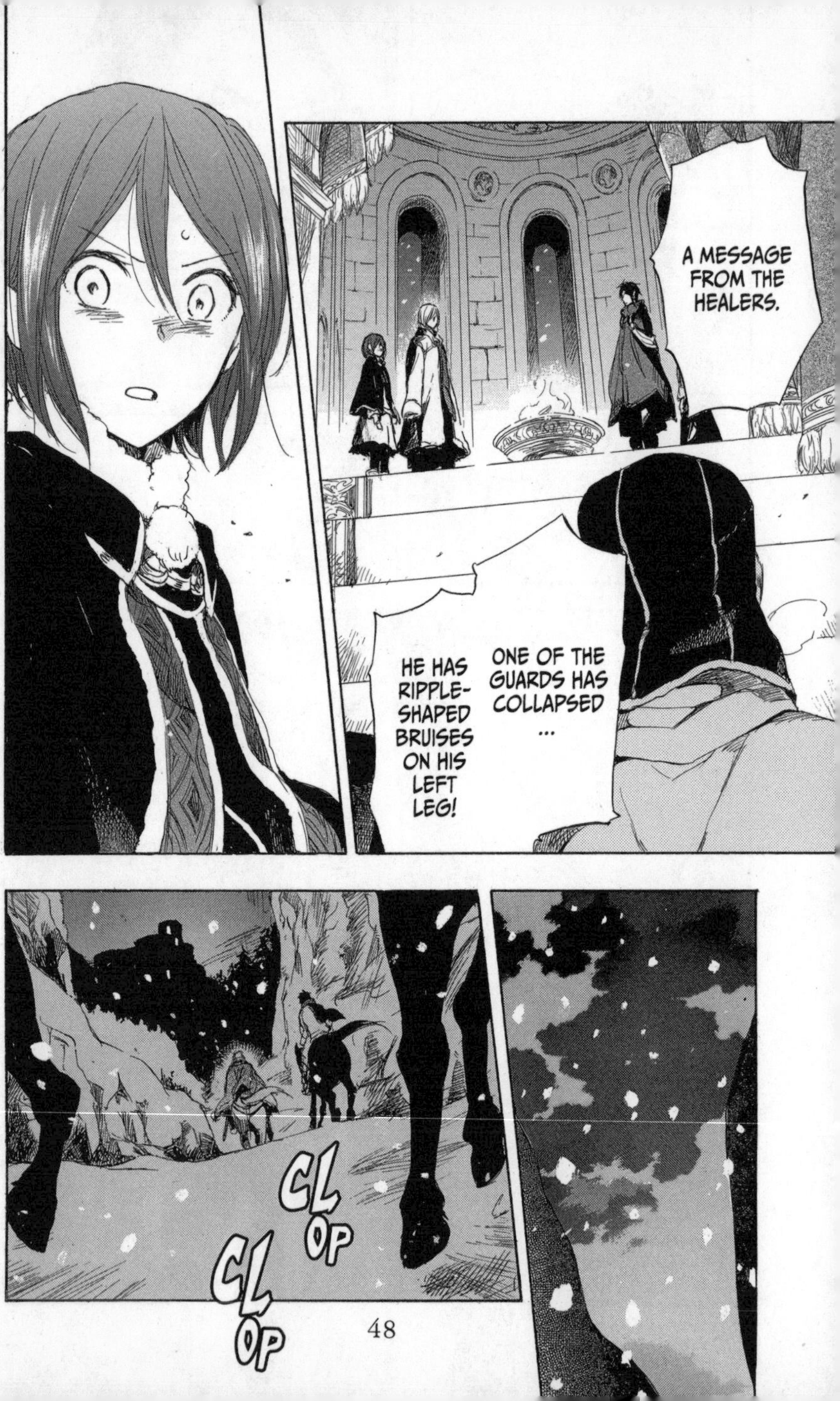
A MESSAGE FROM THE HEALERS.
ONE OF THE GUARDS HAS COLLAPSED ...
HE HAS RIPPLE-SHAPED BRUISES ON HIS LEFT LEG!
CLOP
CLOP

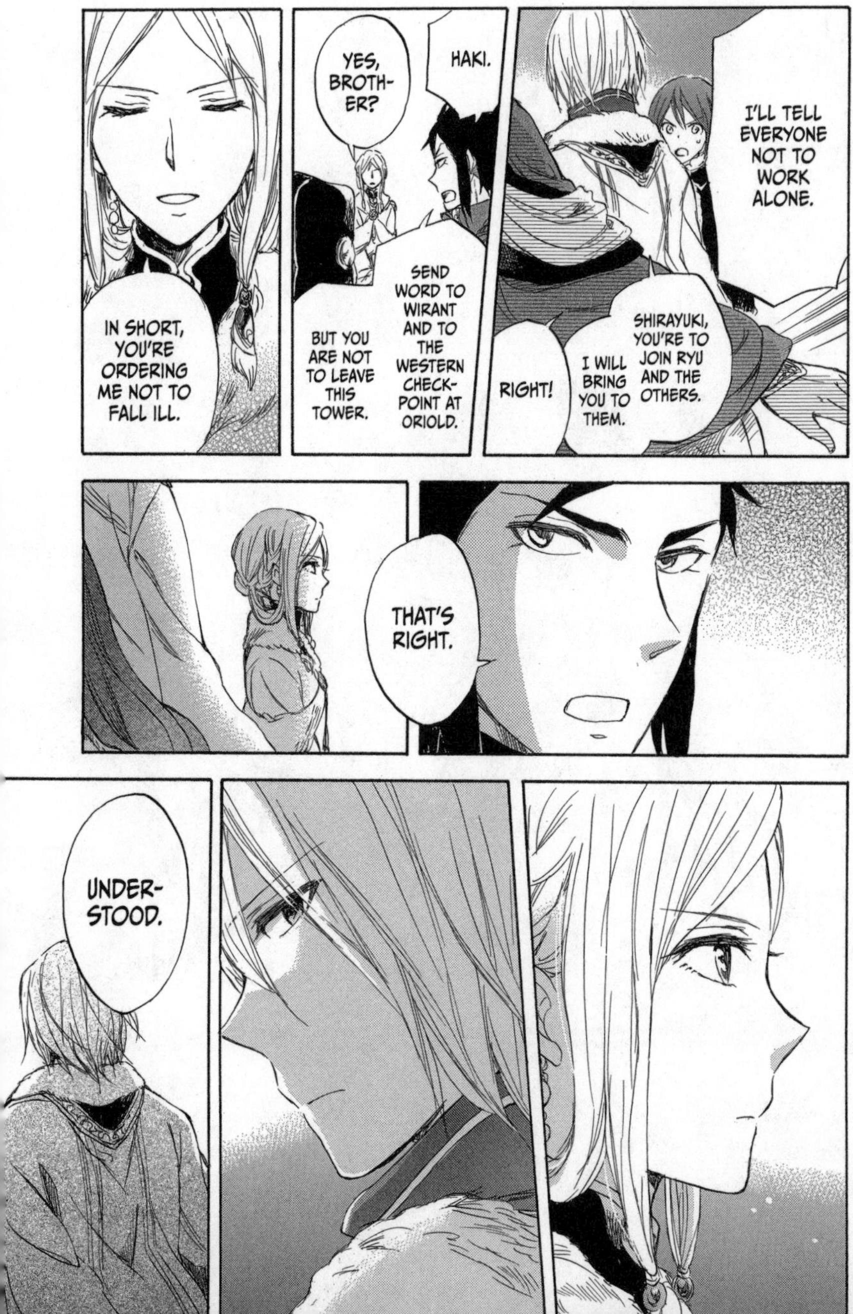
I'LL TELL EVERYONE NOT TO WORK ALONE.
SHIRAYUKI, YOU'RE TO JOIN RYU AND THE OTHERS.
I WILL BRING YOU TO THEM.
RIGHT!
HAKI.
YES, BROTHER?
SEND WORD TO WIRANT AND TO THE WESTERN CHECKPOINT AT ORIOLD.
BUT YOU ARE NOT TO LEAVE THIS TOWER.
IN SHORT, YOU'RE ORDERING ME NOT TO FALL ILL.
THAT'S RIGHT.
UNDERSTOOD.

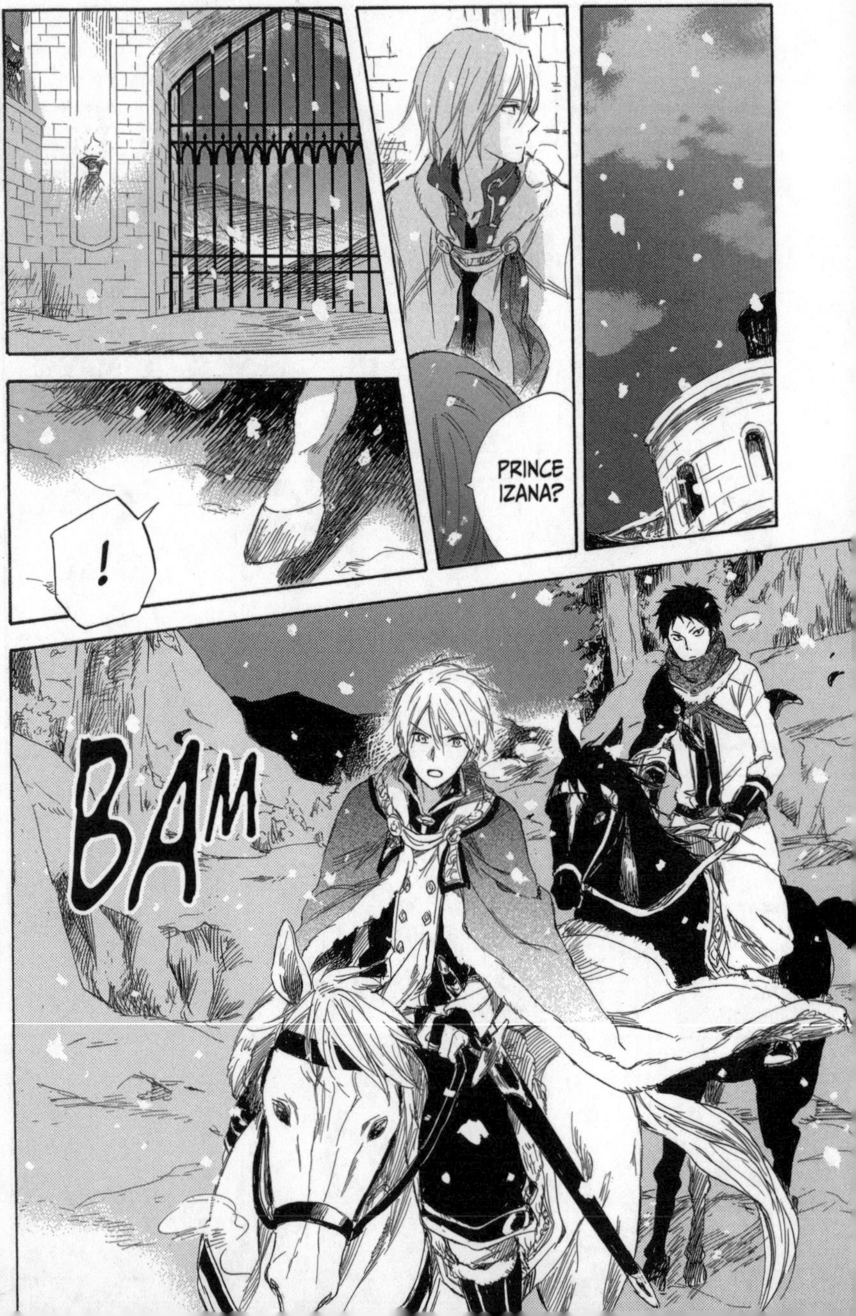
PRINCE IZANA?
!
BAM

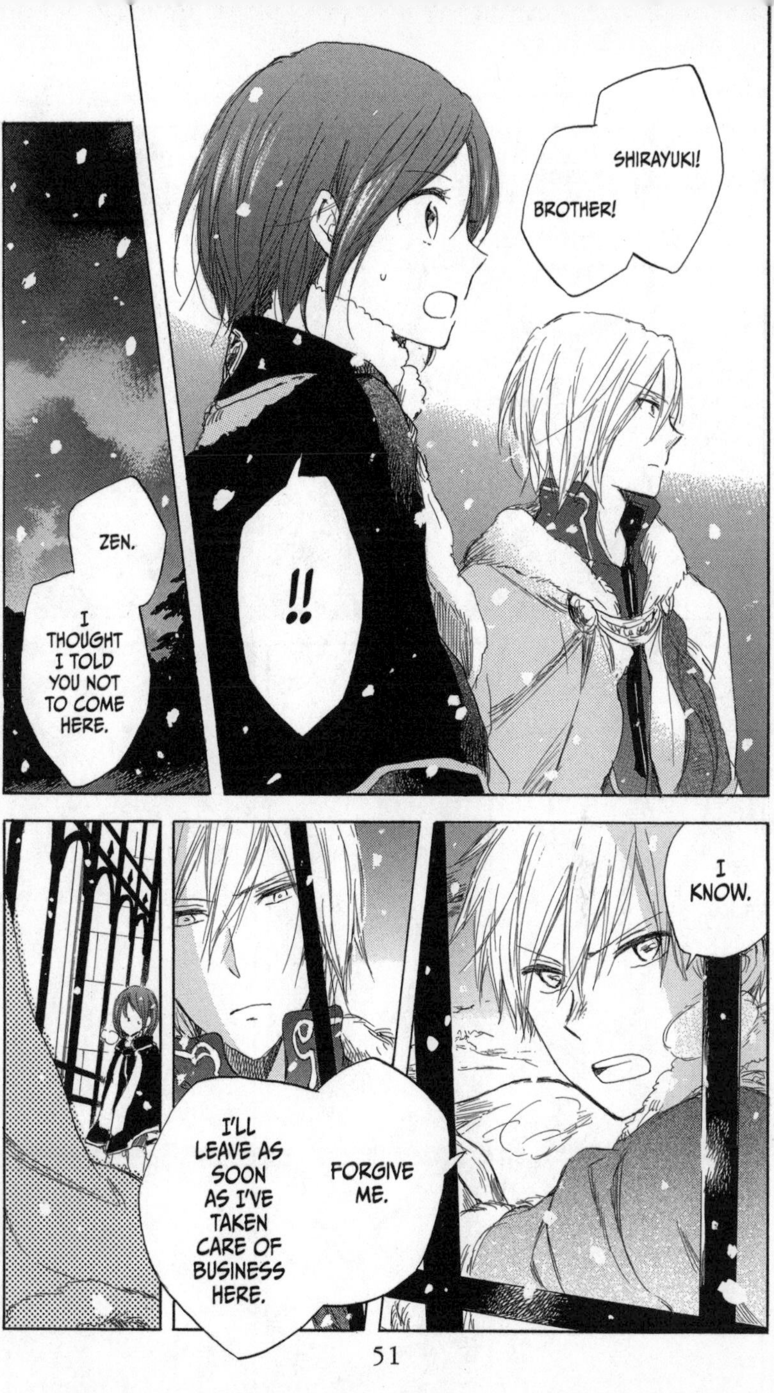
SHIRAYUKI!
BROTHER!
!!
ZEN.
I THOUGHT I TOLD YOU NOT TO COME HERE.
I KNOW.
FORGIVE ME.
I'LL LEAVE AS SOON AS I'VE TAKEN CARE OF BUSINESS HERE.

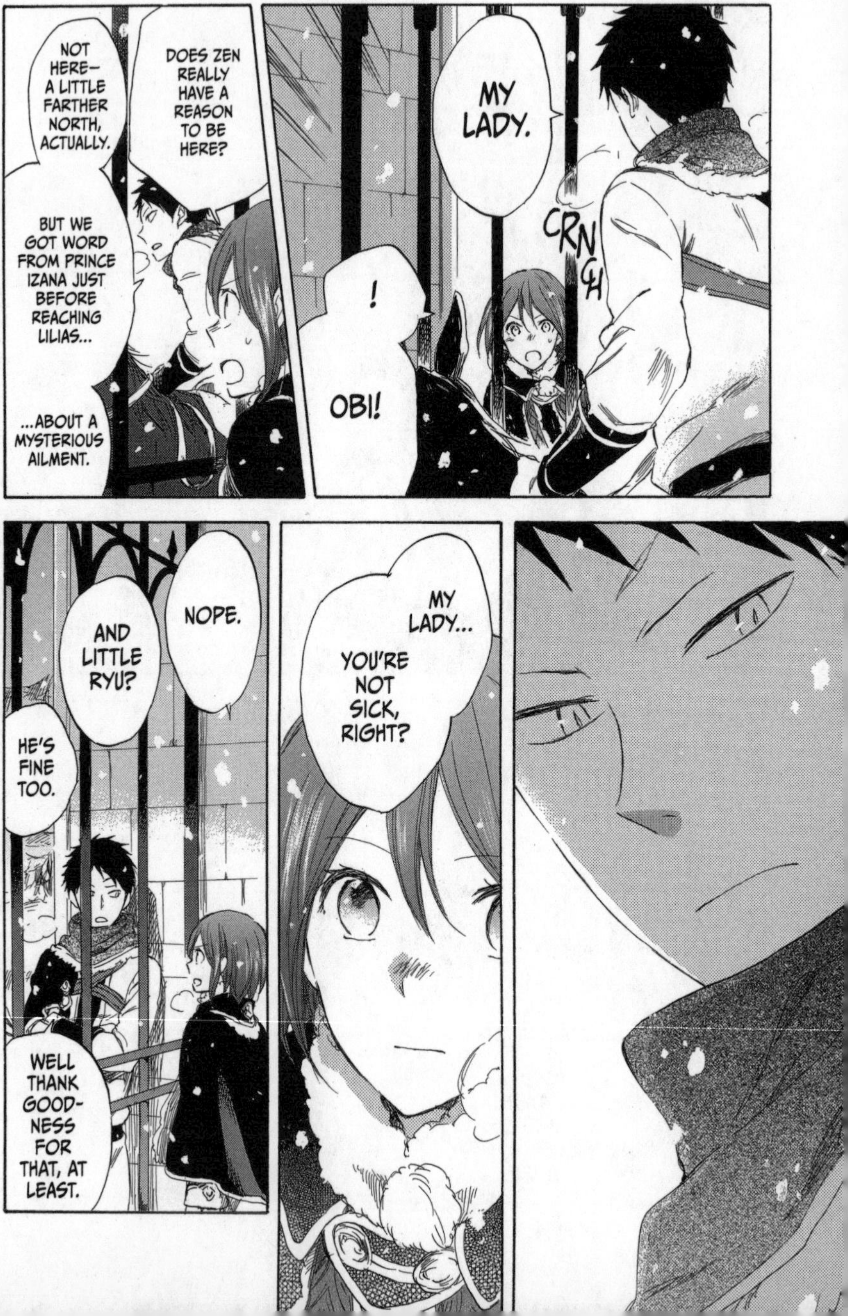
MY LADY.
CRNCH
!
OBI!
DOES ZEN REALLY HAVE A REASON TO BE HERE?
NOT HERE— A LITTLE FARTHER NORTH, ACTUALLY.
BUT WE GOT WORD FROM PRINCE IZANA JUST BEFORE REACHING LILIAS...
...ABOUT A MYSTERIOUS AILMENT.
MY LADY... YOU'RE NOT SICK, RIGHT?
NOPE.
AND LITTLE RYU?
HE'S FINE TOO.
WELL THANK GOOD-NESS FOR THAT, AT LEAST.

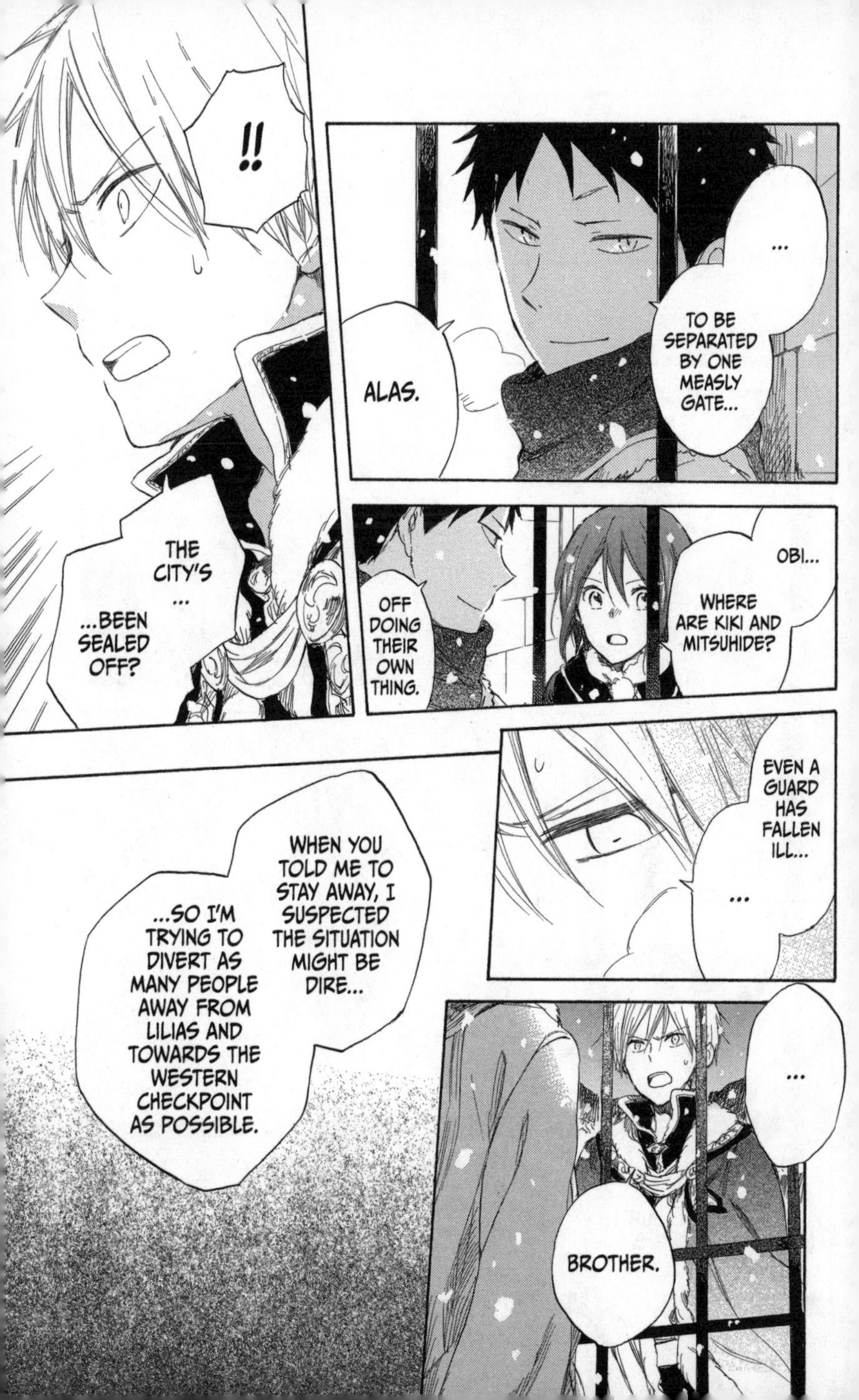
...
TO BE SEPARATED BY ONE MEASLY GATE...
ALAS.
OBI...
WHERE ARE KIKI AND MITSUHIDE?
OFF DOING THEIR OWN THING.
!!
THE CITY'S ...
...BEEN SEALED OFF?
EVEN A GUARD HAS FALLEN ILL...
...
...
BROTHER.
WHEN YOU TOLD ME TO STAY AWAY, I SUSPECTED THE SITUATION MIGHT BE DIRE...
...SO I'M TRYING TO DIVERT AS MANY PEOPLE AWAY FROM LILIAS AND TOWARDS THE WESTERN CHECKPOINT AS POSSIBLE.

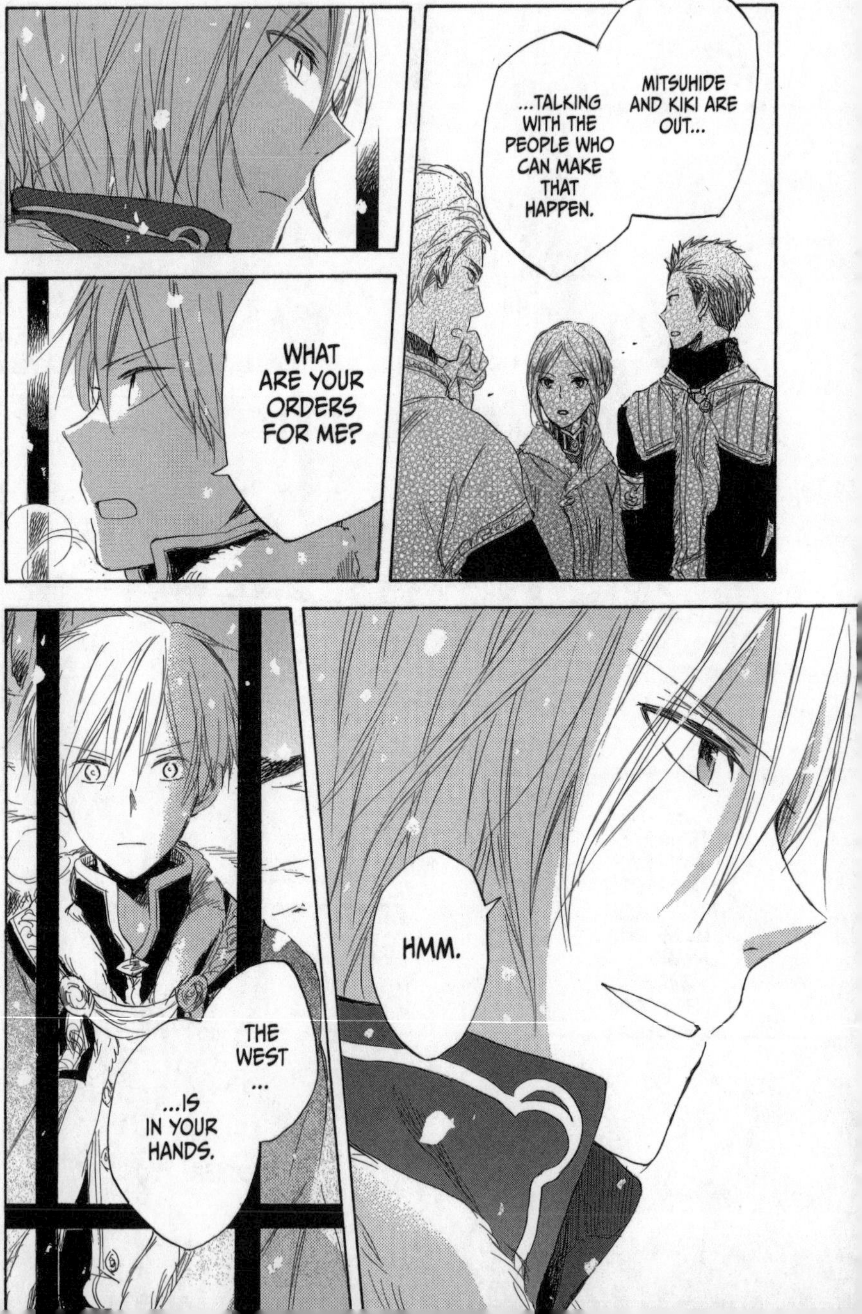
MITSUHIDE AND KIKI ARE OUT...
...TALKING WITH THE PEOPLE WHO CAN MAKE THAT HAPPEN.
WHAT ARE YOUR ORDERS FOR ME?
HMM.
THE WEST ...
...IS IN YOUR HANDS.

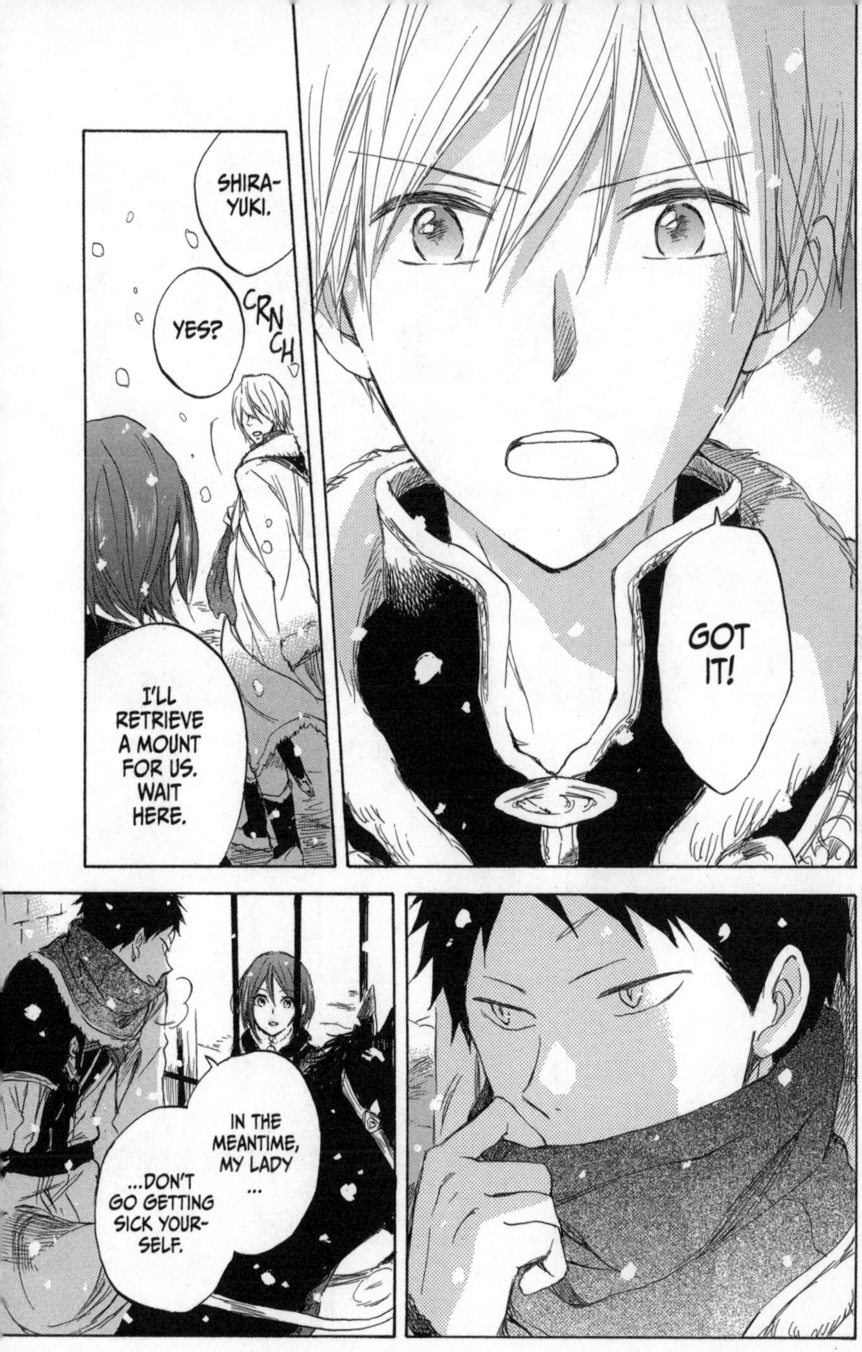
GOT IT!
SHIRA-YUKI.
YES?
CRNCH
I'LL RETRIEVE A MOUNT FOR US. WAIT HERE.
IN THE MEANTIME, MY LADY ...
...DON'T GO GETTING SICK YOUR-SELF.

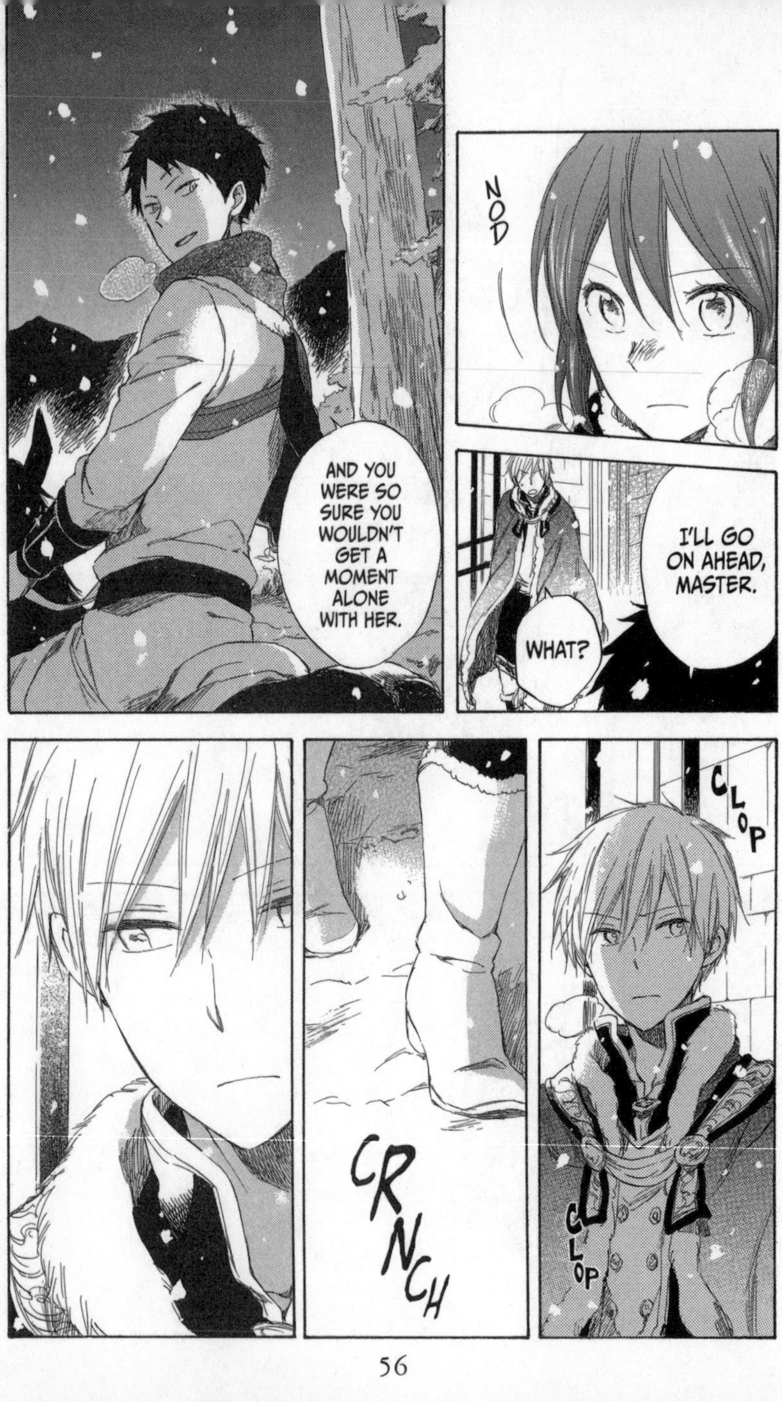
NOD
I'LL GO ON AHEAD, MASTER.
WHAT?
AND YOU WERE SO SURE YOU WOULDN'T GET A MOMENT ALONE WITH HER.
CLOP
CLOP
CRNCH

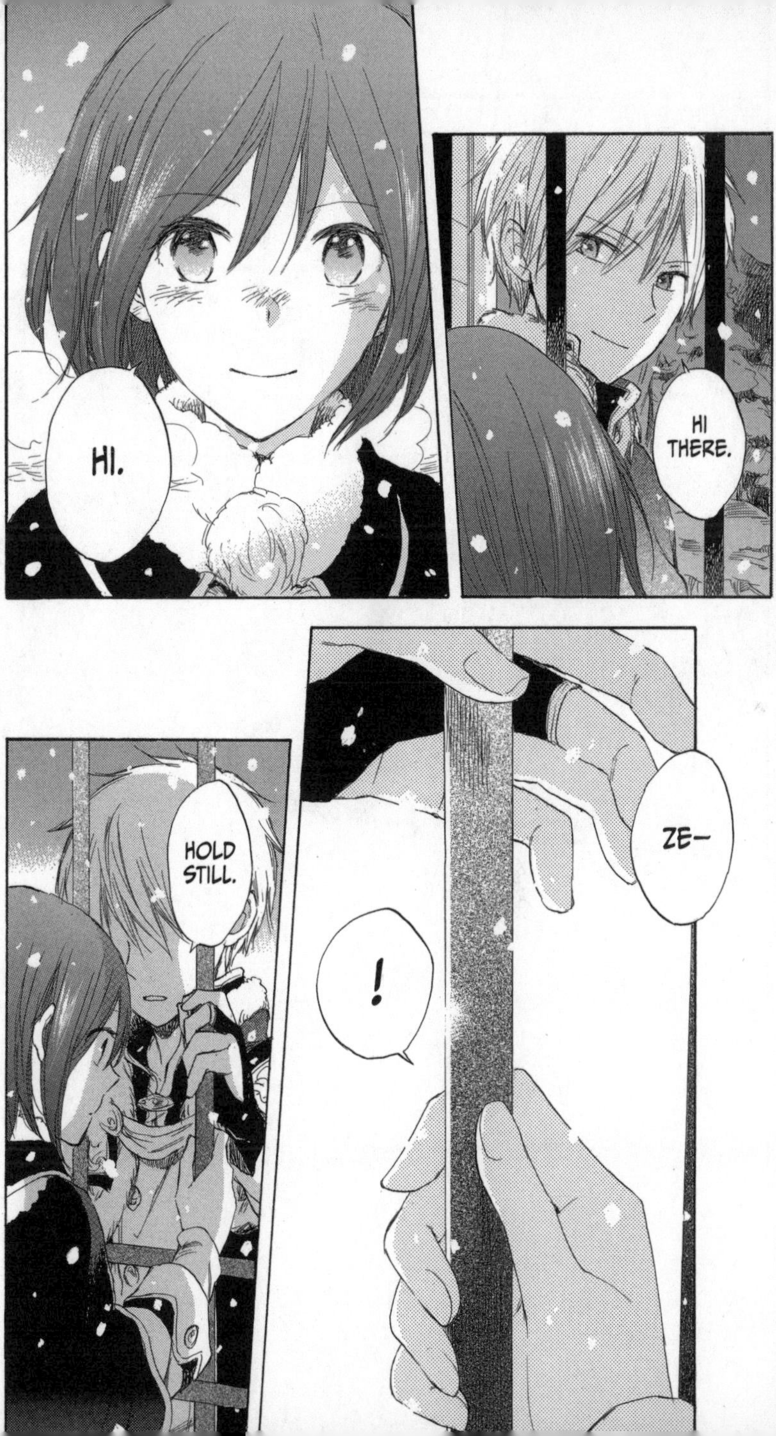
HI THERE.
HI.
ZE—
!
HOLD STILL.

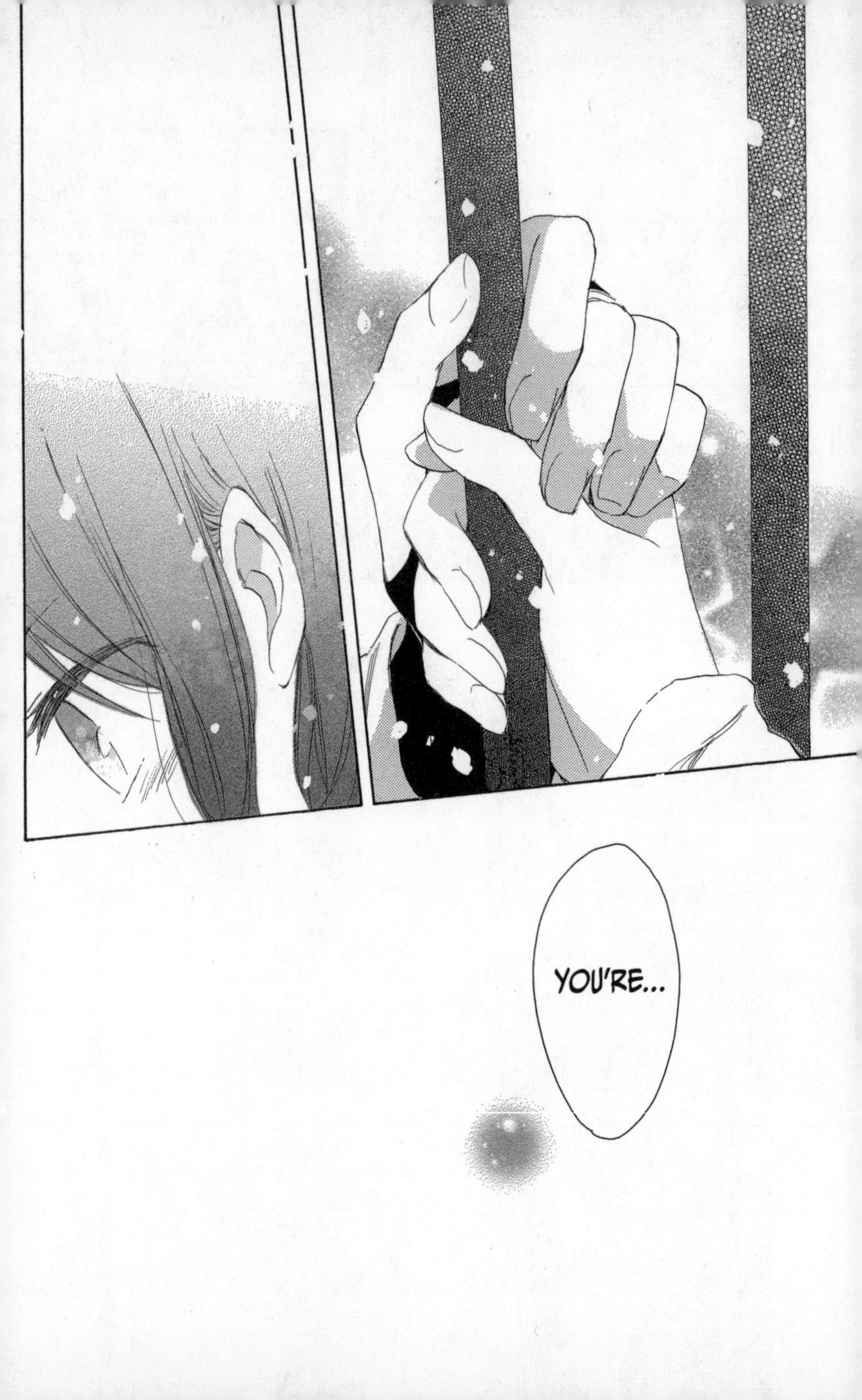
YOU'RE...

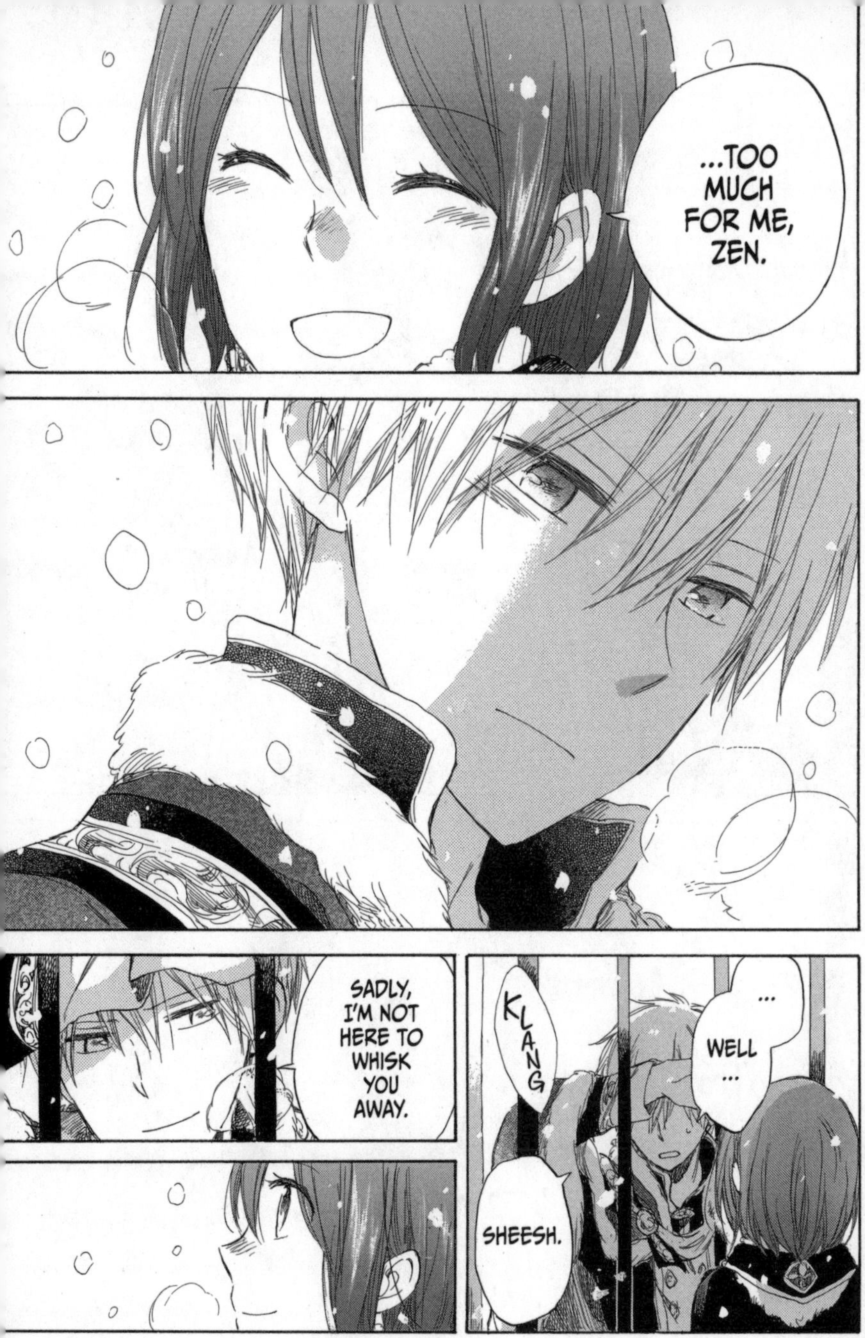
...TOO MUCH FOR ME, ZEN.
... WELL ...
KLANG
SHEESH.
SADLY, I'M NOT HERE TO WHISK YOU AWAY.

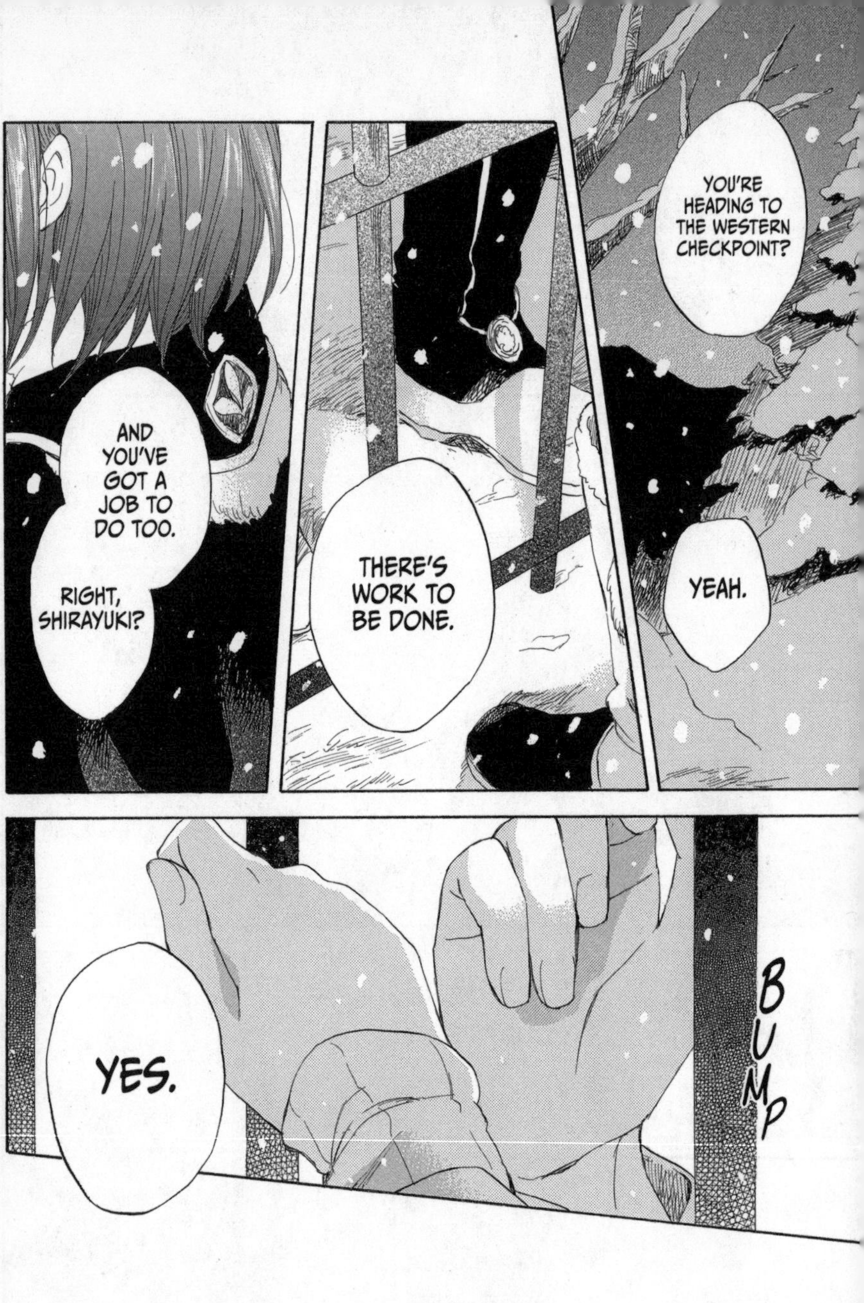
YOU'RE HEADING TO THE WESTERN CHECKPOINT?
YEAH.
THERE'S WORK TO BE DONE.
AND YOU'VE GOT A JOB TO DO TOO.
RIGHT, SHIRAYUKI?
BUMP
YES.

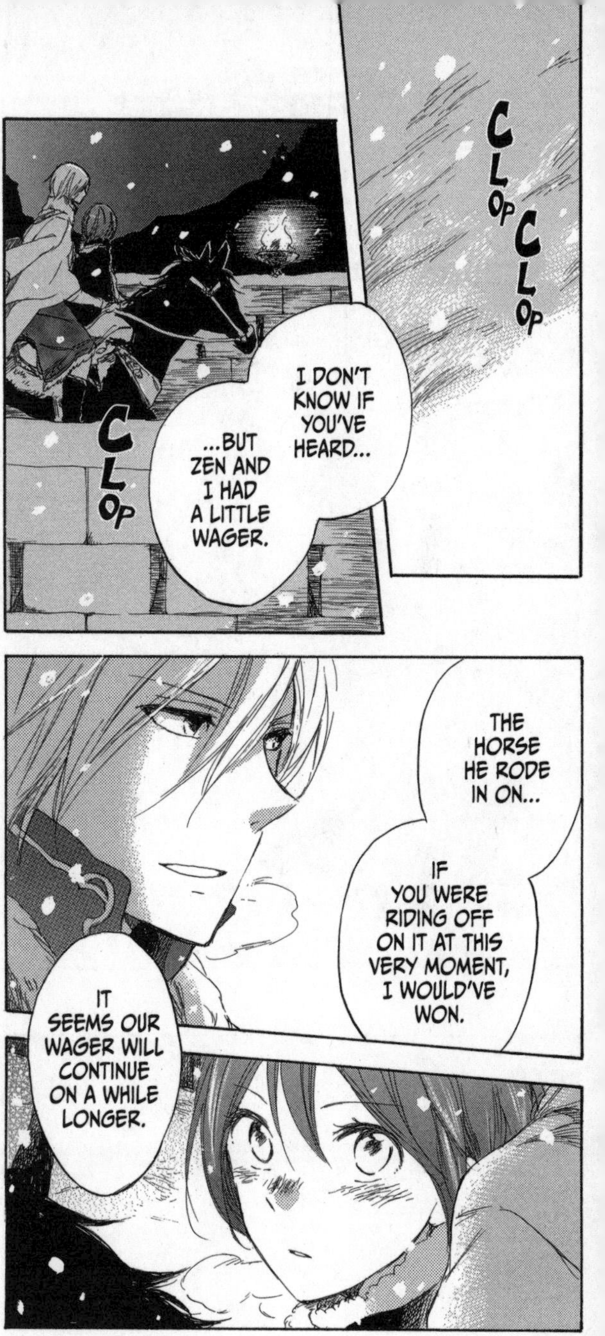
CLOP CLOP CLOP
CLOP
I DON'T KNOW IF YOU'VE HEARD...
...BUT ZEN AND I HAD A LITTLE WAGER.
THE HORSE HE RODE IN ON...
IF YOU WERE RIDING OFF ON IT AT THIS VERY MOMENT, I WOULD'VE WON.
IT SEEMS OUR WAGER WILL CONTINUE ON A WHILE LONGER.

TRIP

In November 2012, I took a trip to Izumo.

Since I went during Kamiarizuki (the month when gods are present, according to Japan's old calendar), I thought maybe I'd see some little deities hanging out on the lanterns at the Grand Shrine...

I saw so many lovely sights while walking around there.

But I didn't know anything about the palace, so my friend Hachi (Toki Yajima) had to explain everything.

Hachi spent a lot of time reflecting on the fact that we were in Izumo... Maybe she was moved by the city's distinct double-bun hairstyle...

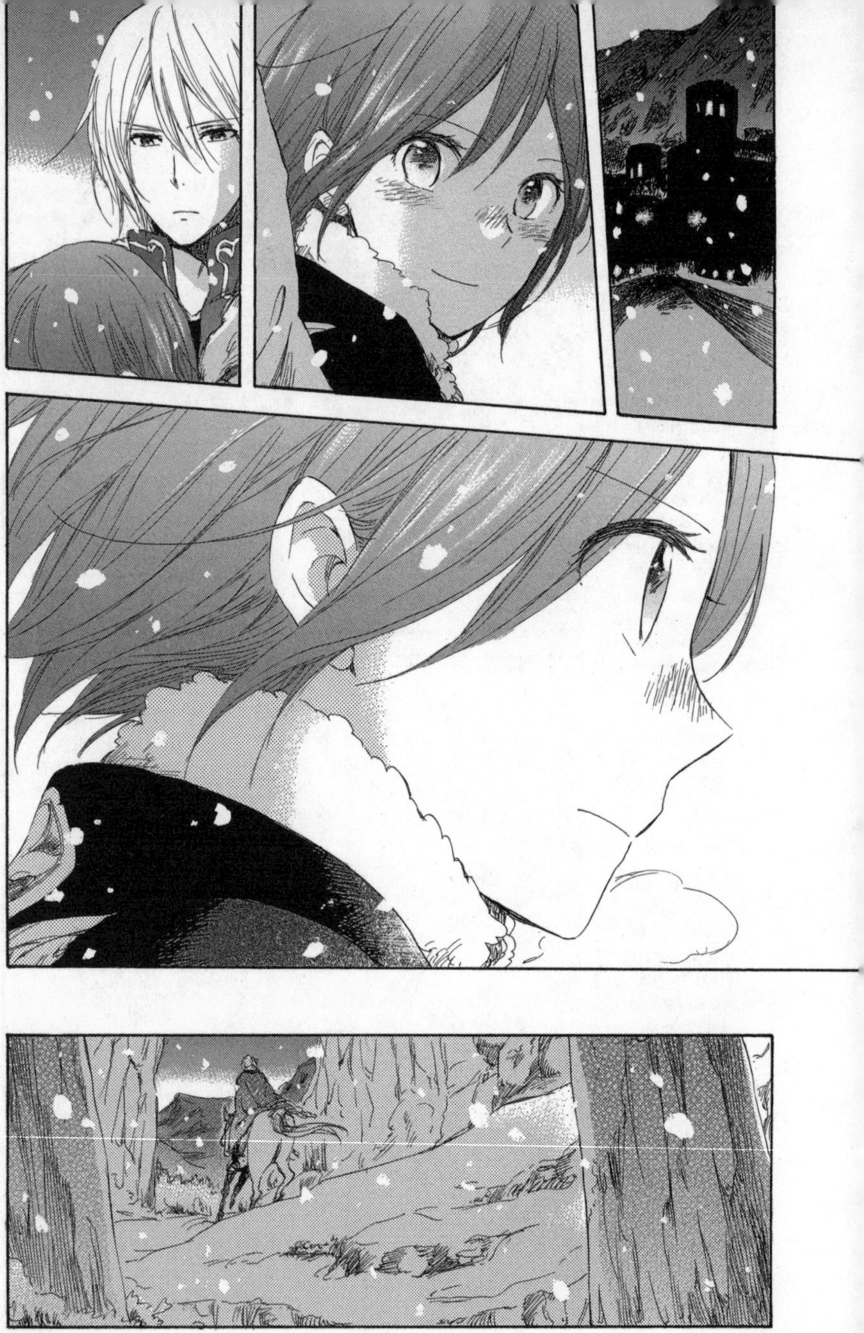

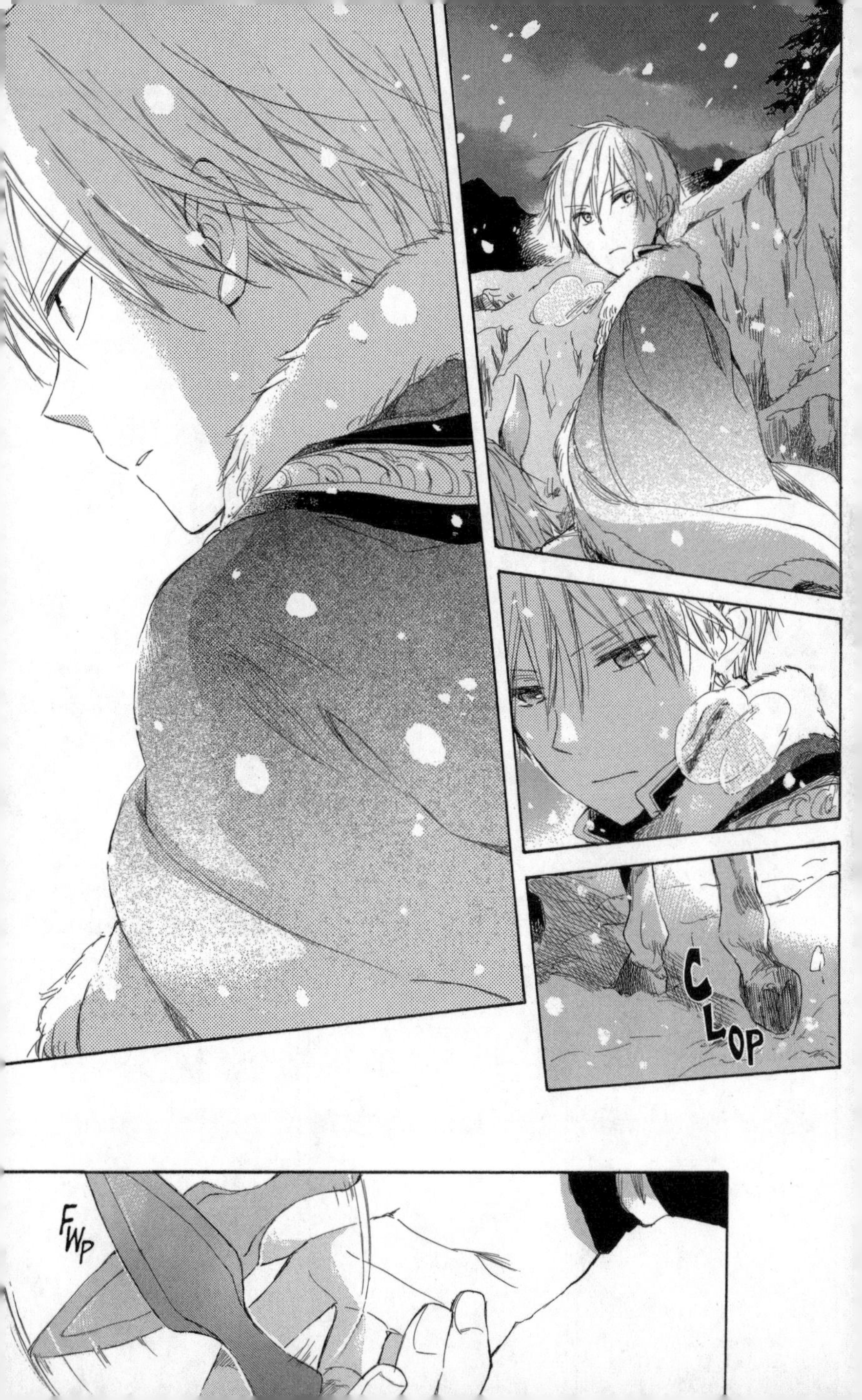
CLOP
FWP

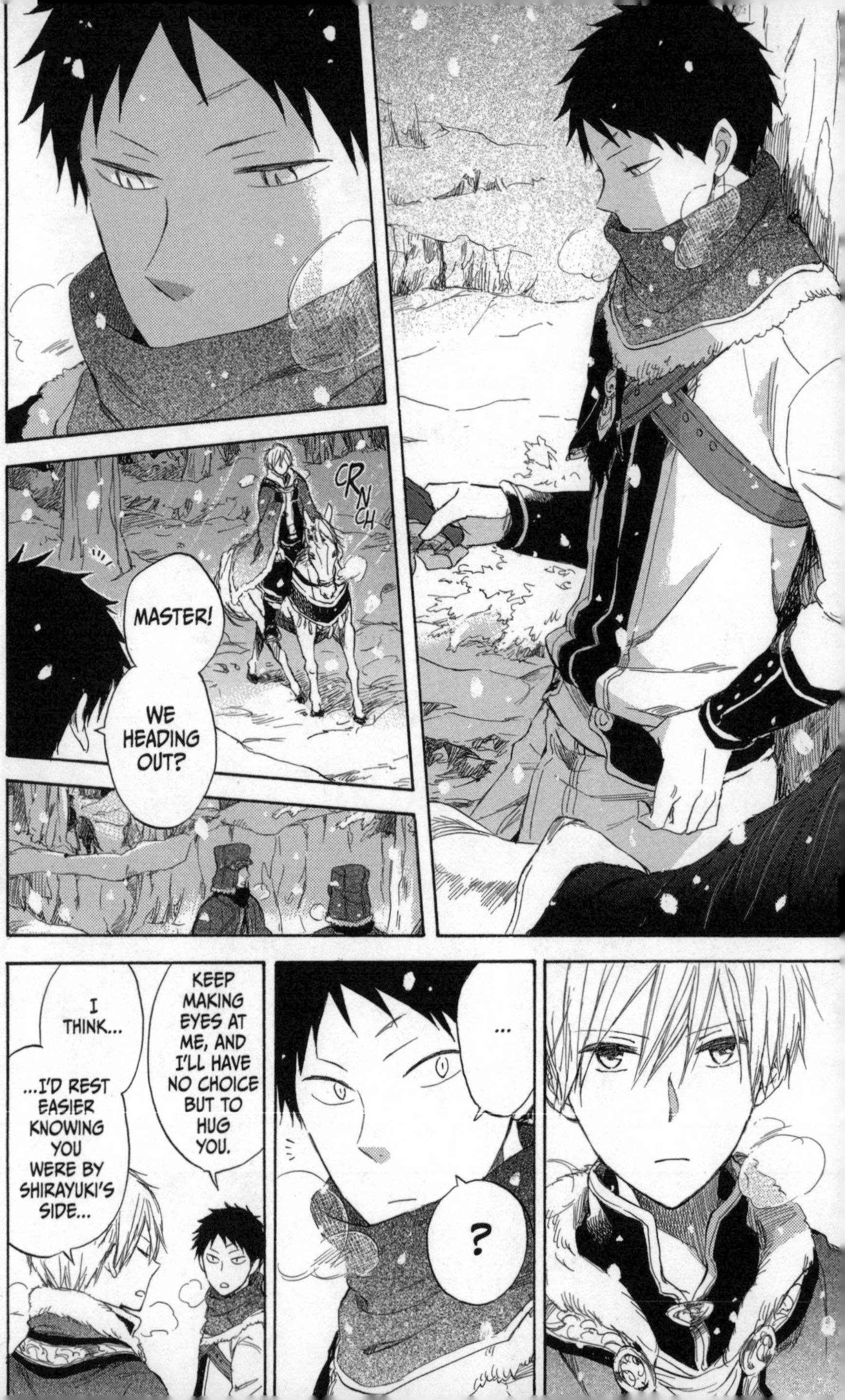
CRNCH
MASTER!
WE HEADING OUT?
...
?
KEEP MAKING EYES AT ME, AND I'LL HAVE NO CHOICE BUT TO HUG YOU.
I THINK...
...I'D REST EASIER KNOWING YOU WERE BY SHIRAYUKI'S SIDE...

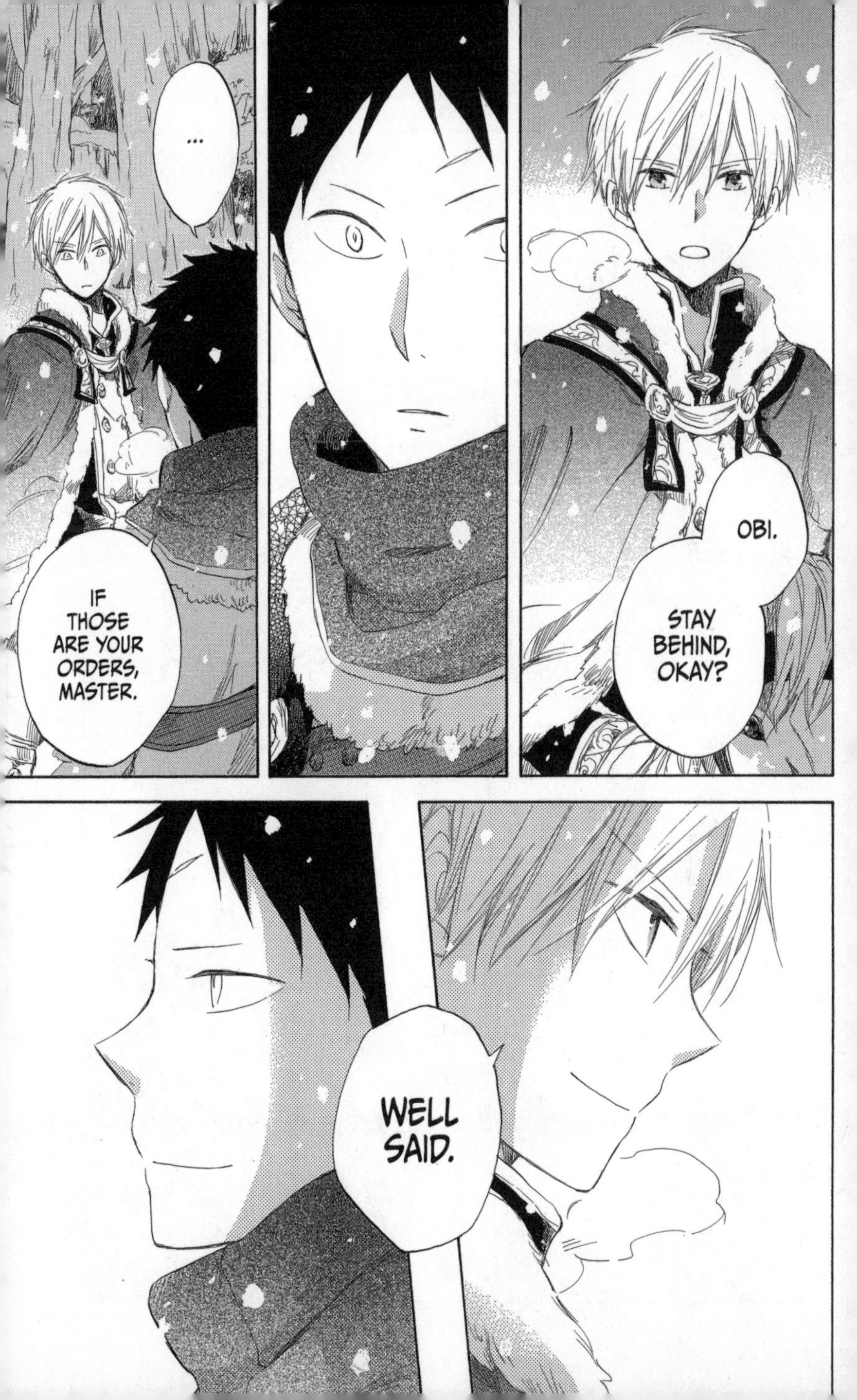
OBI.
STAY BEHIND, OKAY?
...
IF THOSE ARE YOUR ORDERS, MASTER.
WELL SAID.

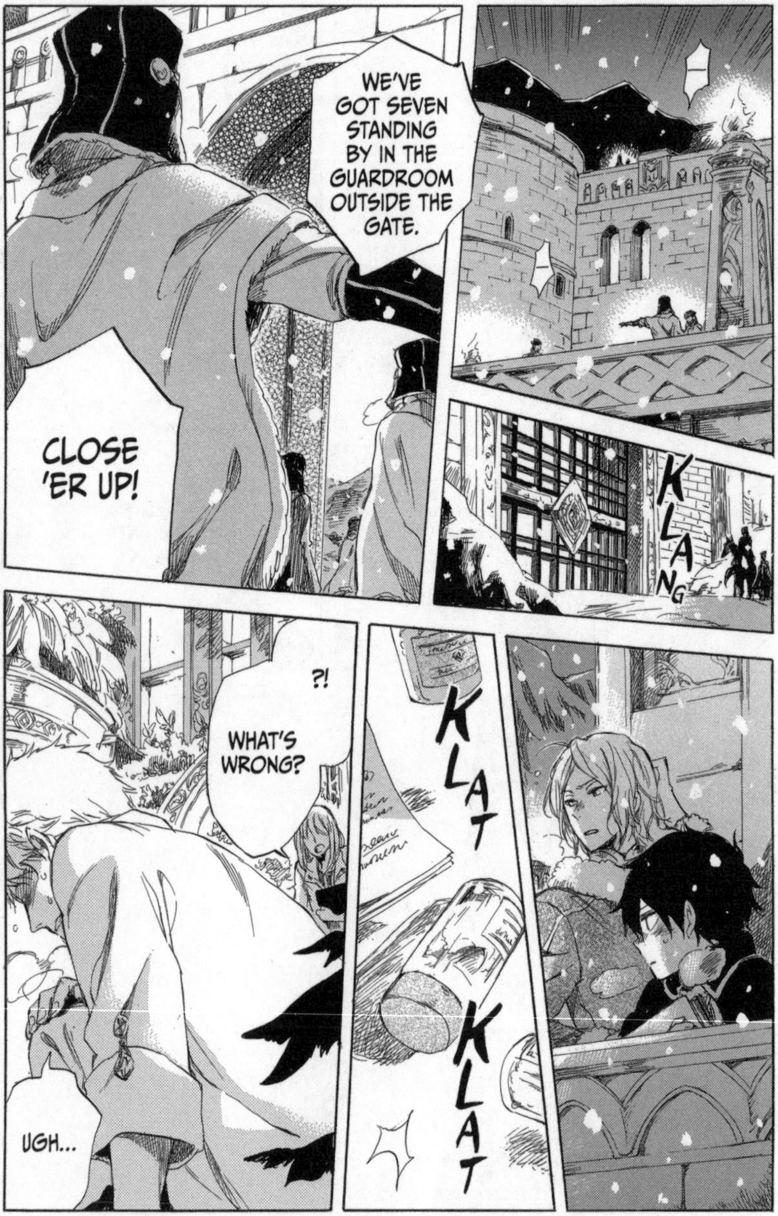
KLANG
WE'VE GOT SEVEN STANDING BY IN THE GUARDROOM OUTSIDE THE GATE.
CLOSE 'ER UP!
KLAT
KLAT
?!
WHAT'S WRONG?
UGH...

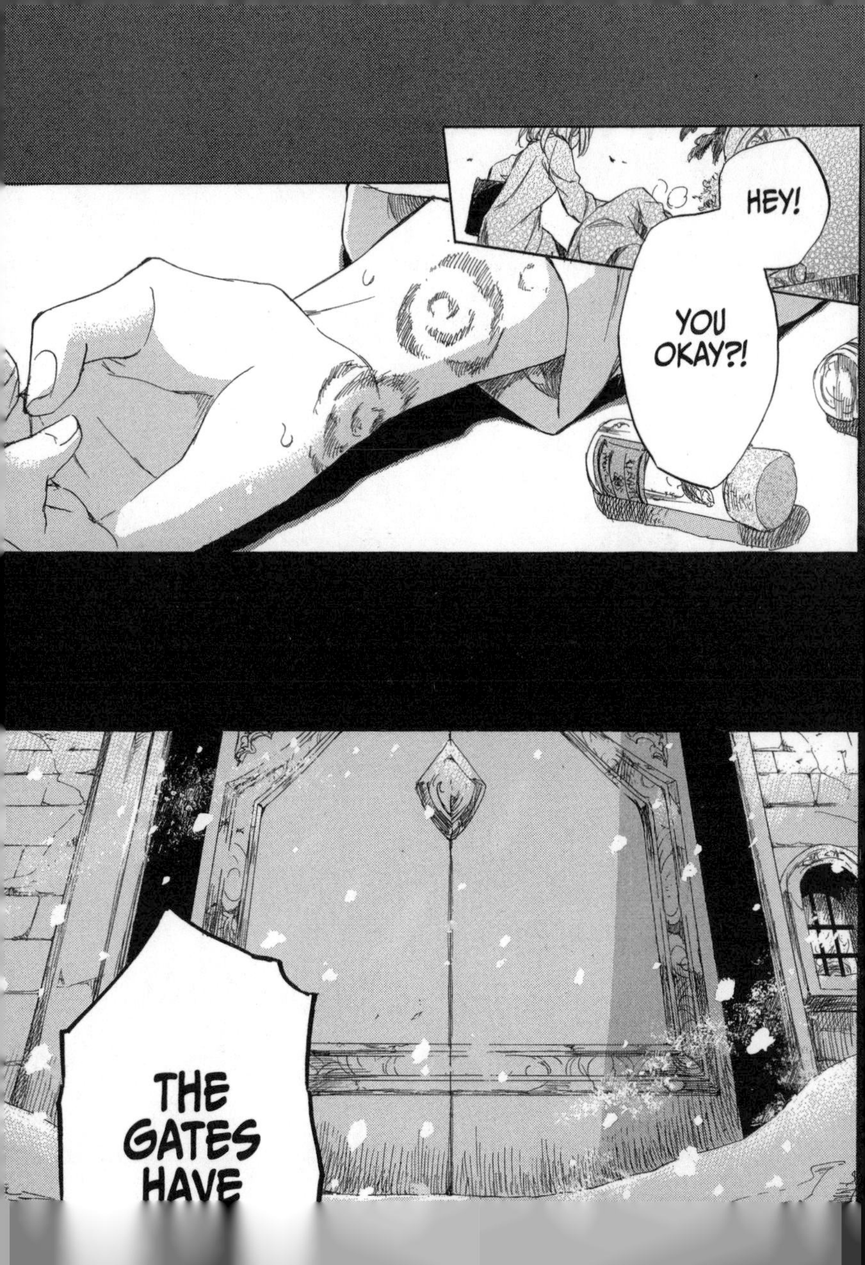
HEY!
YOU OKAY?!
THE GATES HAVE

Chapter 37

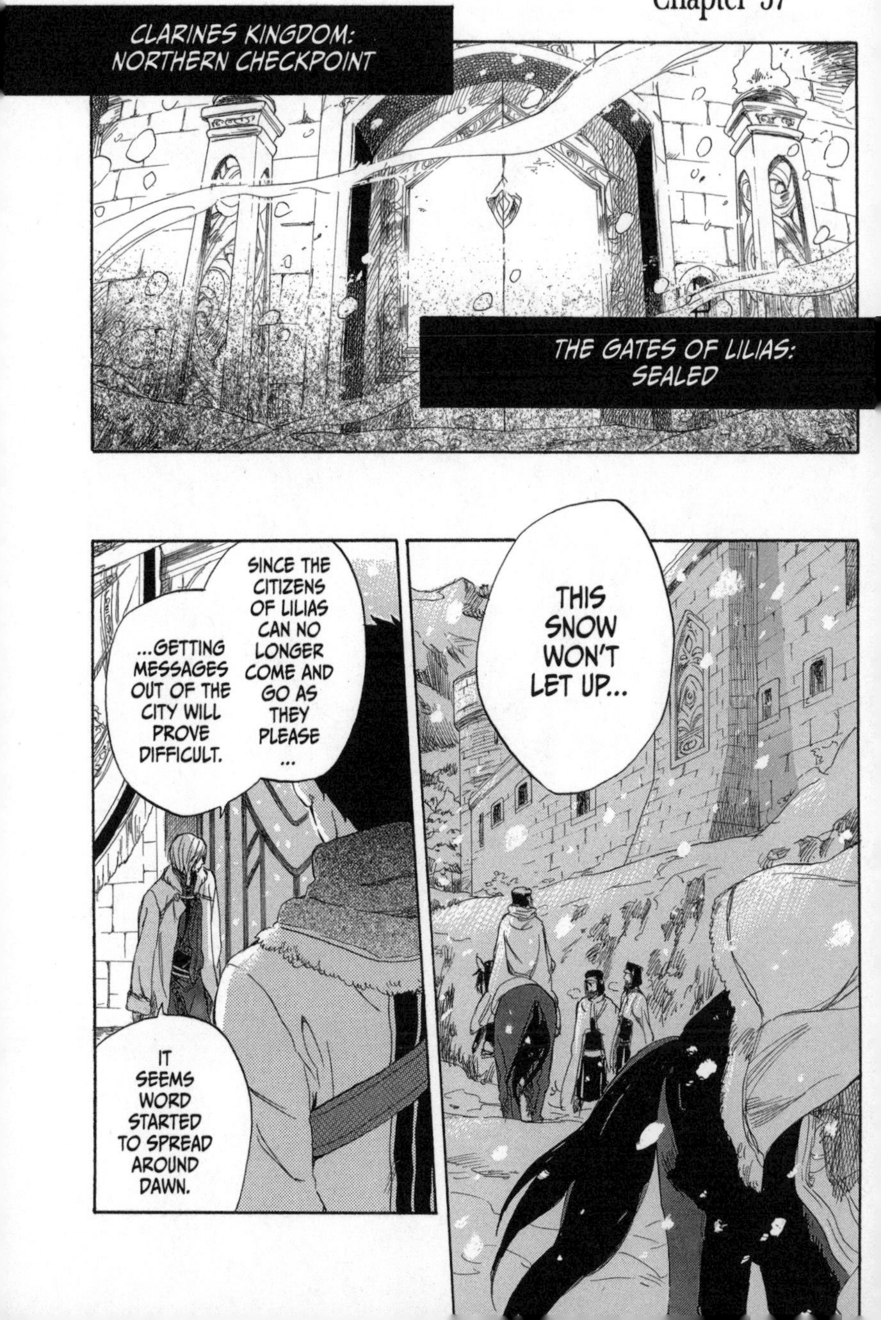
CLARINES KINGDOM: NORTHERN CHECKPOINT
THE GATES OF LILIAS: SEALED
THIS SNOW WON'T LET UP...
SINCE THE CITIZENS OF LILIAS CAN NO LONGER COME AND GO AS THEY PLEASE ...
...GETTING MESSAGES OUT OF THE CITY WILL PROVE DIFFICULT.
IT SEEMS WORD STARTED TO SPREAD AROUND DAWN.

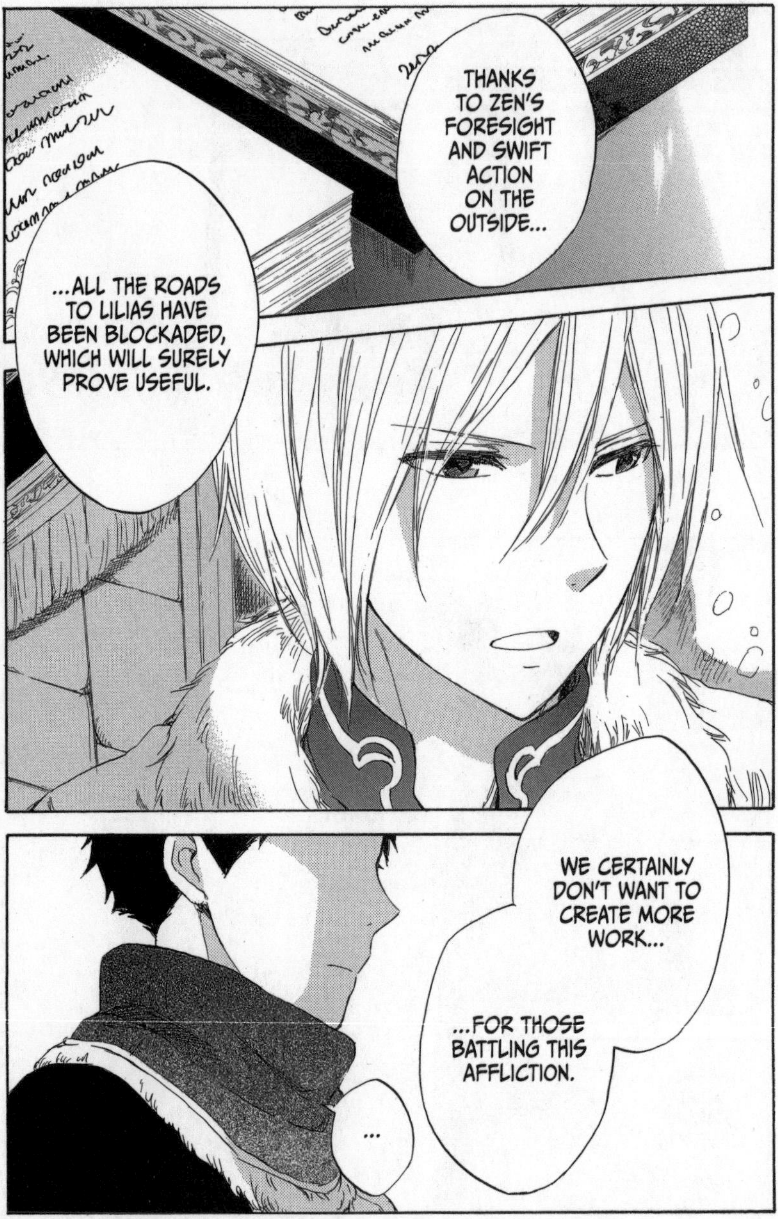
THANKS TO ZEN'S FORESIGHT AND SWIFT ACTION ON THE OUTSIDE...
...ALL THE ROADS TO LILIAS HAVE BEEN BLOCKADED, WHICH WILL SURELY PROVE USEFUL.
WE CERTAINLY DON'T WANT TO CREATE MORE WORK...
...FOR THOSE BATTLING THIS AFFLICTION.
...

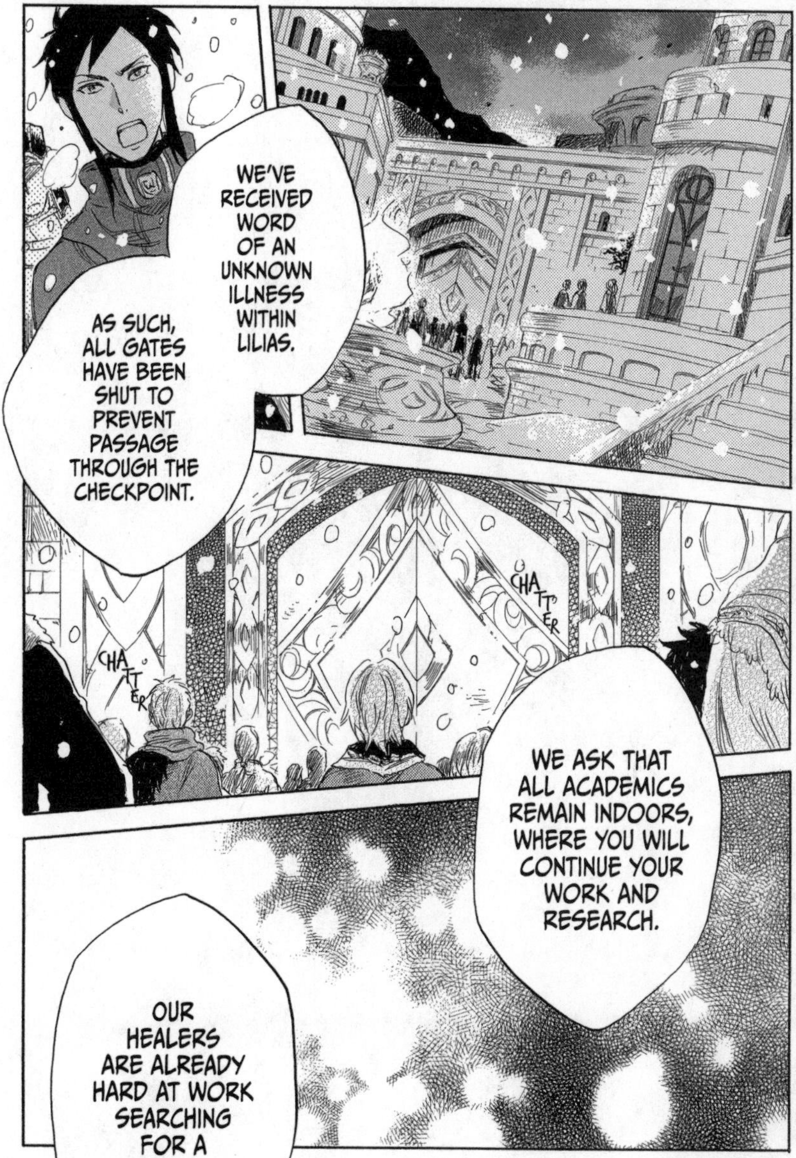
WE'VE RECEIVED WORD OF AN UNKNOWN ILLNESS WITHIN LILIAS.
AS SUCH, ALL GATES HAVE BEEN SHUT TO PREVENT PASSAGE THROUGH THE CHECKPOINT.
CHATTER
CHATTER
WE ASK THAT ALL ACADEMICS REMAIN INDOORS, WHERE YOU WILL CONTINUE YOUR WORK AND RESEARCH.
OUR HEALERS ARE ALREADY HARD AT WORK SEARCHING FOR A CURE.

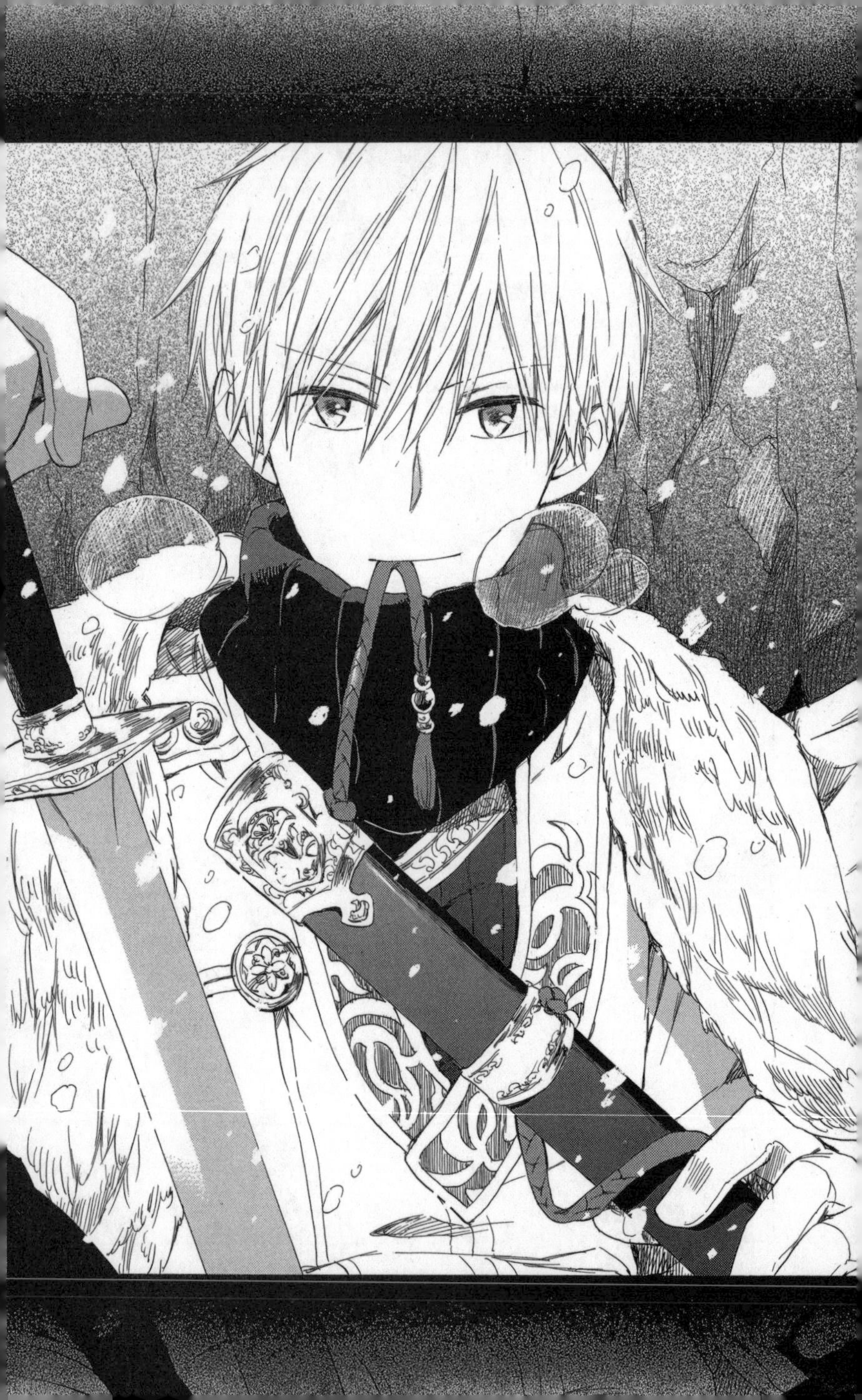

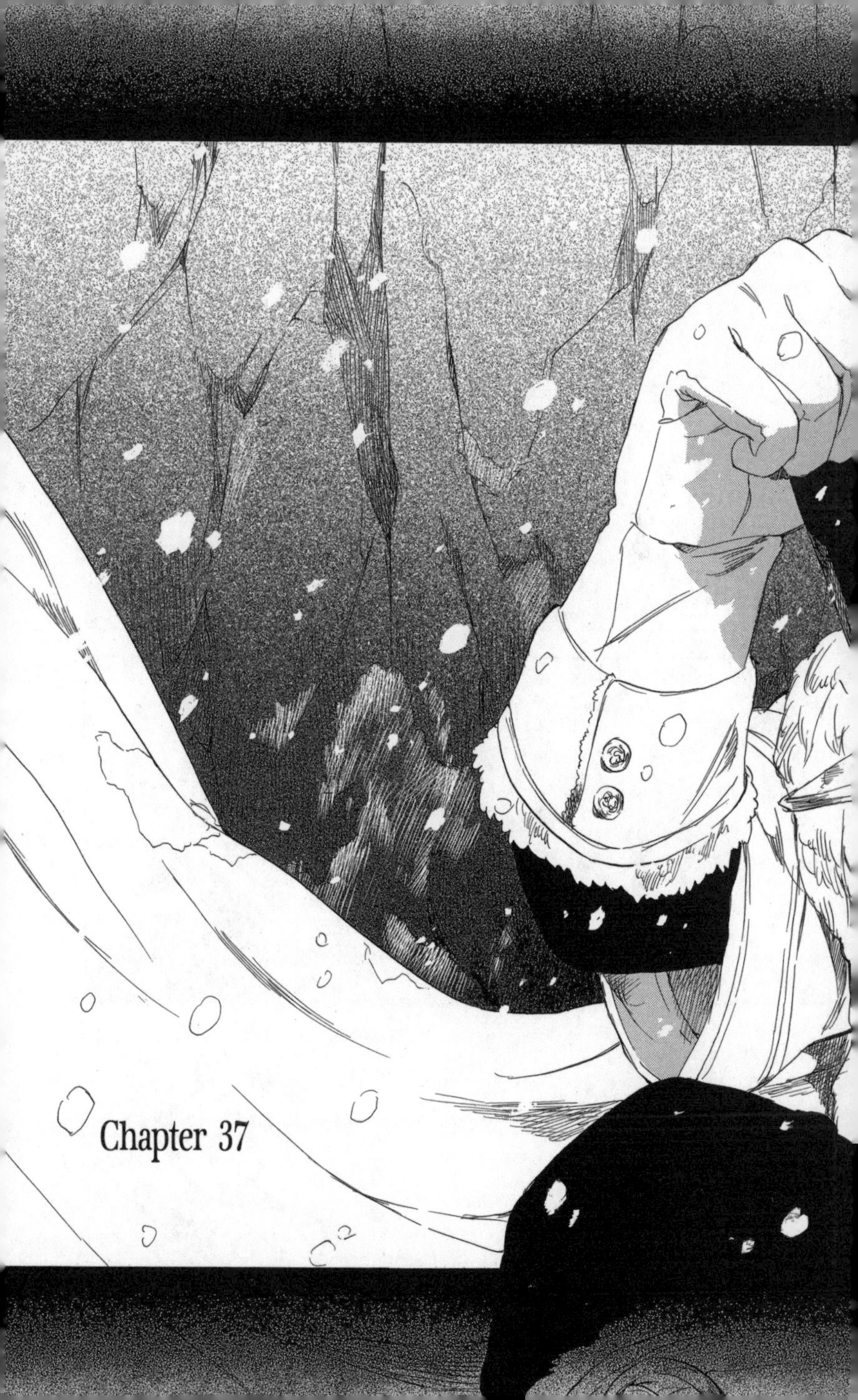
Chapter 37

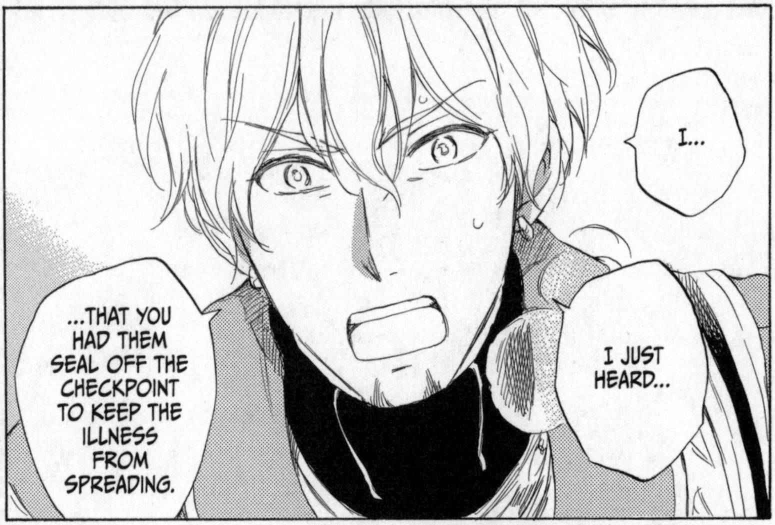
I...
I JUST HEARD...
...THAT YOU HAD THEM SEAL OFF THE CHECKPOINT TO KEEP THE ILLNESS FROM SPREADING.

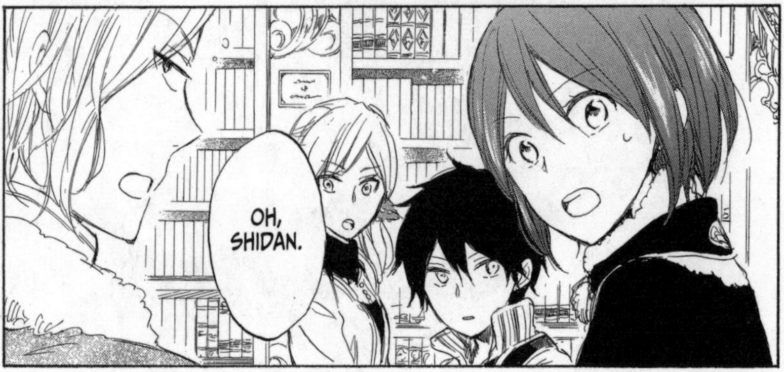
OH, SHIDAN.

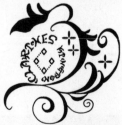

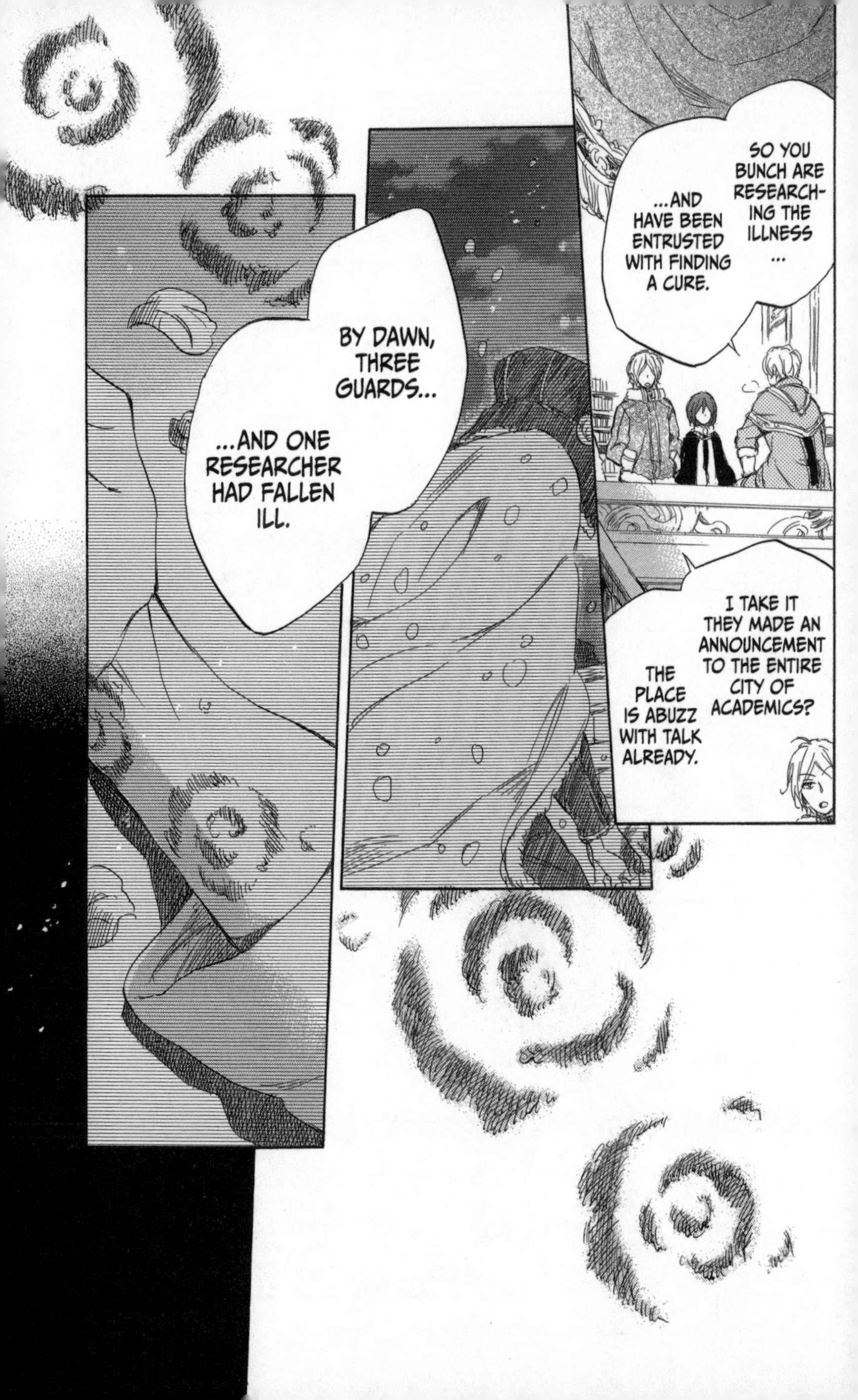
SO YOU BUNCH ARE RESEARCHING THE ILLNESS...
...AND HAVE BEEN ENTRUSTED WITH FINDING A CURE.
I TAKE IT THEY MADE AN ANNOUNCEMENT TO THE ENTIRE CITY OF ACADEMICS?
THE PLACE IS ABUZZ WITH TALK ALREADY.
BY DAWN, THREE GUARDS...
...AND ONE RESEARCHER HAD FALLEN ILL.

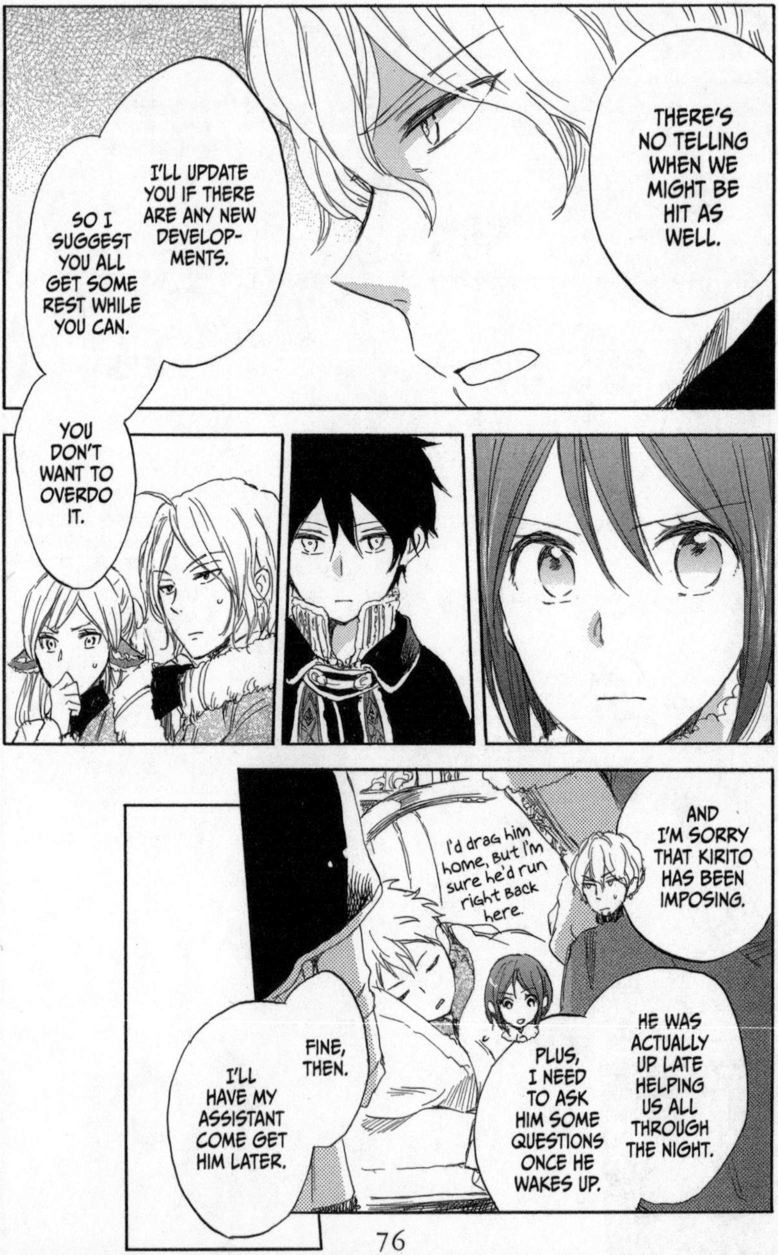
THERE'S NO TELLING WHEN WE MIGHT BE HIT AS WELL.
I'LL UPDATE YOU IF THERE ARE ANY NEW DEVELOPMENTS.
SO I SUGGEST YOU ALL GET SOME REST WHILE YOU CAN.
YOU DON'T WANT TO OVERDO IT.
AND I'M SORRY THAT KIRITO HAS BEEN IMPOSING.
I'd drag him home, but I'm sure he'd run right back here.
HE WAS ACTUALLY UP LATE HELPING US ALL THROUGH THE NIGHT.
PLUS, I NEED TO ASK HIM SOME QUESTIONS ONCE HE WAKES UP.
FINE, THEN.
I'LL HAVE MY ASSISTANT COME GET HIM LATER.

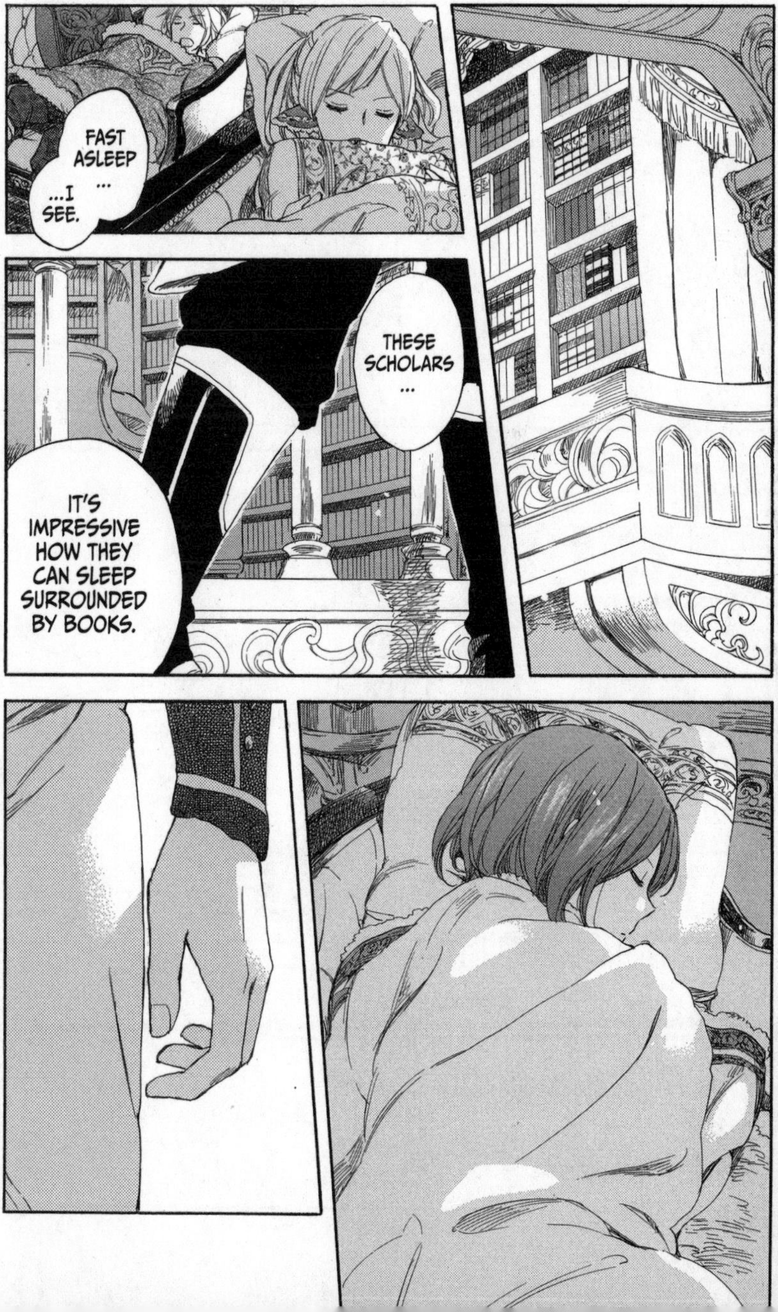
FAST ASLEEP ...
...I SEE.
THESE SCHOLARS ...
IT'S IMPRESSIVE HOW THEY CAN SLEEP SURROUNDED BY BOOKS.

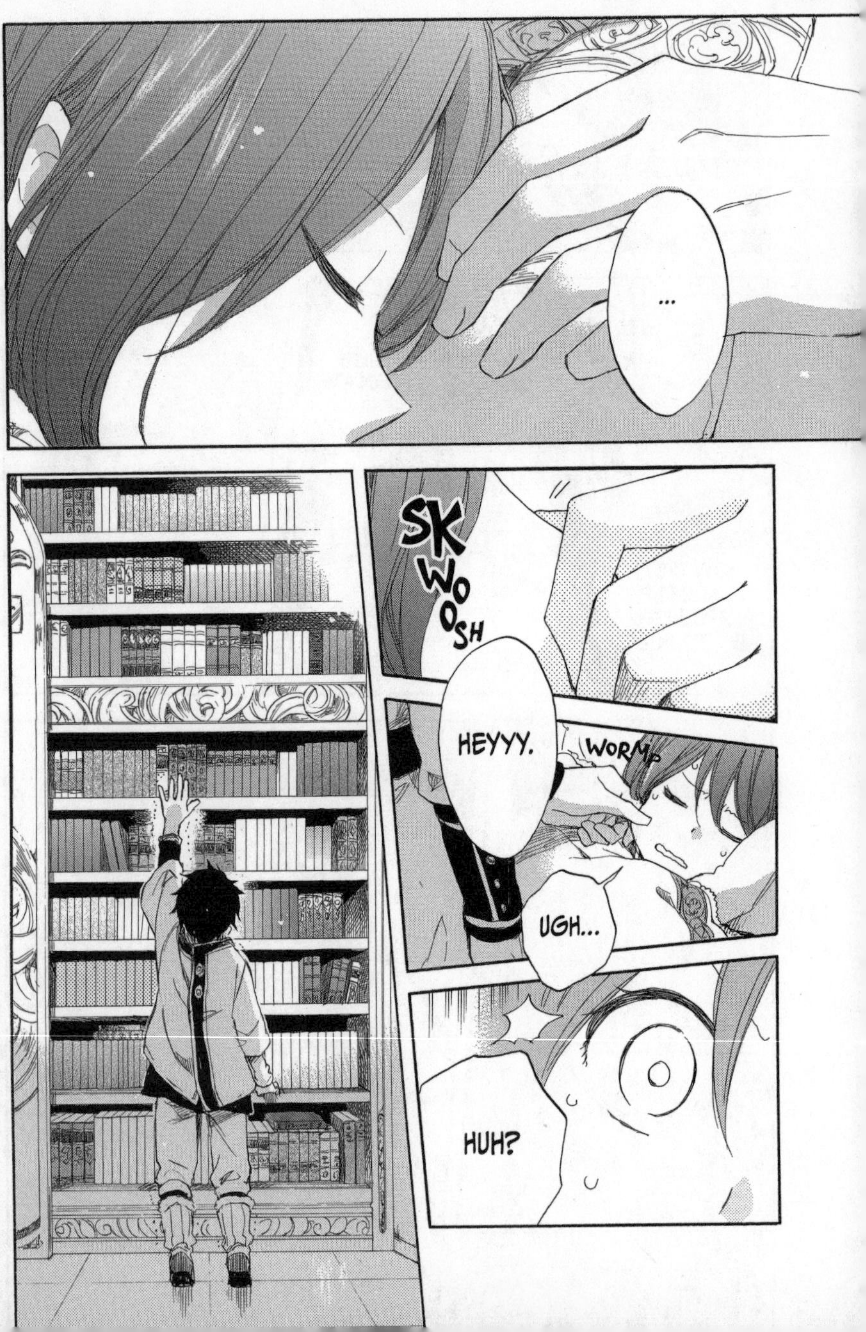
...
SKWOOSH
HEYYY.
WORMP
UGH...
HUH?

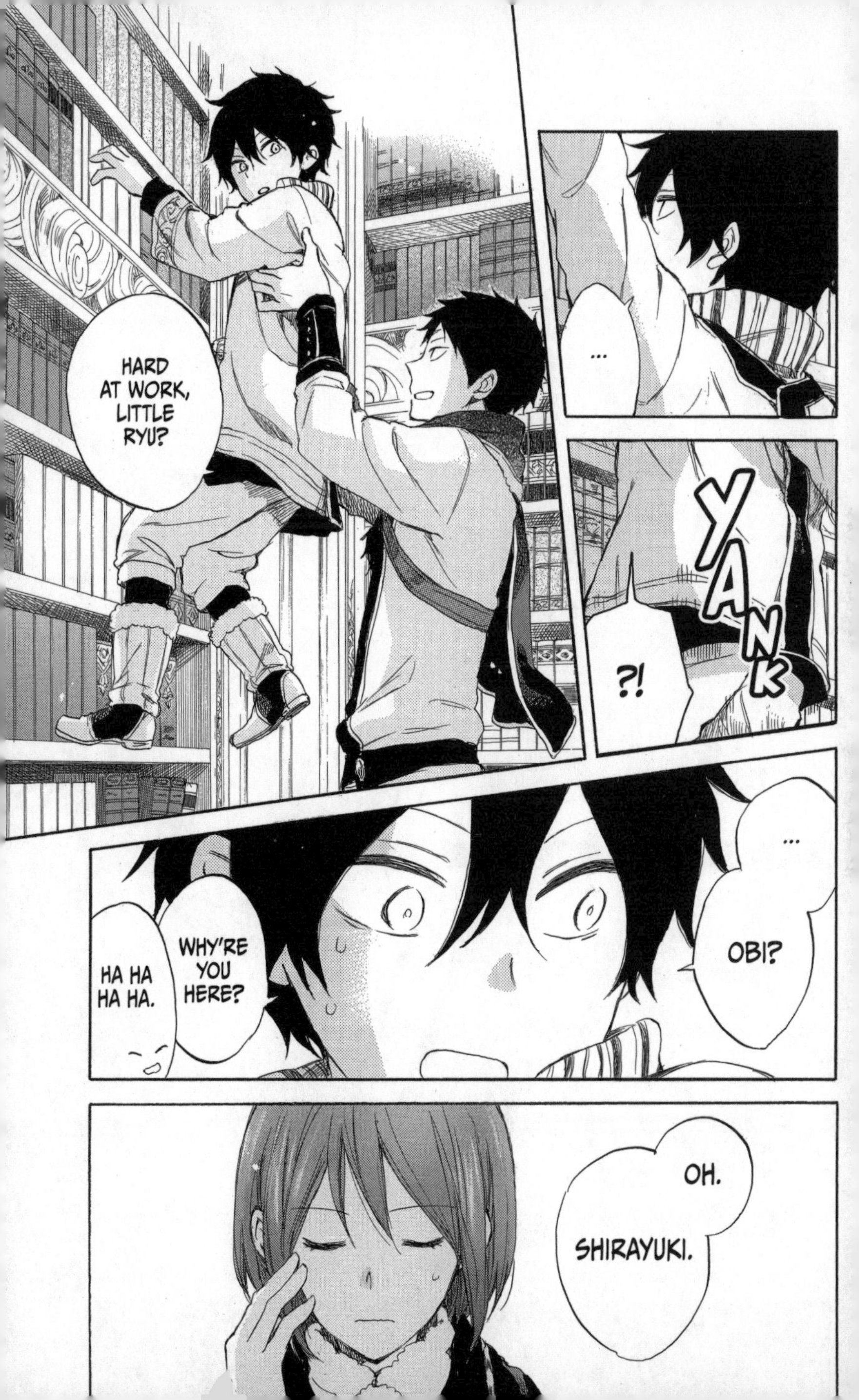
...
YANK
?!
HARD AT WORK, LITTLE RYU?
... OBI?
WHY'RE YOU HERE?
HA HA HA HA.
OH. SHIRAYUKI.

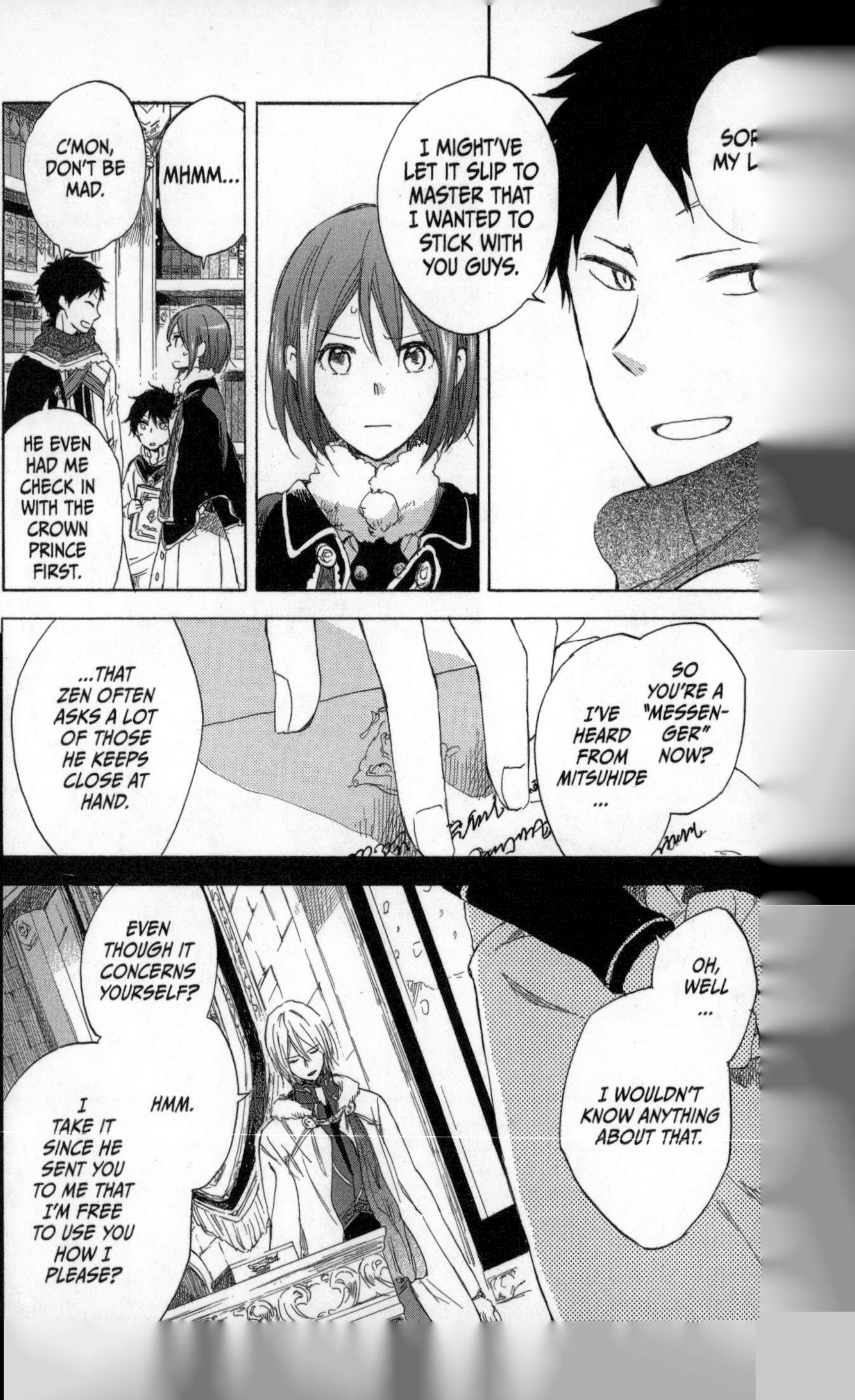
SOR
MY L
I MIGHT'VE LET IT SLIP TO MASTER THAT I WANTED TO STICK WITH YOU GUYS.
MHMM...
C'MON, DON'T BE MAD.
HE EVEN HAD ME CHECK IN WITH THE CROWN PRINCE FIRST.
SO YOU'RE A "MESSENGER" NOW?
I'VE HEARD FROM MITSUHIDE...
...THAT ZEN OFTEN ASKS A LOT OF THOSE HE KEEPS CLOSE AT HAND.
OH, WELL...
I WOULDN'T KNOW ANYTHING ABOUT THAT.
EVEN THOUGH IT CONCERNS YOURSELF?
HMM.
I TAKE IT SINCE HE SENT YOU TO ME THAT I'M FREE TO USE YOU HOW I PLEASE?

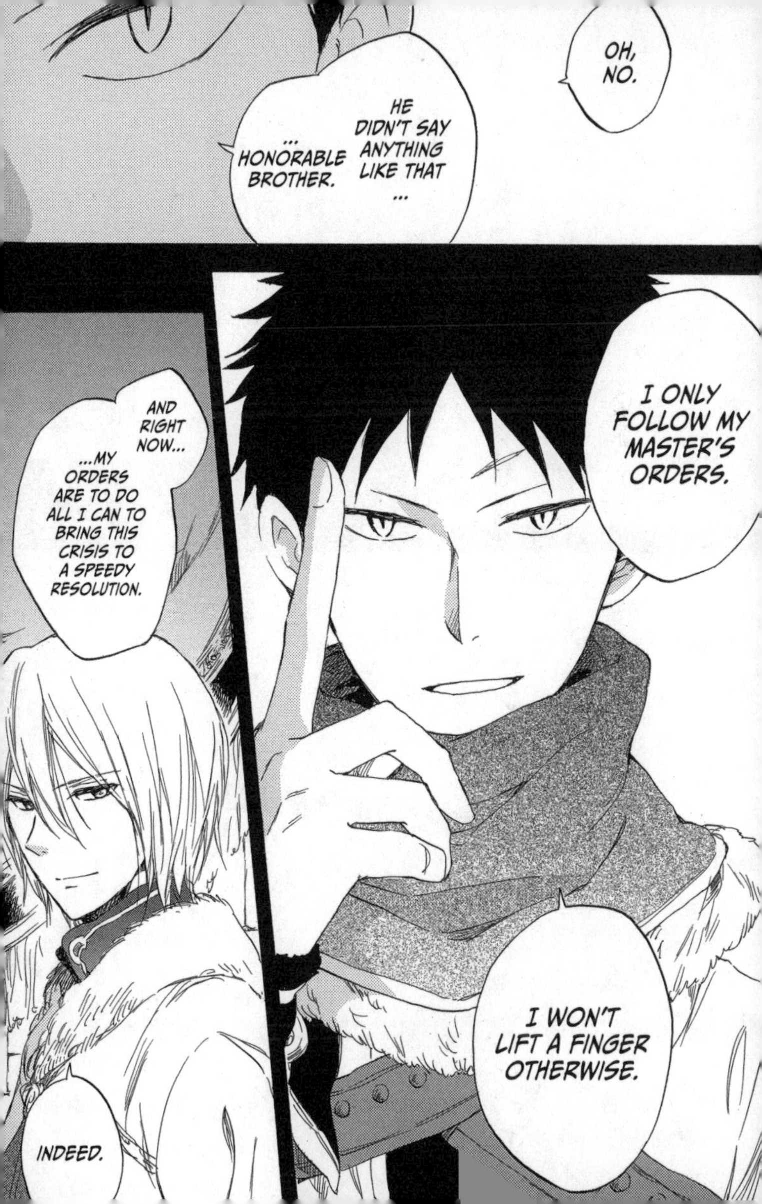
OH, NO.
HE DIDN'T SAY ANYTHING LIKE THAT... ...HONORABLE BROTHER.
I ONLY FOLLOW MY MASTER'S ORDERS.
I WON'T LIFT A FINGER OTHERWISE.
AND RIGHT NOW... ...MY ORDERS ARE TO DO ALL I CAN TO BRING THIS CRISIS TO A SPEEDY RESOLUTION.
INDEED.

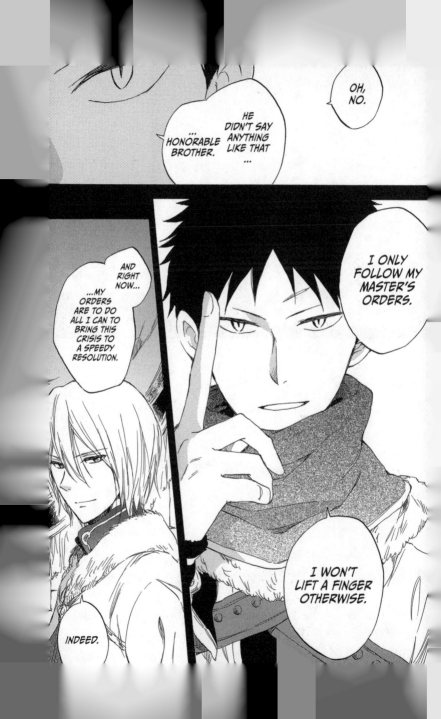

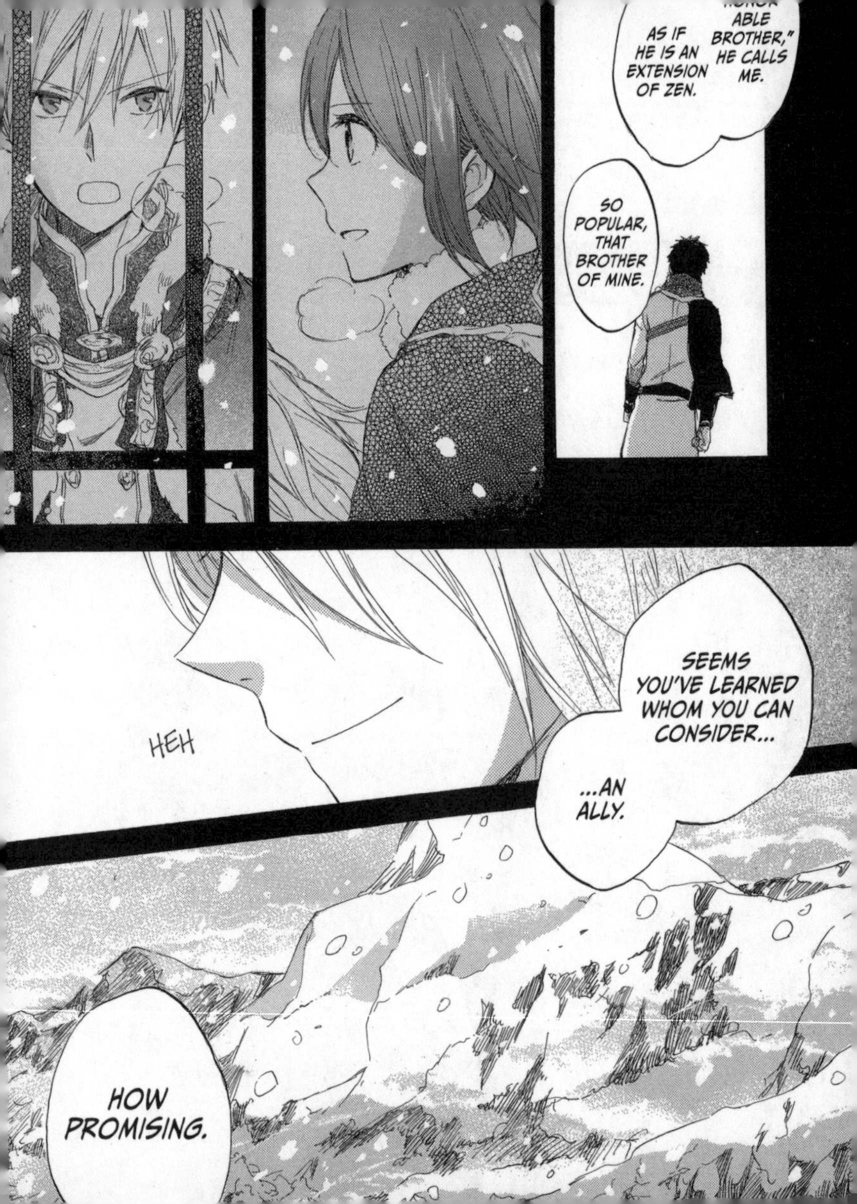
ABLE BROTHER,” HE CALLS ME.
AS IF HE IS AN EXTENSION OF ZEN.
SO POPULAR, THAT BROTHER OF MINE.
SEEMS YOU'VE LEARNED WHOM YOU CAN CONSIDER...
...AN ALLY.
HEH
HOW PROMISING.

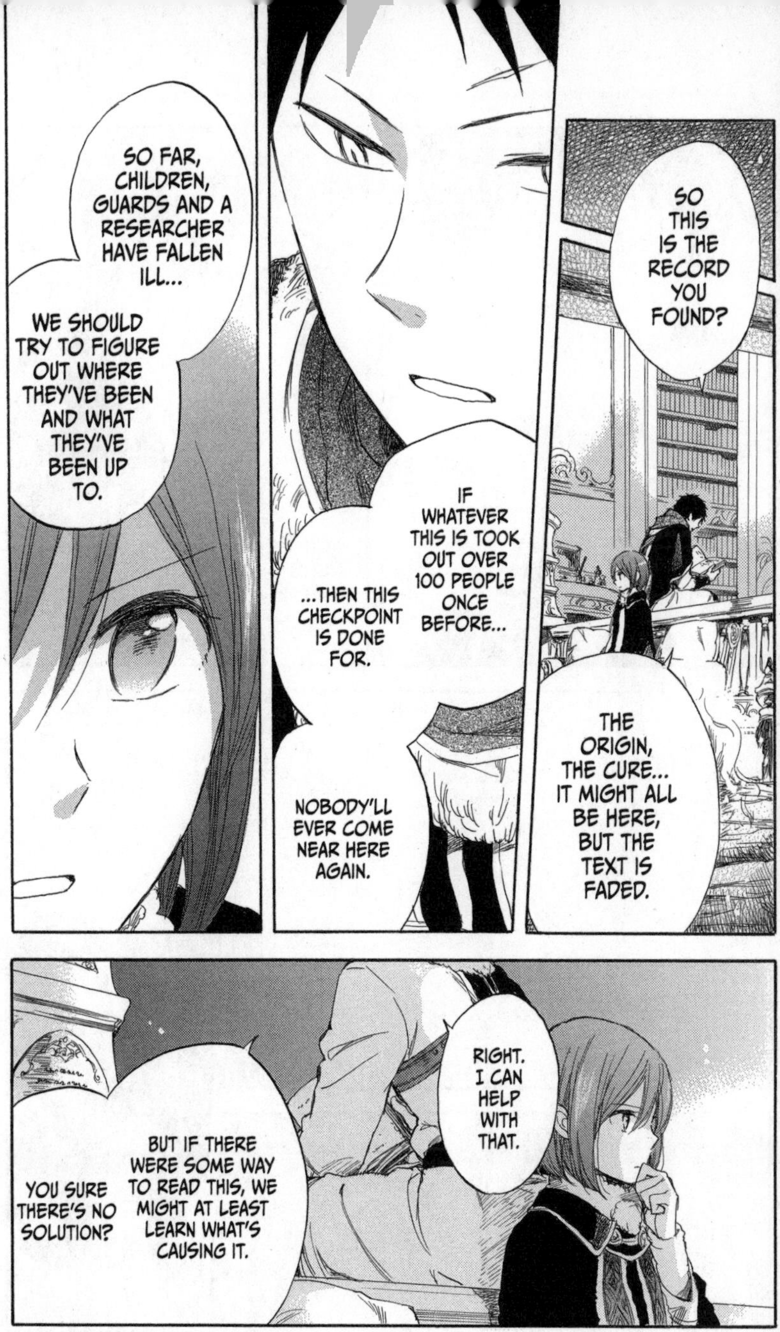
SO THIS IS THE RECORD YOU FOUND?
THE ORIGIN, THE CURE... IT MIGHT ALL BE HERE, BUT THE TEXT IS FADED.
IF WHATEVER THIS IS TOOK OUT OVER 100 PEOPLE ONCE BEFORE...
...THEN THIS CHECKPOINT IS DONE FOR.
NOBODY'LL EVER COME NEAR HERE AGAIN.
SO FAR, CHILDREN, GUARDS AND A RESEARCHER HAVE FALLEN ILL...
WE SHOULD TRY TO FIGURE OUT WHERE THEY'VE BEEN AND WHAT THEY'VE BEEN UP TO.
RIGHT. I CAN HELP WITH THAT.
BUT IF THERE WERE SOME WAY TO READ THIS, WE MIGHT AT LEAST LEARN WHAT'S CAUSING IT.
YOU SURE THERE'S NO SOLUTION?

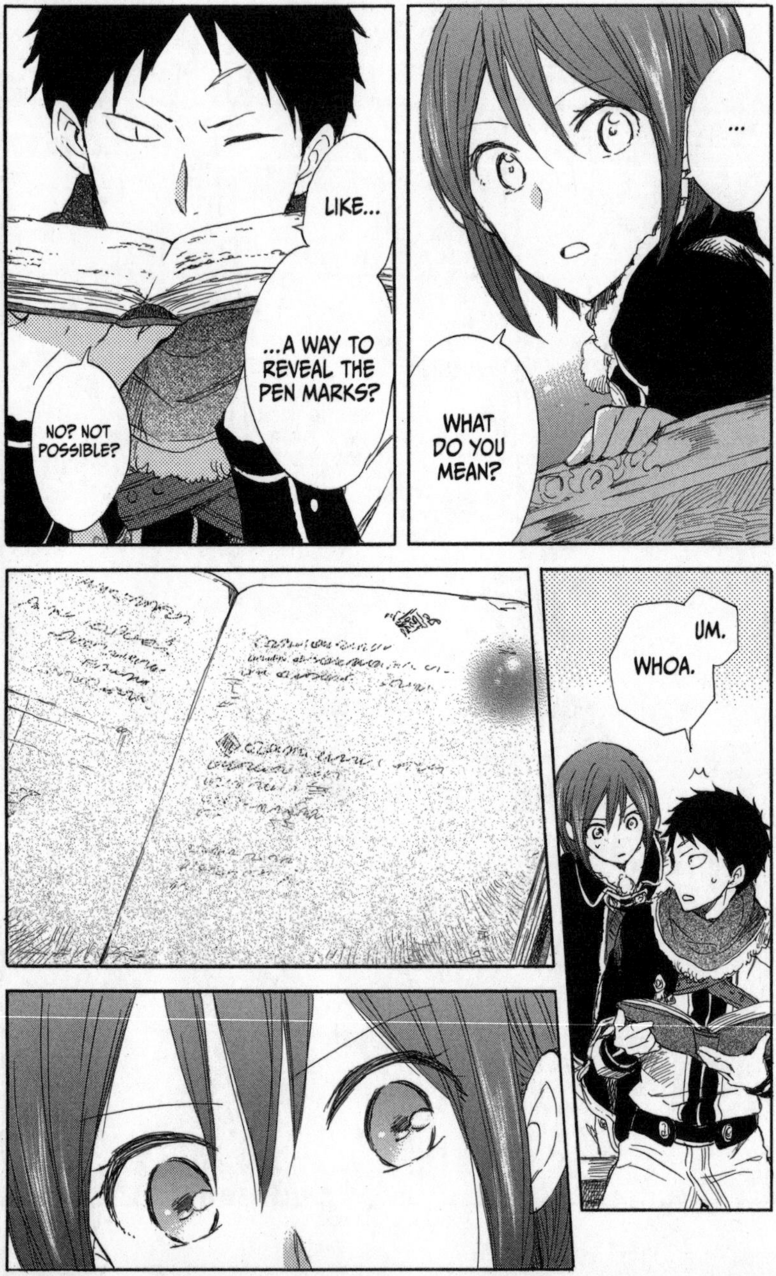
...
WHAT DO YOU MEAN?
LIKE...
...A WAY TO REVEAL THE PEN MARKS?
NO? NOT POSSIBLE?
UM. WHOA.

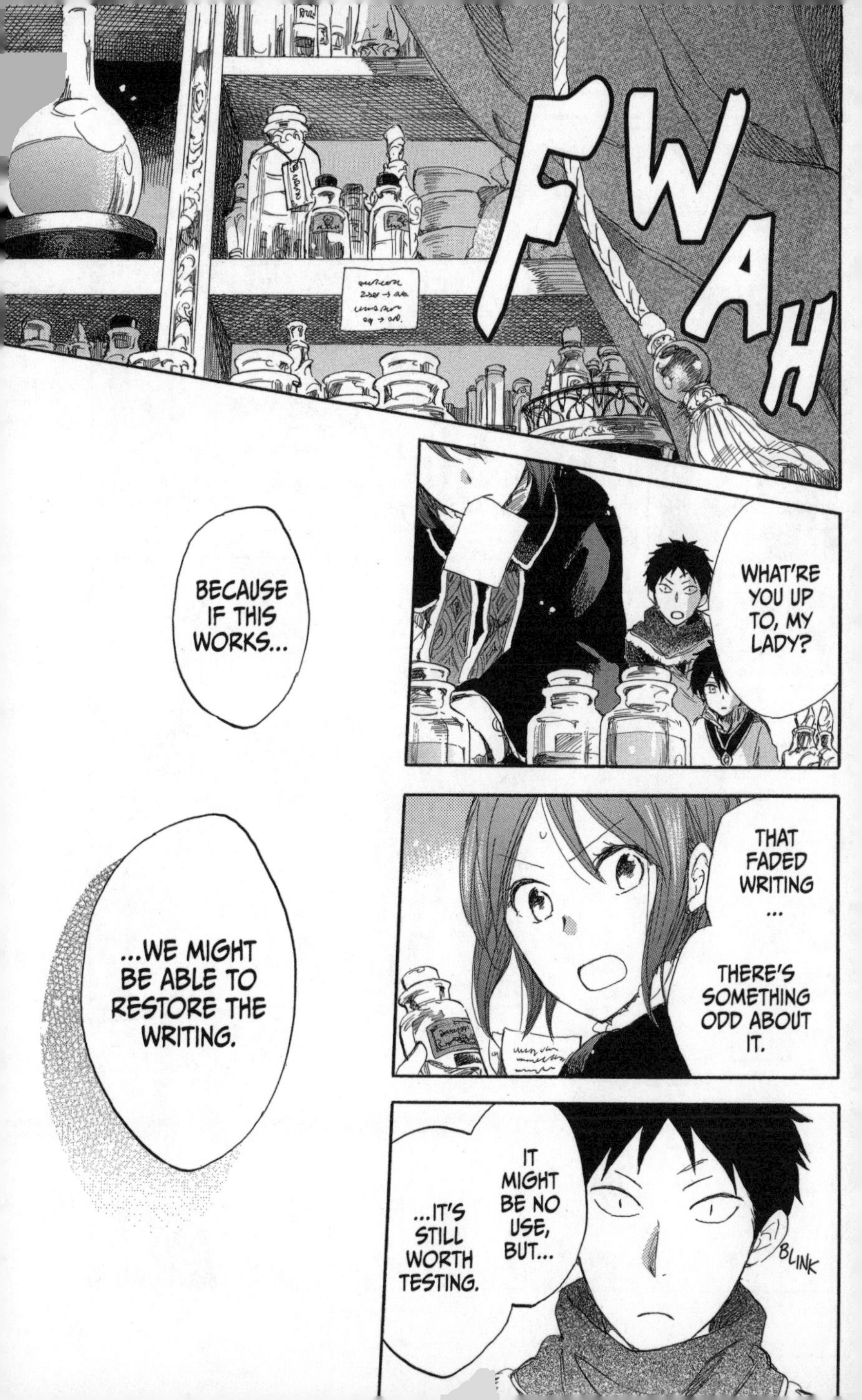
FWAH
WHAT'RE YOU UP TO, MY LADY?
BECAUSE IF THIS WORKS...
THAT FADED WRITING...
THERE'S SOMETHING ODD ABOUT IT.
...WE MIGHT BE ABLE TO RESTORE THE WRITING.
IT MIGHT BE NO USE, BUT...
...IT'S STILL WORTH TESTING.
BLINK

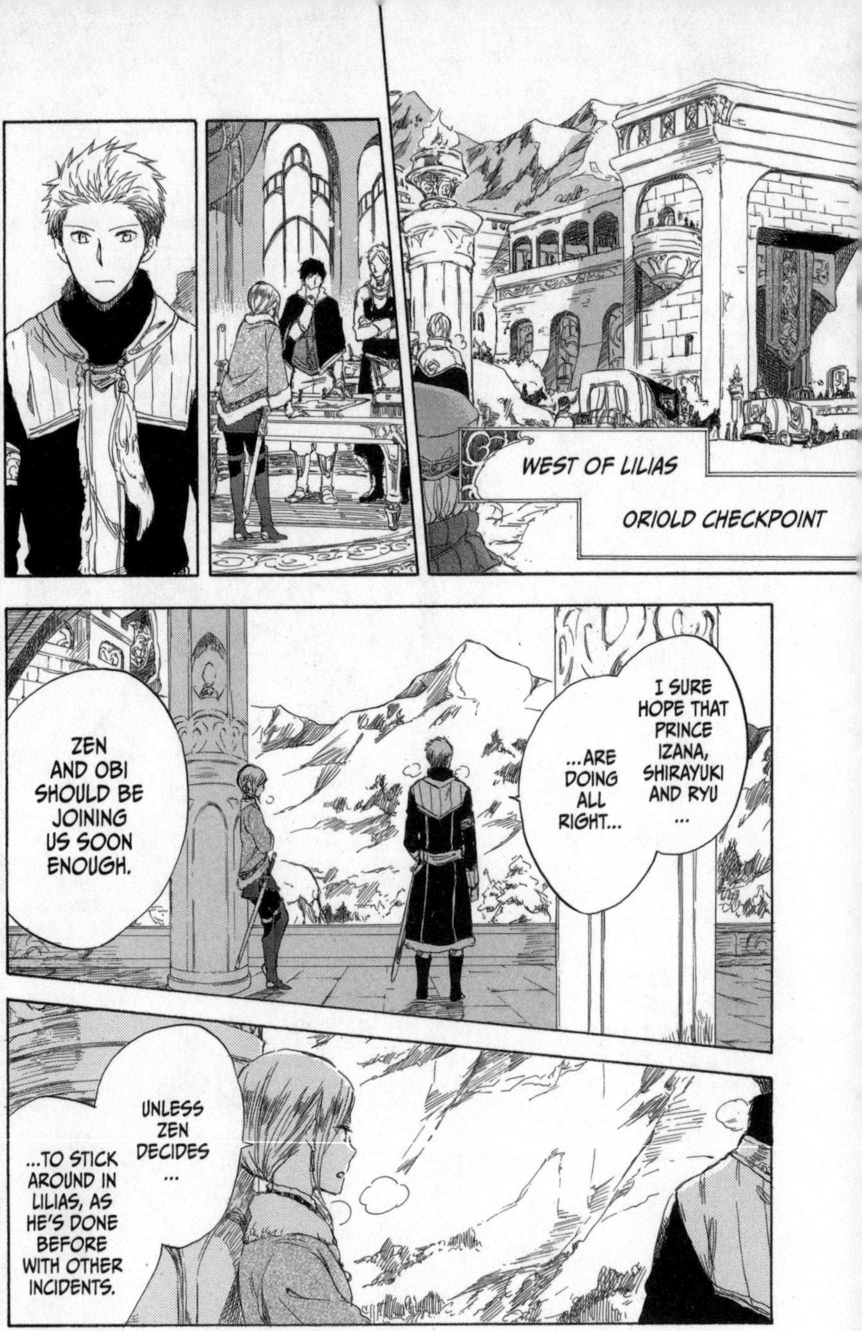
WEST OF LILIAS
ORIOLD CHECKPOINT
I SURE HOPE THAT PRINCE IZANA, SHIRAYUKI AND RYU ...
...ARE DOING ALL RIGHT...
ZEN AND OBI SHOULD BE JOINING US SOON ENOUGH.
UNLESS ZEN DECIDES ...
...TO STICK AROUND IN LILIAS, AS HE'S DONE BEFORE WITH OTHER INCIDENTS.

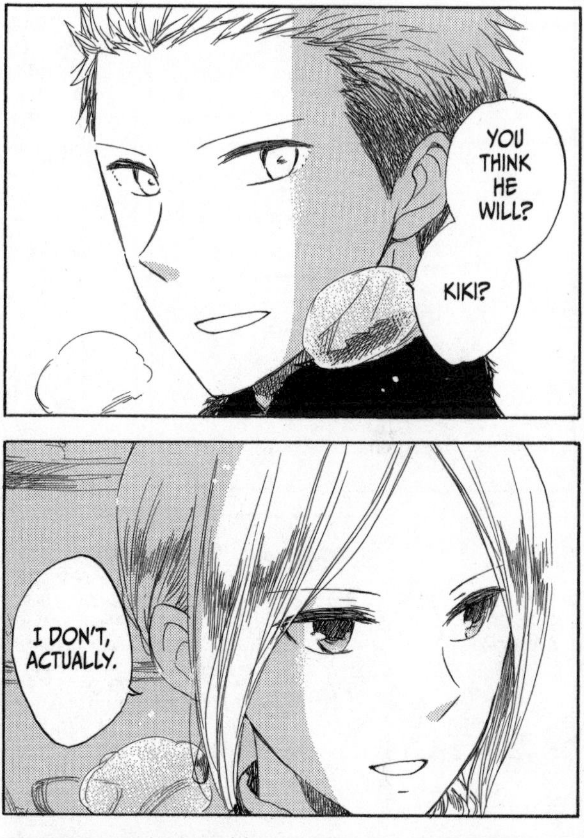
YOU THINK HE WILL?
KIKI?
I DON'T, ACTUALLY.
... I SUPPOSE IT DEPENDS ON WHAT IZANA SAID TO HIM...
THOUGH, ZEN DOESN'T SEEM TO HAVE A PROBLEM STANDING UP TO IZANA ANYMORE ...
...SO I DON'T THINK WE HAVE ANYTHING TO WORRY ABOUT...

TRIP 2

No talk about Izumo is complete without including the famous love knot!

And *zenzai* (red bean soup)!

I didn't realize before, but zenzai originally came from Izumo.

I got to eat some at the shop facing the Grand Shrine. The place was decorated with tatami mats and had a very relaxing atmosphere.

And the zenzai itself went down really smooth (the beans and hot water were served separately). So delicious.

The pickled turnip was also great... I brought some back as a souvenir.

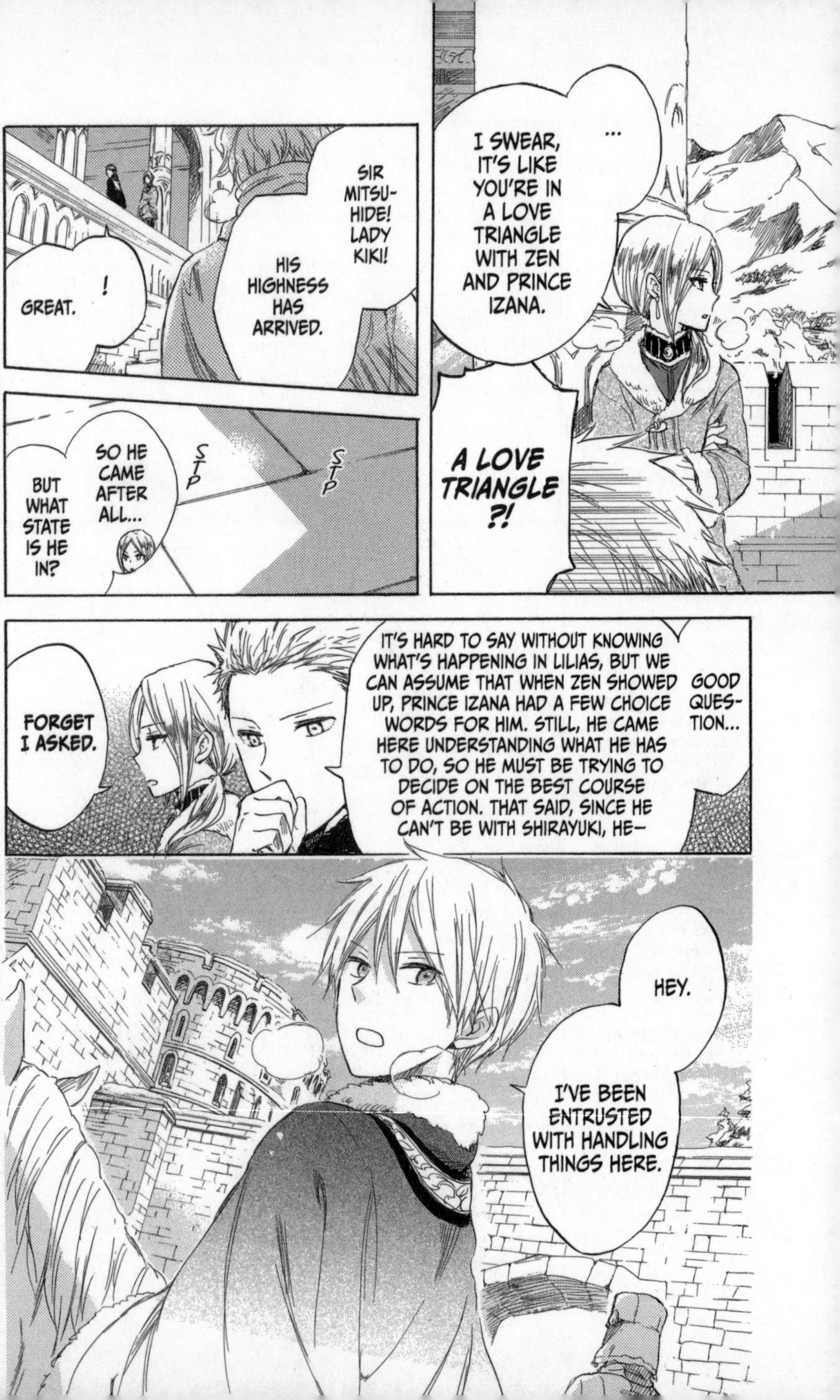
...
I SWEAR, IT'S LIKE YOU'RE IN A LOVE TRIANGLE WITH ZEN AND PRINCE IZANA.
A LOVE TRIANGLE ?!
SIR MITSU-HIDE! LADY KIKI!
HIS HIGHNESS HAS ARRIVED.
!
GREAT.
STP
STP
SO HE CAME AFTER ALL...
BUT WHAT STATE IS HE IN?
GOOD QUES-TION...
IT'S HARD TO SAY WITHOUT KNOWING WHAT'S HAPPENING IN LILIAS, BUT WE CAN ASSUME THAT WHEN ZEN SHOWED UP, PRINCE IZANA HAD A FEW CHOICE WORDS FOR HIM. STILL, HE CAME HERE UNDERSTANDING WHAT HE HAS TO DO, SO HE MUST BE TRYING TO DECIDE ON THE BEST COURSE OF ACTION. THAT SAID, SINCE HE CAN'T BE WITH SHIRAYUKI, HE—
FORGET I ASKED.
HEY.
I'VE BEEN ENTRUSTED WITH HANDLING THINGS HERE.

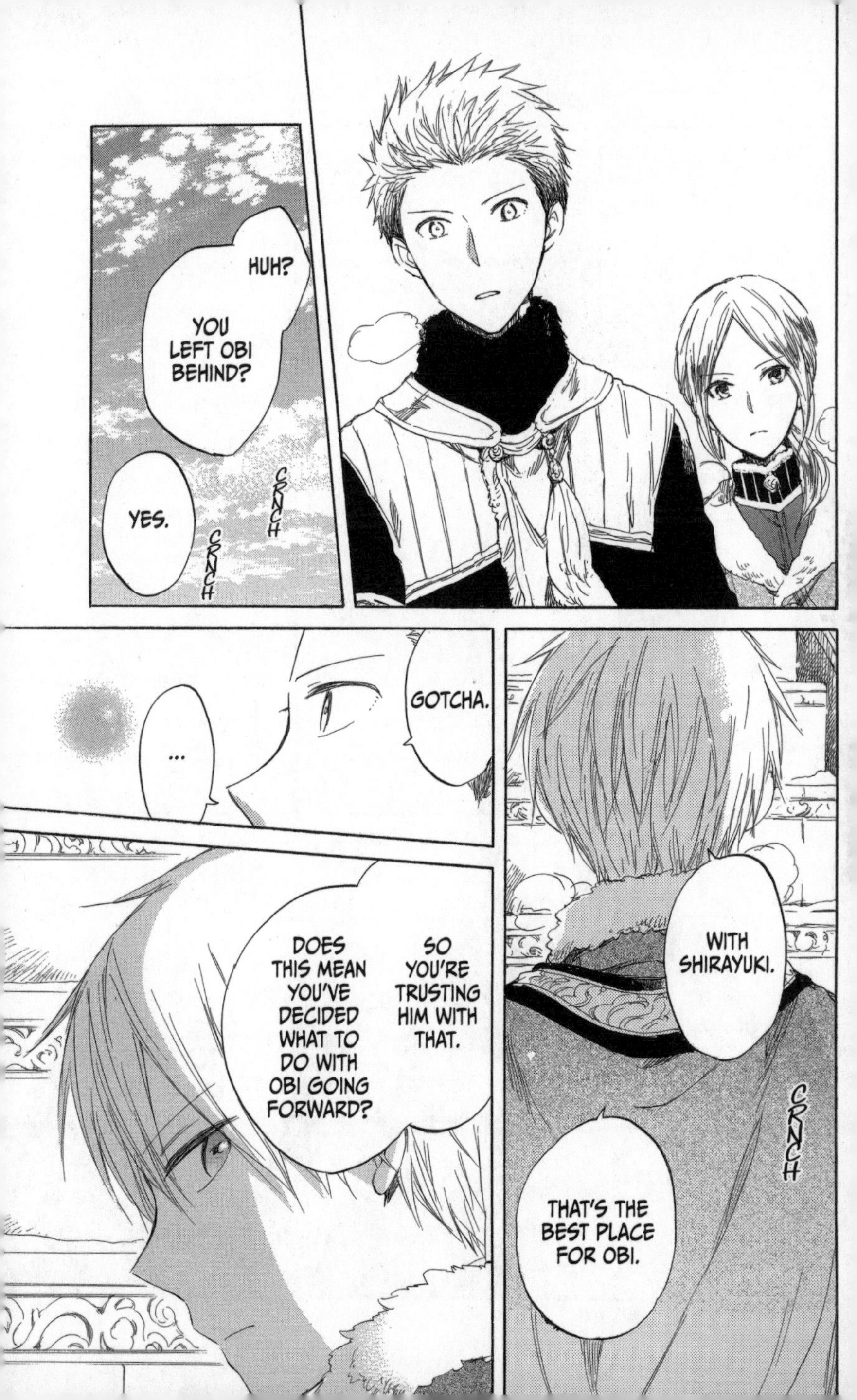
HUH?
YOU LEFT OBI BEHIND?
CRNCH
YES.
CRNCH
WITH SHIRAYUKI.
CRNCH
THAT'S THE BEST PLACE FOR OBI.
GOTCHA.
...
SO YOU'RE TRUSTING HIM WITH THAT.
DOES THIS MEAN YOU'VE DECIDED WHAT TO DO WITH OBI GOING FORWARD?

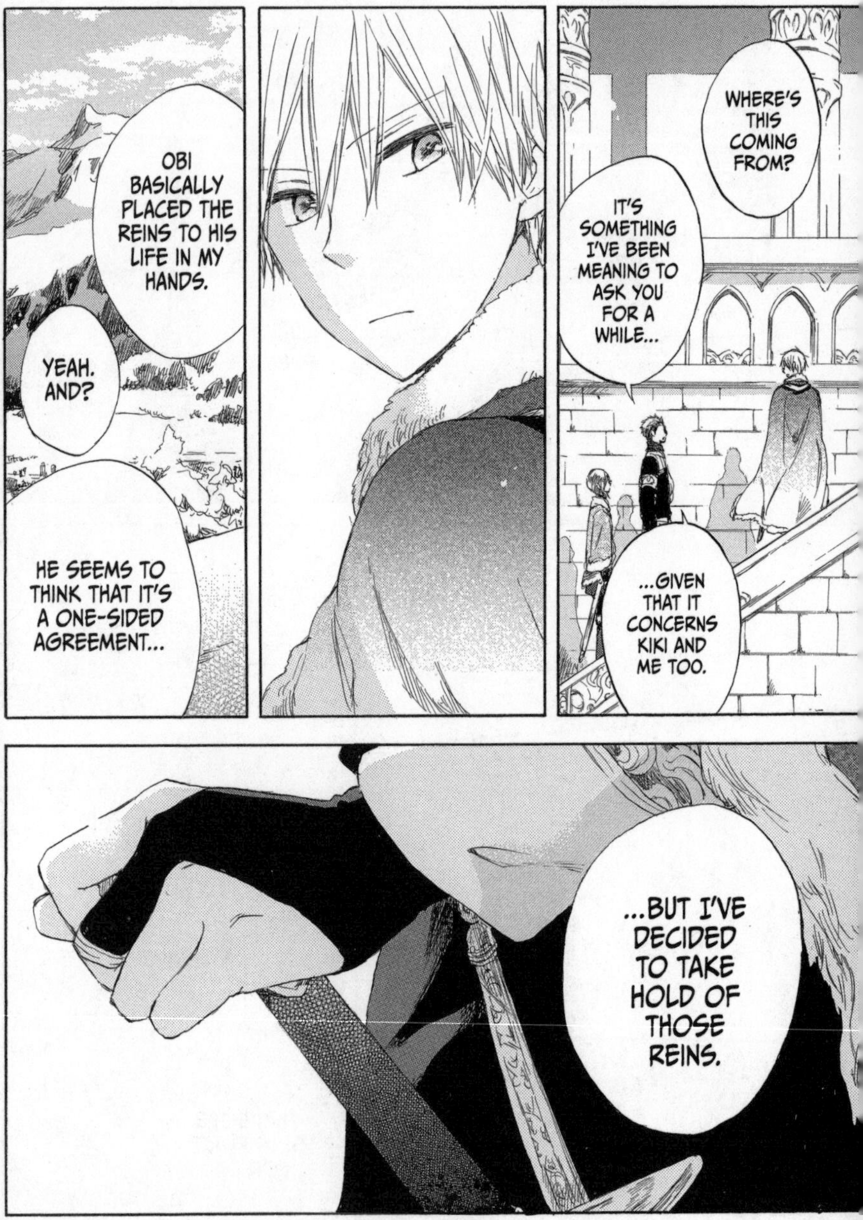
WHERE'S THIS COMING FROM?
IT'S SOMETHING I'VE BEEN MEANING TO ASK YOU FOR A WHILE...
...GIVEN THAT IT CONCERNS KIKI AND ME TOO.
OBI BASICALLY PLACED THE REINS TO HIS LIFE IN MY HANDS.
YEAH. AND?
HE SEEMS TO THINK THAT IT'S A ONE-SIDED AGREEMENT...
...BUT I'VE DECIDED TO TAKE HOLD OF THOSE REINS.

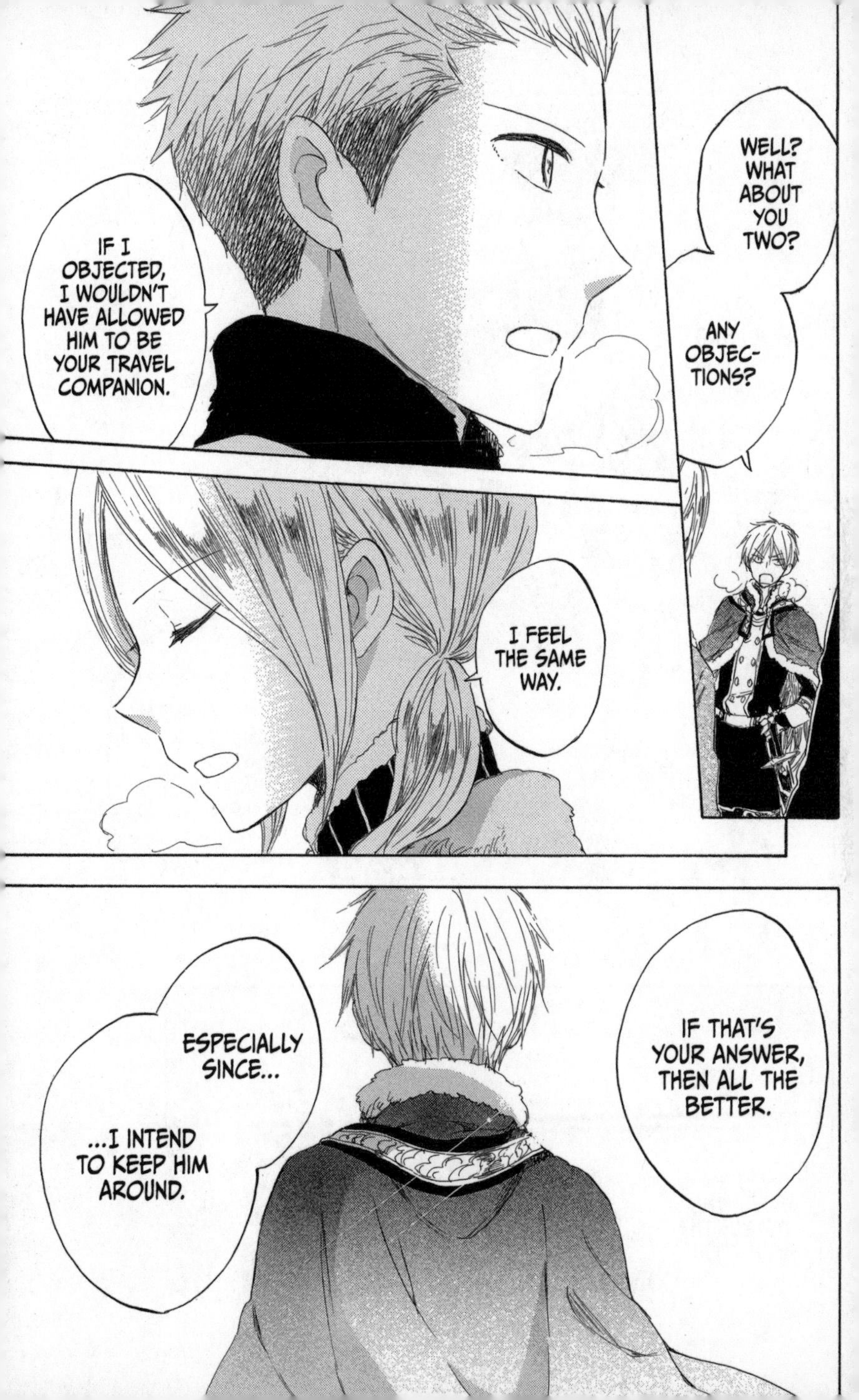
WELL? WHAT ABOUT YOU TWO?
ANY OBJEC-TIONS?
IF I OBJECTED, I WOULDN'T HAVE ALLOWED HIM TO BE YOUR TRAVEL COMPANION.
I FEEL THE SAME WAY.
IF THAT'S YOUR ANSWER, THEN ALL THE BETTER.
ESPECIALLY SINCE...
...I INTEND TO KEEP HIM AROUND.

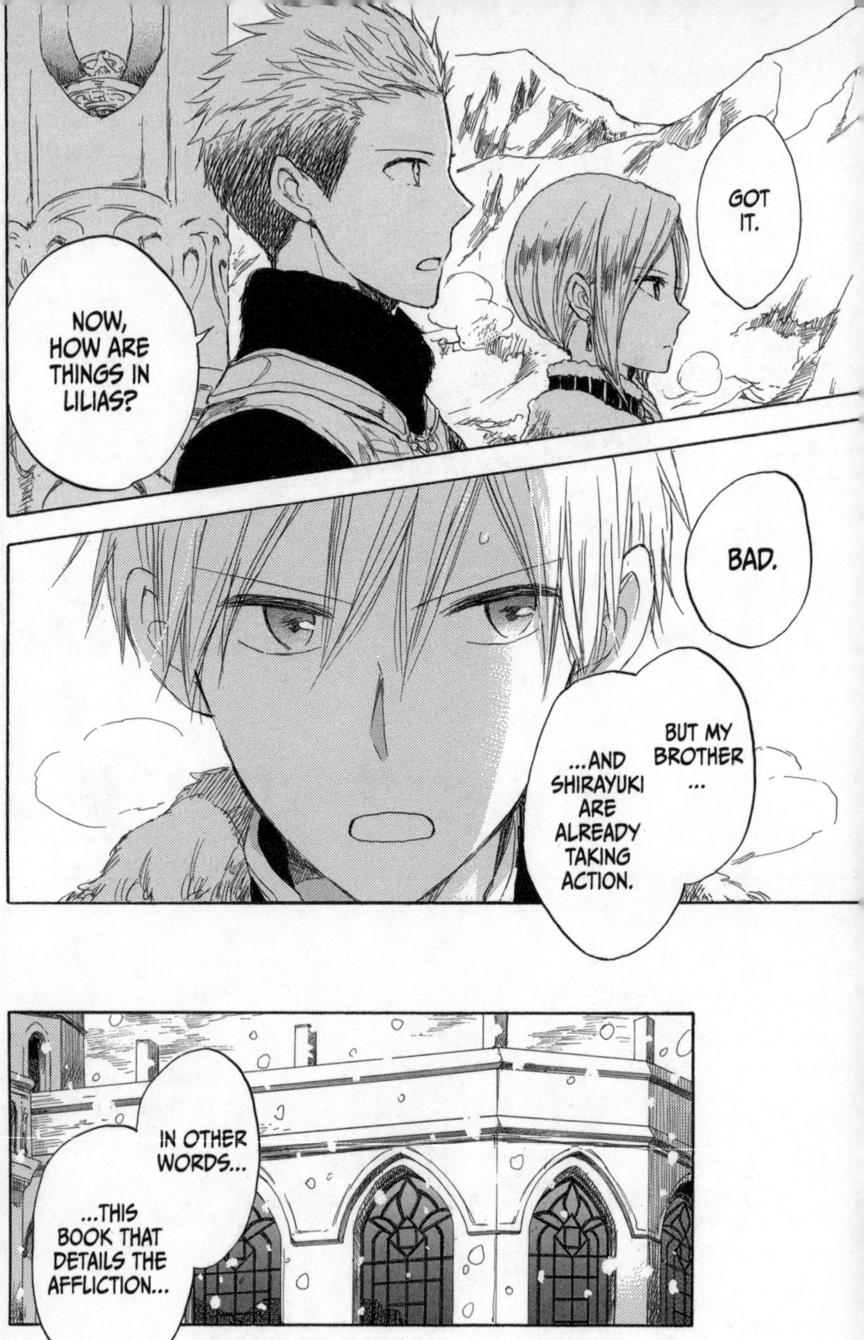
GOT IT.
NOW, HOW ARE THINGS IN LILIAS?
BAD.
BUT MY BROTHER...
...AND SHIRAYUKI ARE ALREADY TAKING ACTION.
IN OTHER WORDS...
...THIS BOOK THAT DETAILS THE AFFLICTION...

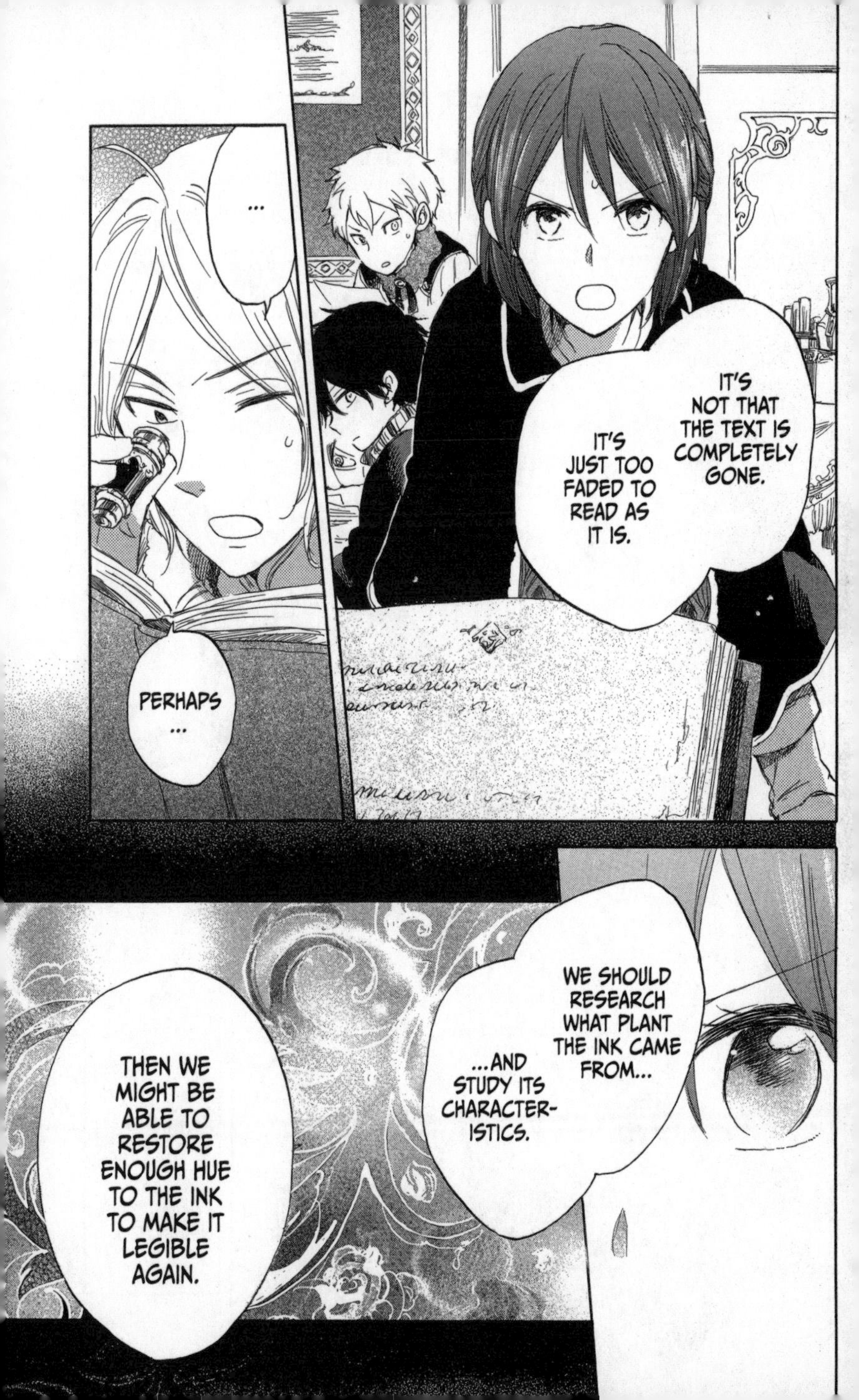
IT'S NOT THAT THE TEXT IS COMPLETELY GONE.
IT'S JUST TOO FADED TO READ AS IT IS.
...
PERHAPS...
WE SHOULD RESEARCH WHAT PLANT THE INK CAME FROM...
...AND STUDY ITS CHARACTER-ISTICS.
THEN WE MIGHT BE ABLE TO RESTORE ENOUGH HUE TO THE INK TO MAKE IT LEGIBLE AGAIN.

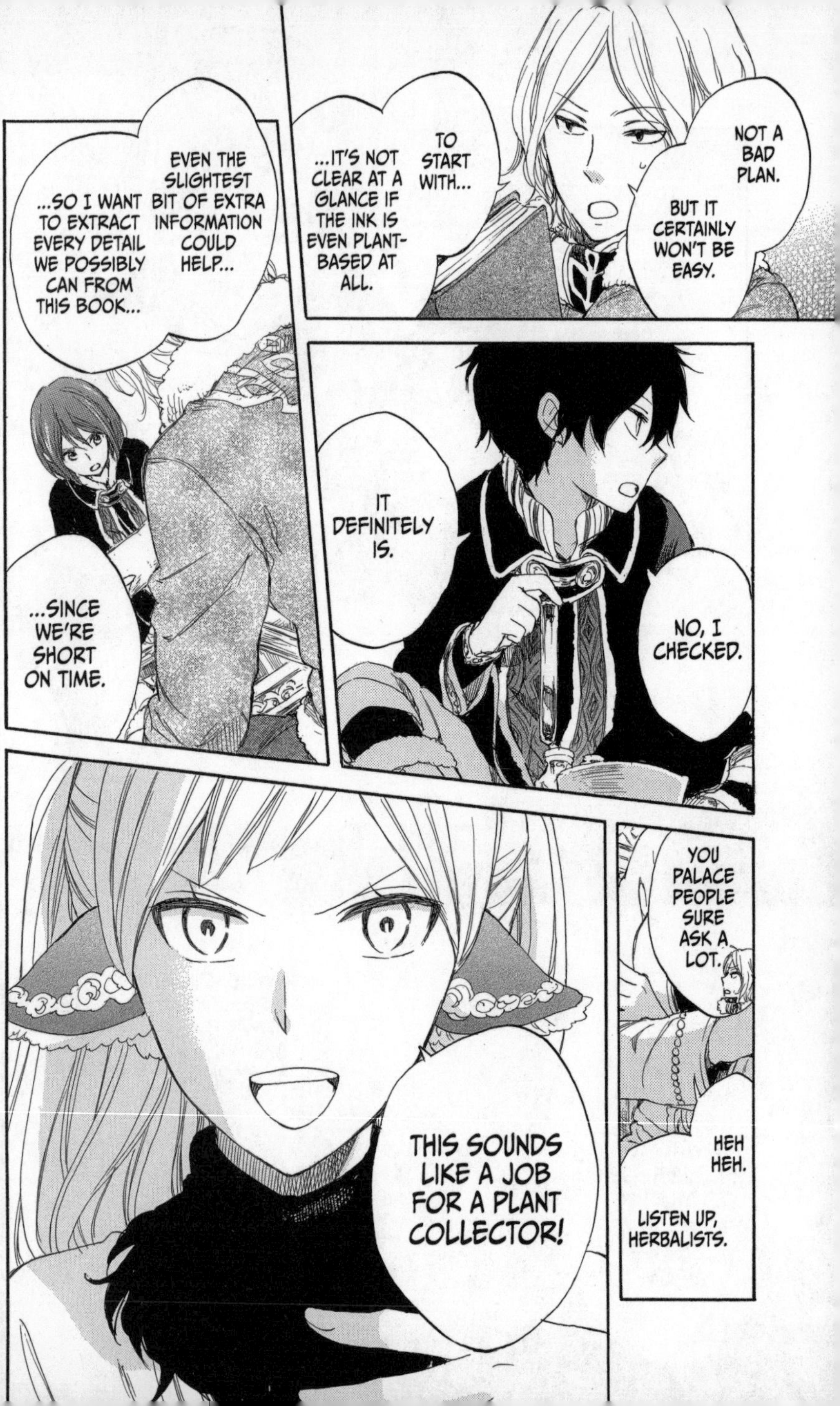
NOT A BAD PLAN.
BUT IT CERTAINLY WON'T BE EASY.
TO START WITH...
...IT'S NOT CLEAR AT A GLANCE IF THE INK IS EVEN PLANT-BASED AT ALL.
NO, I CHECKED.
IT DEFINITELY IS.
EVEN THE SLIGHTEST BIT OF EXTRA INFORMATION COULD HELP...
...SO I WANT TO EXTRACT EVERY DETAIL WE POSSIBLY CAN FROM THIS BOOK...
...SINCE WE'RE SHORT ON TIME.
YOU PALACE PEOPLE SURE ASK A LOT.
HEH HEH.
LISTEN UP, HERBALISTS.
THIS SOUNDS LIKE A JOB FOR A PLANT COLLECTOR!

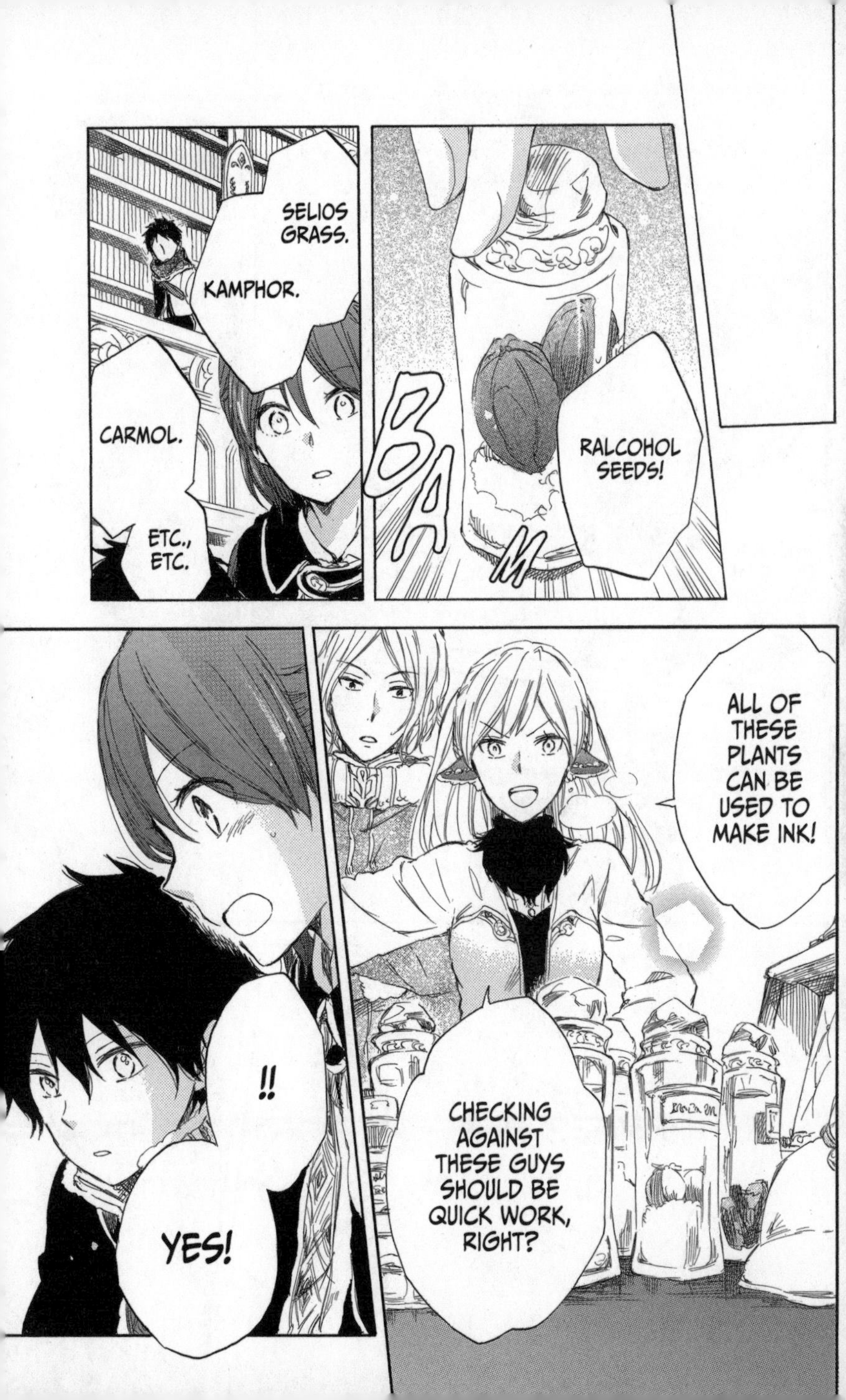
BAM
RALCOHOL SEEDS!
SELIOS GRASS.
KAMPHOR.
CARMOL.
ETC., ETC.
ALL OF THESE PLANTS CAN BE USED TO MAKE INK!
CHECKING AGAINST THESE GUYS SHOULD BE QUICK WORK, RIGHT?
!!
YES!

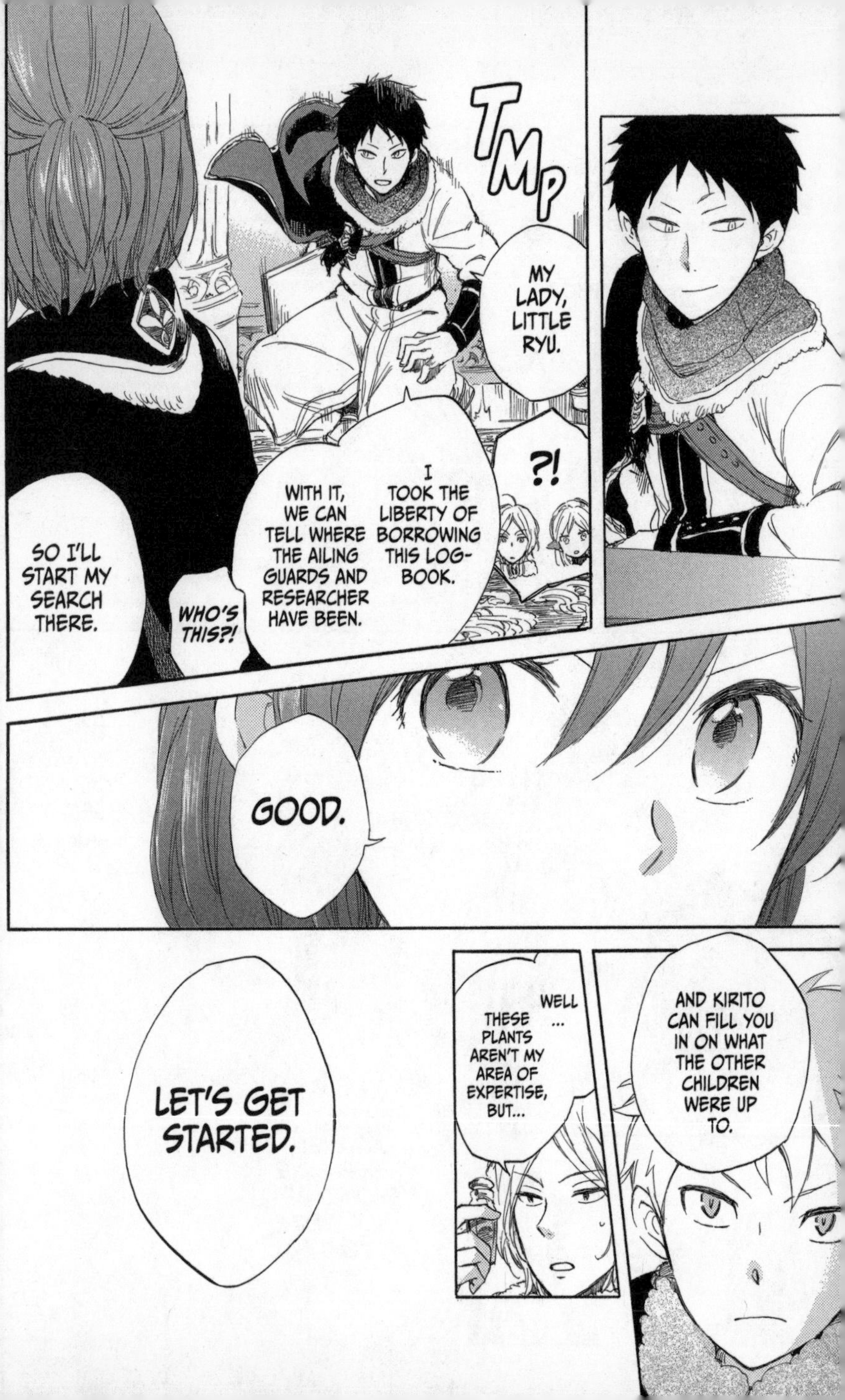
TMP
MY LADY, LITTLE RYU.
?!
I TOOK THE LIBERTY OF BORROWING THIS LOG-BOOK.
WITH IT, WE CAN TELL WHERE THE AILING GUARDS AND RESEARCHER HAVE BEEN.
WHO'S THIS?!
SO I'LL START MY SEARCH THERE.
GOOD.
AND KIRITO CAN FILL YOU IN ON WHAT THE OTHER CHILDREN WERE UP TO.
WELL... THESE PLANTS AREN'T MY AREA OF EXPERTISE, BUT...
LET'S GET STARTED.

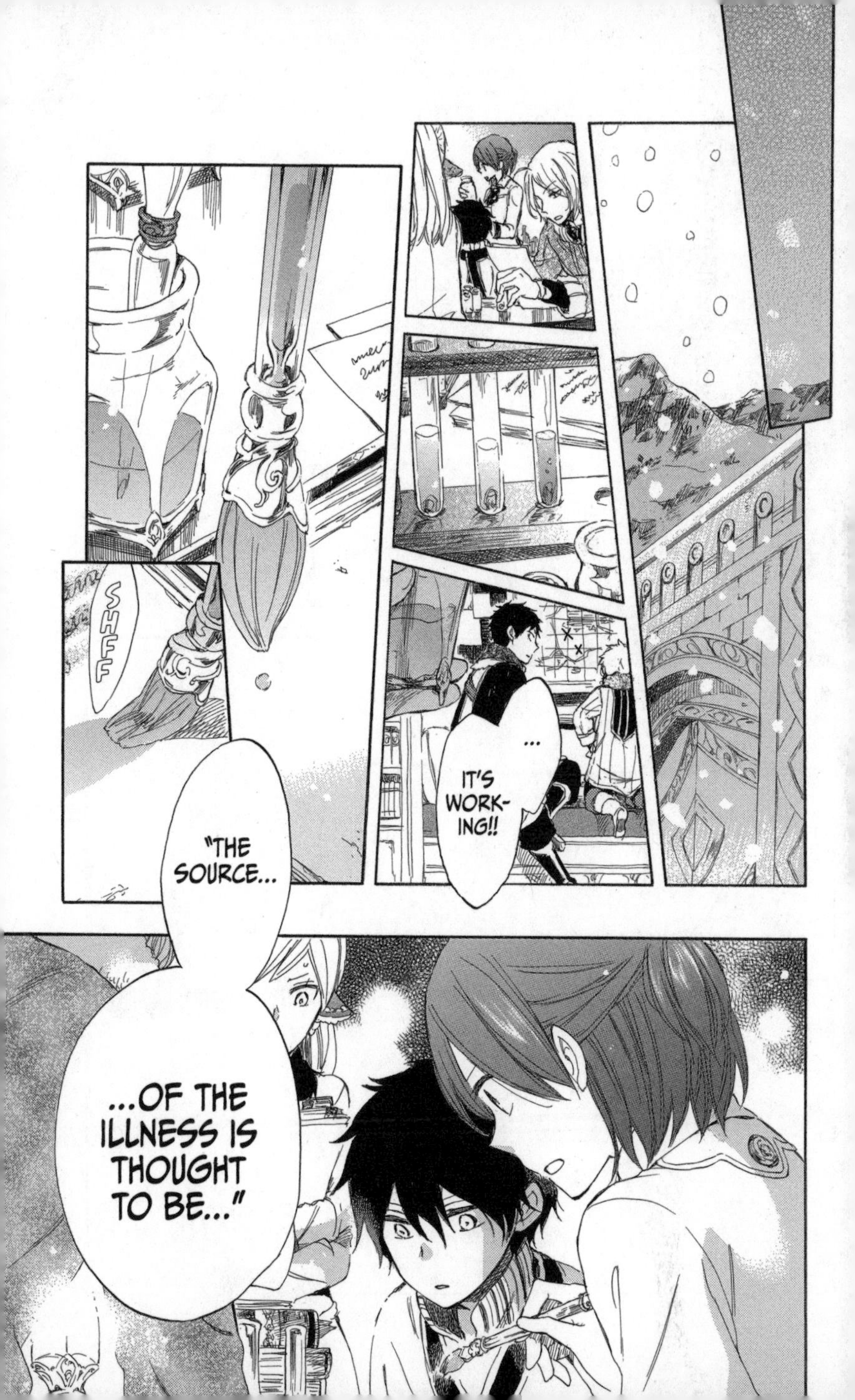
...
IT'S WORK-ING!!
SHFF
"THE SOURCE...
...OF THE ILLNESS IS THOUGHT TO BE..."

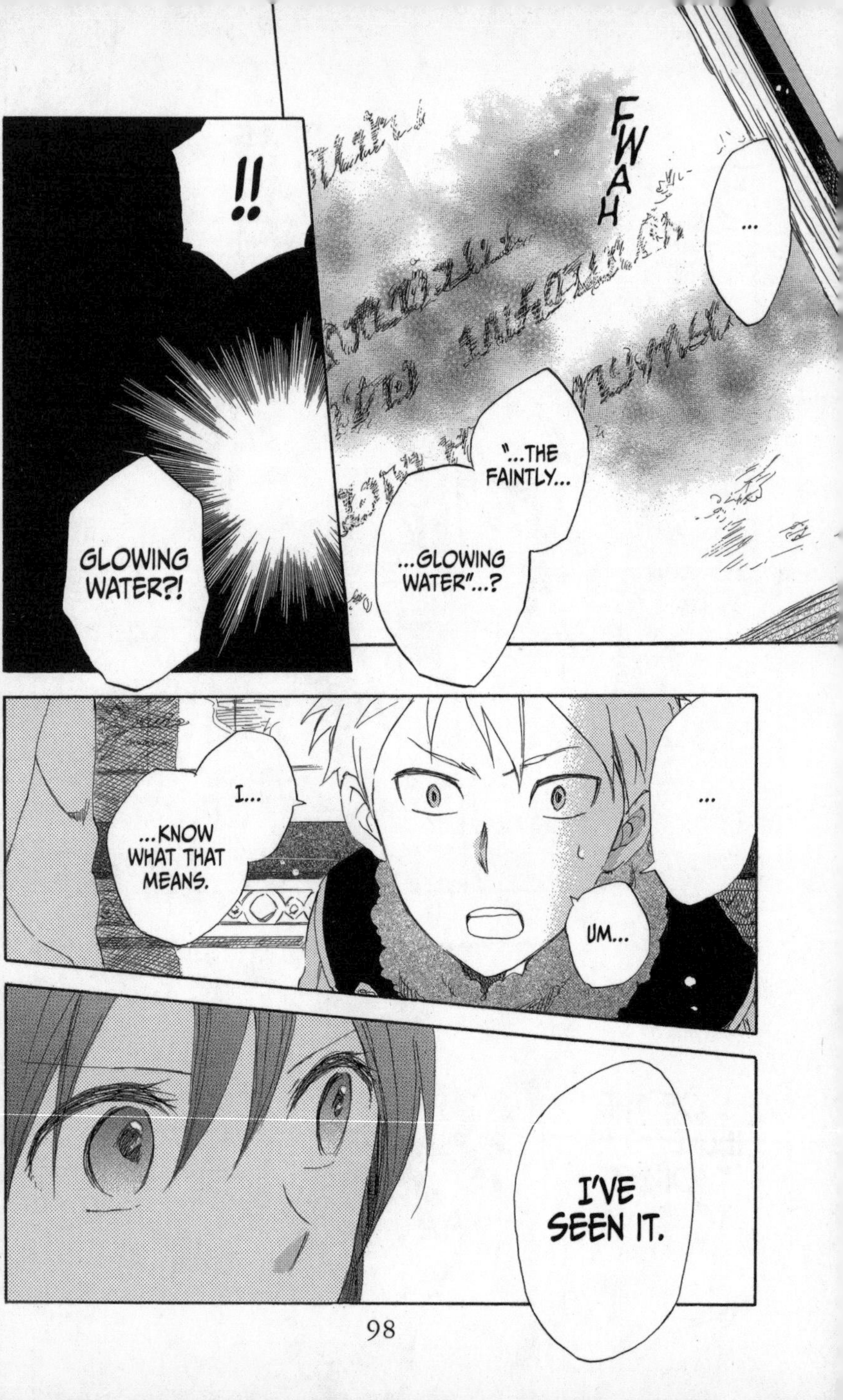
...
FWAH
"...THE FAINTLY...
...GLOWING WATER"...?
!!
GLOWING WATER?!
...
UM...
I...
...KNOW WHAT THAT MEANS.
I'VE SEEN IT.

Chapter 38

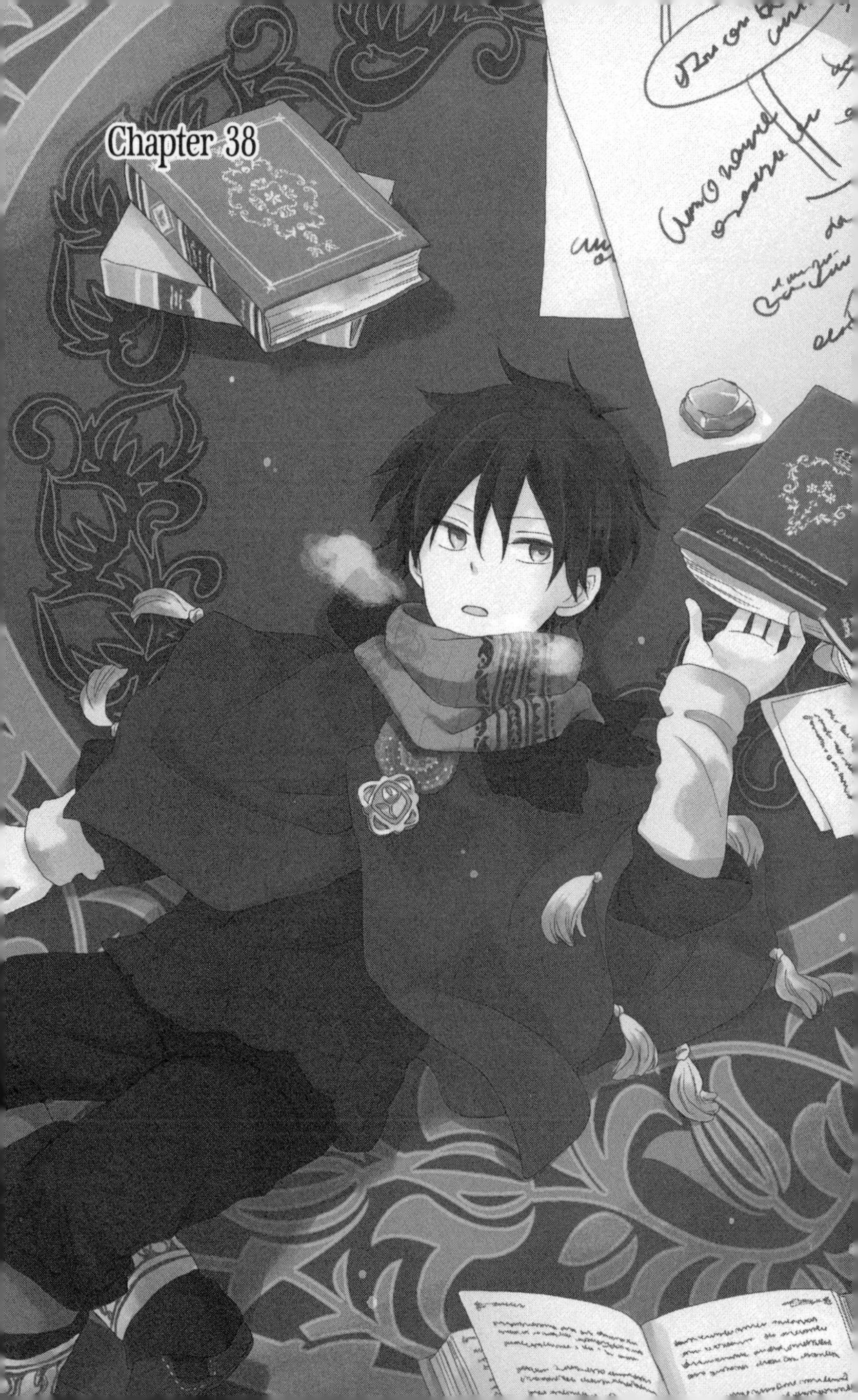

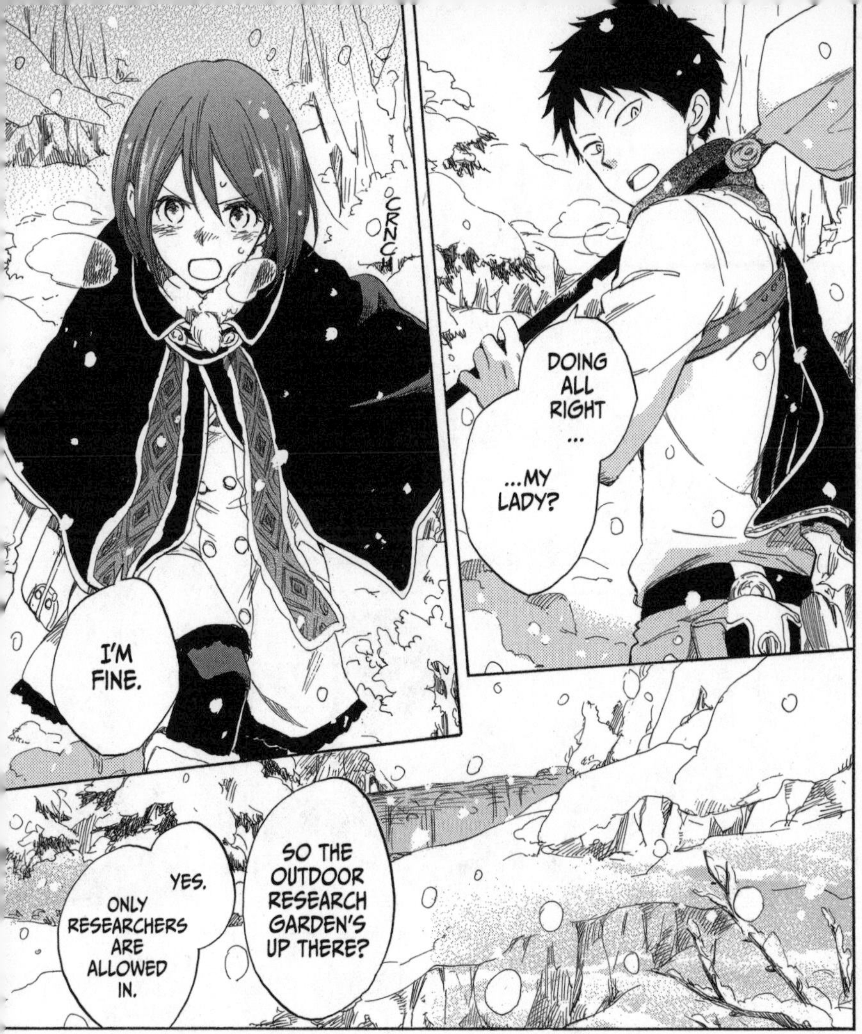
DOING ALL RIGHT ...
...MY LADY?
CRNCH
I'M FINE.
SO THE OUTDOOR RESEARCH GARDEN'S UP THERE?
YES.
ONLY RESEARCHERS ARE ALLOWED IN.

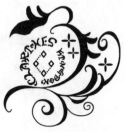

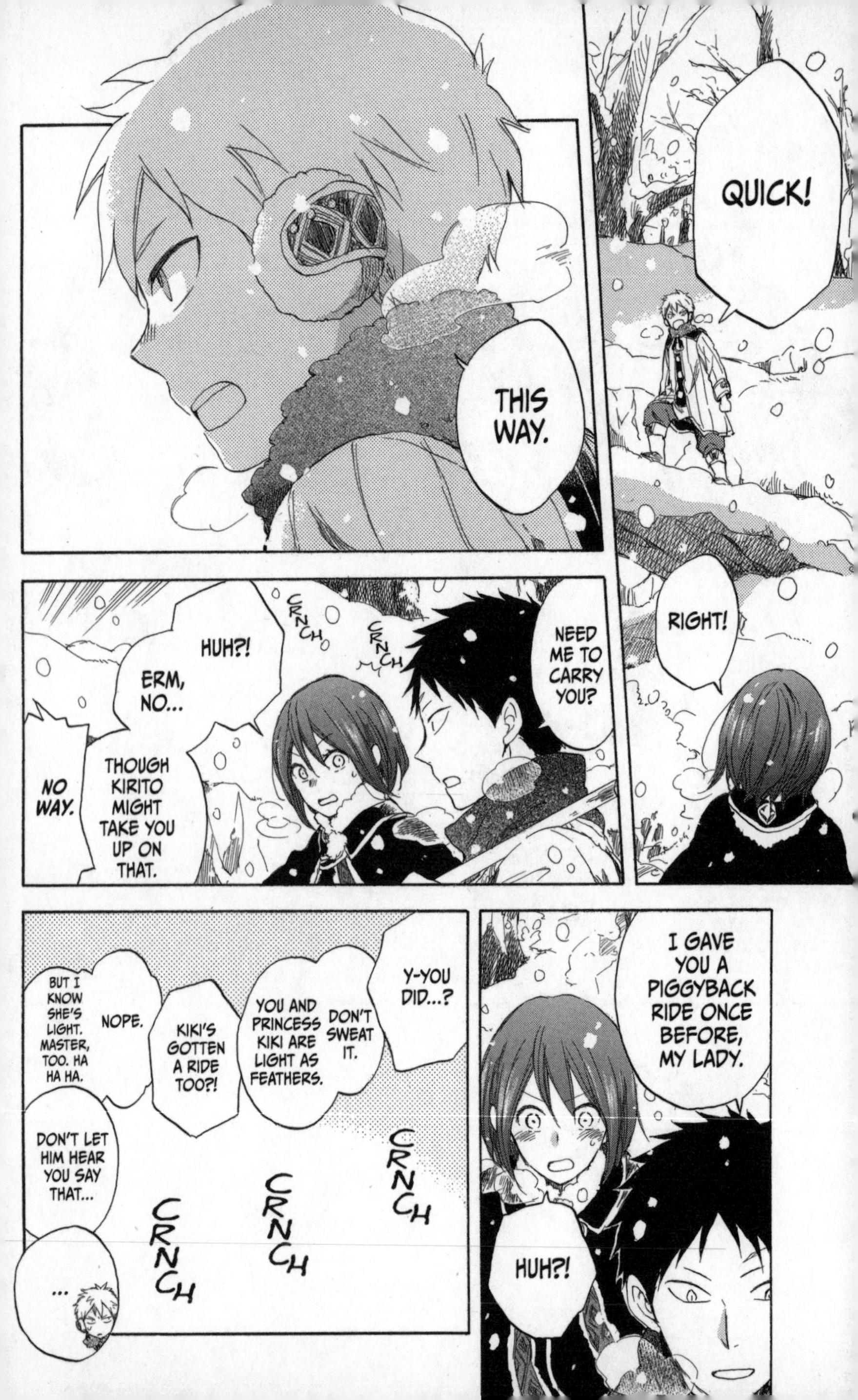
QUICK!
THIS WAY.
RIGHT!
NEED ME TO CARRY YOU?
CRNCH
CRNCH
HUH?!
ERM, NO...
THOUGH KIRITO MIGHT TAKE YOU UP ON THAT.
NO WAY.
I GAVE YOU A PIGGYBACK RIDE ONCE BEFORE, MY LADY.
HUH?!
Y-YOU DID...?
DON'T SWEAT IT.
YOU AND PRINCESS KIKI ARE LIGHT AS FEATHERS.
KIKI'S GOTTEN A RIDE TOO?!
NOPE.
BUT I KNOW SHE'S LIGHT. MASTER, TOO. HA HA HA.
DON'T LET HIM HEAR YOU SAY THAT...
CRNCH
CRNCH
CRNCH
...

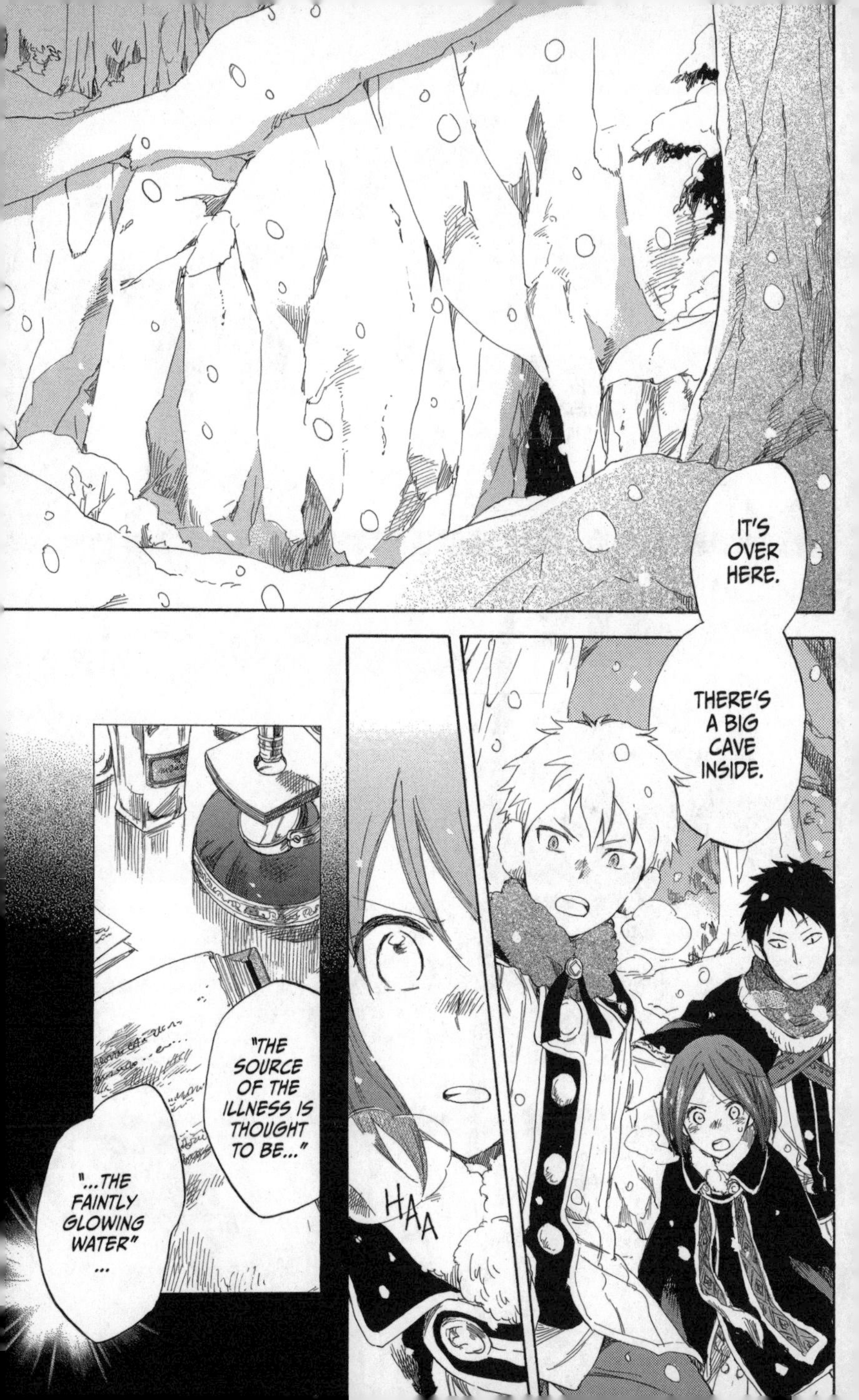
IT'S OVER HERE.
THERE'S A BIG CAVE INSIDE.
HAA
"THE SOURCE OF THE ILLNESS IS THOUGHT TO BE..."
"...THE FAINTLY GLOWING WATER" ...

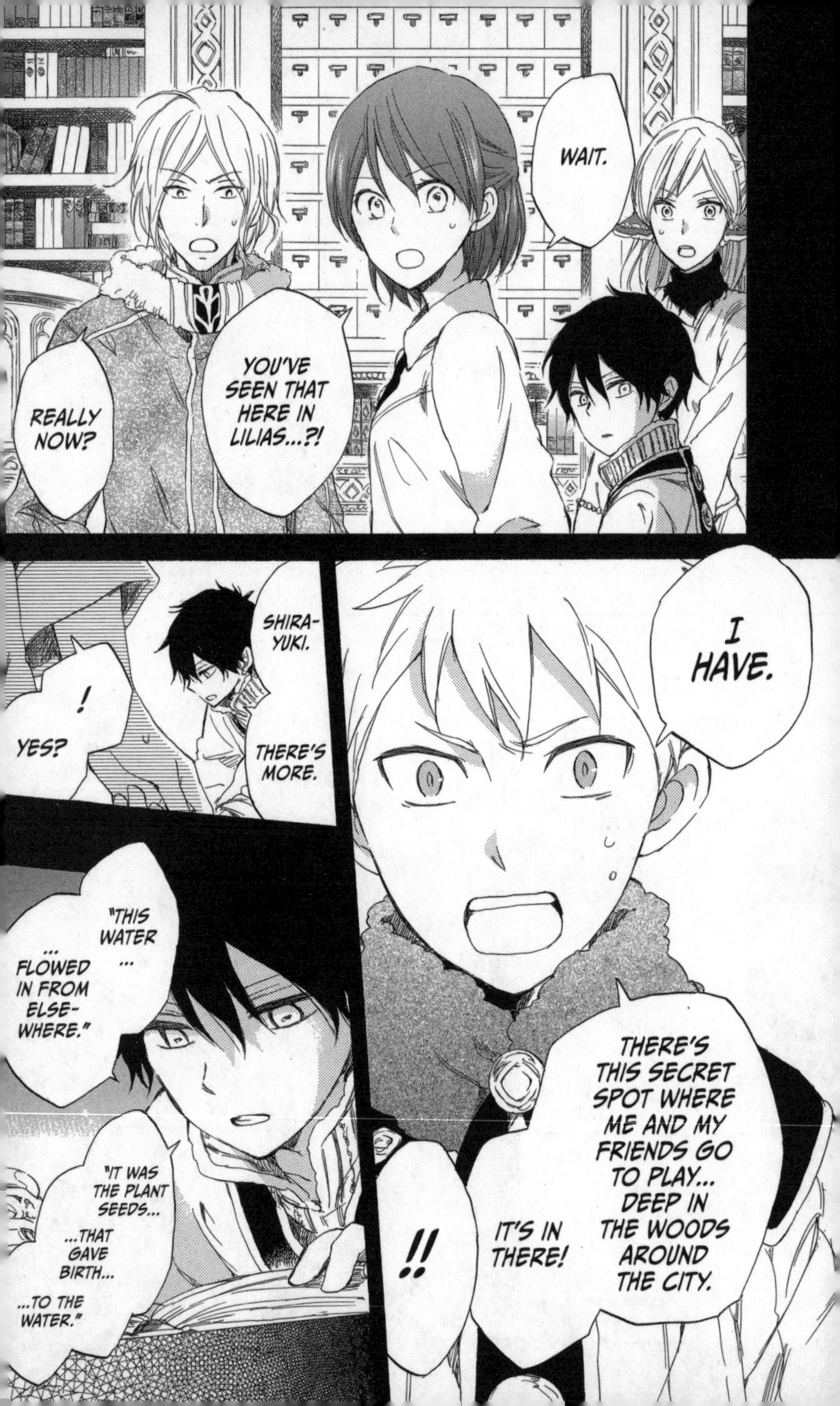
WAIT.
YOU'VE SEEN THAT HERE IN LILIAS...?!
REALLY NOW?
I HAVE.
THERE'S THIS SECRET SPOT WHERE ME AND MY FRIENDS GO TO PLAY... DEEP IN THE WOODS AROUND THE CITY.
IT'S IN THERE!
!!
SHIRAYUKI.
THERE'S MORE.
!
YES?
"THIS WATER ...
... FLOWED IN FROM ELSEWHERE."
"IT WAS THE PLANT SEEDS...
...THAT GAVE BIRTH...
...TO THE WATER."

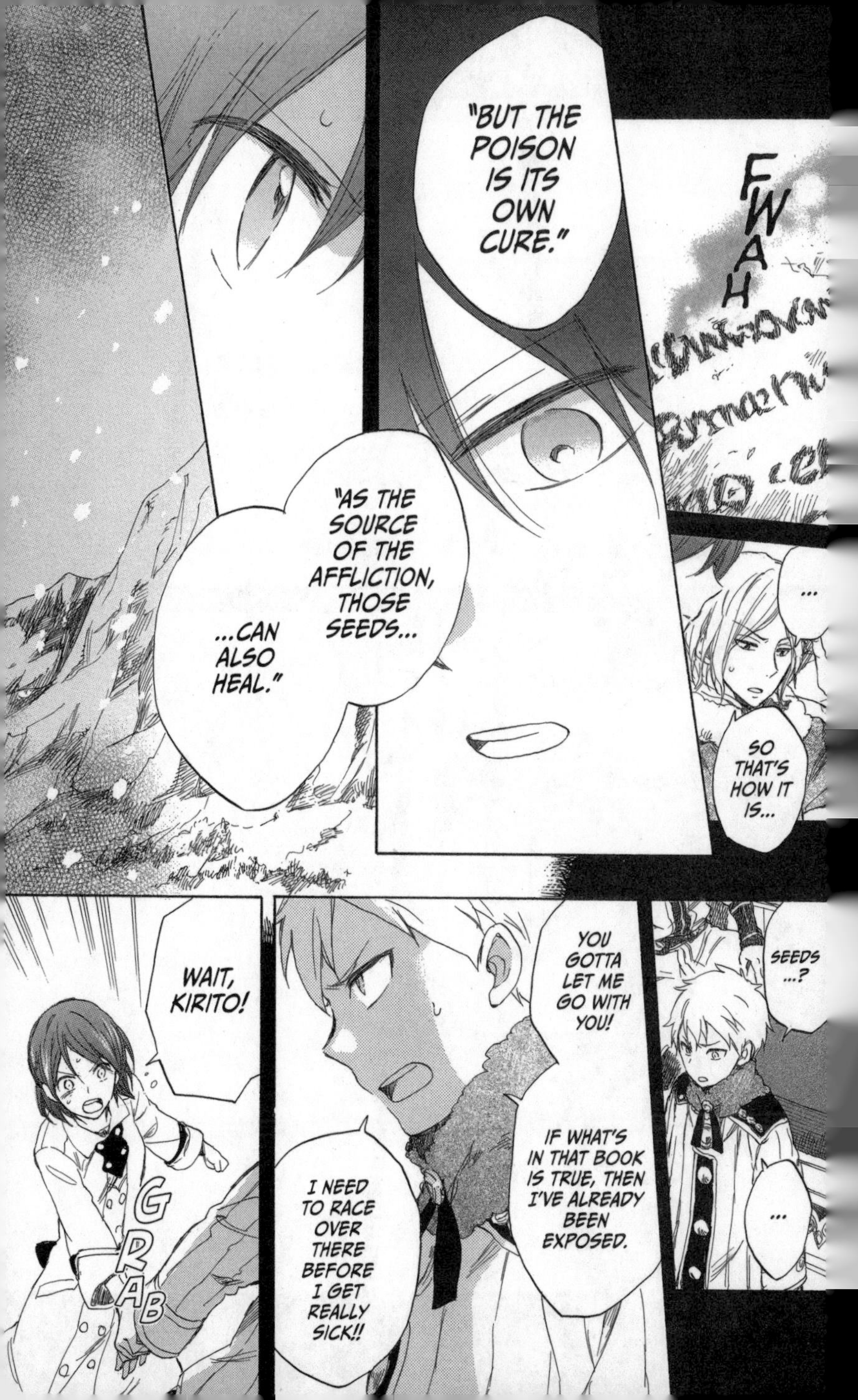
FWAH
...
SO THAT'S HOW IT IS...
"BUT THE POISON IS ITS OWN CURE."
"AS THE SOURCE OF THE AFFLICTION, THOSE SEEDS...
...CAN ALSO HEAL."
SEEDS ...?
...
YOU GOTTA LET ME GO WITH YOU!
IF WHAT'S IN THAT BOOK IS TRUE, THEN I'VE ALREADY BEEN EXPOSED.
I NEED TO RACE OVER THERE BEFORE I GET REALLY SICK!!
WAIT, KIRITO!
GRAB

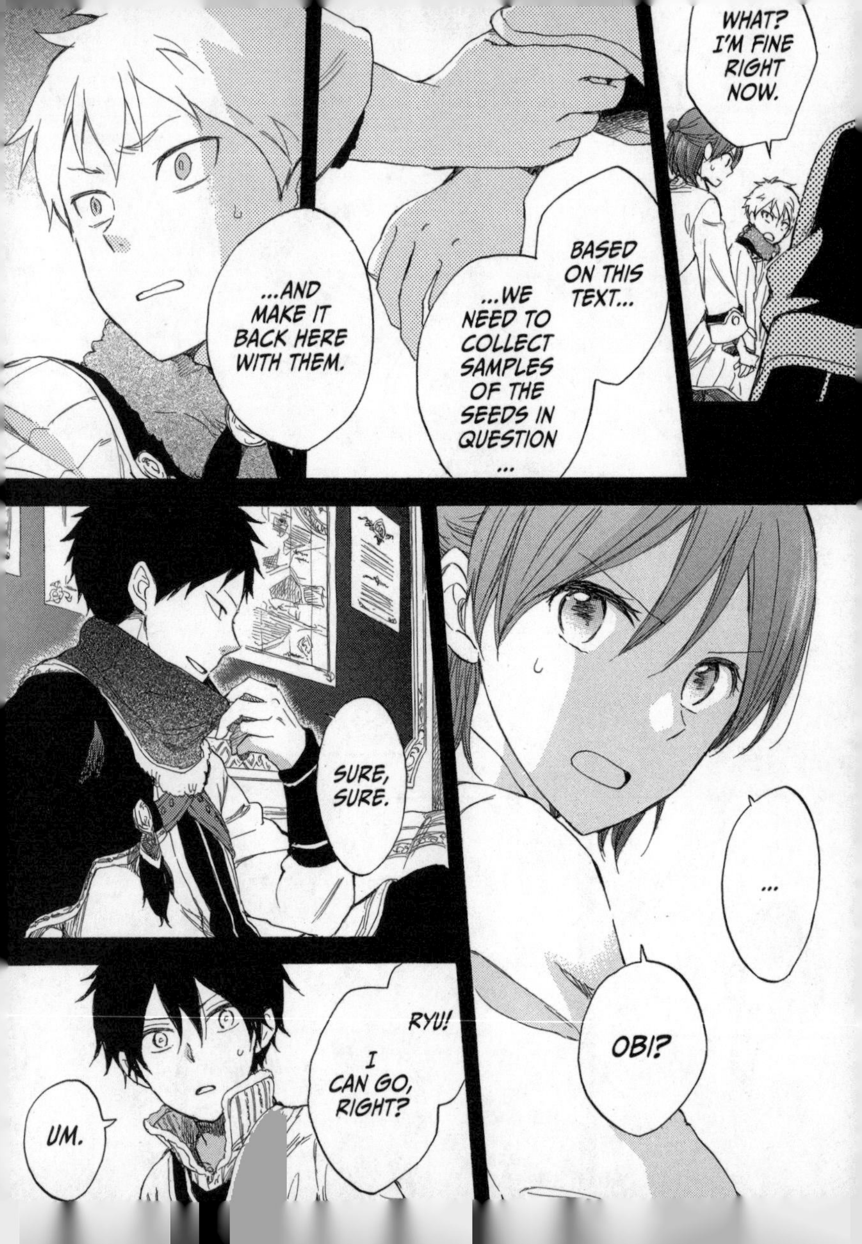
WHAT? I'M FINE RIGHT NOW.
BASED ON THIS TEXT...
...WE NEED TO COLLECT SAMPLES OF THE SEEDS IN QUESTION...
...AND MAKE IT BACK HERE WITH THEM.
...
OBI?
SURE, SURE.
RYU!
I CAN GO, RIGHT?
UM.

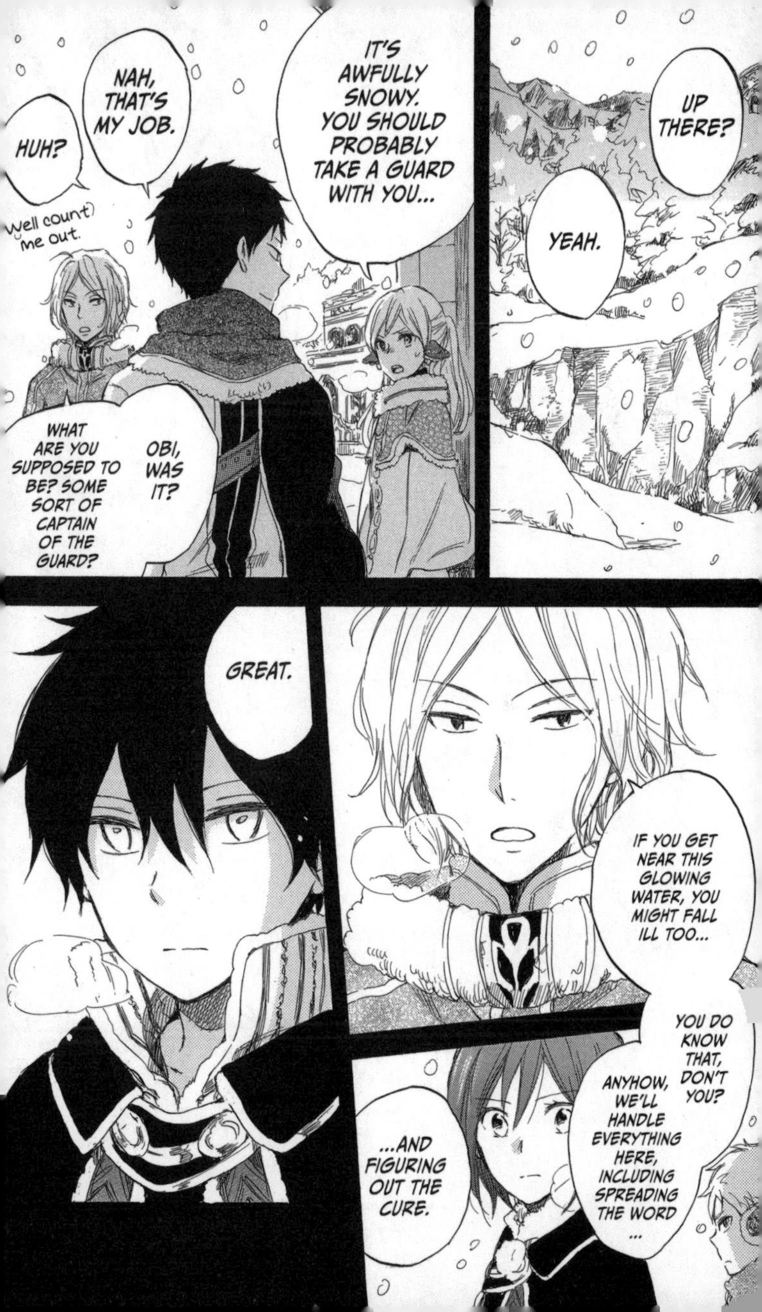
UP THERE?
YEAH.
IT'S AWFULLY SNOWY. YOU SHOULD PROBABLY TAKE A GUARD WITH YOU...
NAH, THAT'S MY JOB.
HUH?
Well count me out.
OBI, WAS IT?
WHAT ARE YOU SUPPOSED TO BE? SOME SORT OF CAPTAIN OF THE GUARD?
IF YOU GET NEAR THIS GLOWING WATER, YOU MIGHT FALL ILL TOO...
YOU DO KNOW THAT, DON'T YOU?
ANYHOW, WE'LL HANDLE EVERYTHING HERE, INCLUDING SPREADING THE WORD...
...AND FIGURING OUT THE CURE.
GREAT.

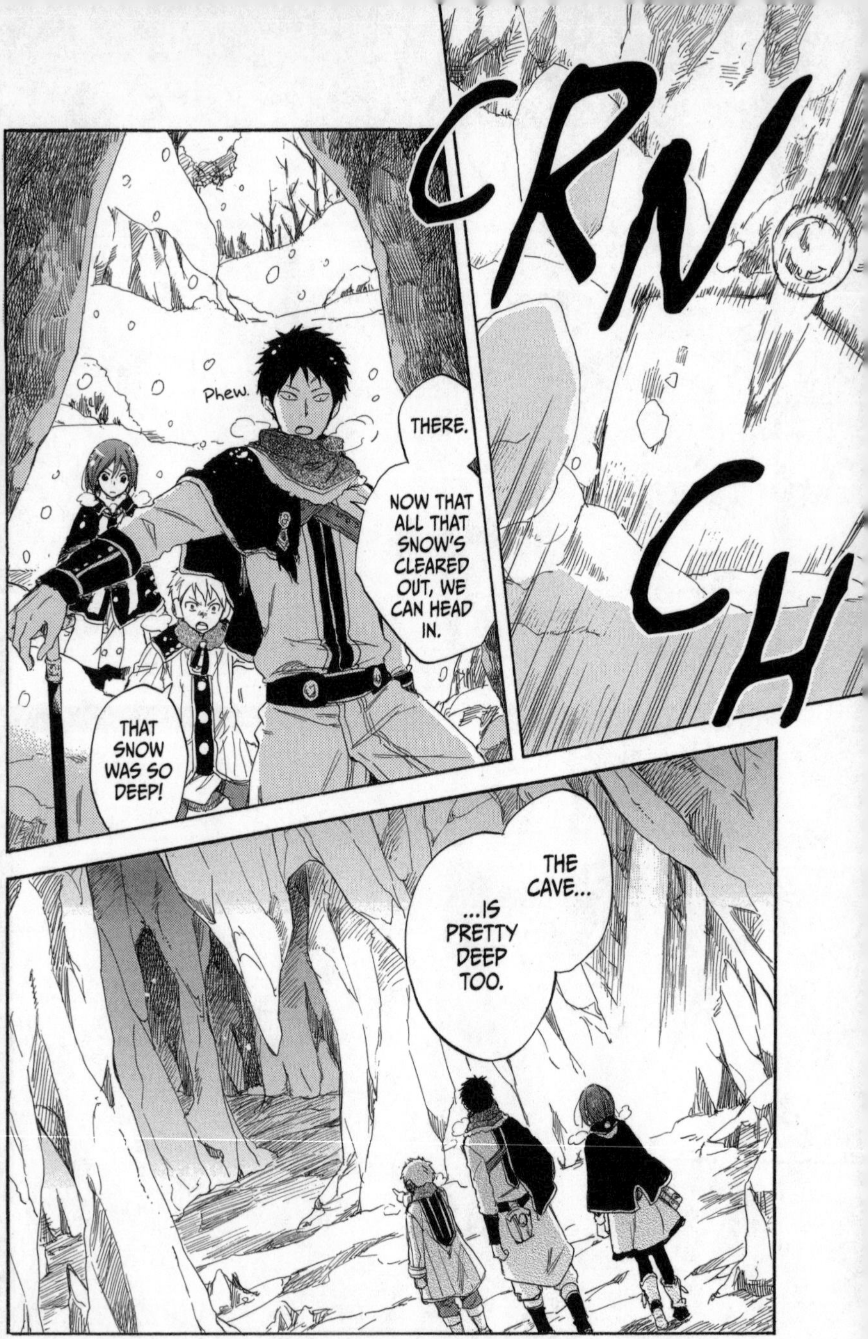
CRNCH
THERE.
NOW THAT ALL THAT SNOW'S CLEARED OUT, WE CAN HEAD IN.
Phew.
THAT SNOW WAS SO DEEP!
THE CAVE...
...IS PRETTY DEEP TOO.

TRIP ③

By the way, I went on this trip with three other manga artists. We also visited Tamatsukuri Hot Springs!

Thank the heavens for giant public baths!

I love the sounds you hear in those high-ceilinged bathing areas. It makes for a unique atmosphere...

You might even call it steamy....

We also paid a visit to Yaegaki Shrine.

I participated in a special type of fortune-telling where you have pieces of paper float up in a pond, but I lost track of which piece of paper was mine. Now I'll never know my fortune...

Was it "good luck" or "extra super-duper good luck"...?

(I'm an optimist.)

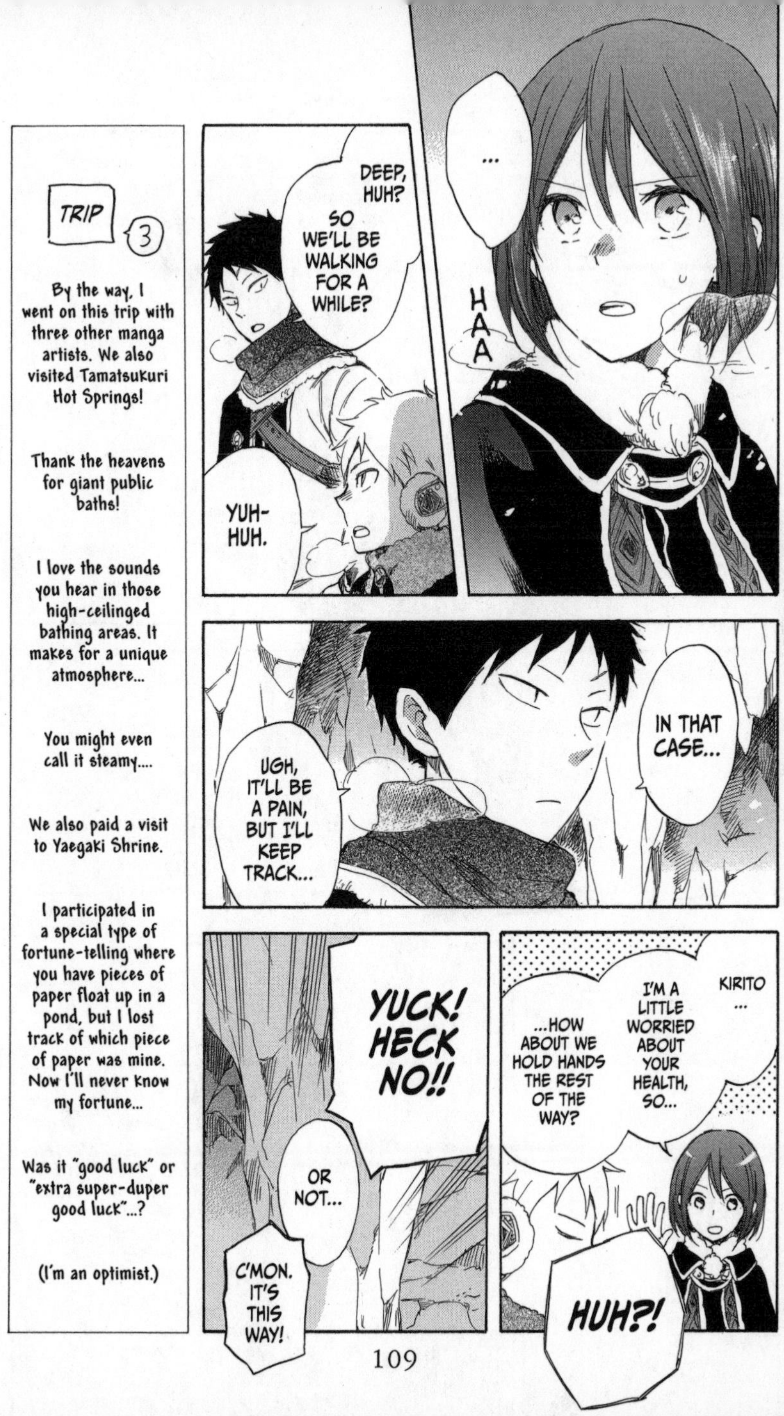
...
HAA
DEEP, HUH?
SO WE'LL BE WALKING FOR A WHILE?
YUH-HUH.
IN THAT CASE...
UGH, IT'LL BE A PAIN, BUT I'LL KEEP TRACK...
KIRITO ...
I'M A LITTLE WORRIED ABOUT YOUR HEALTH, SO...
...HOW ABOUT WE HOLD HANDS THE REST OF THE WAY?
HUH?!
YUCK! HECK NO!!
OR NOT...
C'MON. IT'S THIS WAY!

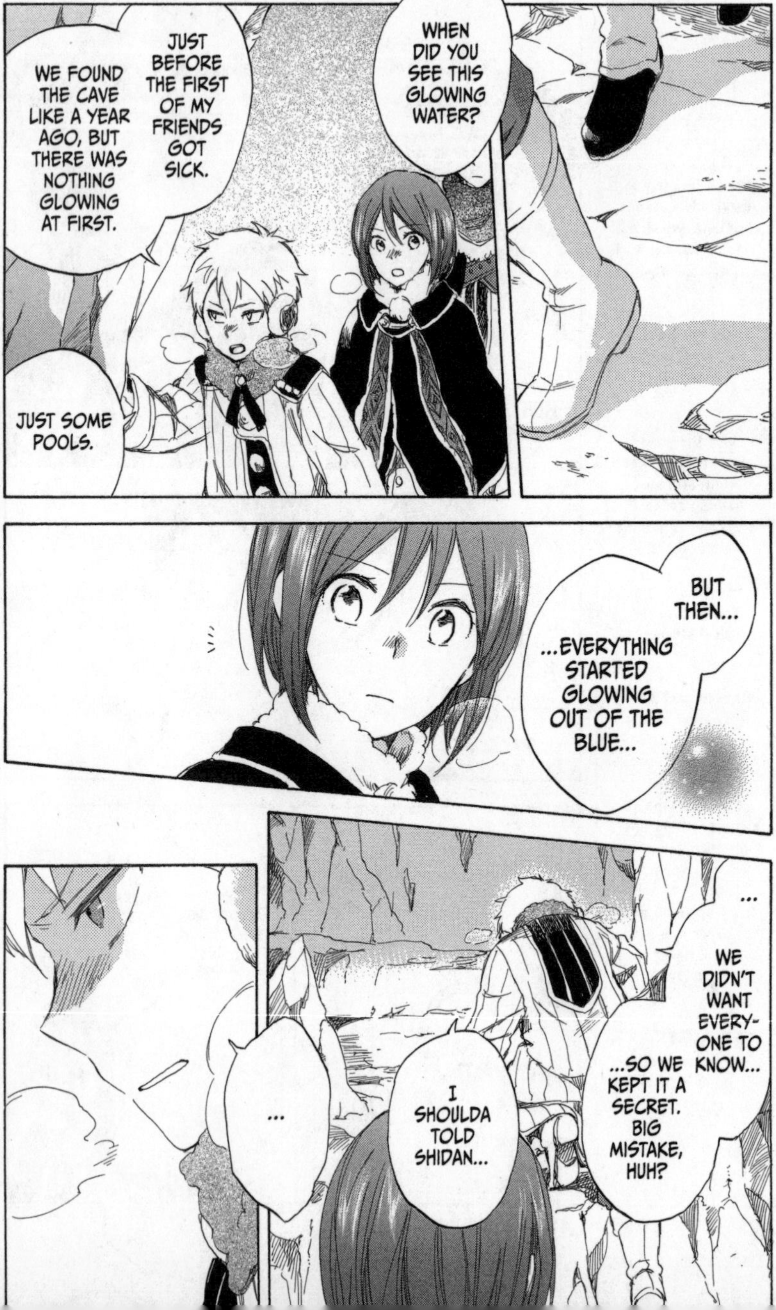
WHEN DID YOU SEE THIS GLOWING WATER?
JUST BEFORE THE FIRST OF MY FRIENDS GOT SICK.
WE FOUND THE CAVE LIKE A YEAR AGO, BUT THERE WAS NOTHING GLOWING AT FIRST.
JUST SOME POOLS.
BUT THEN...
...EVERYTHING STARTED GLOWING OUT OF THE BLUE...
...
WE DIDN'T WANT EVERY-ONE TO KNOW...
...SO WE KEPT IT A SECRET. BIG MISTAKE, HUH?
I SHOULDA TOLD SHIDAN...
...

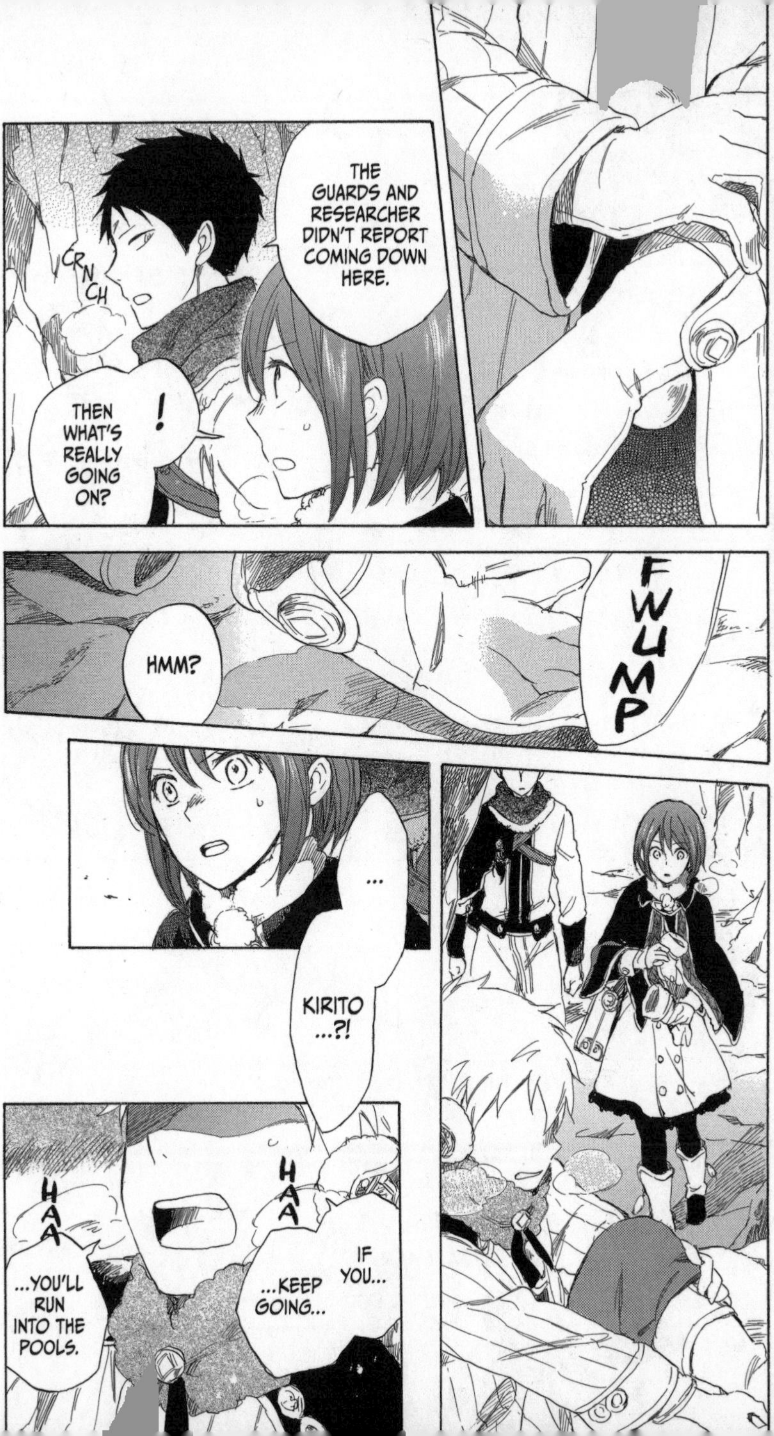
THE GUARDS AND RESEARCHER DIDN'T REPORT COMING DOWN HERE.
!
CRNCH
THEN WHAT'S REALLY GOING ON?
FWUMP
HMM?
...
KIRITO ...?!
HAA
IF YOU...
...KEEP GOING...
HAA
...YOU'LL RUN INTO THE POOLS.

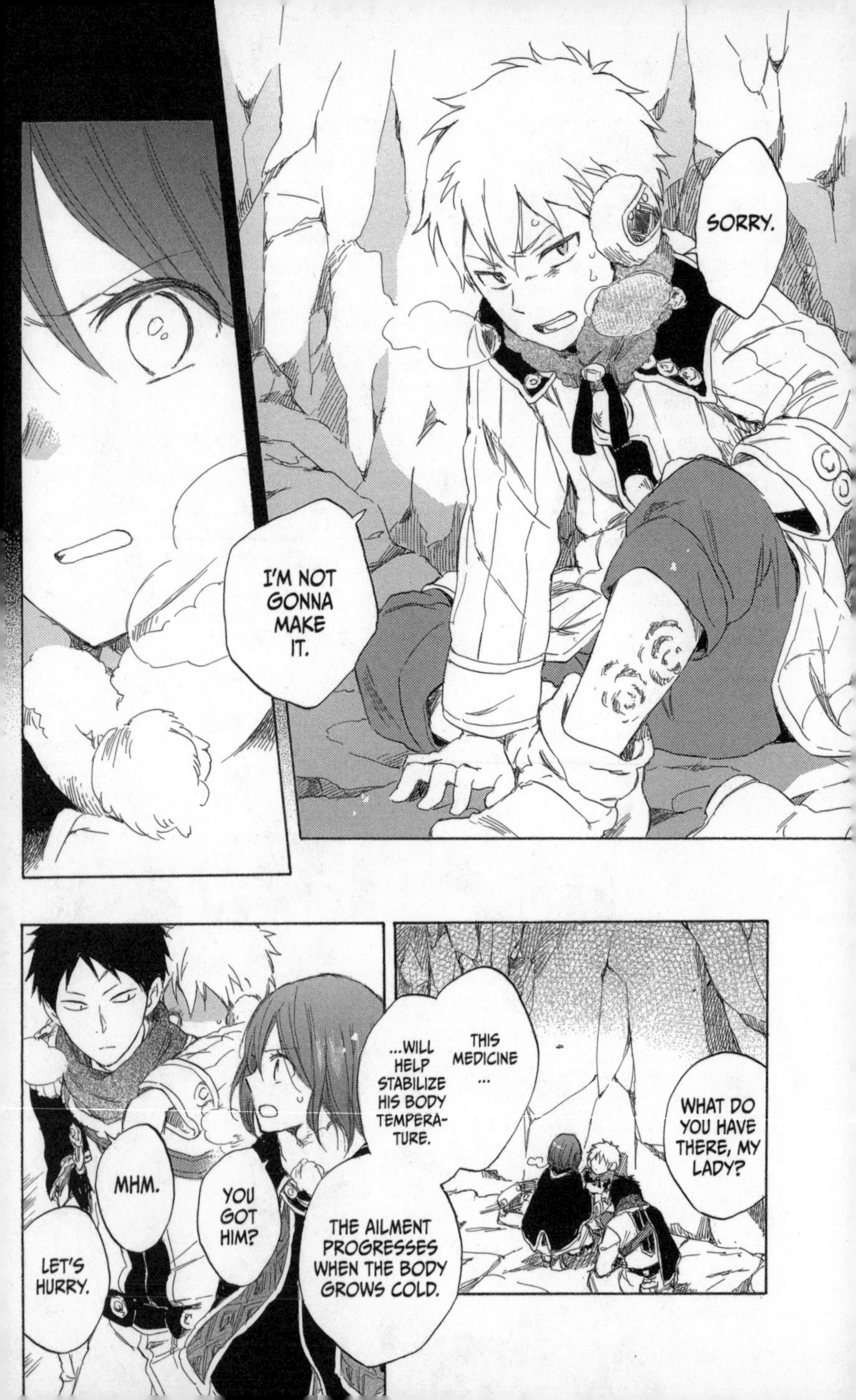
SORRY.
I'M NOT GONNA MAKE IT.
WHAT DO YOU HAVE THERE, MY LADY?
THIS MEDICINE...
...WILL HELP STABILIZE HIS BODY TEMPERA-TURE.
THE AILMENT PROGRESSES WHEN THE BODY GROWS COLD.
YOU GOT HIM?
MHM.
LET'S HURRY.

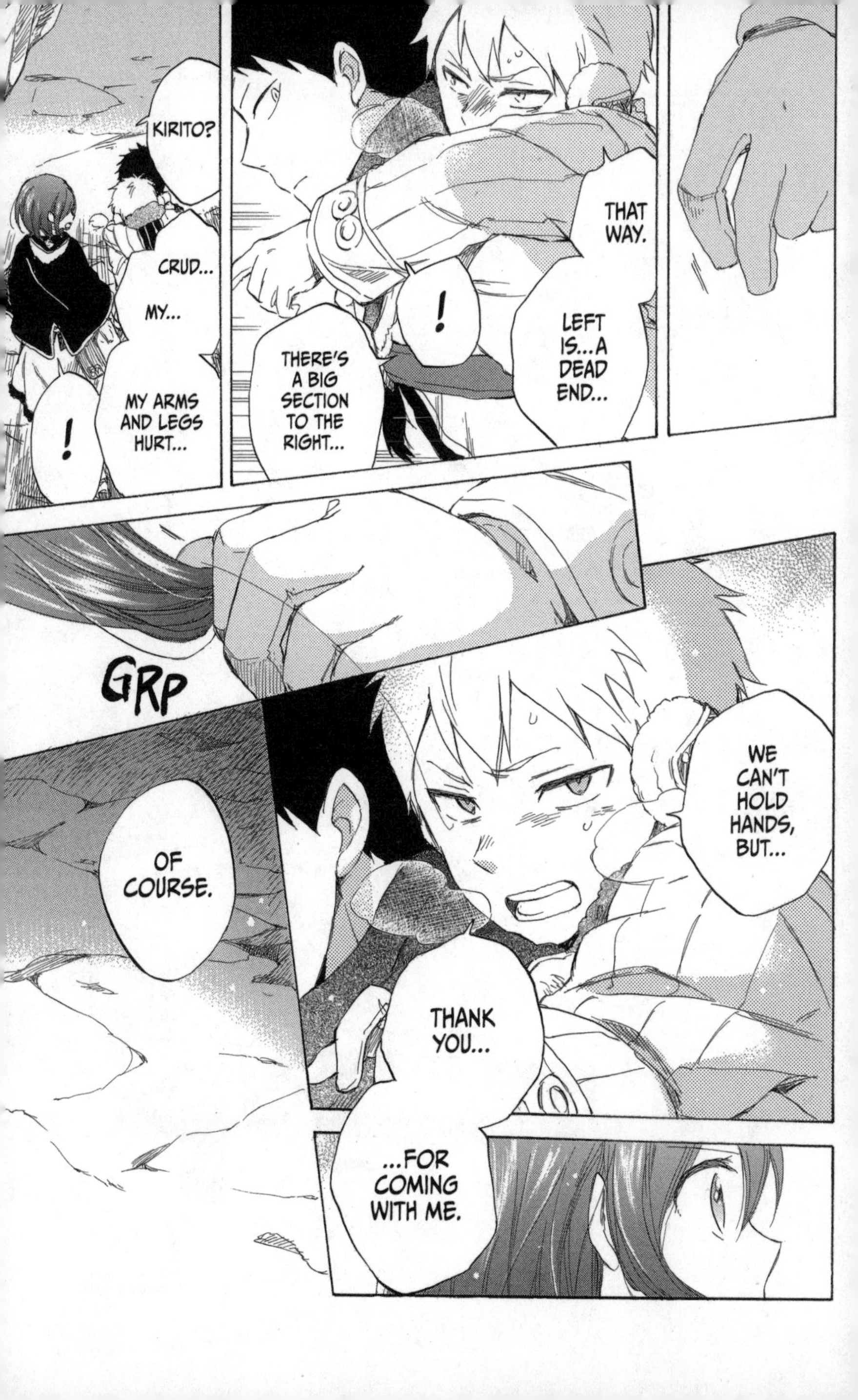
THAT WAY.
LEFT IS...A DEAD END...
!
THERE'S A BIG SECTION TO THE RIGHT...
KIRITO?
CRUD...
MY...
MY ARMS AND LEGS HURT...
!
GRP
WE CAN'T HOLD HANDS, BUT...
THANK YOU...
...FOR COMING WITH ME.
OF COURSE.

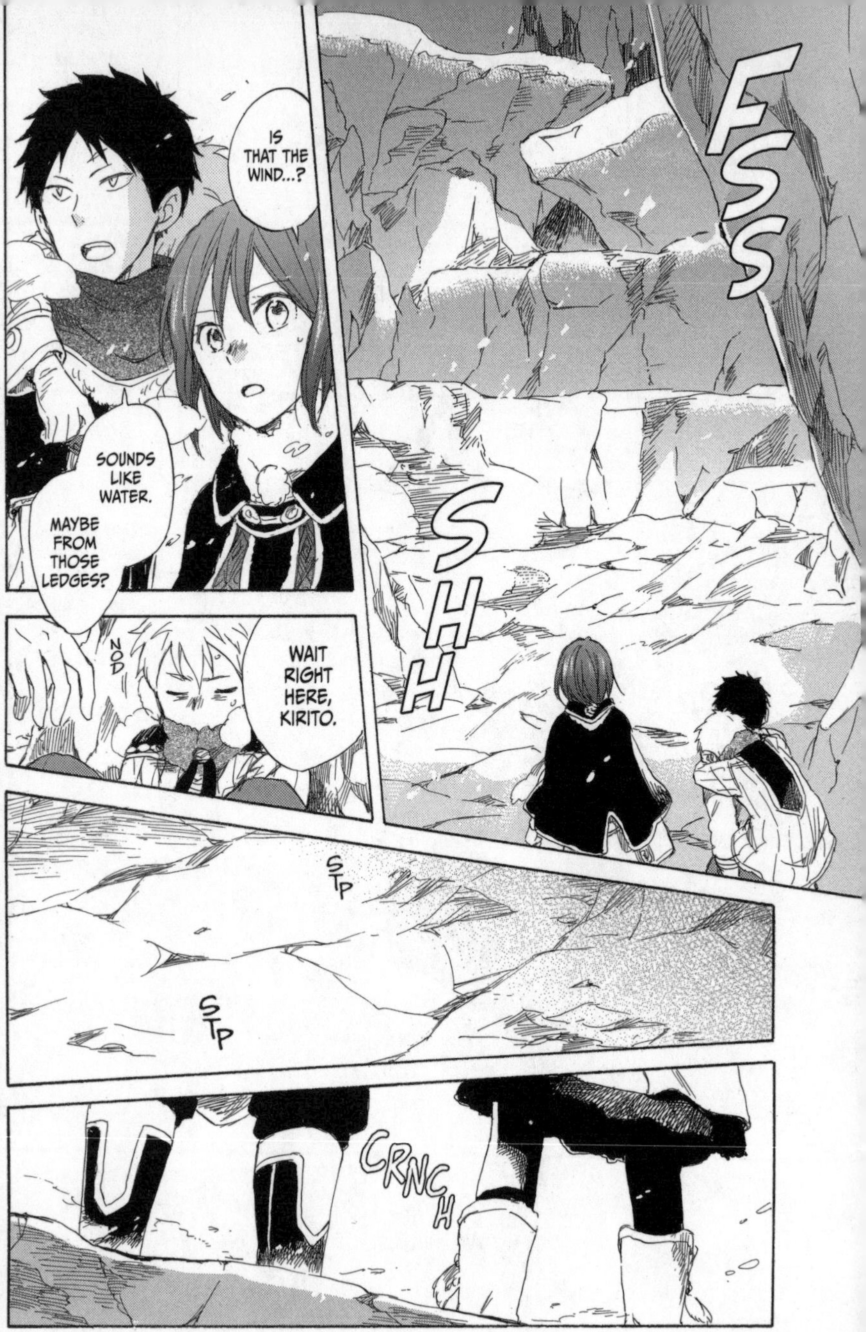
FSS
SHHH
IS THAT THE WIND...?
SOUNDS LIKE WATER.
MAYBE FROM THOSE LEDGES?
WAIT RIGHT HERE, KIRITO.
NOD
STP
STP
CRNCH

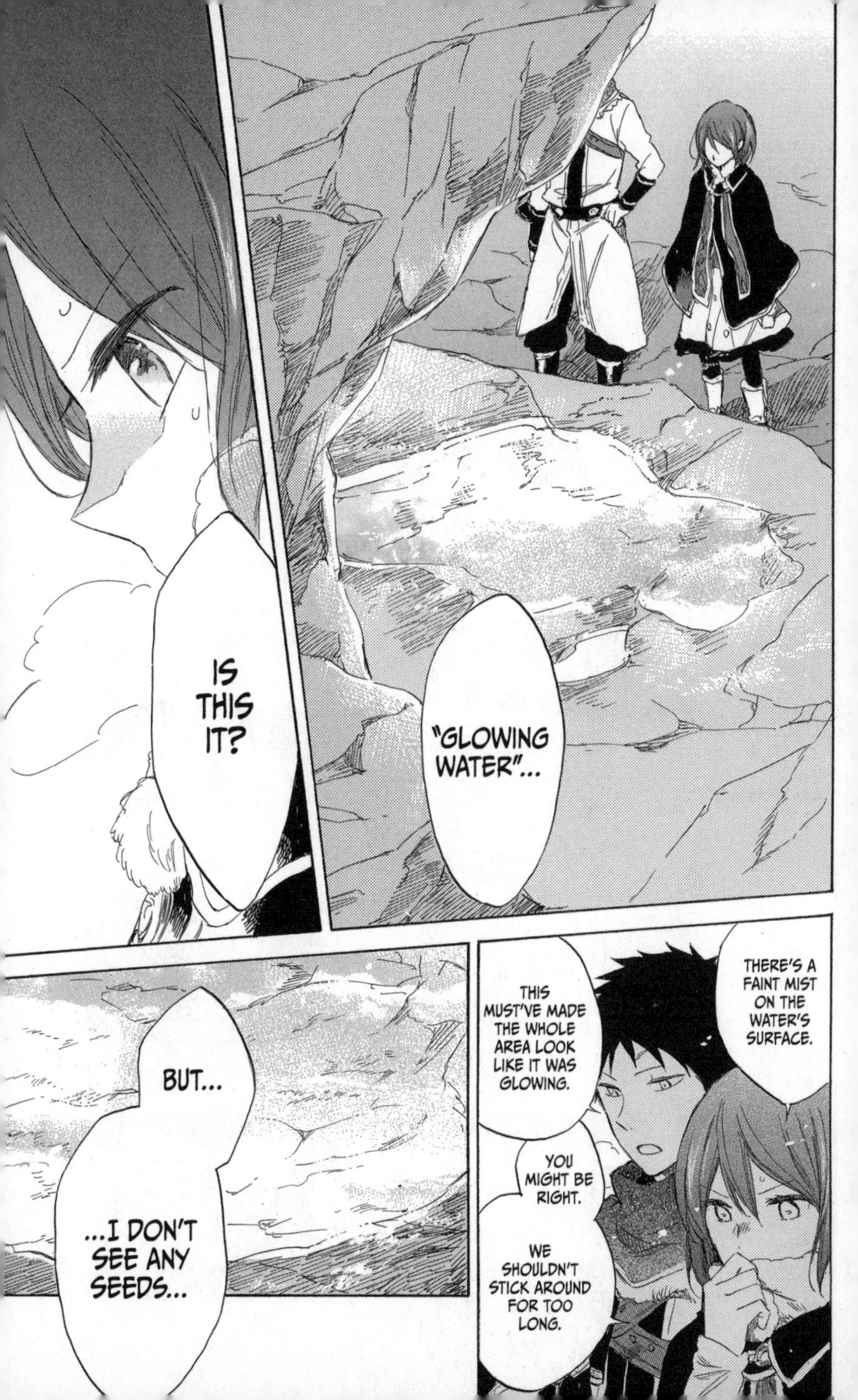
"GLOWING WATER"...
IS THIS IT?
THERE'S A FAINT MIST ON THE WATER'S SURFACE.
THIS MUST'VE MADE THE WHOLE AREA LOOK LIKE IT WAS GLOWING.
YOU MIGHT BE RIGHT.
WE SHOULDN'T STICK AROUND FOR TOO LONG.
BUT...
...I DON'T SEE ANY SEEDS...

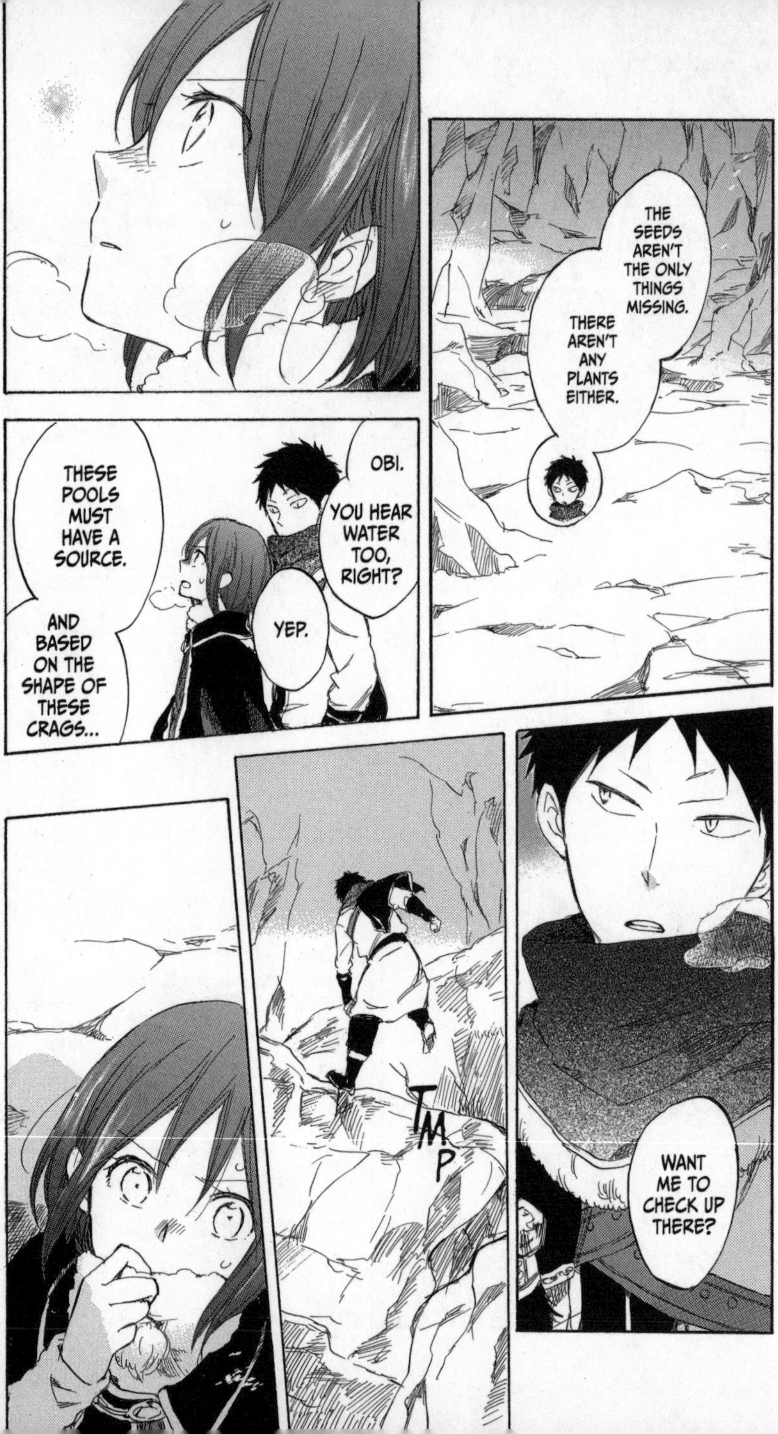
THE SEEDS AREN'T THE ONLY THINGS MISSING.
THERE AREN'T ANY PLANTS EITHER.
OBI.
YOU HEAR WATER TOO, RIGHT?
YEP.
THESE POOLS MUST HAVE A SOURCE.
AND BASED ON THE SHAPE OF THESE CRAGS...
WANT ME TO CHECK UP THERE?
TMP

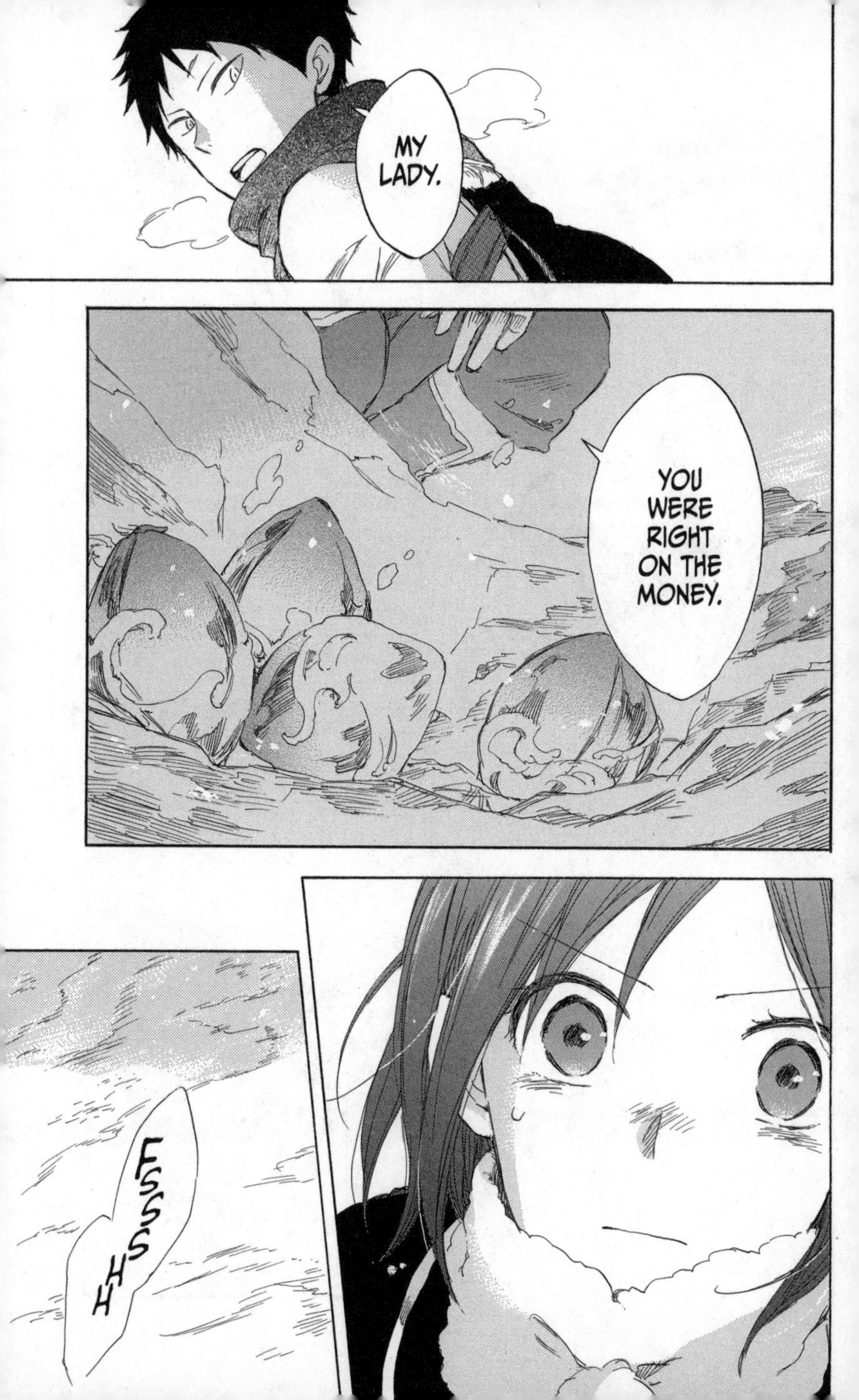
MY LADY.
YOU WERE RIGHT ON THE MONEY.
FSSSHH

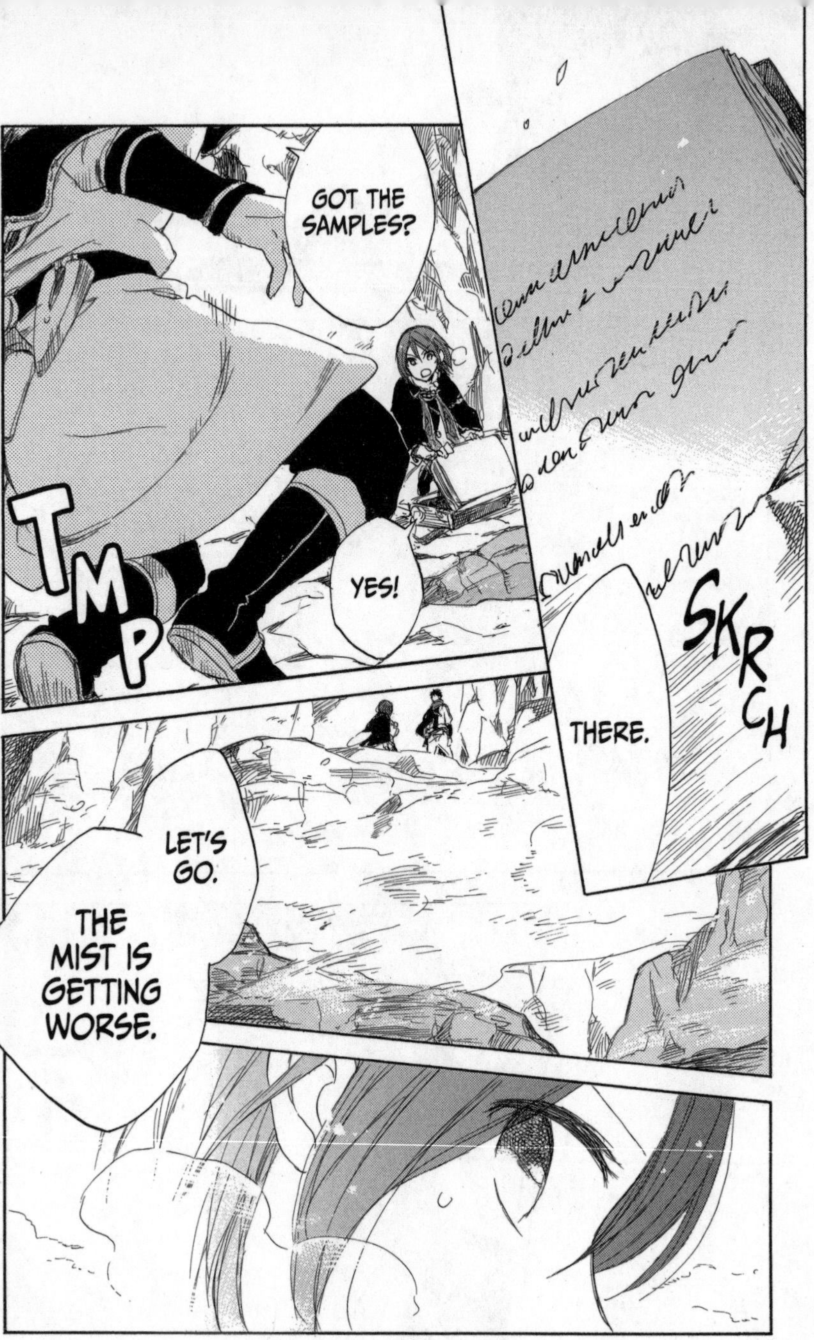
SKRCH
THERE.
GOT THE SAMPLES?
YES!
TMP
LET'S GO.
THE MIST IS GETTING WORSE.

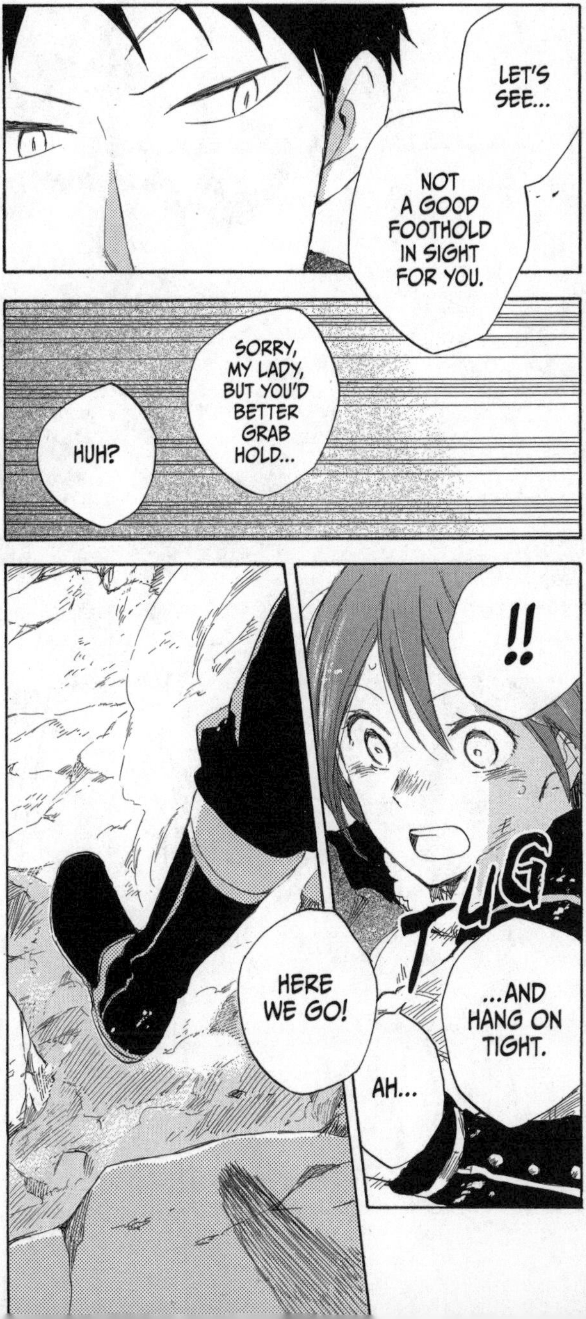
LET'S SEE...
NOT A GOOD FOOTHOLD IN SIGHT FOR YOU.
SORRY, MY LADY, BUT YOU'D BETTER GRAB HOLD...
HUH?
!!
TUG
...AND HANG ON TIGHT.
AH...
HERE WE GO!

Just when I thought I was done compiling this volume, I panicked and realized I had another one of these sidebars to write.

W-what should I write about...? Zenzai...? More about zenzai...?

Anyhow, last night I encountered writer's block while working on a rough draft for a chapter of *Snow White*. So to clear my head a bit, I tried to come up with a school romance one-shot. But I even failed at doing that.

So, I decided to make it about a middle school boy.

Once I switched gears, the ideas started flowing.

Behold, the power of the middle school boy.

Though I still haven't drawn out the story.

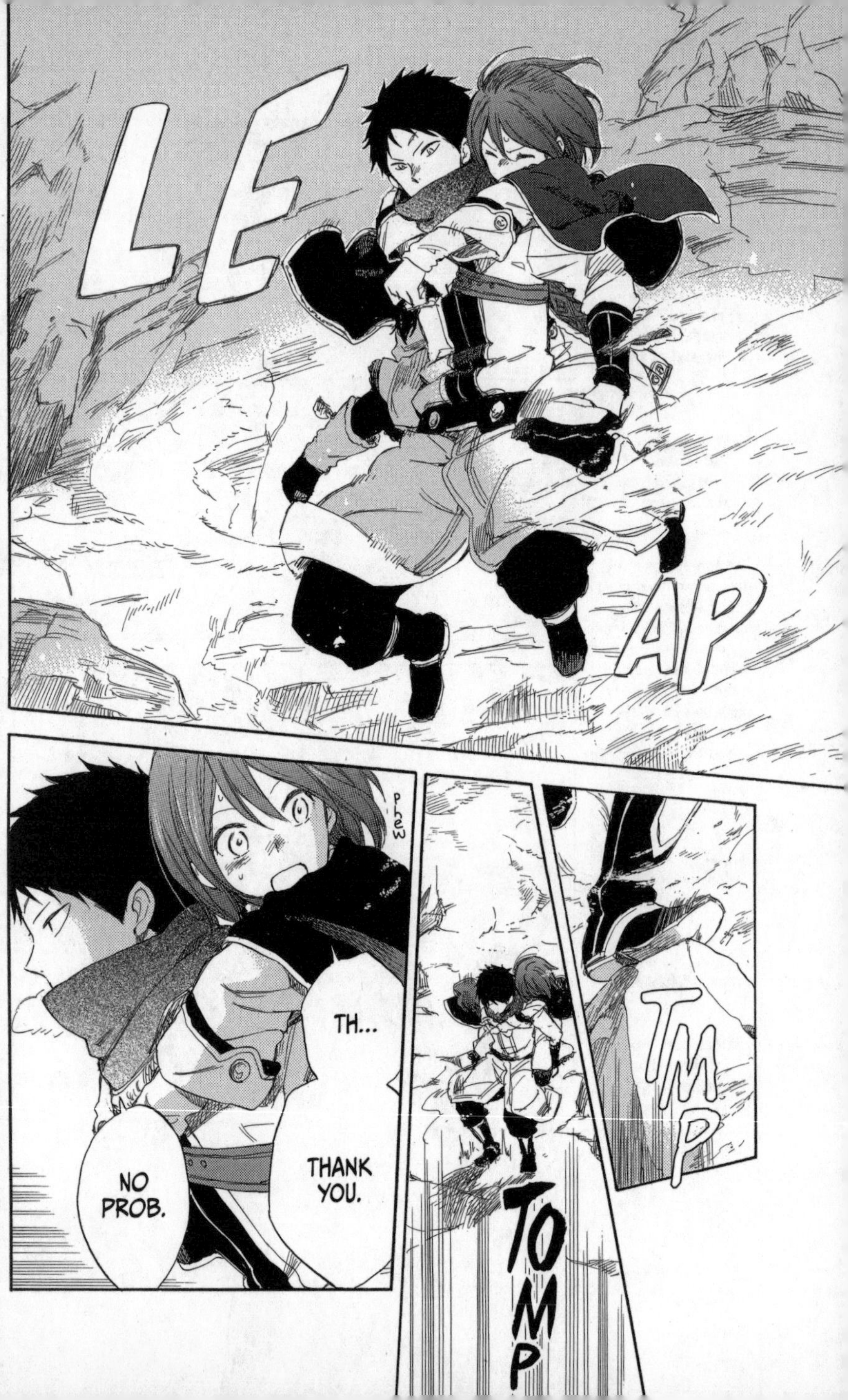
LE
AP
TMP
TOMP
phew
TH...
THANK YOU.
NO PROB.

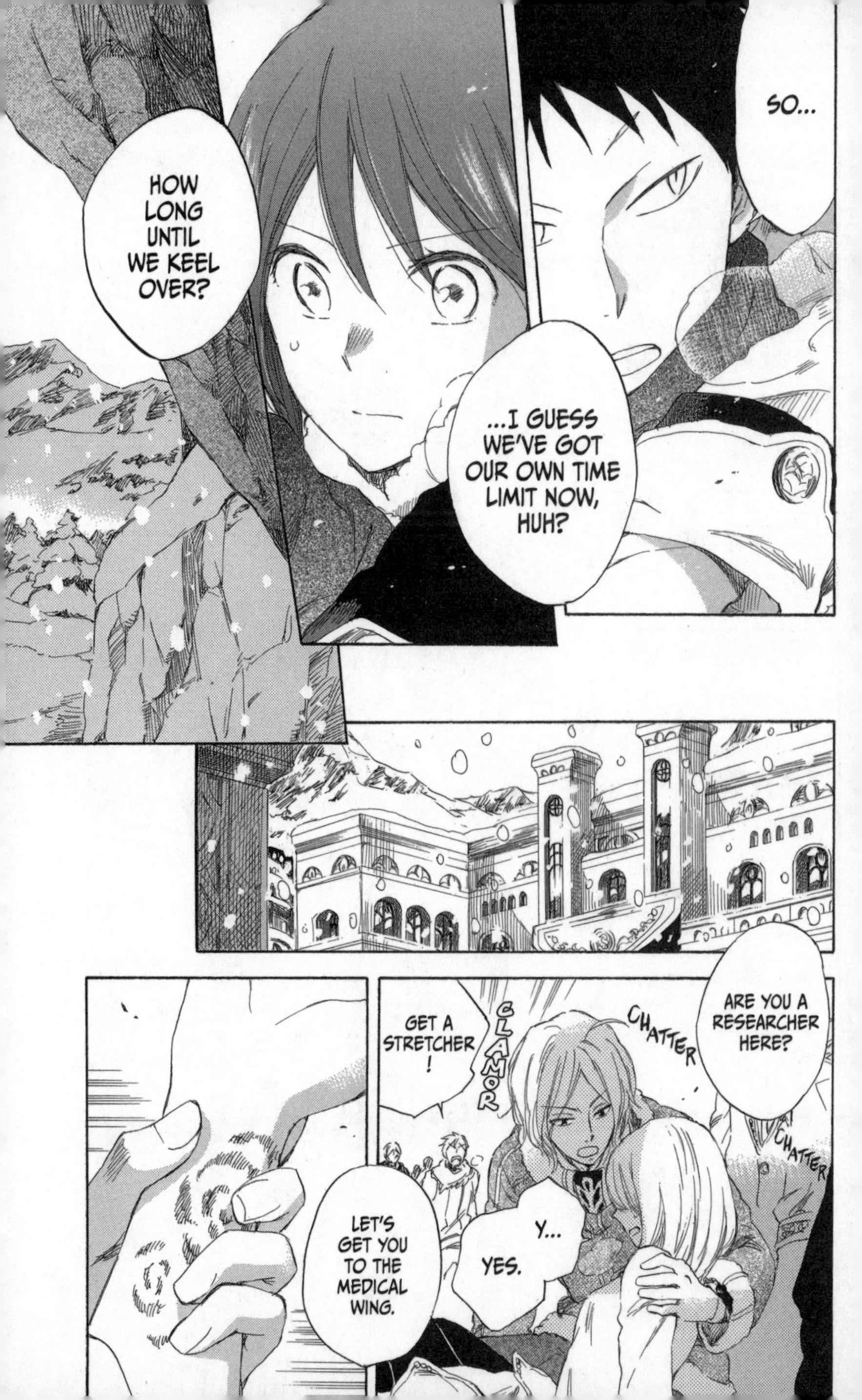
SO...
...I GUESS WE'VE GOT OUR OWN TIME LIMIT NOW, HUH?
HOW LONG UNTIL WE KEEL OVER?
ARE YOU A RESEARCHER HERE?
CHATTER
CHATTER
CLAMOR
GET A STRETCHER!
Y...
YES.
LET'S GET YOU TO THE MEDICAL WING.

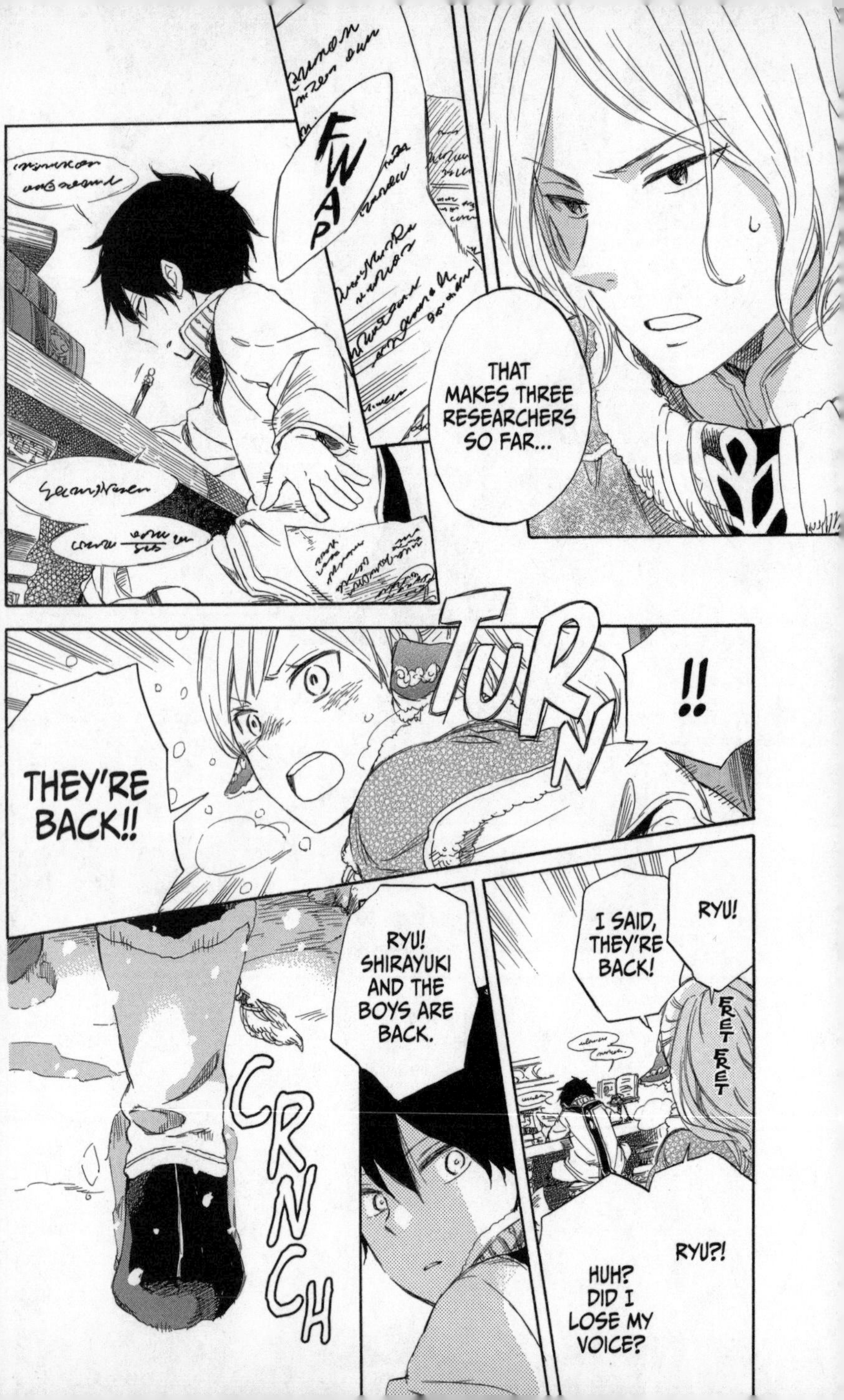
THAT MAKES THREE RESEARCHERS SO FAR...
FWAP
TURN
!!
THEY'RE BACK!!
RYU!
I SAID, THEY'RE BACK!
ERET ERET
RYU?!
HUH? DID I LOSE MY VOICE?
RYU! SHIRAYUKI AND THE BOYS ARE BACK.
CRNCH

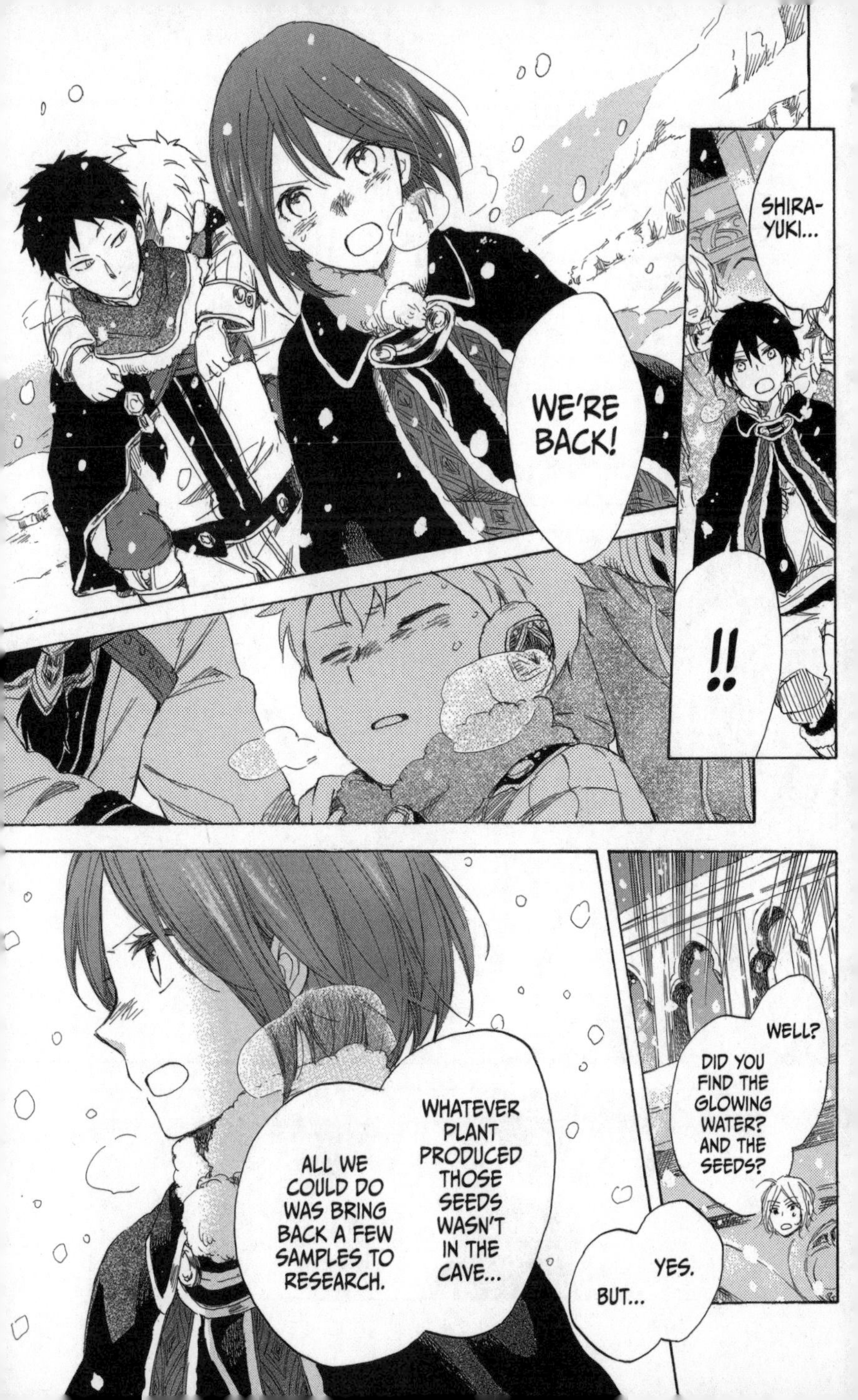
SHIRA-YUKI...
!!
WE'RE BACK!
WELL?
DID YOU FIND THE GLOWING WATER? AND THE SEEDS?
YES.
BUT...
WHATEVER PLANT PRODUCED THOSE SEEDS WASN'T IN THE CAVE...
ALL WE COULD DO WAS BRING BACK A FEW SAMPLES TO RESEARCH.

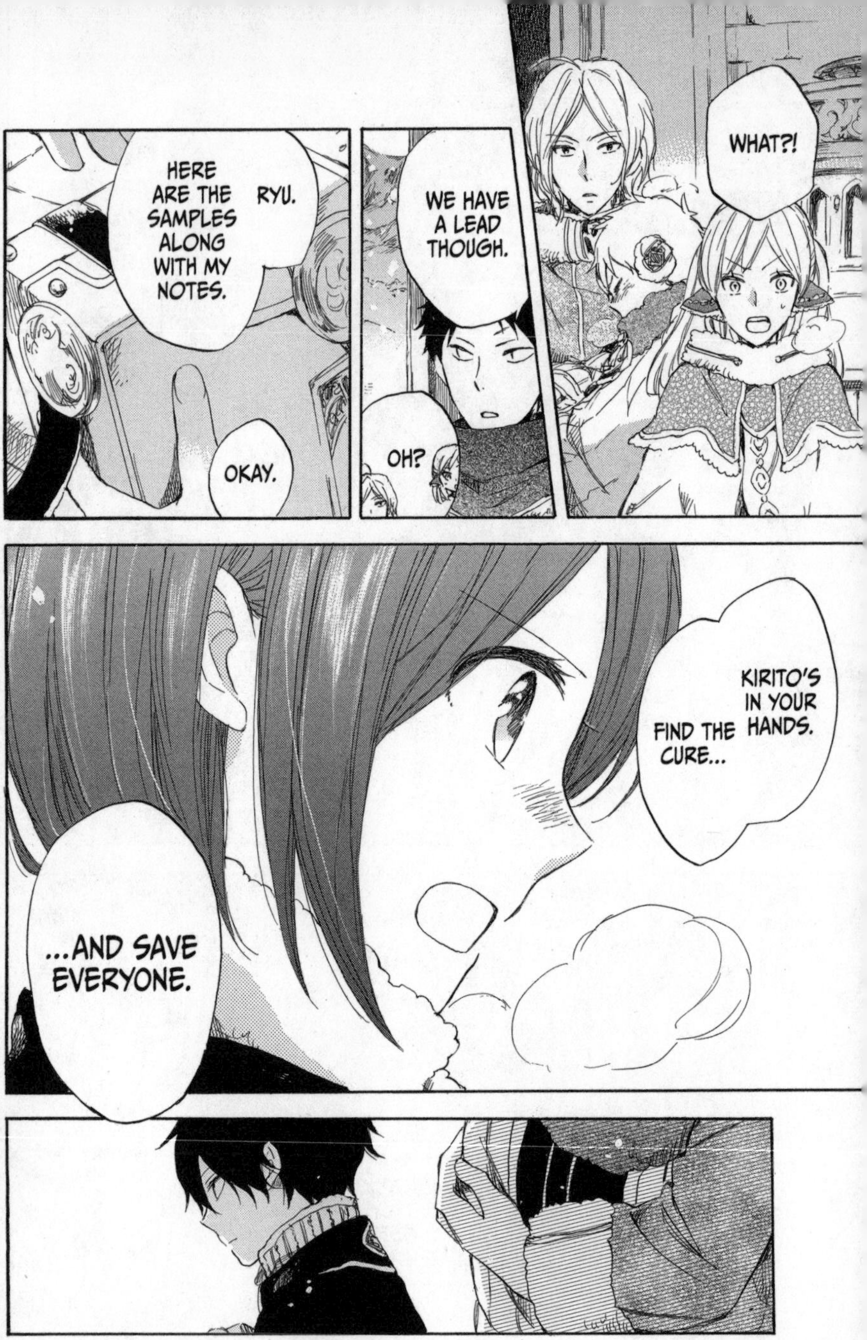
WHAT?!
WE HAVE A LEAD THOUGH.
OH?
RYU.
HERE ARE THE SAMPLES ALONG WITH MY NOTES.
OKAY.
KIRITO'S IN YOUR HANDS.
FIND THE CURE...
...AND SAVE EVERYONE.

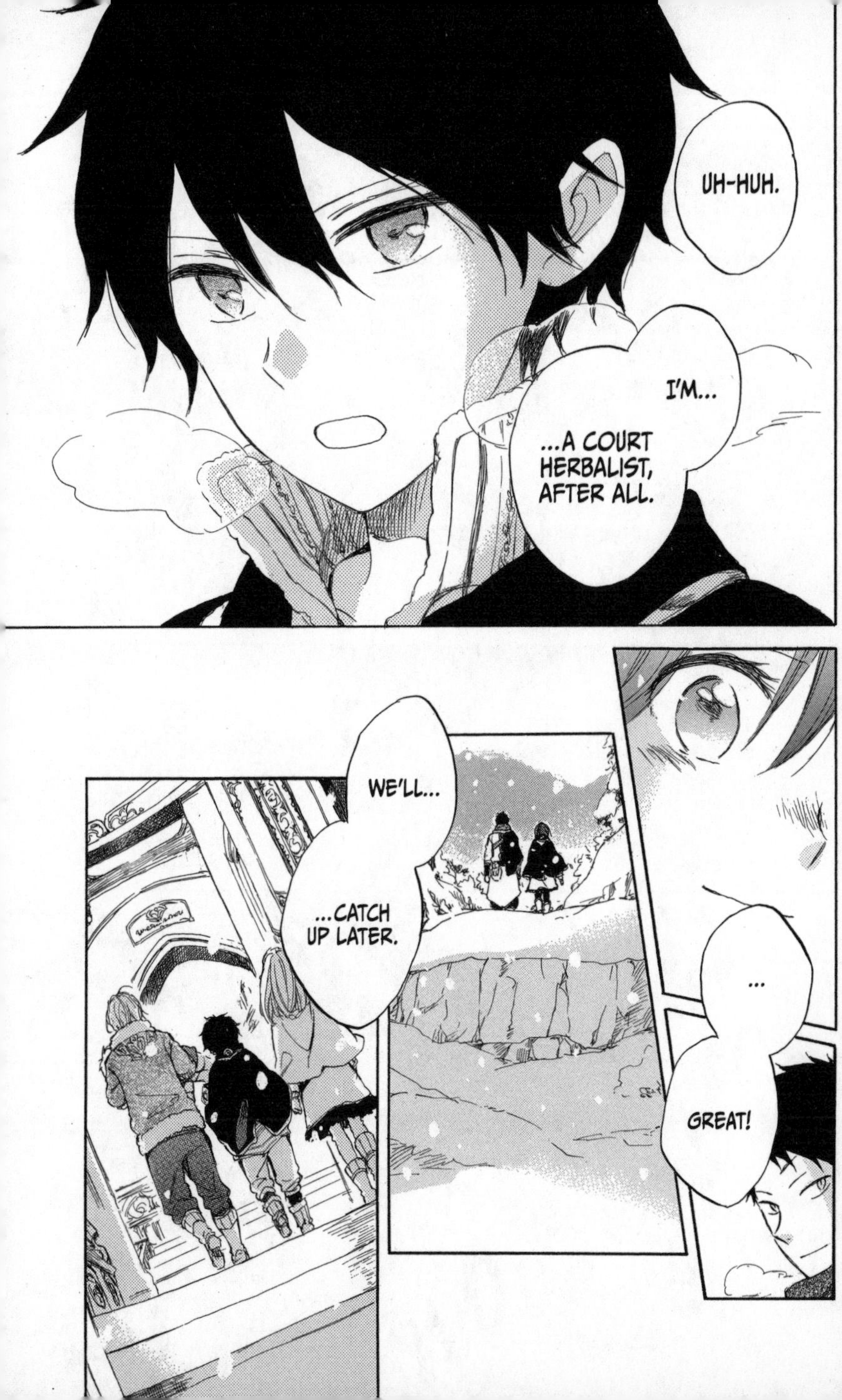
UH-HUH.
I'M...
...A COURT HERBALIST, AFTER ALL.
...
GREAT!
WE'LL...
...CATCH UP LATER.

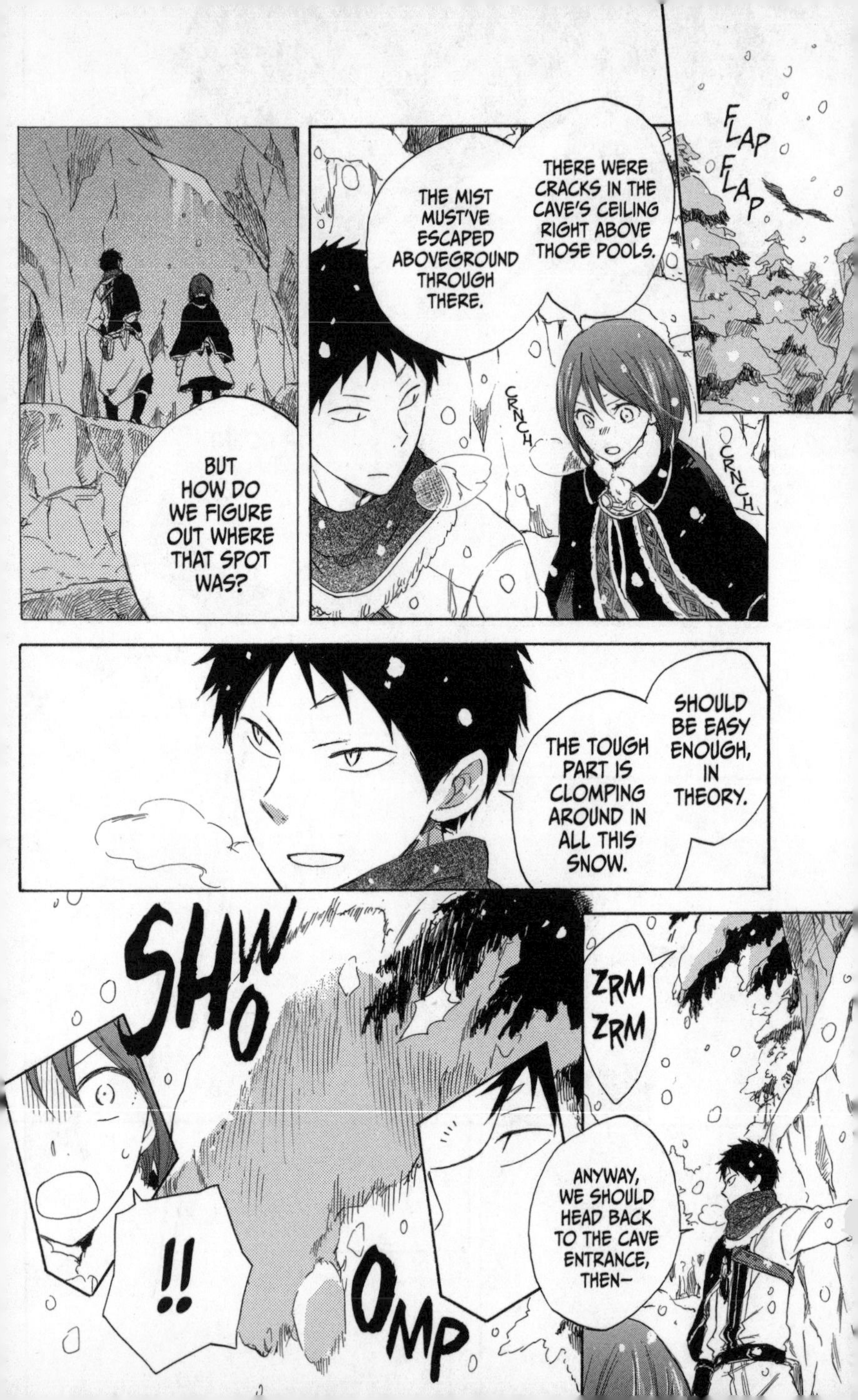
FLAP FLAP
THERE WERE CRACKS IN THE CAVE'S CEILING RIGHT ABOVE THOSE POOLS.
THE MIST MUST'VE ESCAPED ABOVEGROUND THROUGH THERE.
CRNCH
CRNCH
BUT HOW DO WE FIGURE OUT WHERE THAT SPOT WAS?
SHOULD BE EASY ENOUGH, IN THEORY.
THE TOUGH PART IS CLOMPING AROUND IN ALL THIS SNOW.
ZRM ZRM
ANYWAY, WE SHOULD HEAD BACK TO THE CAVE ENTRANCE, THEN—
SHWOMP
!!

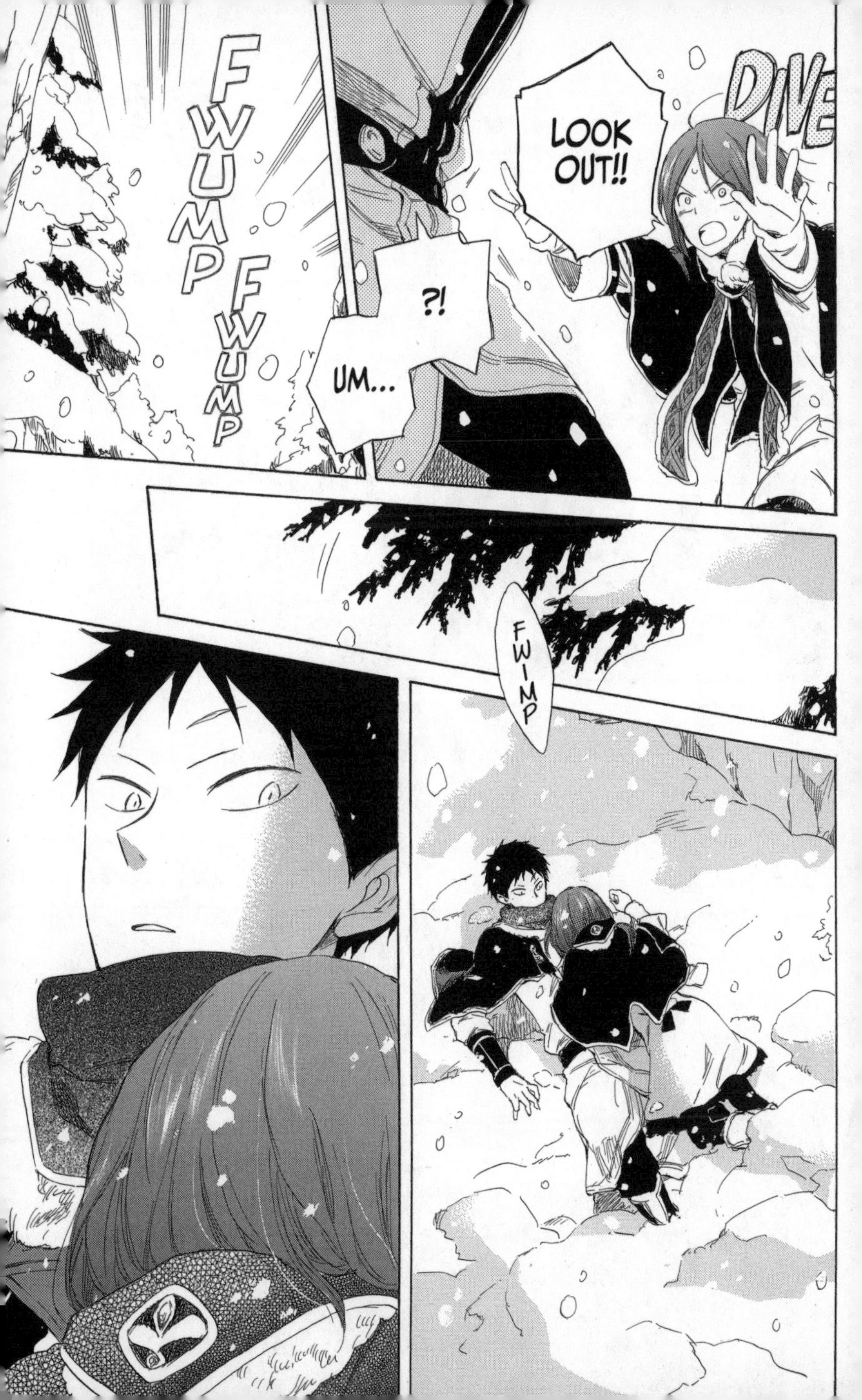
DIVE
LOOK OUT!!
?!
UM...
FWUMP
FWUMP
FWIMP

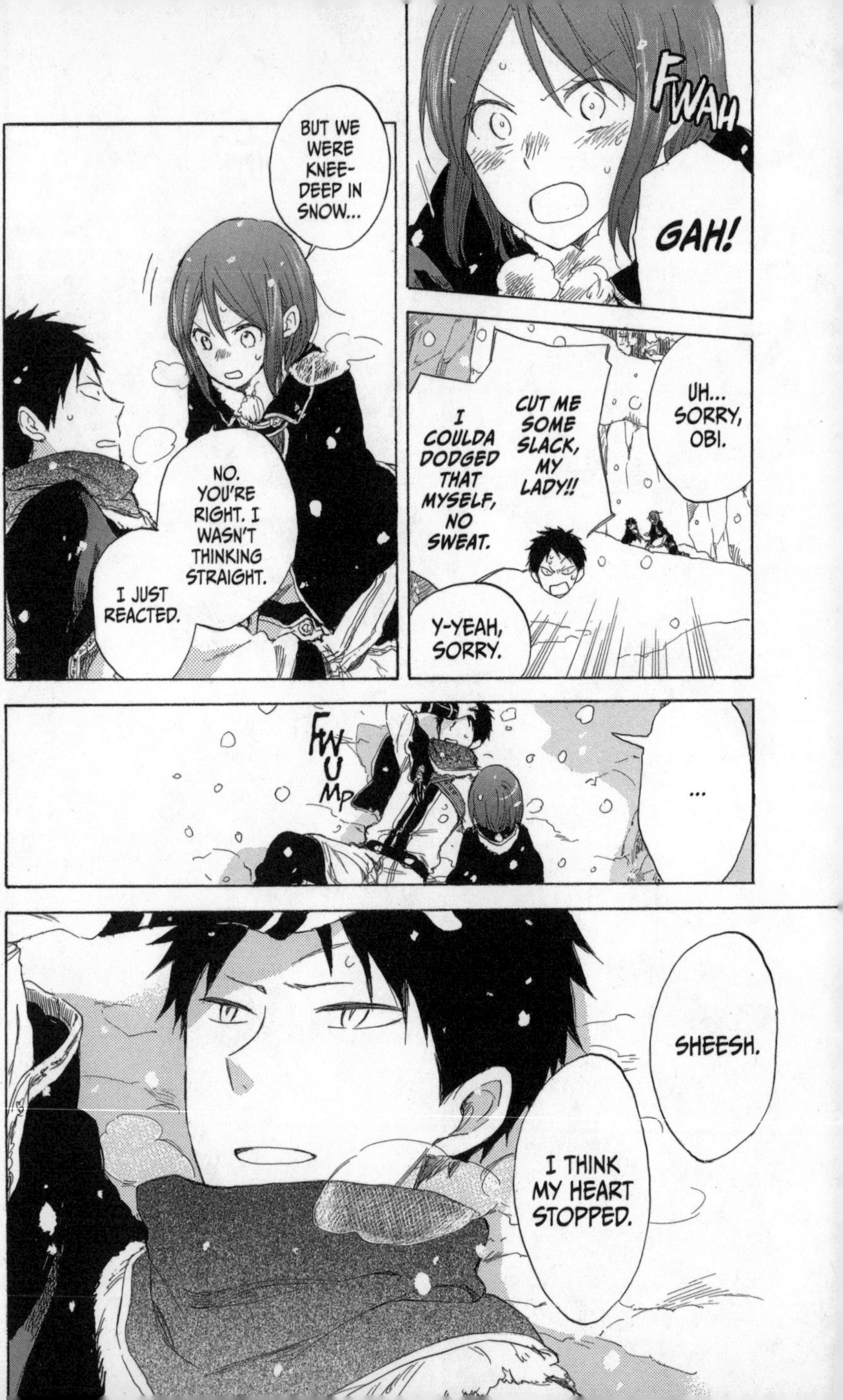
FWAH
GAH!
UH... SORRY, OBI.
CUT ME SOME SLACK, MY LADY!!
I COULDA DODGED THAT MYSELF, NO SWEAT.
Y-YEAH, SORRY.
BUT WE WERE KNEE-DEEP IN SNOW...
NO. YOU'RE RIGHT. I WASN'T THINKING STRAIGHT.
I JUST REACTED.
...
FWUMP
SHEESH.
I THINK MY HEART STOPPED.

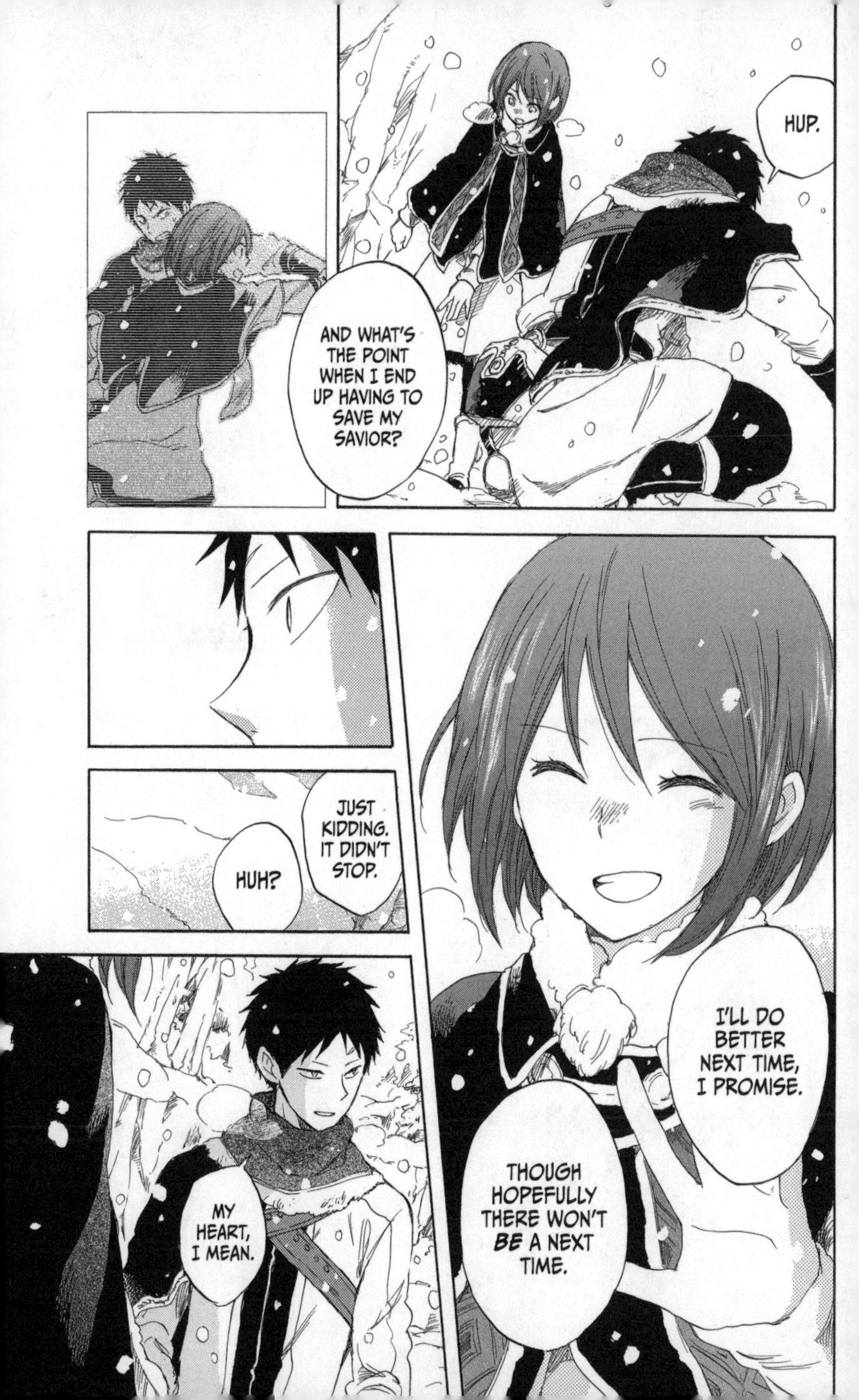
HUP.
AND WHAT'S THE POINT WHEN I END UP HAVING TO SAVE MY SAVIOR?
I'LL DO BETTER NEXT TIME, I PROMISE.
THOUGH HOPEFULLY THERE WON'T *BE* A NEXT TIME.
JUST KIDDING. IT DIDN'T STOP.
HUH?
MY HEART, I MEAN.

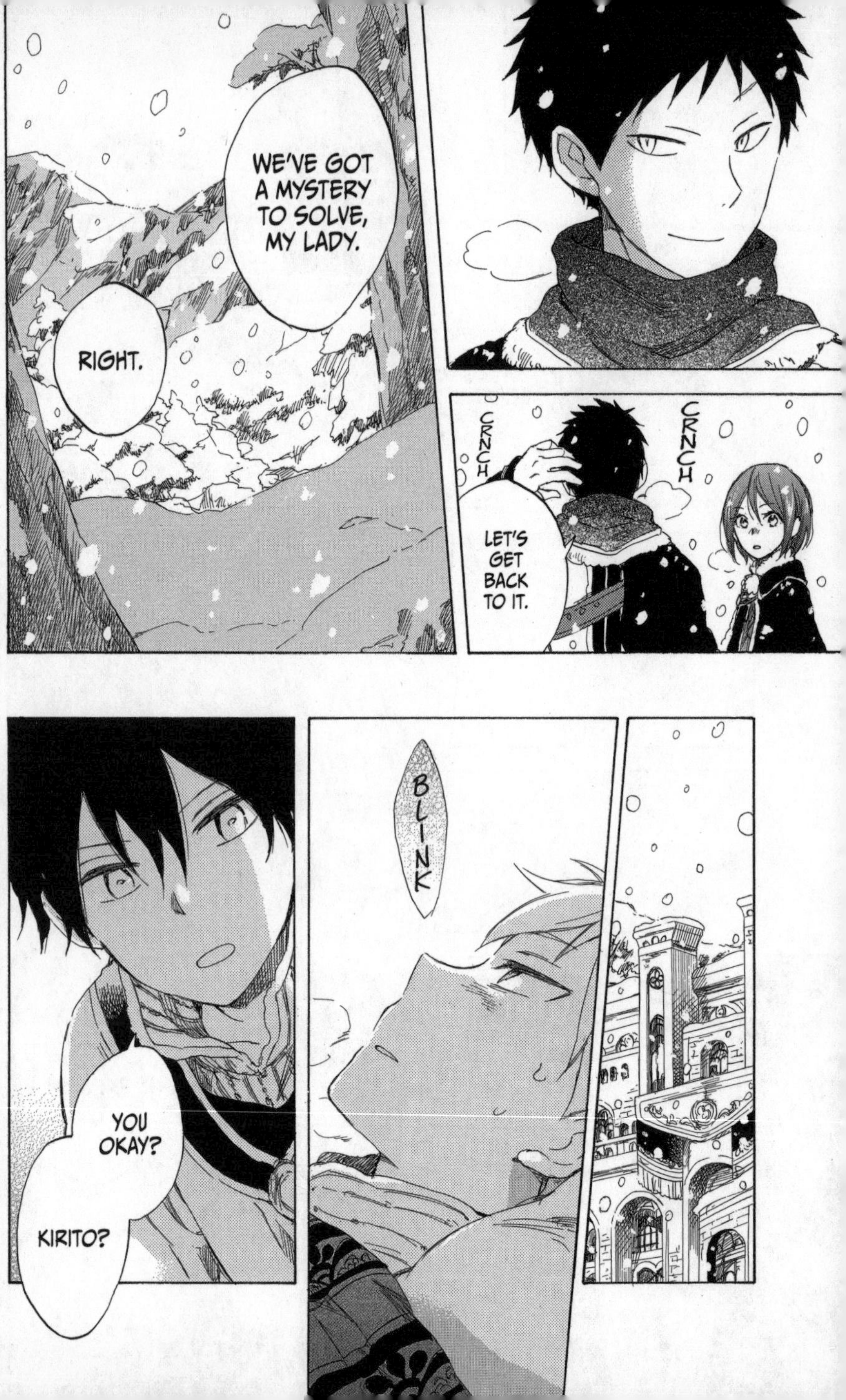
CRNCH
CRNCH
LET'S GET BACK TO IT.
WE'VE GOT A MYSTERY TO SOLVE, MY LADY.
RIGHT.
BLINK
YOU OKAY?
KIRITO?

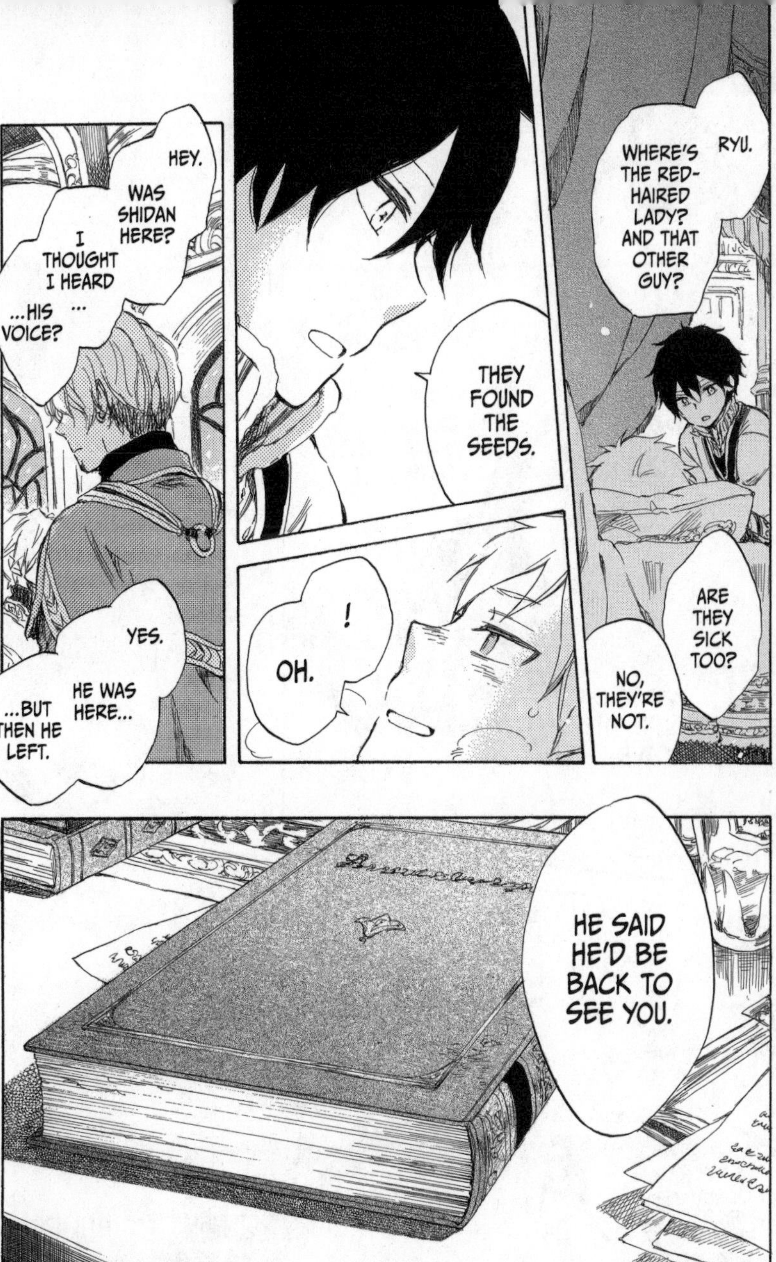
RYU.
WHERE'S THE RED-HAIRED LADY? AND THAT OTHER GUY?
ARE THEY SICK TOO?
NO, THEY'RE NOT.
THEY FOUND THE SEEDS.
!
OH.
HEY.
WAS SHIDAN HERE?
I THOUGHT I HEARD ...
...HIS VOICE?
YES.
HE WAS HERE...
...BUT THEN HE LEFT.
HE SAID HE'D BE BACK TO SEE YOU.

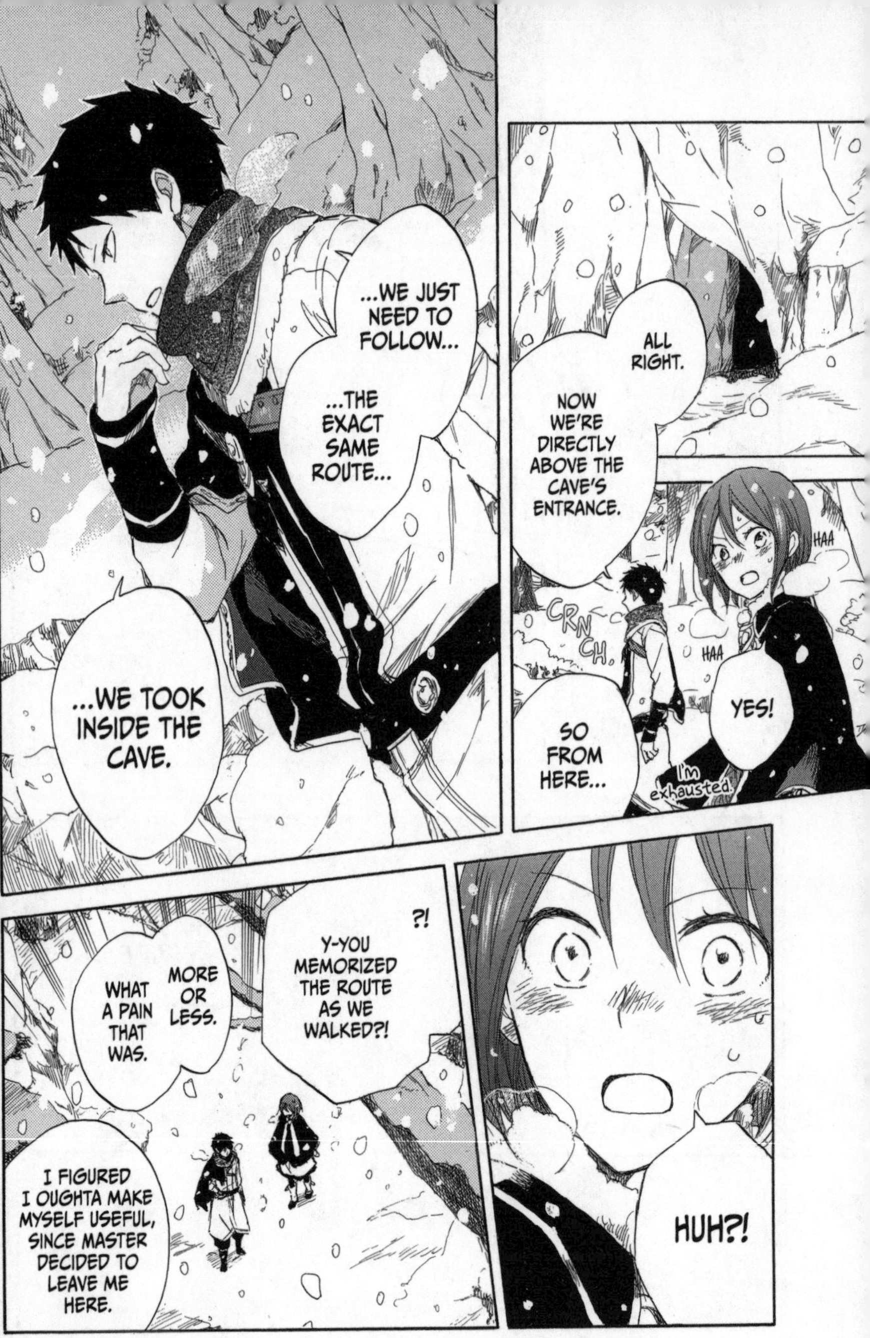
ALL RIGHT.
NOW WE'RE DIRECTLY ABOVE THE CAVE'S ENTRANCE.
HAA
CRNCH
HAA
YES!
I'm exhausted.
SO FROM HERE...
...WE JUST NEED TO FOLLOW...
...THE EXACT SAME ROUTE...
...WE TOOK INSIDE THE CAVE.
HUH?!
?!
Y-YOU MEMORIZED THE ROUTE AS WE WALKED?!
MORE OR LESS.
WHAT A PAIN THAT WAS.
I FIGURED I OUGHTA MAKE MYSELF USEFUL, SINCE MASTER DECIDED TO LEAVE ME HERE.

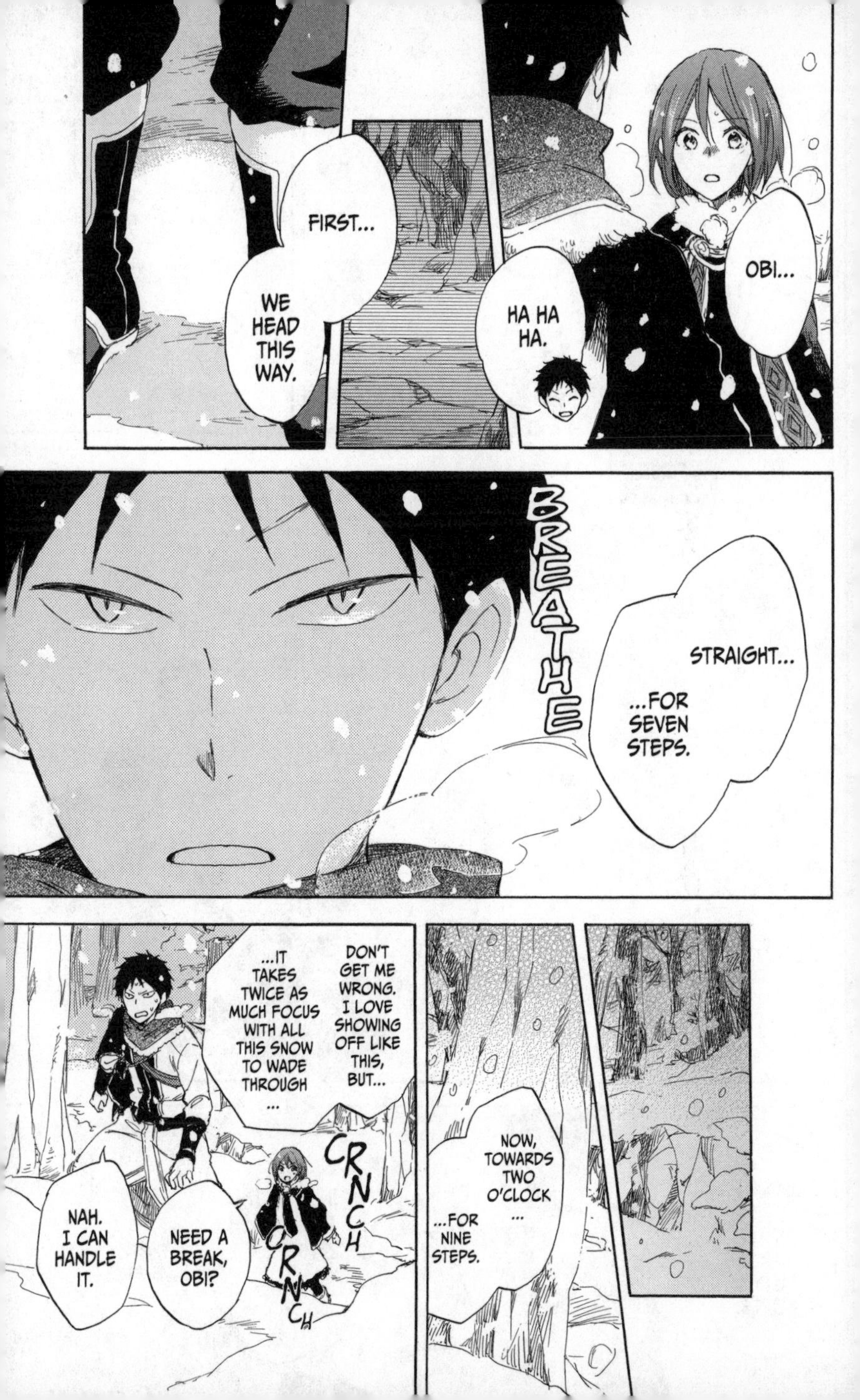
OBI...
HA HA HA.
FIRST...
WE HEAD THIS WAY.
BREATHE
STRAIGHT...
...FOR SEVEN STEPS.
NOW, TOWARDS TWO O'CLOCK ...
...FOR NINE STEPS.
DON'T GET ME WRONG. I LOVE SHOWING OFF LIKE THIS, BUT...
...IT TAKES TWICE AS MUCH FOCUS WITH ALL THIS SNOW TO WADE THROUGH ...
CRNCH
CRNCH
NEED A BREAK, OBI?
NAH. I CAN HANDLE IT.

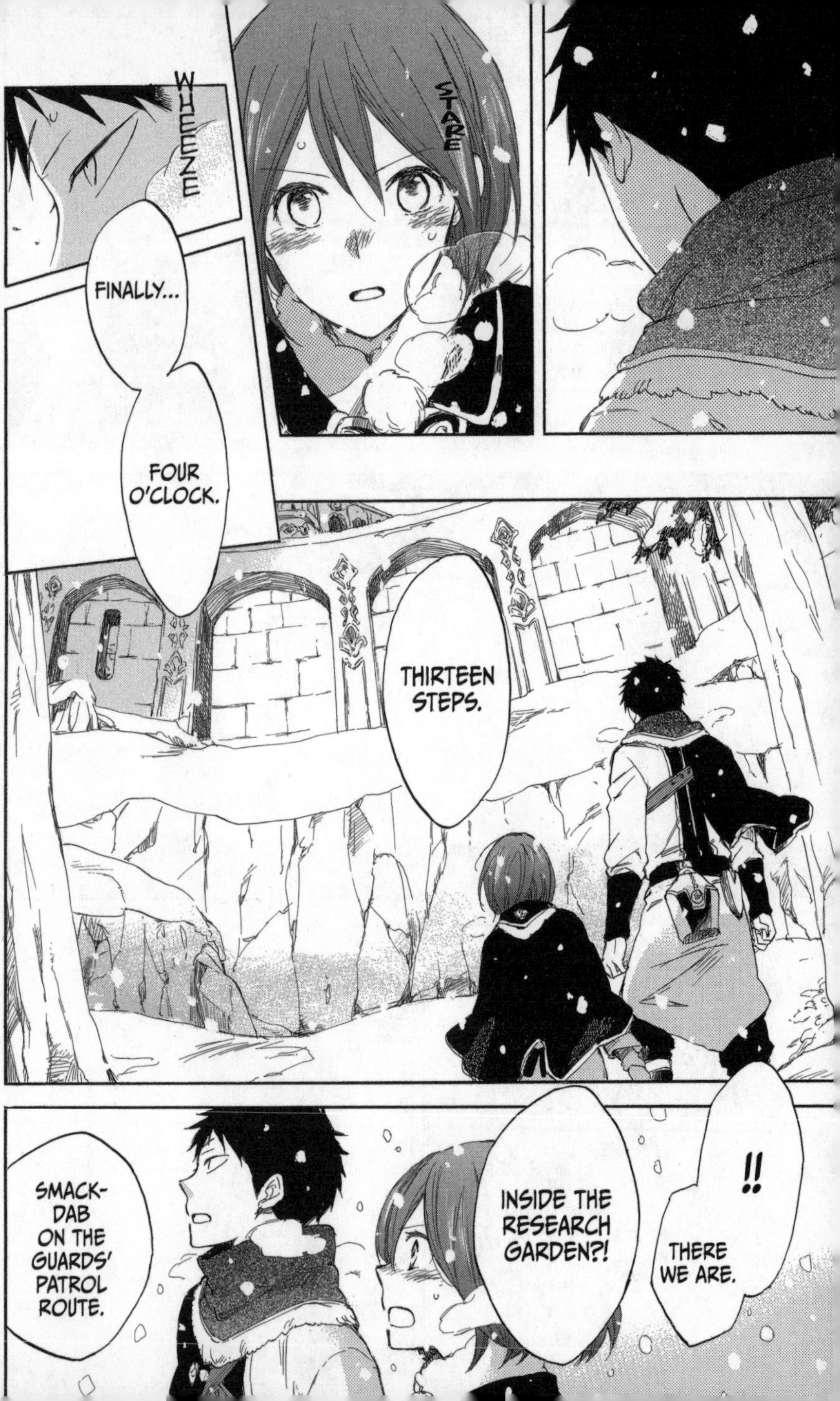
STARE
WHEEZE
FINALLY... FOUR O'CLOCK.
THIRTEEN STEPS.
!!
THERE WE ARE.
INSIDE THE RESEARCH GARDEN?!
SMACK-DAB ON THE GUARDS' PATROL ROUTE.

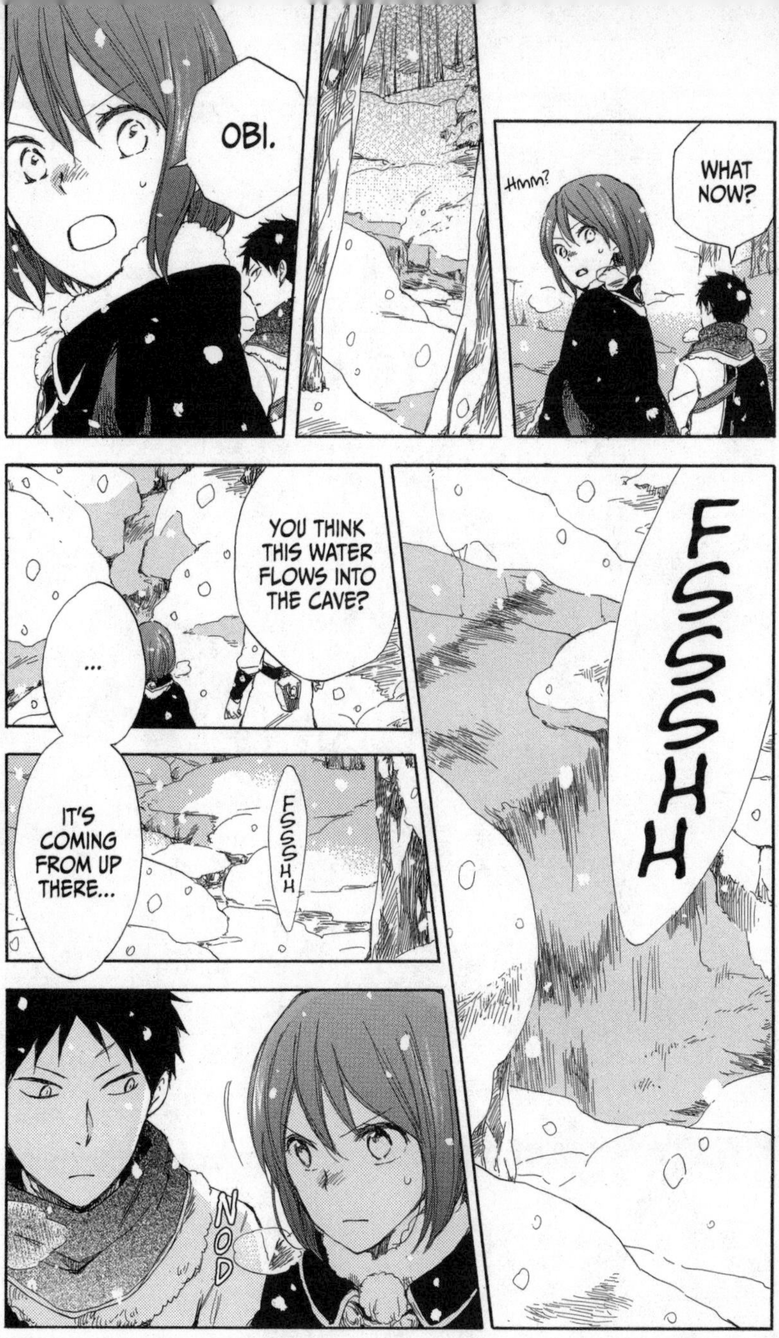
WHAT NOW?
Hmm?
OBI.
FSSSH
YOU THINK THIS WATER FLOWS INTO THE CAVE?
...
FSSSH
IT'S COMING FROM UP THERE...
NOD

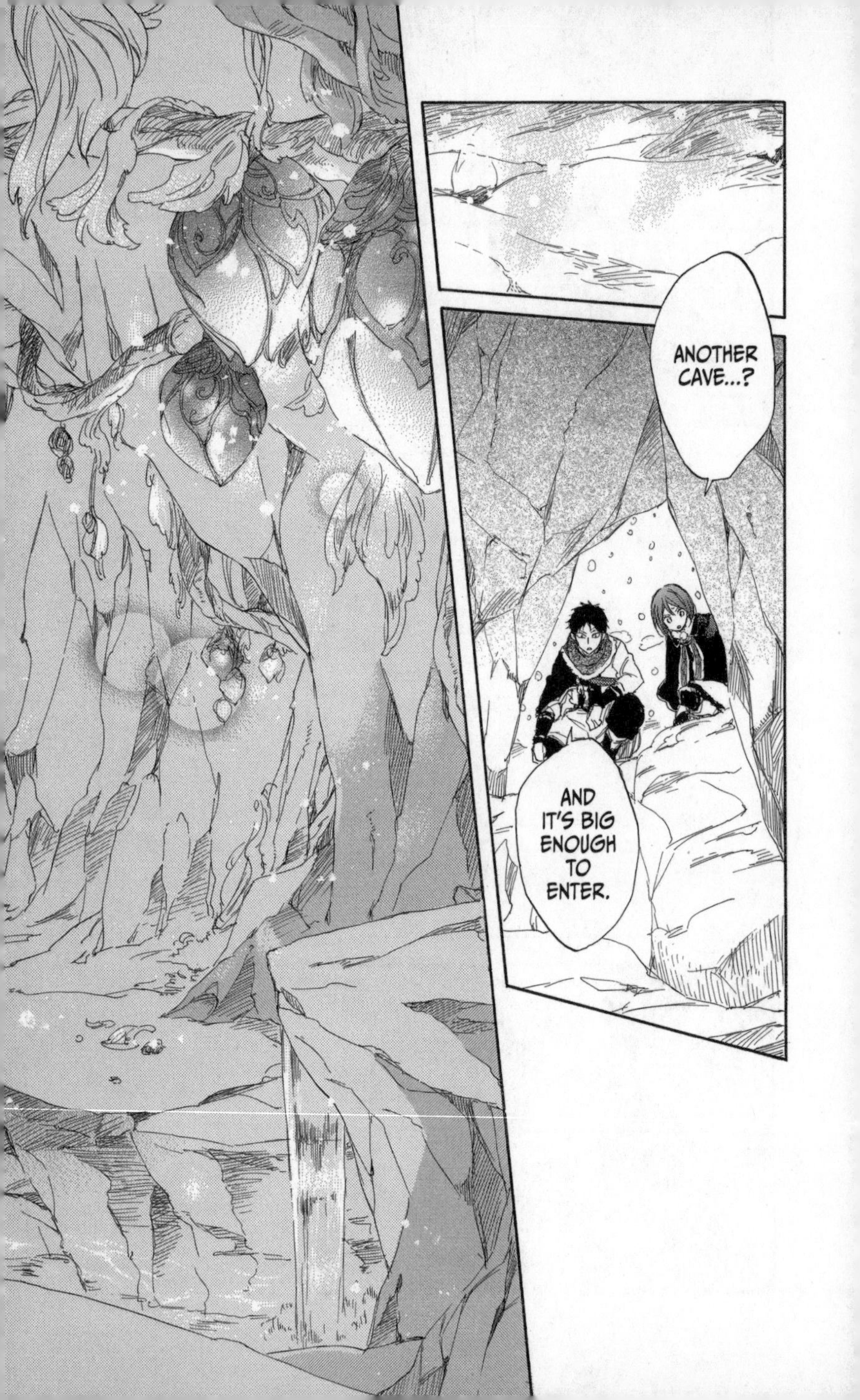
ANOTHER CAVE...?
AND IT'S BIG ENOUGH TO ENTER.

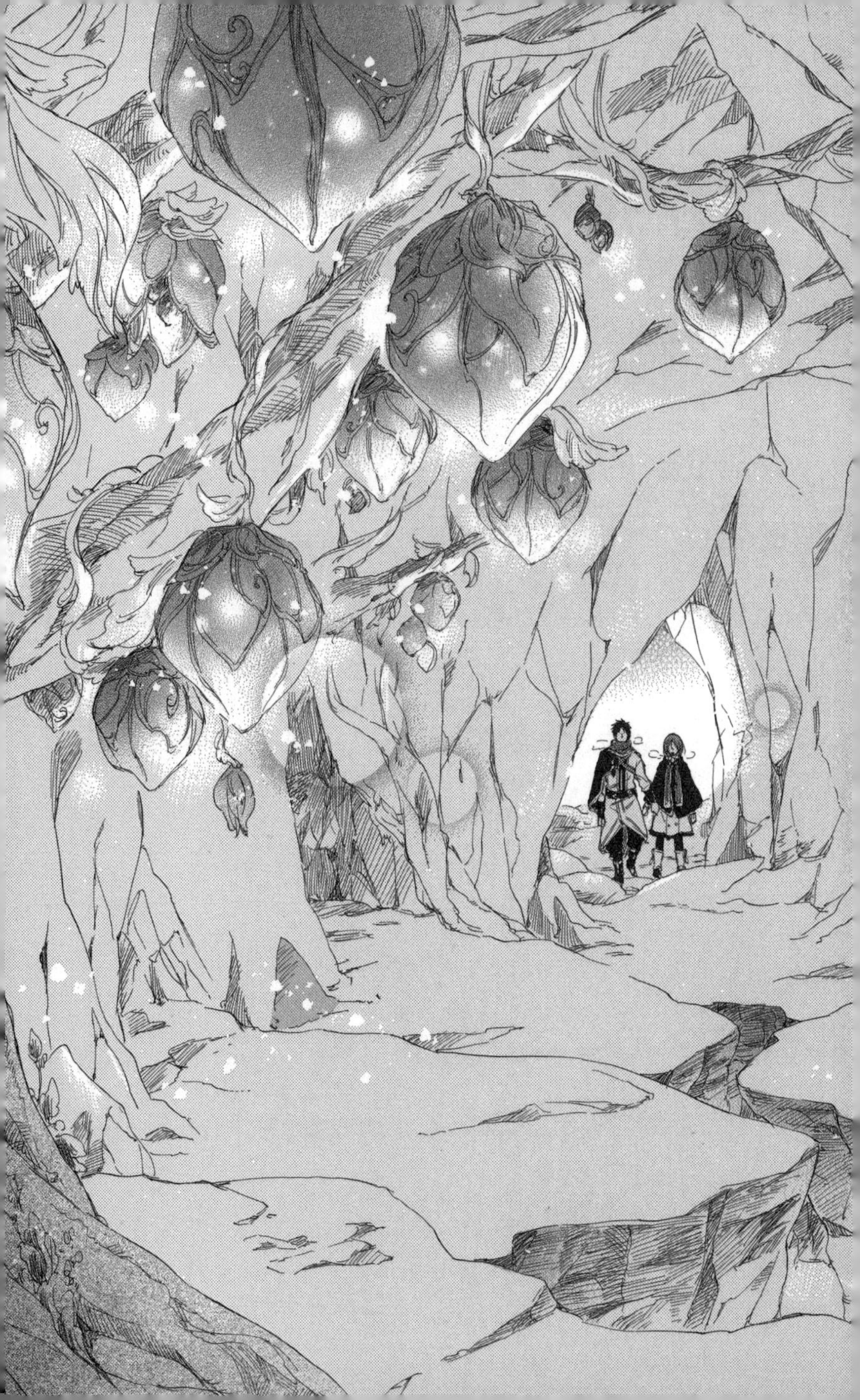

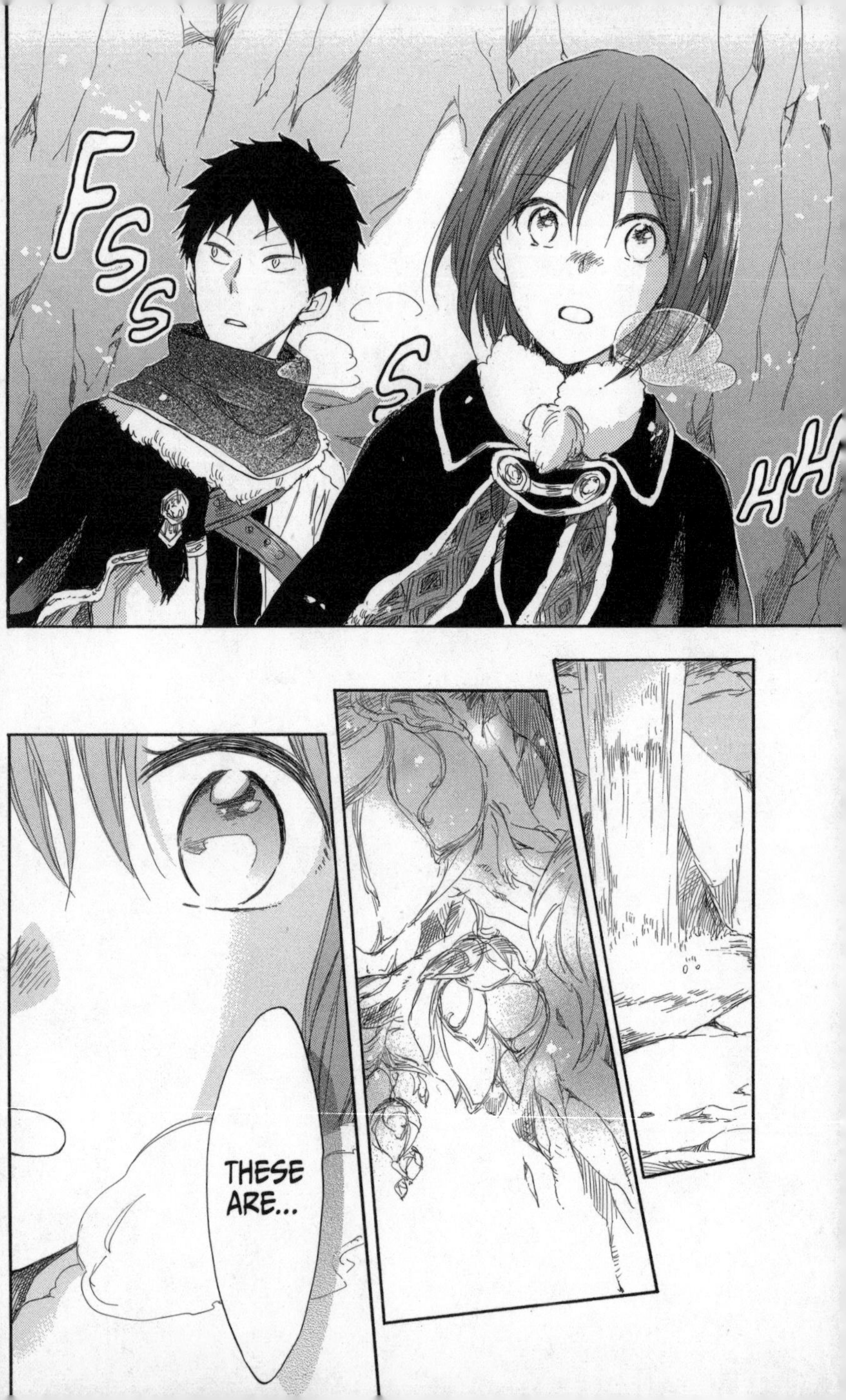
FSSS
S
HH
THESE ARE...

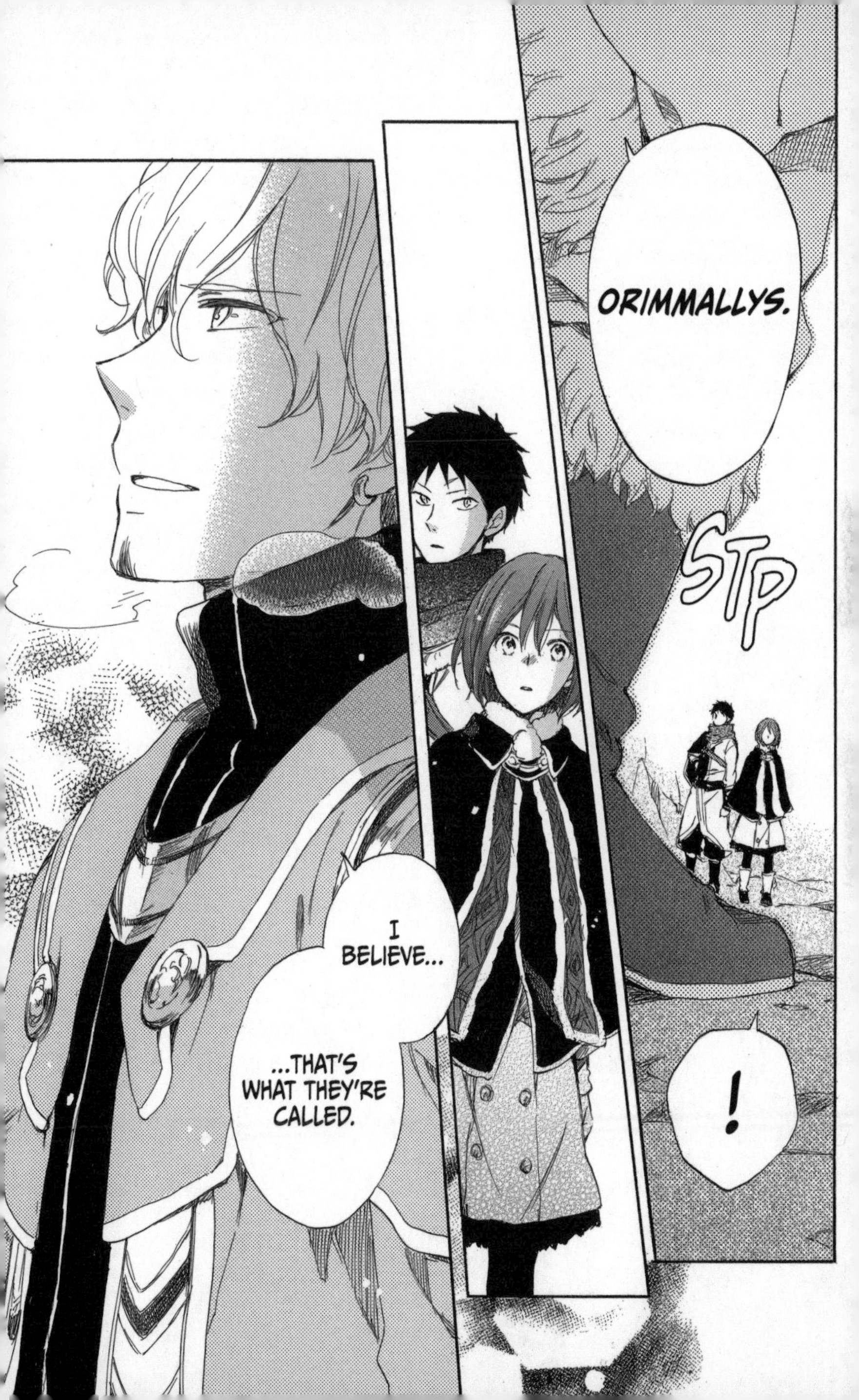
ORIMMALLYS.
STP
!
I BELIEVE...
...THAT'S WHAT THEY'RE CALLED.

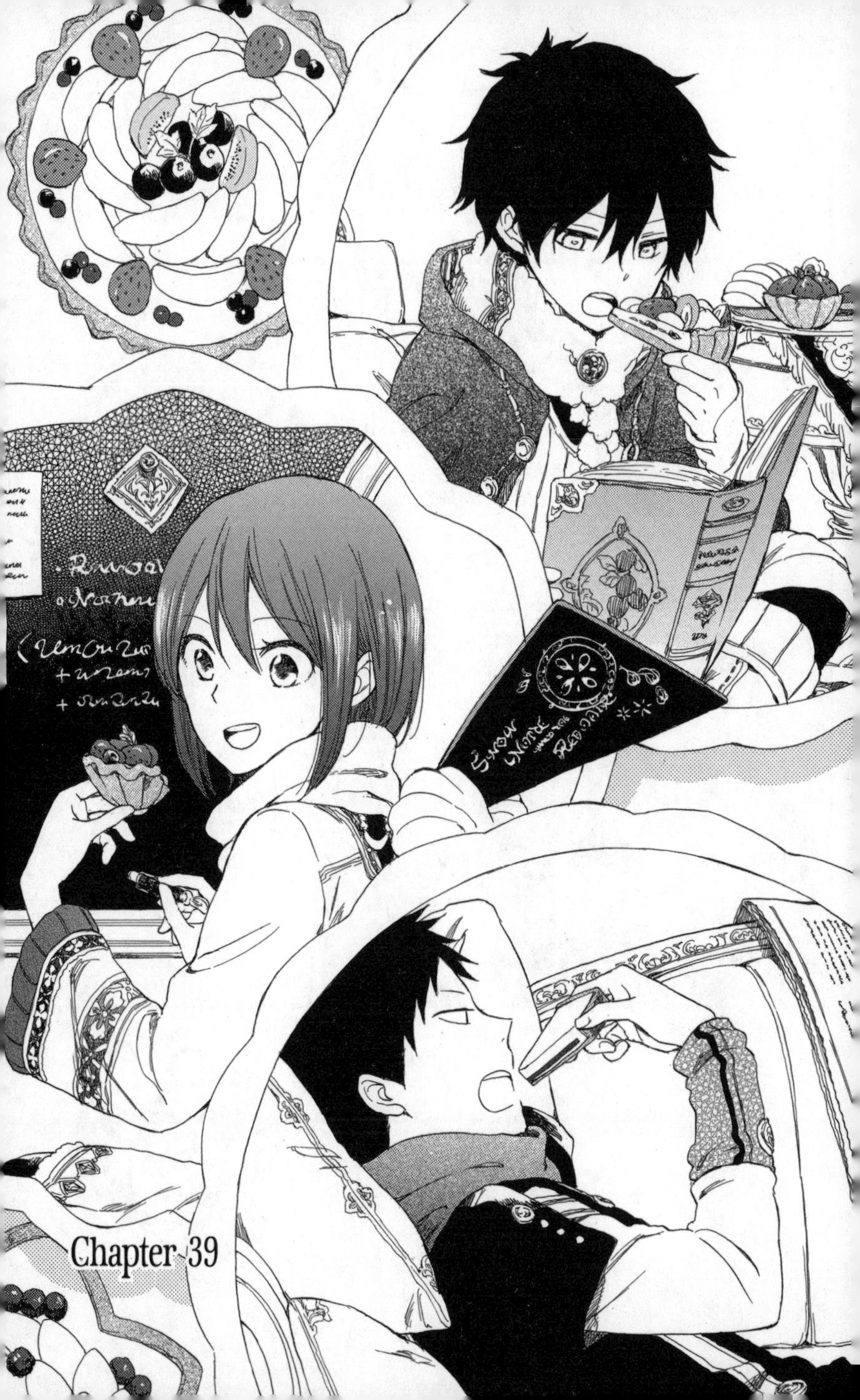
Chapter 39

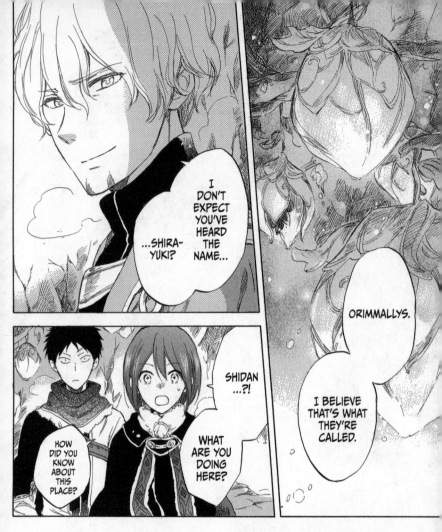

ORIMMALLYS.
I BELIEVE THAT'S WHAT THEY'RE CALLED.
I DON'T EXPECT YOU'VE HEARD THE NAME...
...SHIRA-YUKI?
SHIDAN ...?!
WHAT ARE YOU DOING HERE?
HOW DID YOU KNOW ABOUT THIS PLACE?

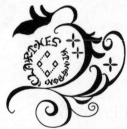

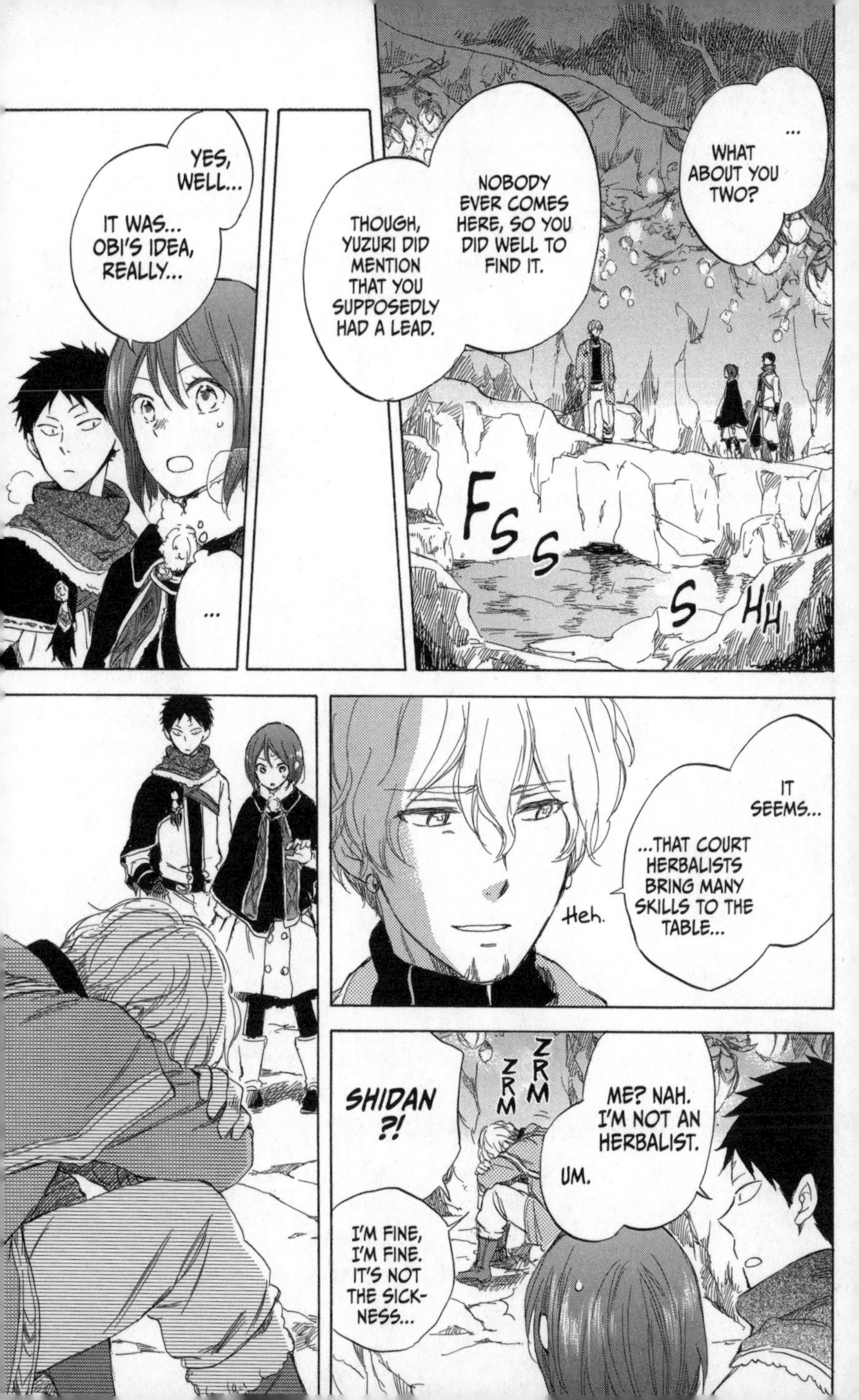
...
WHAT ABOUT YOU TWO?
NOBODY EVER COMES HERE, SO YOU DID WELL TO FIND IT.
THOUGH, YUZURI DID MENTION THAT YOU SUPPOSEDLY HAD A LEAD.
FSSSHH
YES, WELL...
IT WAS... OBI'S IDEA, REALLY...
...
IT SEEMS...
...THAT COURT HERBALISTS BRING MANY SKILLS TO THE TABLE...
Heh.
ME? NAH. I'M NOT AN HERBALIST.
UM.
ZRM ZRM
SHIDAN ?!
I'M FINE, I'M FINE. IT'S NOT THE SICK-NESS...

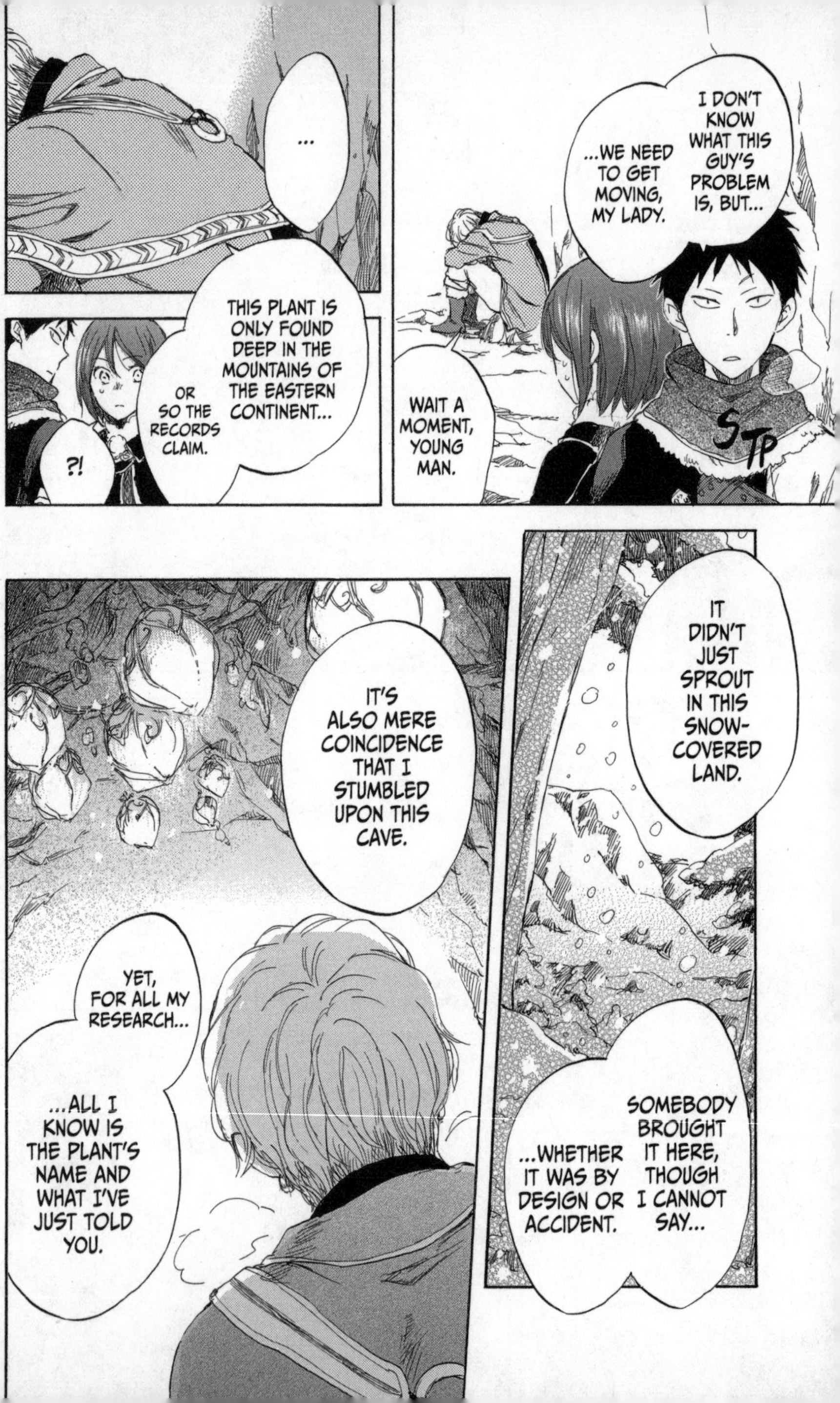
I DON'T KNOW WHAT THIS GUY'S PROBLEM IS, BUT...
...WE NEED TO GET MOVING, MY LADY.
STP
WAIT A MOMENT, YOUNG MAN.
...
THIS PLANT IS ONLY FOUND DEEP IN THE MOUNTAINS OF THE EASTERN CONTINENT...
OR SO THE RECORDS CLAIM.
?!
IT DIDN'T JUST SPROUT IN THIS SNOW-COVERED LAND.
SOMEBODY BROUGHT IT HERE, THOUGH I CANNOT SAY...
...WHETHER IT WAS BY DESIGN OR ACCIDENT.
IT'S ALSO MERE COINCIDENCE THAT I STUMBLED UPON THIS CAVE.
YET, FOR ALL MY RESEARCH...
...ALL I KNOW IS THE PLANT'S NAME AND WHAT I'VE JUST TOLD YOU.

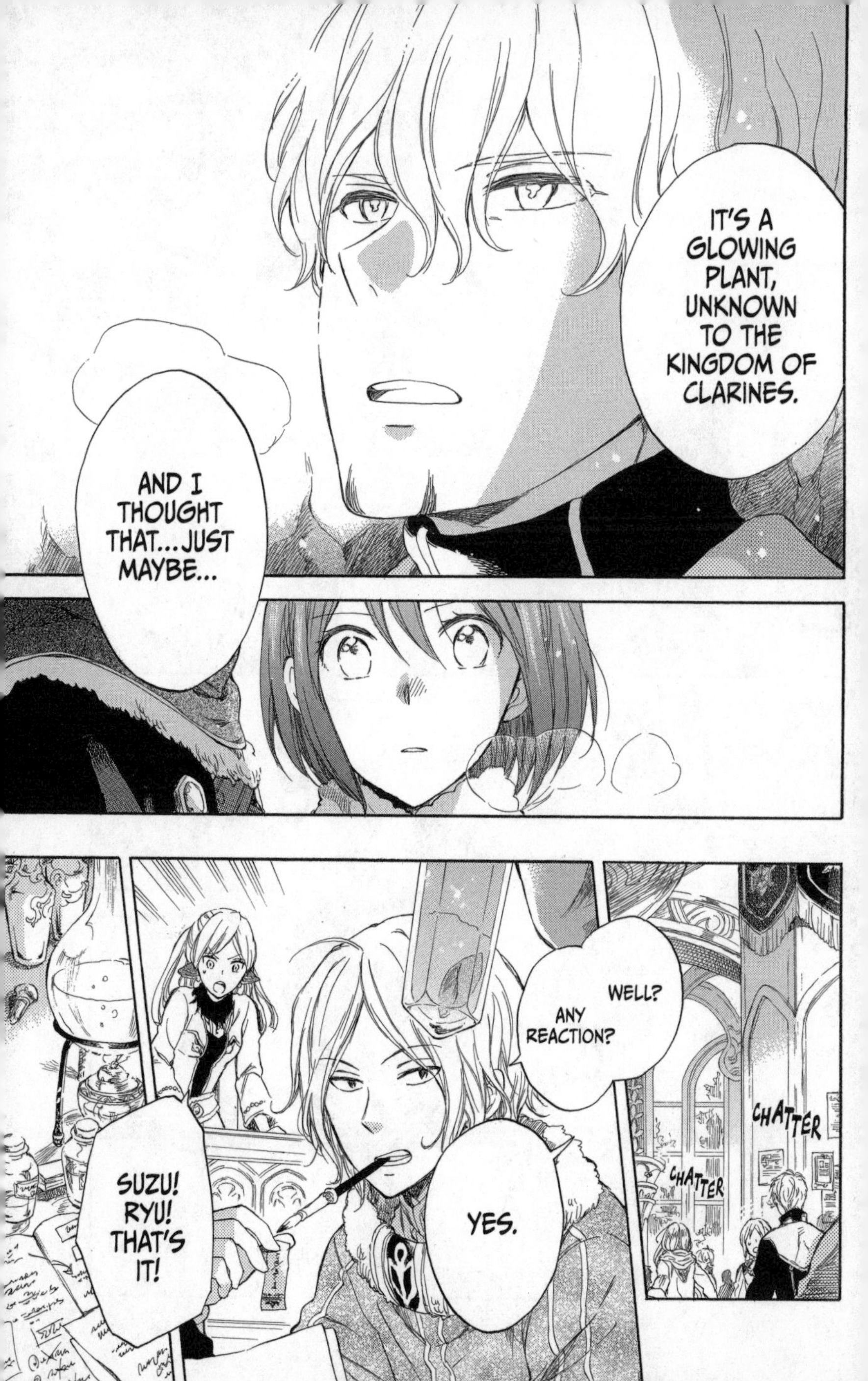
IT'S A GLOWING PLANT, UNKNOWN TO THE KINGDOM OF CLARINES.
AND I THOUGHT THAT...JUST MAYBE...
CHATTER
CHATTER
WELL? ANY REACTION?
YES.
SUZU! RYU! THAT'S IT!

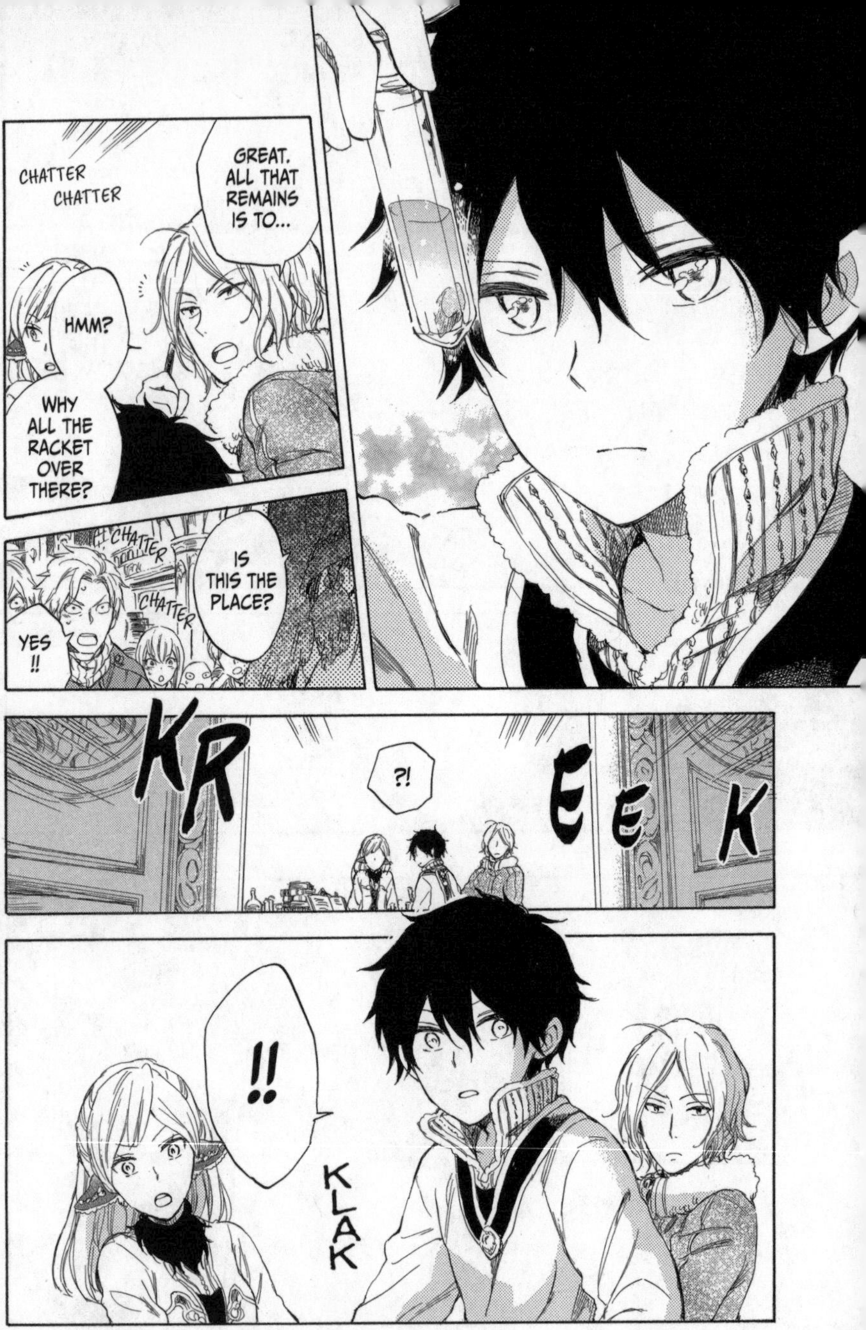
GREAT. ALL THAT REMAINS IS TO...
CHATTER CHATTER
HMM?
WHY ALL THE RACKET OVER THERE?
IS THIS THE PLACE?
CHATTER CHATTER
YES !!
KR
?!
EEK
!!
KLAK

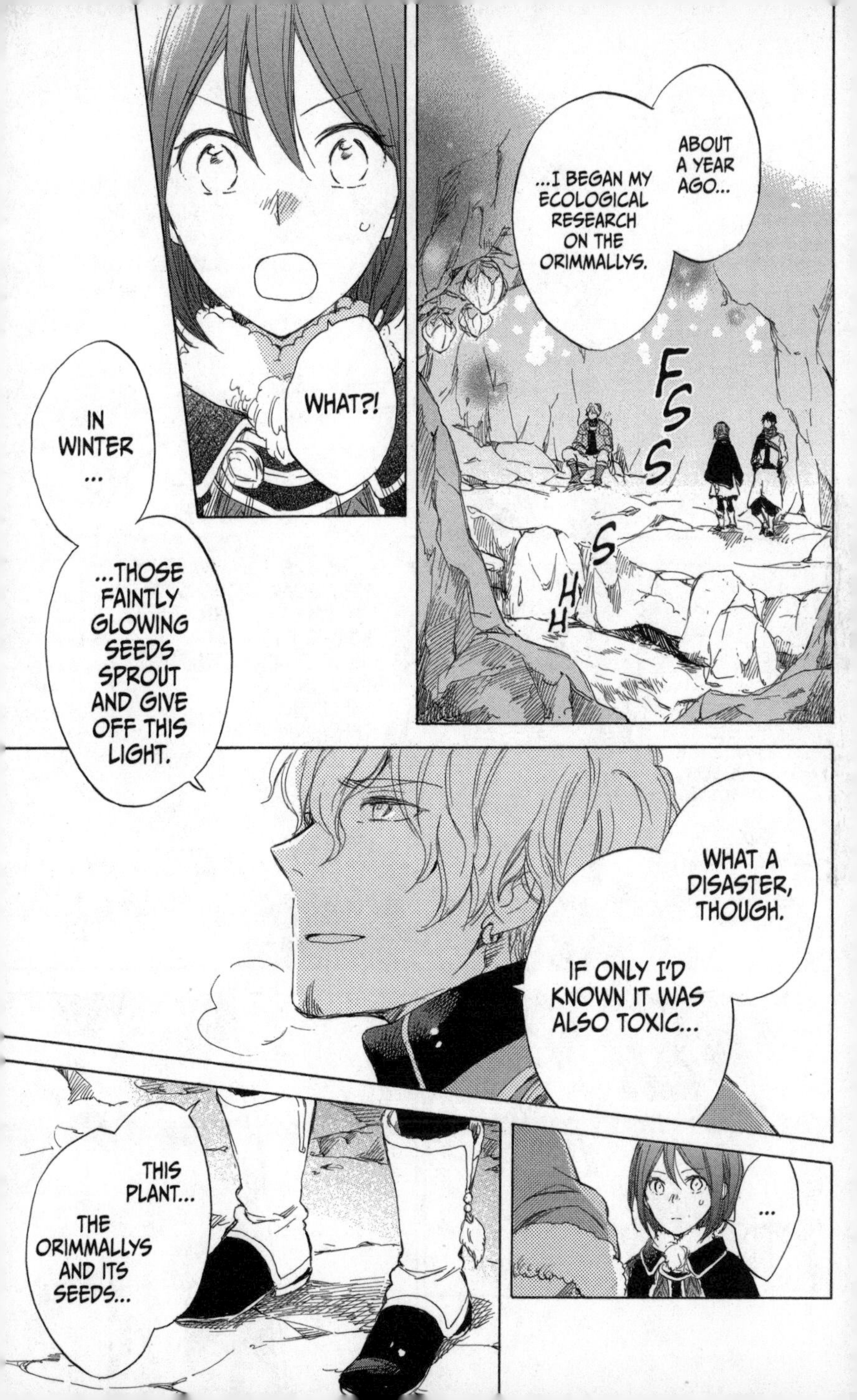
ABOUT A YEAR AGO...
...I BEGAN MY ECOLOGICAL RESEARCH ON THE ORIMMALLYS.
FSSSHH
WHAT?!
IN WINTER ...
...THOSE FAINTLY GLOWING SEEDS SPROUT AND GIVE OFF THIS LIGHT.
WHAT A DISASTER, THOUGH.
IF ONLY I'D KNOWN IT WAS ALSO TOXIC...
...
THIS PLANT...
THE ORIMMALLYS AND ITS SEEDS...

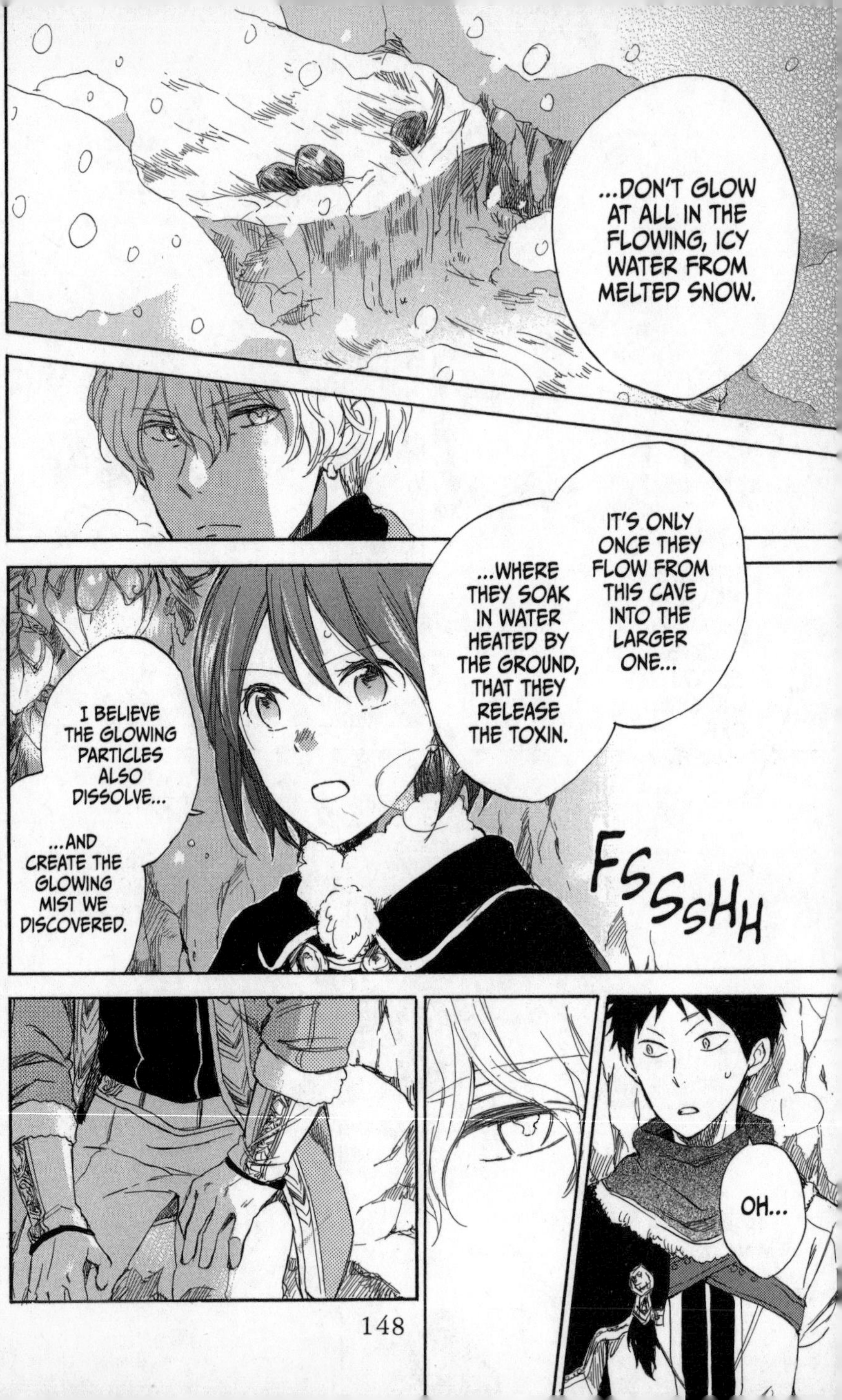
...DON'T GLOW AT ALL IN THE FLOWING, ICY WATER FROM MELTED SNOW.
IT'S ONLY ONCE THEY FLOW FROM THIS CAVE INTO THE LARGER ONE...
...WHERE THEY SOAK IN WATER HEATED BY THE GROUND, THAT THEY RELEASE THE TOXIN.
FSSSHH
I BELIEVE THE GLOWING PARTICLES ALSO DISSOLVE...
...AND CREATE THE GLOWING MIST WE DISCOVERED.
OH...

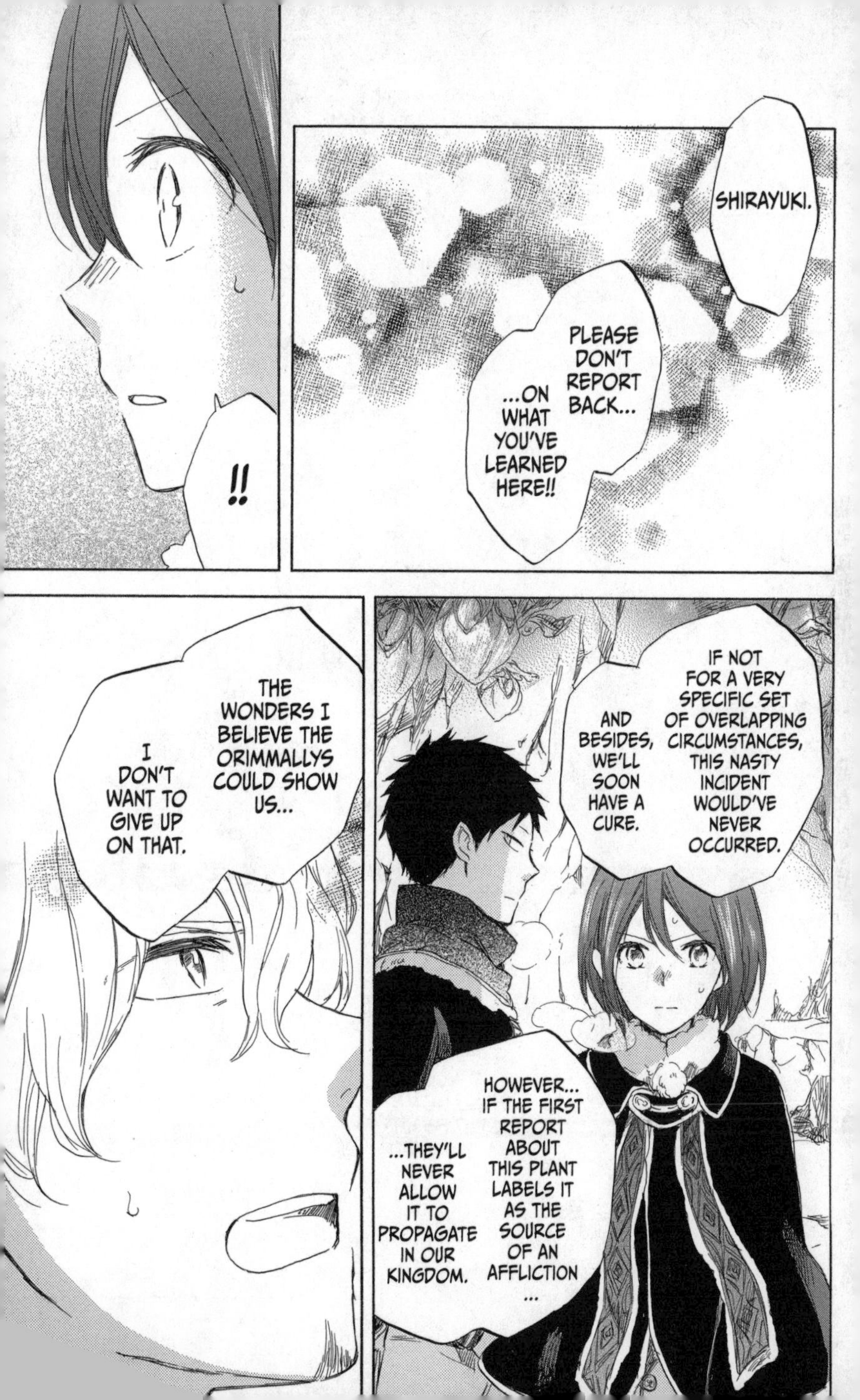
SHIRAYUKI.
PLEASE DON'T REPORT BACK...
...ON WHAT YOU'VE LEARNED HERE!!
!!
IF NOT FOR A VERY SPECIFIC SET OF OVERLAPPING CIRCUMSTANCES, THIS NASTY INCIDENT WOULD'VE NEVER OCCURRED.
AND BESIDES, WE'LL SOON HAVE A CURE.
HOWEVER... IF THE FIRST REPORT ABOUT THIS PLANT LABELS IT AS THE SOURCE OF AN AFFLICTION ...
...THEY'LL NEVER ALLOW IT TO PROPAGATE IN OUR KINGDOM.
THE WONDERS I BELIEVE THE ORIMMALLYS COULD SHOW US...
I DON'T WANT TO GIVE UP ON THAT.

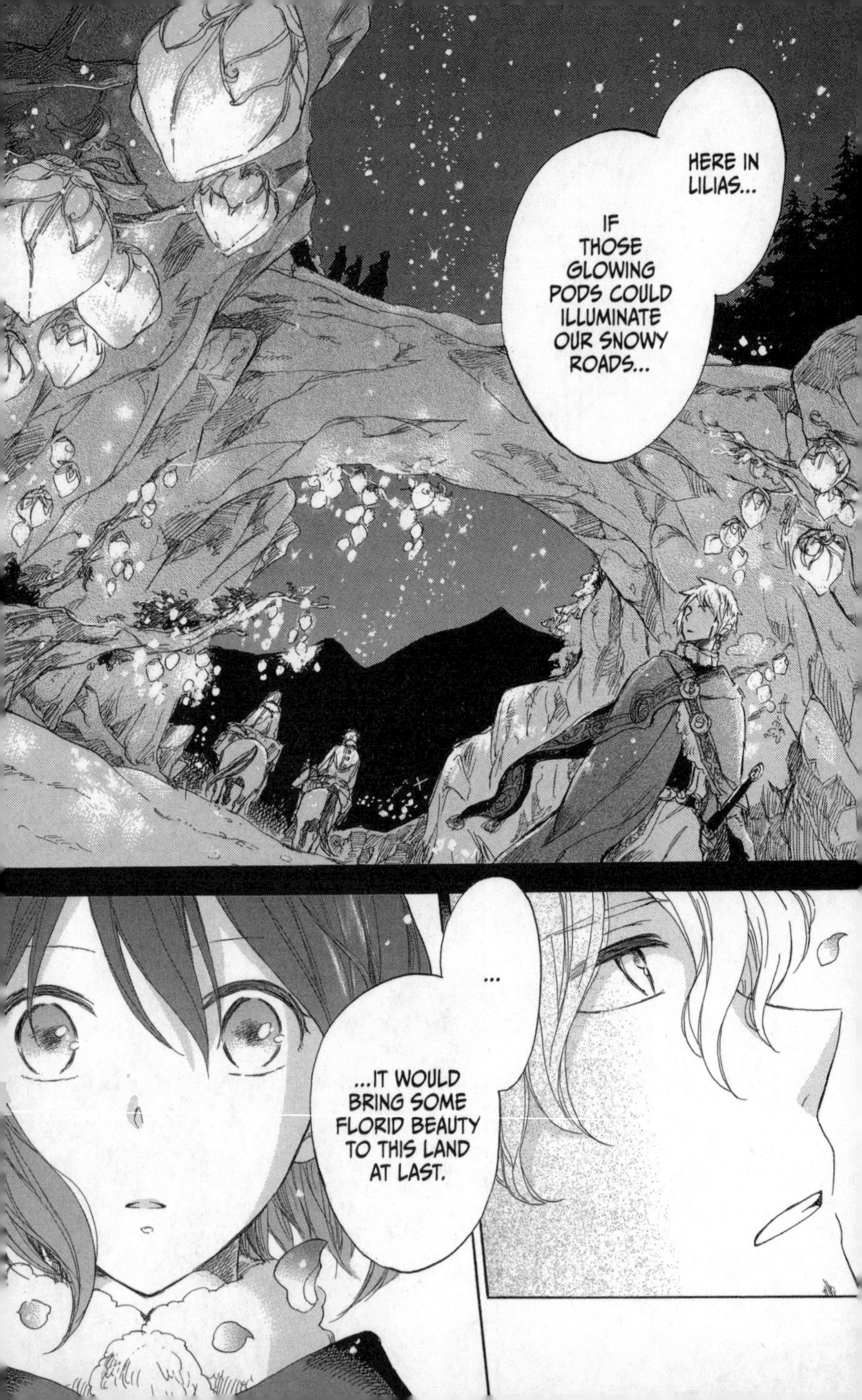
HERE IN LILIAS...
IF THOSE GLOWING PODS COULD ILLUMINATE OUR SNOWY ROADS...
...
...IT WOULD BRING SOME FLORID BEAUTY TO THIS LAND AT LAST.

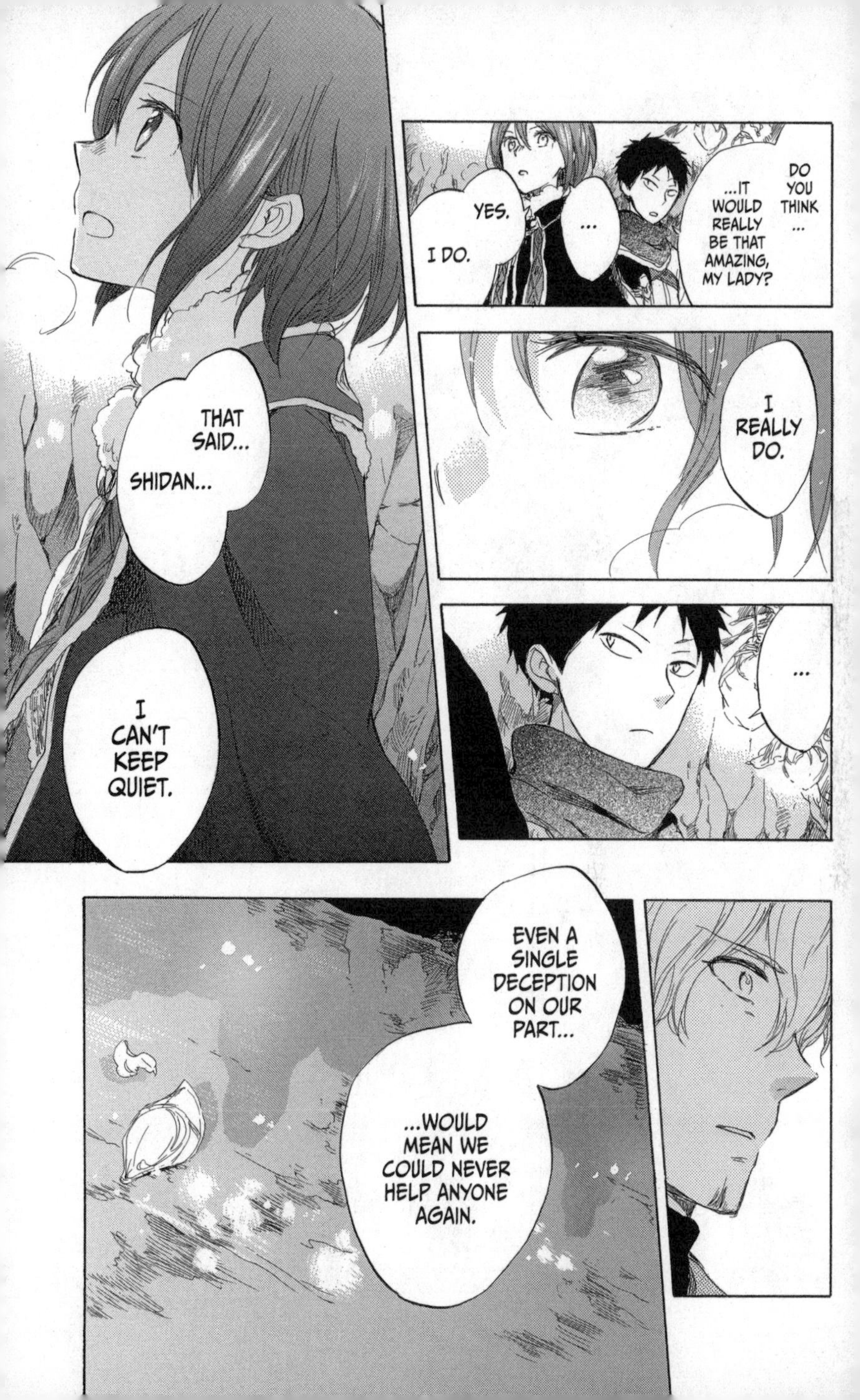
DO YOU THINK ...
...IT WOULD REALLY BE THAT AMAZING, MY LADY?
...
YES.
I DO.
I REALLY DO.
...
THAT SAID...
SHIDAN...
I CAN'T KEEP QUIET.
EVEN A SINGLE DECEPTION ON OUR PART...
...WOULD MEAN WE COULD NEVER HELP ANYONE AGAIN.

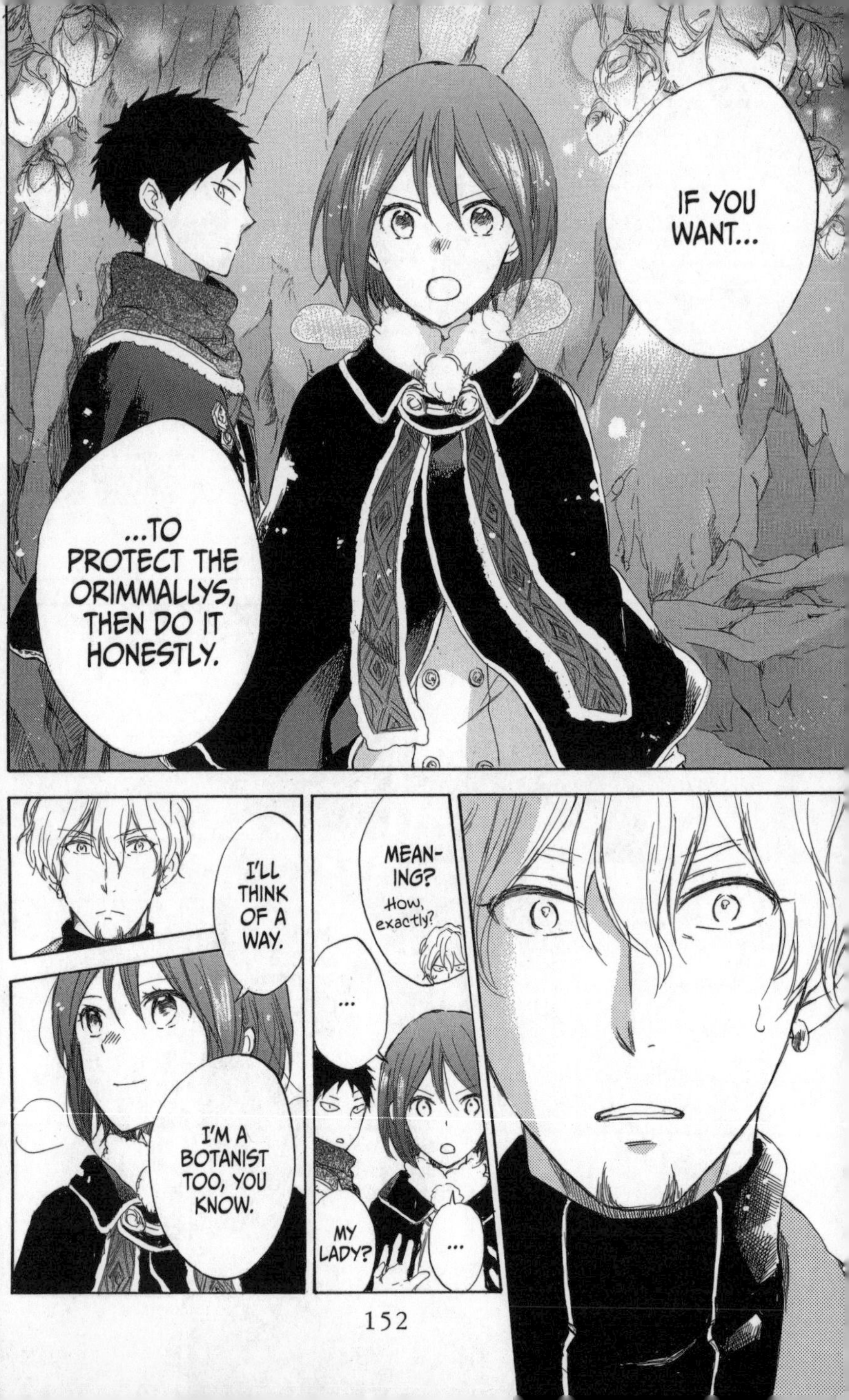
IF YOU WANT...
...TO PROTECT THE ORIMMALLYS, THEN DO IT HONESTLY.
MEAN-ING?
How, exactly?
...
...
MY LADY?
I'LL THINK OF A WAY.
I'M A BOTANIST TOO, YOU KNOW.

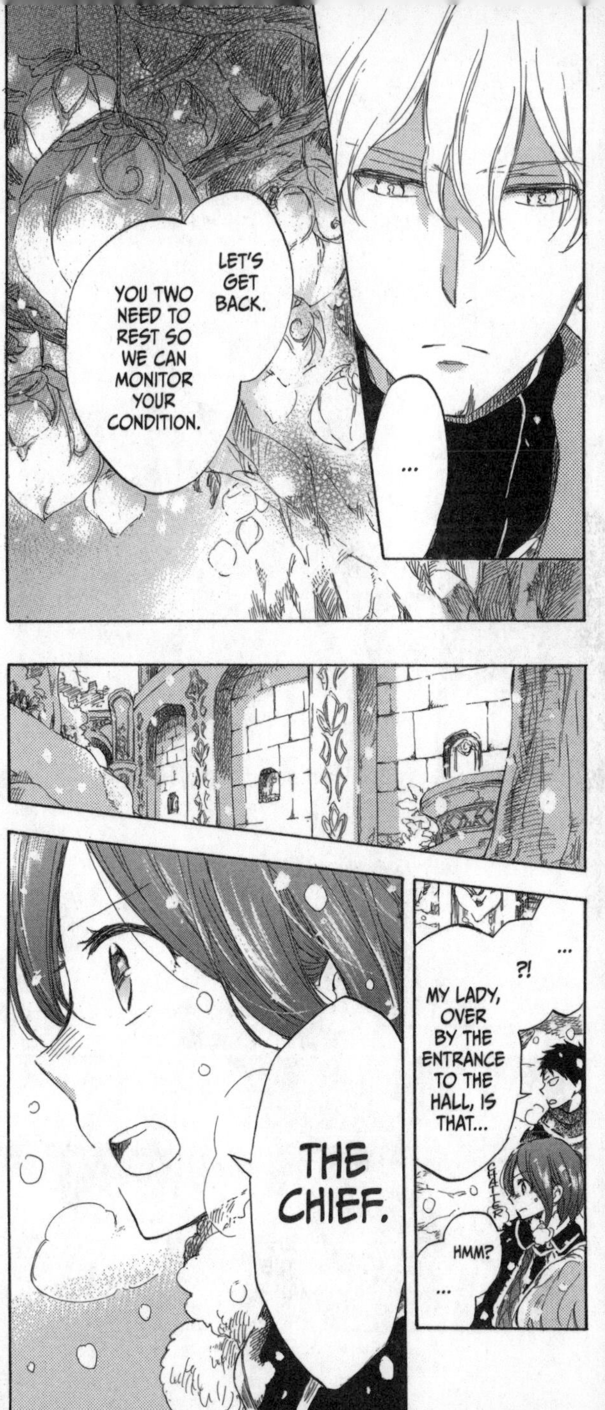
LET'S GET BACK.
YOU TWO NEED TO REST SO WE CAN MONITOR YOUR CONDITION.
...
...
?!
MY LADY, OVER BY THE ENTRANCE TO THE HALL, IS THAT...
CHATTER
HMM?
...
THE CHIEF.

FINAL SIDEBAR

My vacation in Izumo was filled with fun experiences, including shrine visits and a trip to the hot springs.

STEAMY STEAMY

In 2012, I wrote my first one-shot in a school setting in a long while.

It takes place during the height of summer, so it was a lot of fun to draw.

Clarines doesn't seem to have puffy cumulonimbus clouds. Or does it?

Now I'm imagining big thunderheads in the background behind Prince Izana. Ha ha ha ha.

I should've focused more on drawing the four distinct seasons in this story! Maybe we'll visit a kingdom like that someday. And it shall be called...the Kingdom of Castanetal.

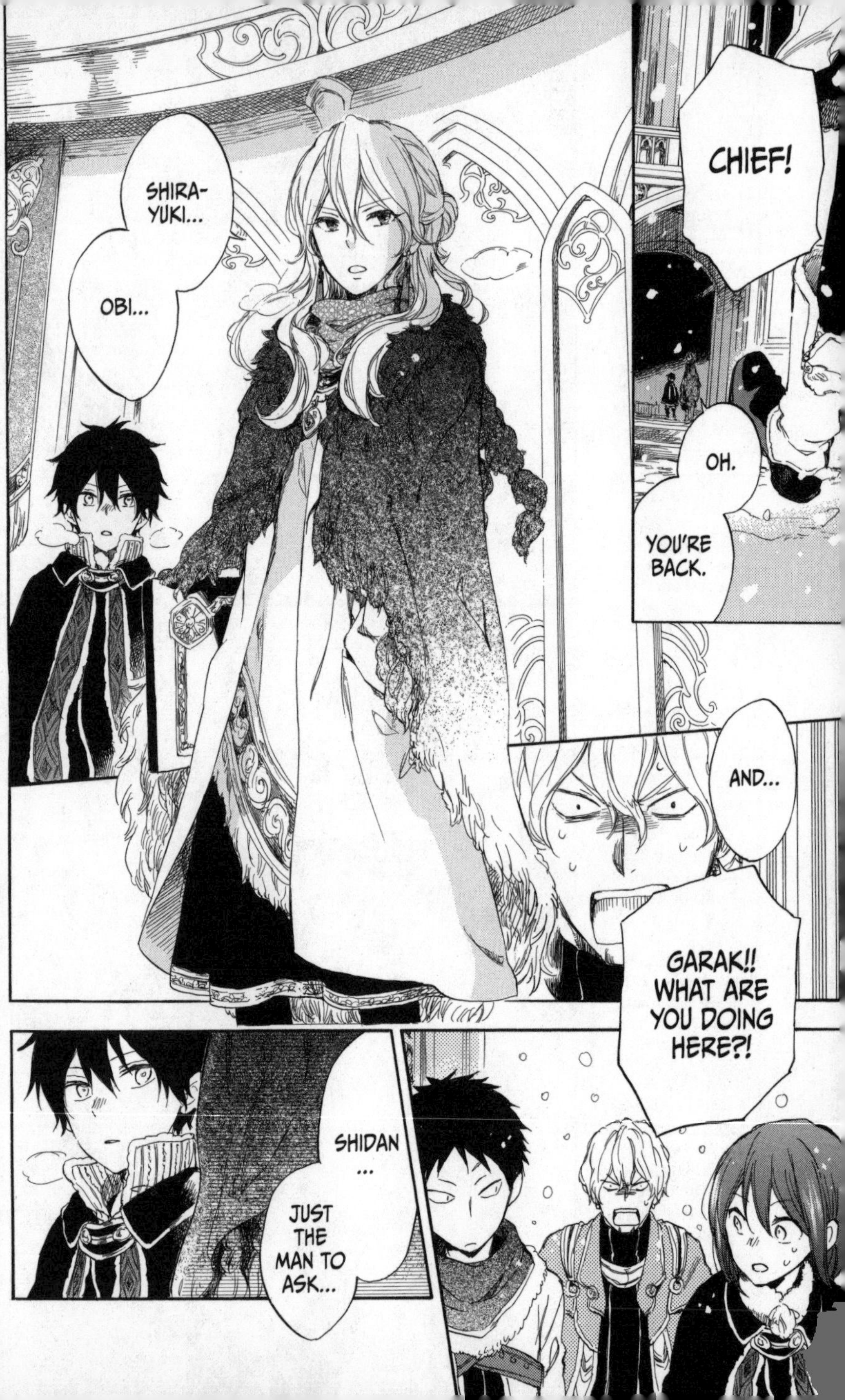
CHIEF!
OH.
YOU'RE BACK.
AND...
GARAK!! WHAT ARE YOU DOING HERE?!
SHIRA-YUKI...
OBI...
SHIDAN...
JUST THE MAN TO ASK...

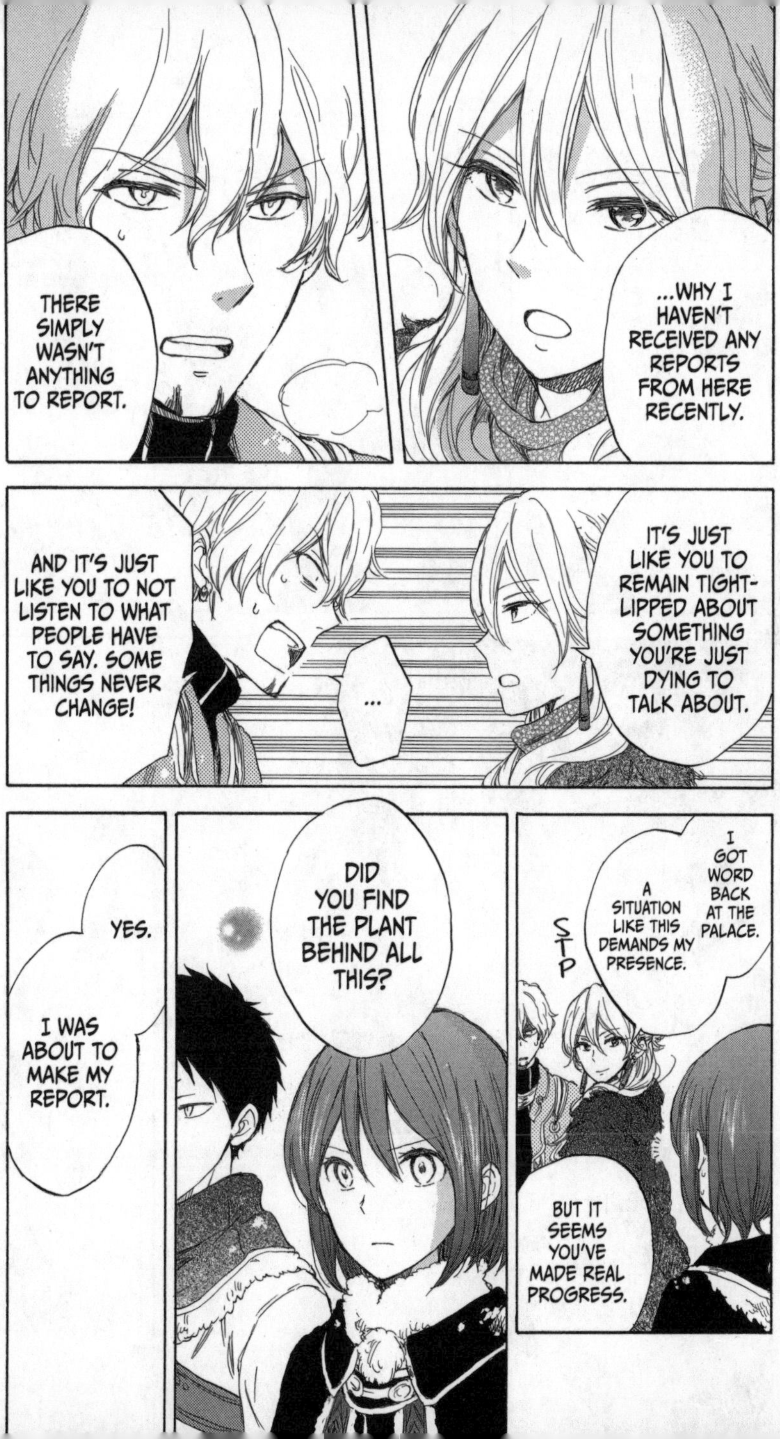
...WHY I HAVEN'T RECEIVED ANY REPORTS FROM HERE RECENTLY.
THERE SIMPLY WASN'T ANYTHING TO REPORT.
IT'S JUST LIKE YOU TO REMAIN TIGHT-LIPPED ABOUT SOMETHING YOU'RE JUST DYING TO TALK ABOUT.
...
AND IT'S JUST LIKE YOU TO NOT LISTEN TO WHAT PEOPLE HAVE TO SAY. SOME THINGS NEVER CHANGE!
I GOT WORD BACK AT THE PALACE.
A SITUATION LIKE THIS DEMANDS MY PRESENCE.
STP
BUT IT SEEMS YOU'VE MADE REAL PROGRESS.
DID YOU FIND THE PLANT BEHIND ALL THIS?
YES.
I WAS ABOUT TO MAKE MY REPORT.

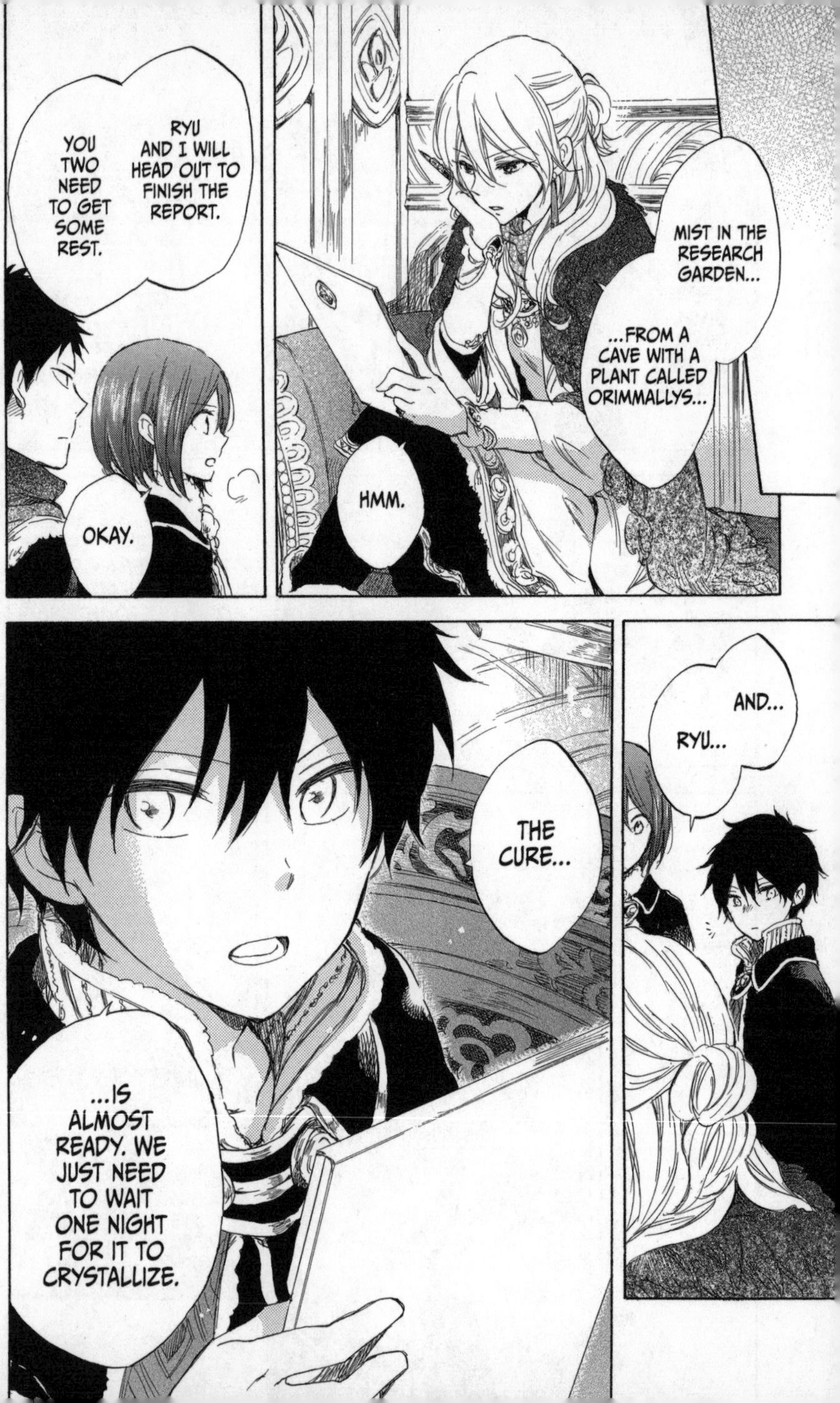
MIST IN THE RESEARCH GARDEN...
...FROM A CAVE WITH A PLANT CALLED ORIMMALLYS...
HMM.
RYU AND I WILL HEAD OUT TO FINISH THE REPORT.
YOU TWO NEED TO GET SOME REST.
OKAY.
AND... RYU...
THE CURE...
...IS ALMOST READY. WE JUST NEED TO WAIT ONE NIGHT FOR IT TO CRYSTALLIZE.

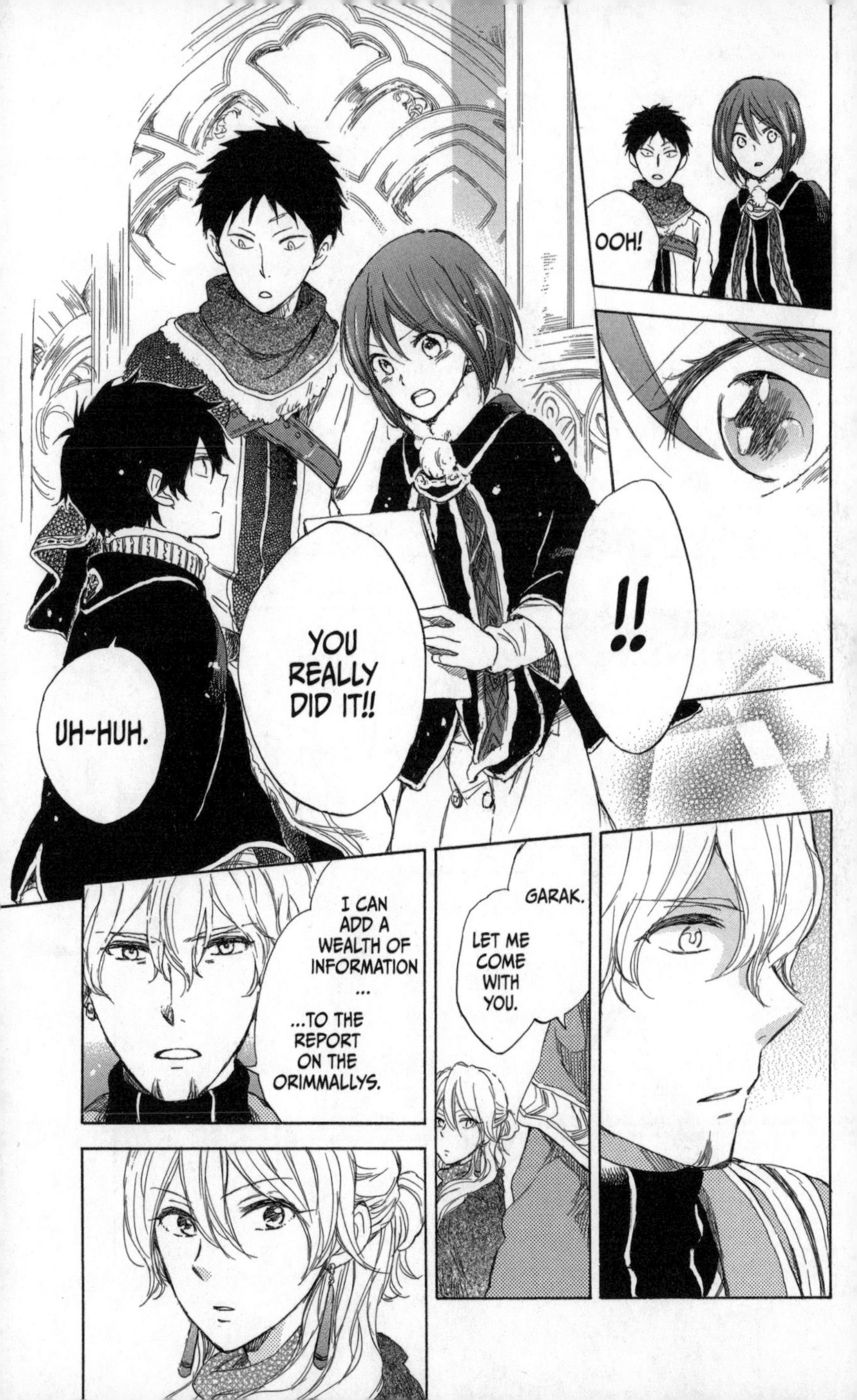
OOH!
!!
YOU REALLY DID IT!!
UH-HUH.
GARAK.
LET ME COME WITH YOU.
I CAN ADD A WEALTH OF INFORMATION...
...TO THE REPORT ON THE ORIMMALLYS.

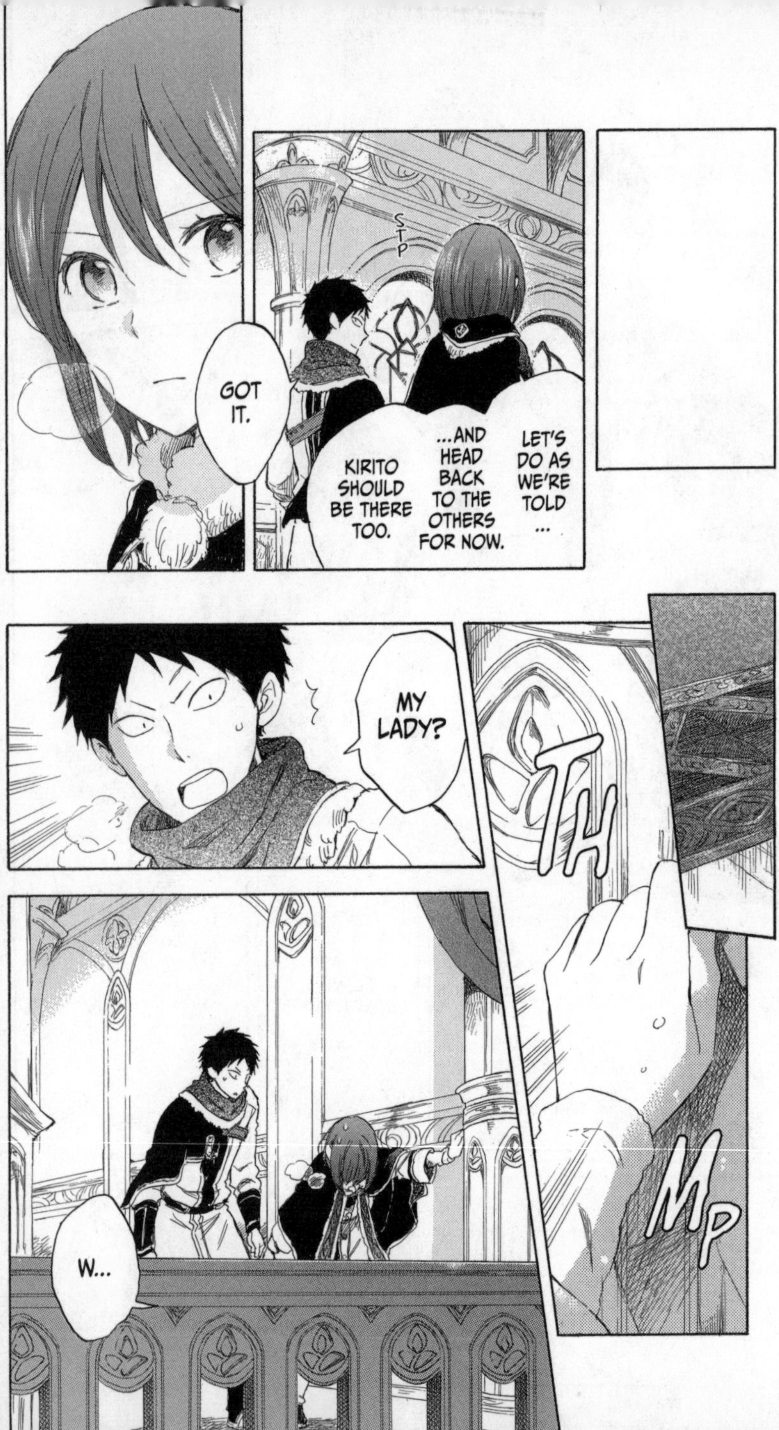
LET'S DO AS WE'RE TOLD ...
...AND HEAD BACK TO THE OTHERS FOR NOW.
KIRITO SHOULD BE THERE TOO.
STP
GOT IT.
TH
MP
MY LADY?
W...

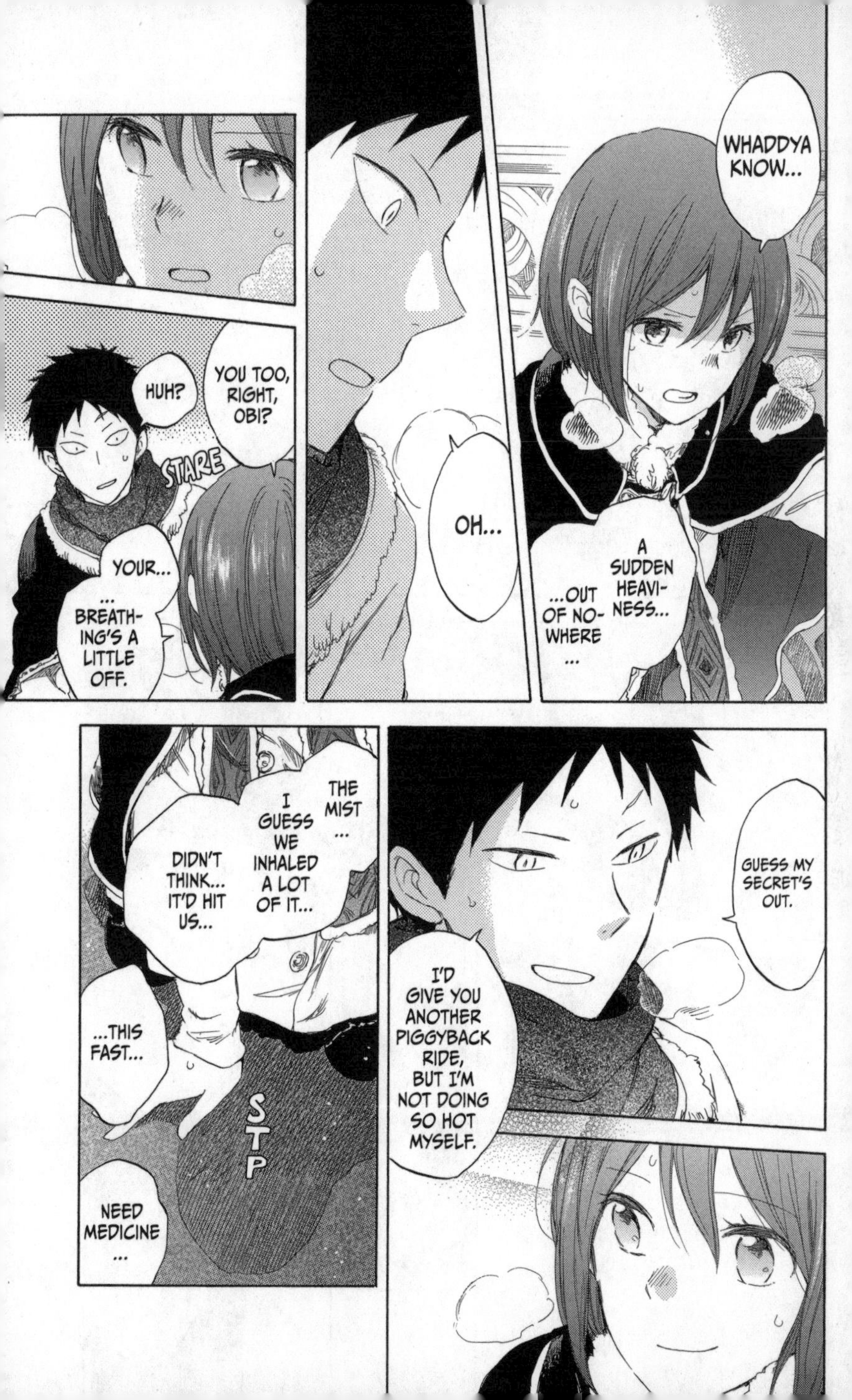
WHADDYA KNOW...
A SUDDEN HEAVINESS...
...OUT OF NOWHERE...
OH...
YOU TOO, RIGHT, OBI?
HUH?
STARE
YOUR...
...BREATHING'S A LITTLE OFF.
GUESS MY SECRET'S OUT.
I'D GIVE YOU ANOTHER PIGGYBACK RIDE, BUT I'M NOT DOING SO HOT MYSELF.
THE MIST...
I GUESS WE INHALED A LOT OF IT...
DIDN'T THINK... IT'D HIT US...
...THIS FAST...
STP
NEED MEDICINE...

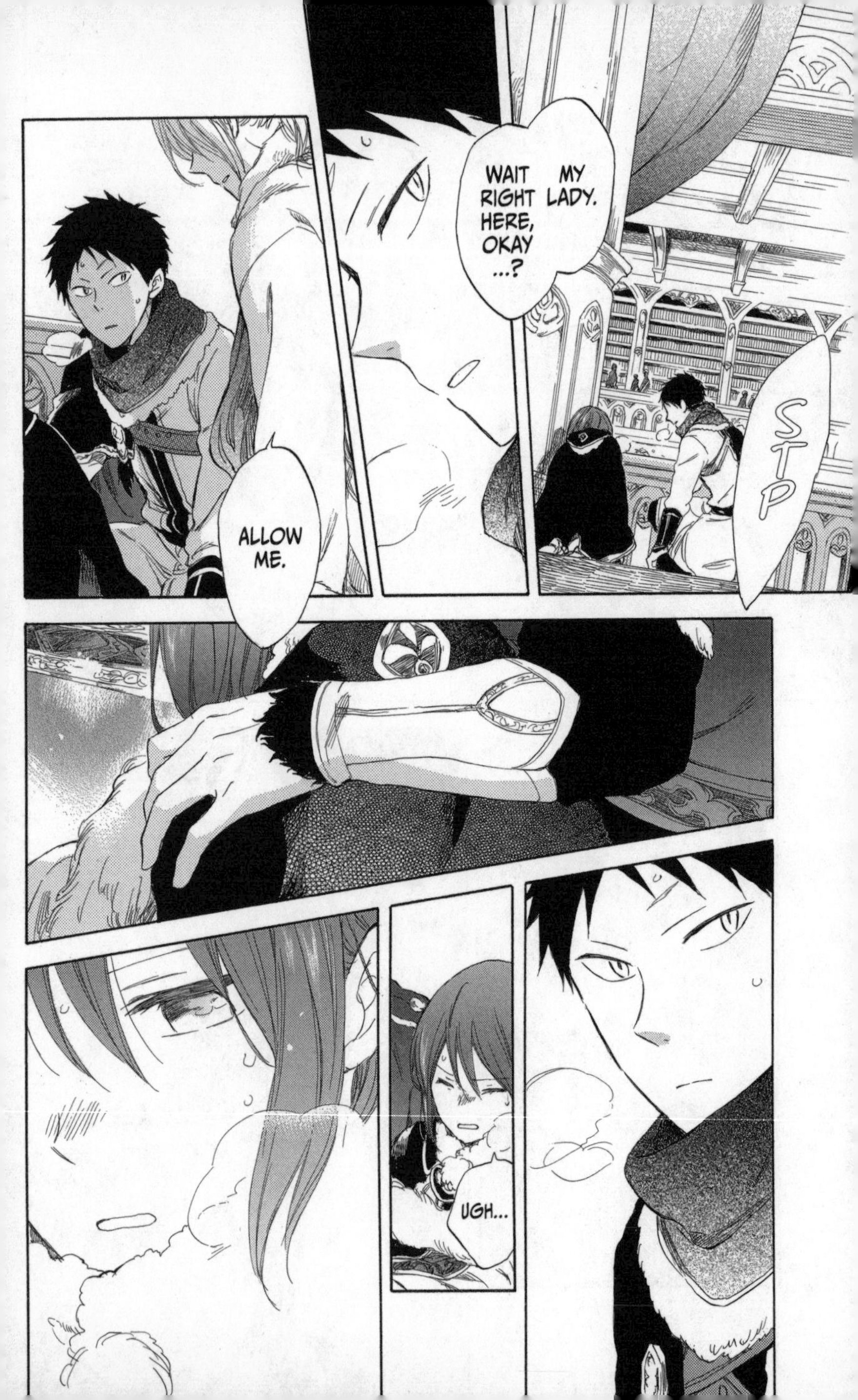
STP
MY LADY.
WAIT RIGHT HERE, OKAY ...?
ALLOW ME.
UGH...

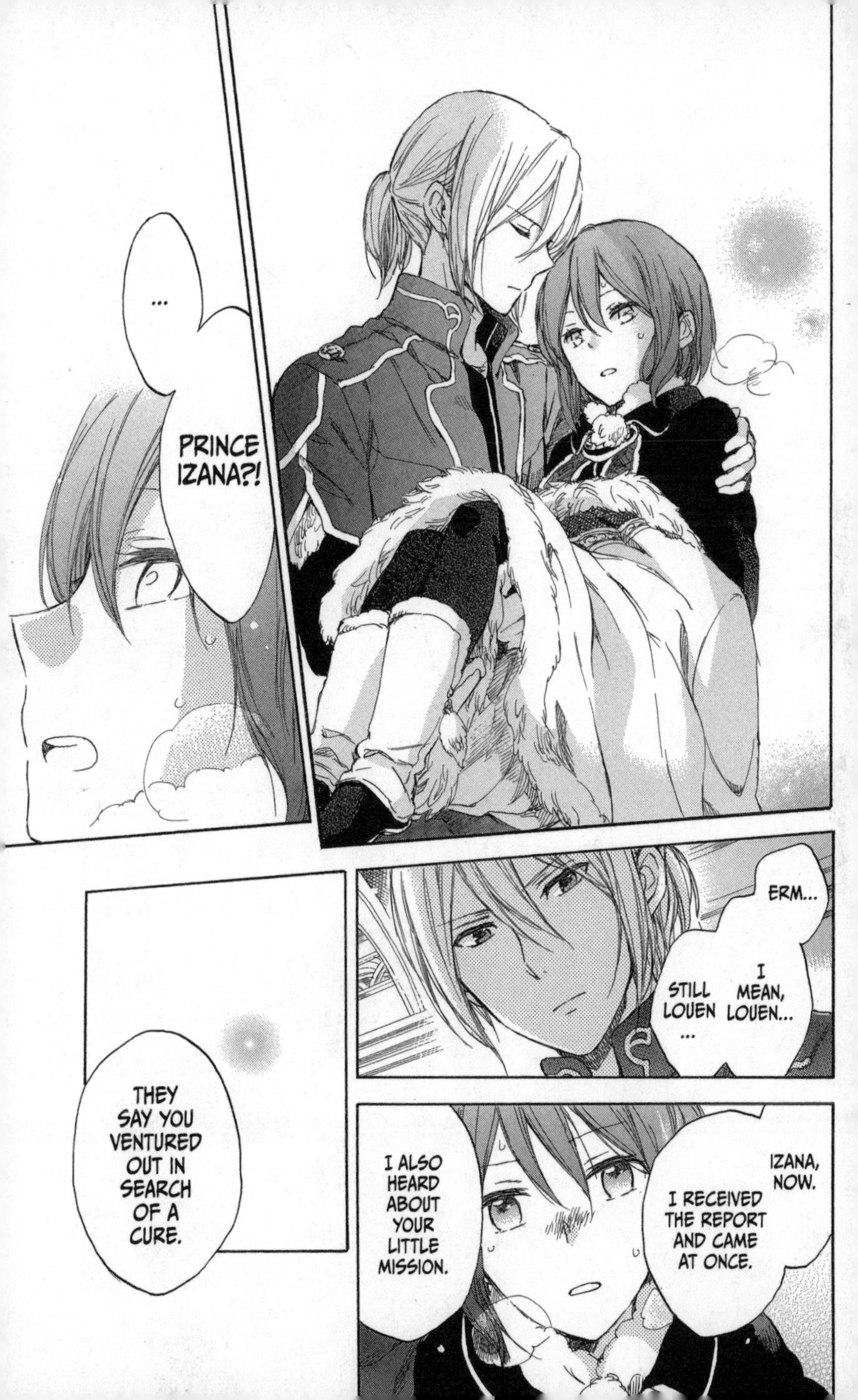
...
PRINCE IZANA?!
ERM...
I MEAN, LOUEN...
STILL LOUEN ...
IZANA, NOW.
I RECEIVED THE REPORT AND CAME AT ONCE.
I ALSO HEARD ABOUT YOUR LITTLE MISSION.
THEY SAY YOU VENTURED OUT IN SEARCH OF A CURE.

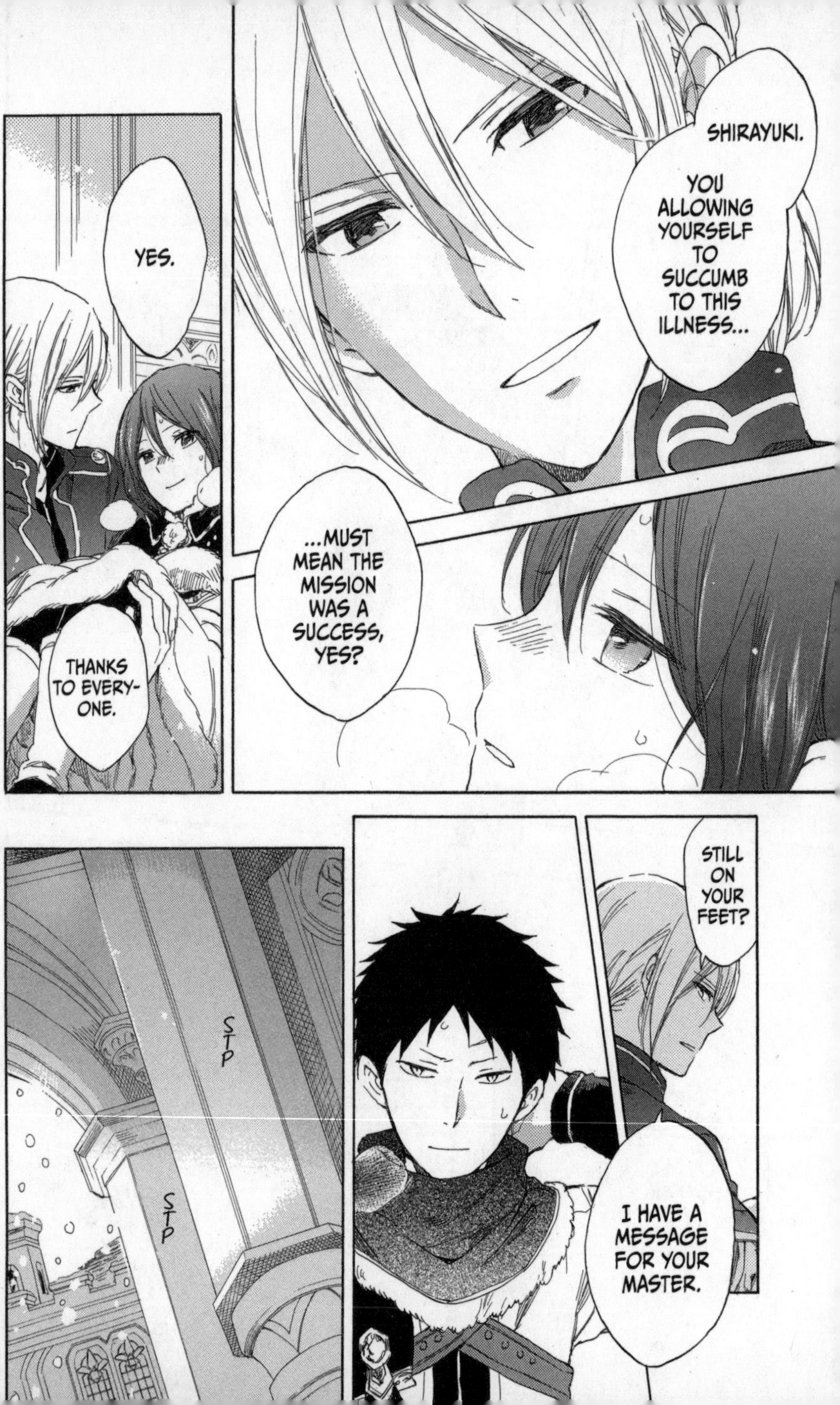
SHIRAYUKI.
YOU ALLOWING YOURSELF TO SUCCUMB TO THIS ILLNESS...
...MUST MEAN THE MISSION WAS A SUCCESS, YES?
YES.
THANKS TO EVERY-ONE.
STILL ON YOUR FEET?
I HAVE A MESSAGE FOR YOUR MASTER.
STP
STP

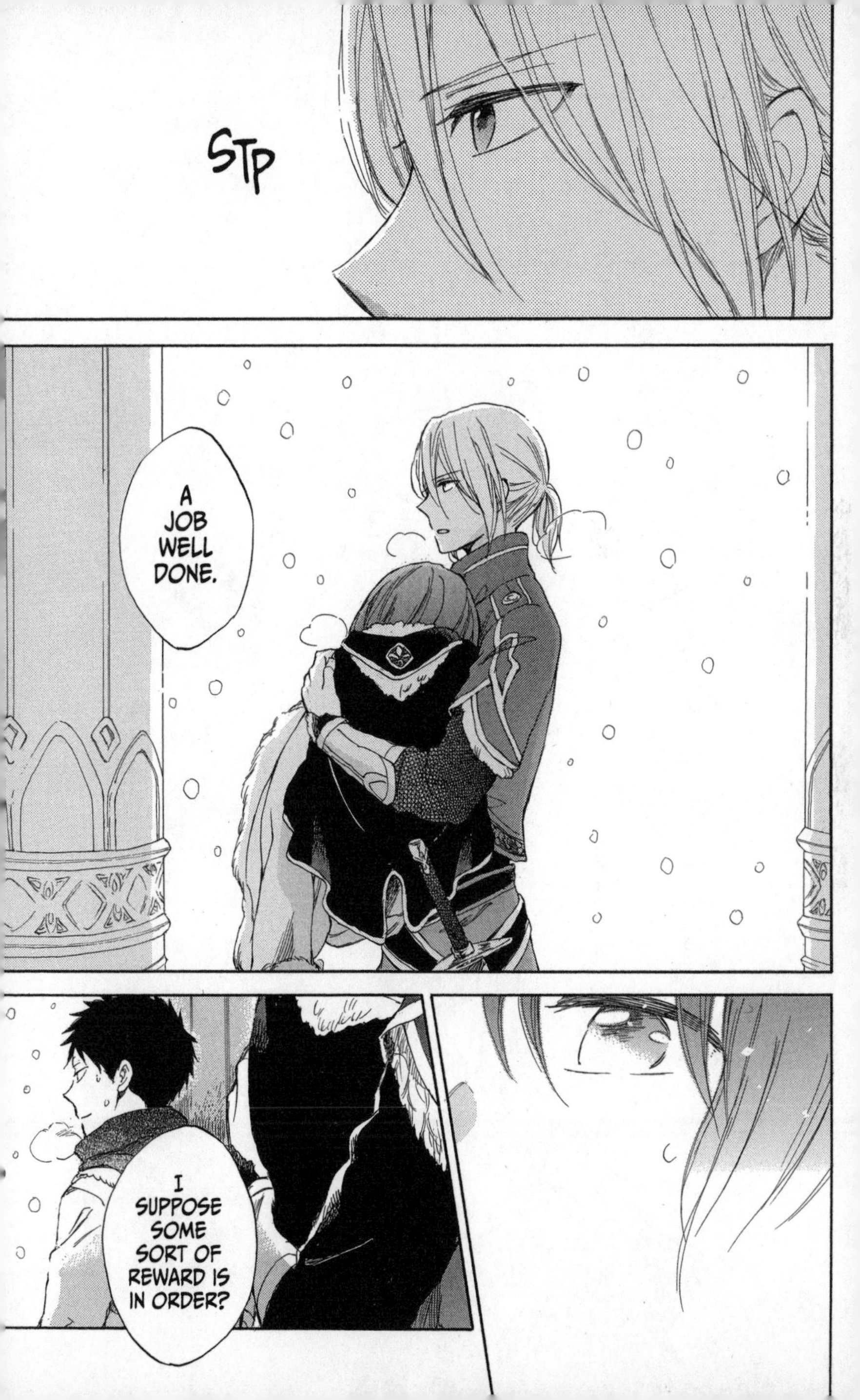
STP
A JOB WELL DONE.
I SUPPOSE SOME SORT OF REWARD IS IN ORDER?

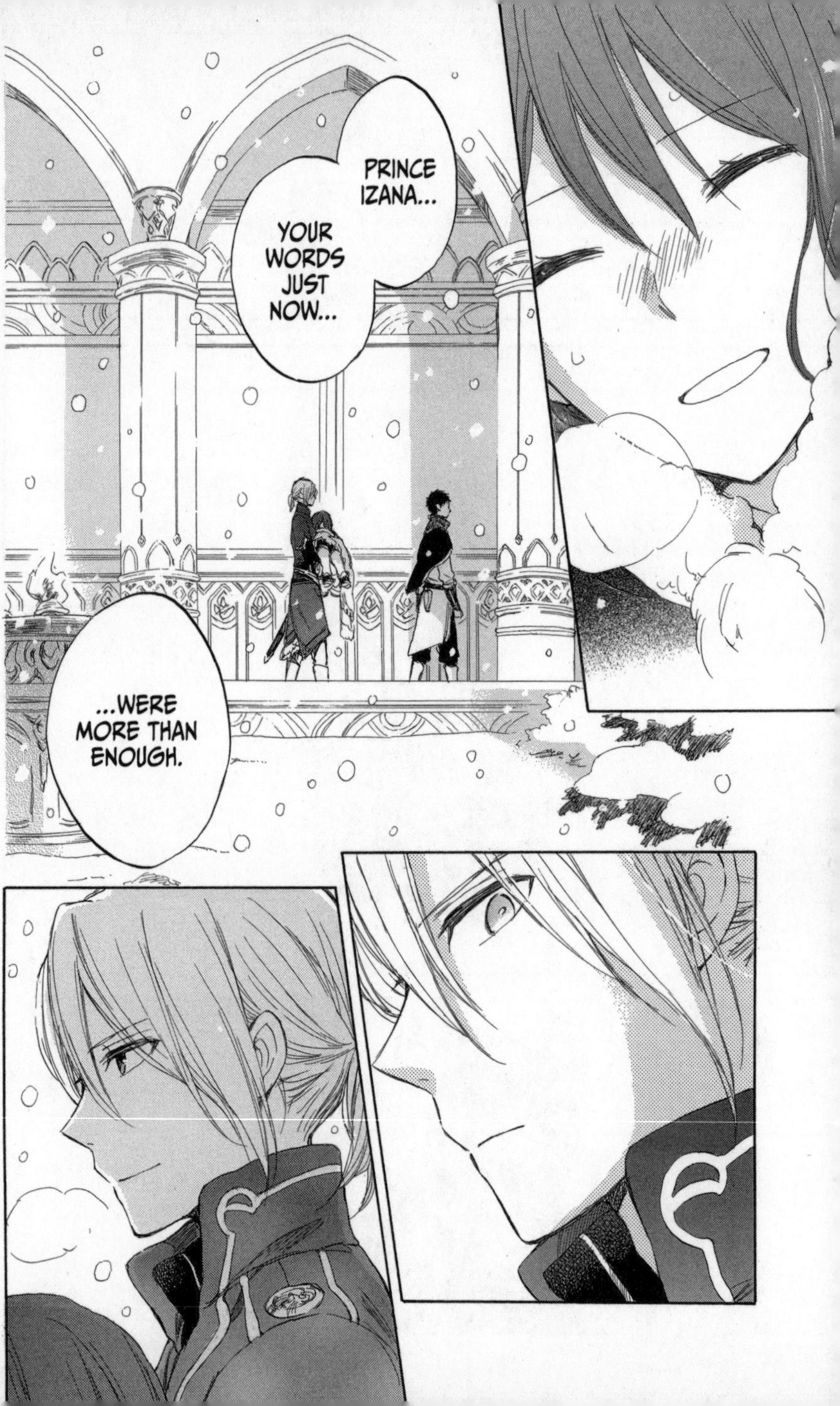
PRINCE IZANA...
YOUR WORDS JUST NOW...
...WERE MORE THAN ENOUGH.

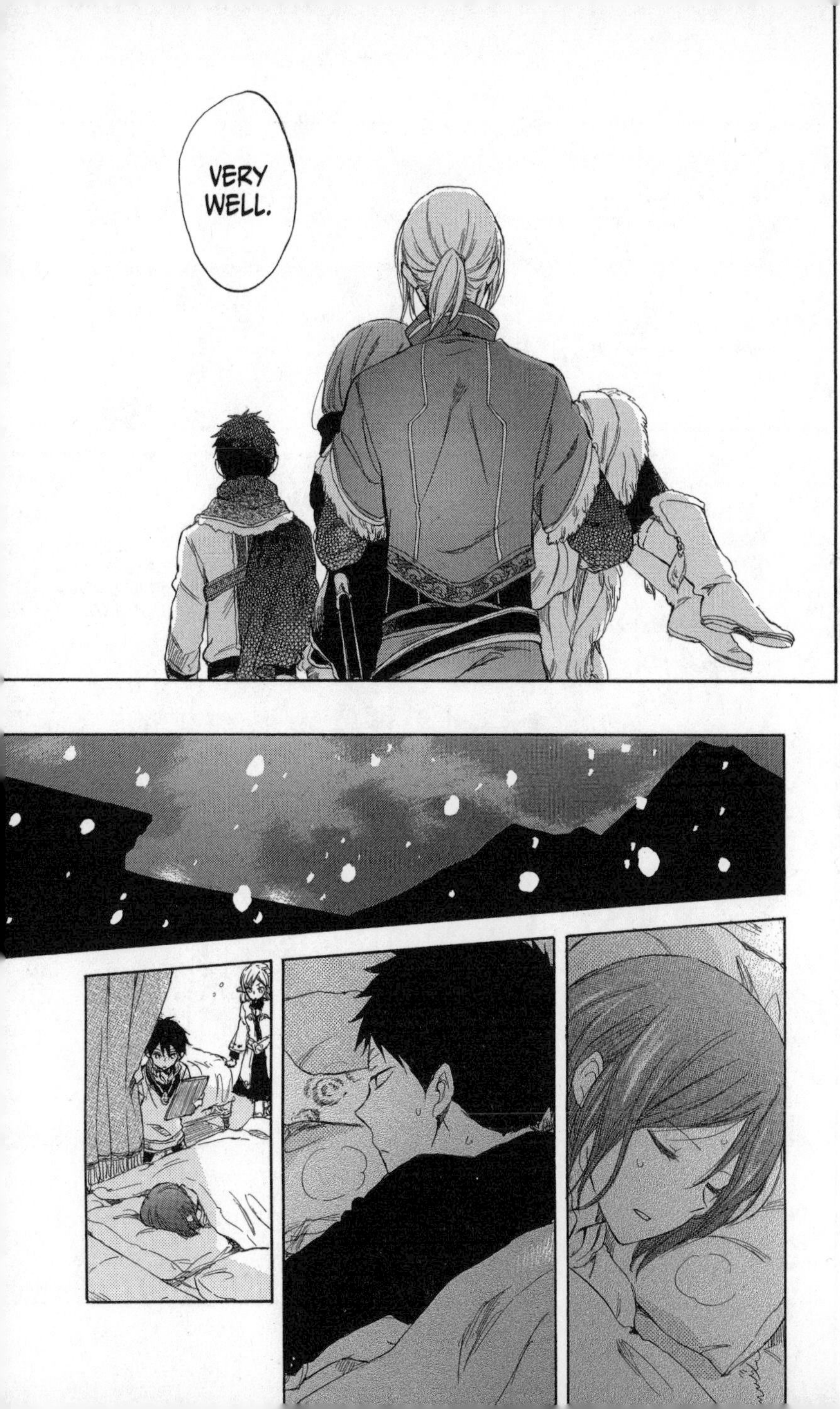
VERY WELL.

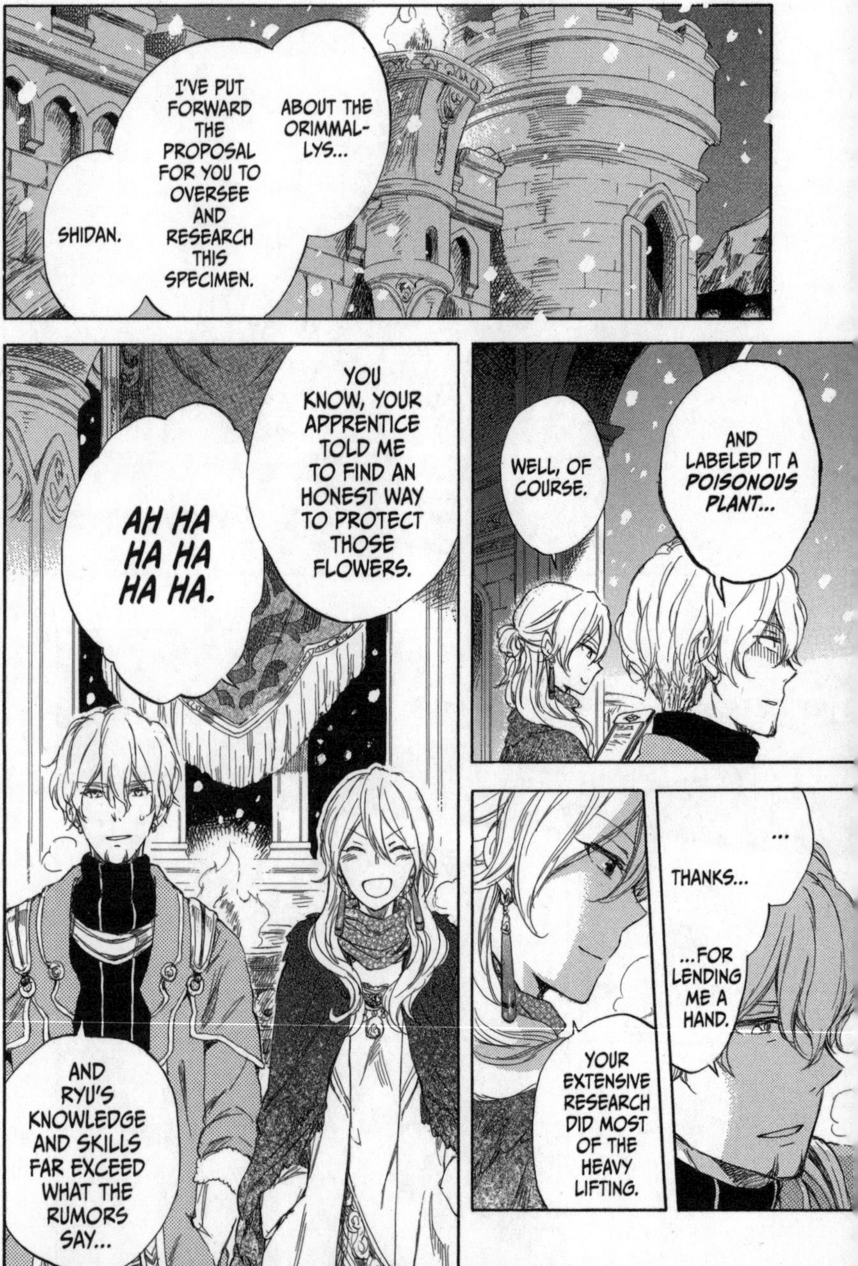
ABOUT THE ORIMMAL-LYS...
I'VE PUT FORWARD THE PROPOSAL FOR YOU TO OVERSEE AND RESEARCH THIS SPECIMEN.
SHIDAN.
AND LABELED IT A *POISONOUS PLANT*...
WELL, OF COURSE.
...
THANKS...
...FOR LENDING ME A HAND.
YOUR EXTENSIVE RESEARCH DID MOST OF THE HEAVY LIFTING.
YOU KNOW, YOUR APPRENTICE TOLD ME TO FIND AN HONEST WAY TO PROTECT THOSE FLOWERS.
AH HA HA HA HA HA.
AND RYU'S KNOWLEDGE AND SKILLS FAR EXCEED WHAT THE RUMORS SAY...

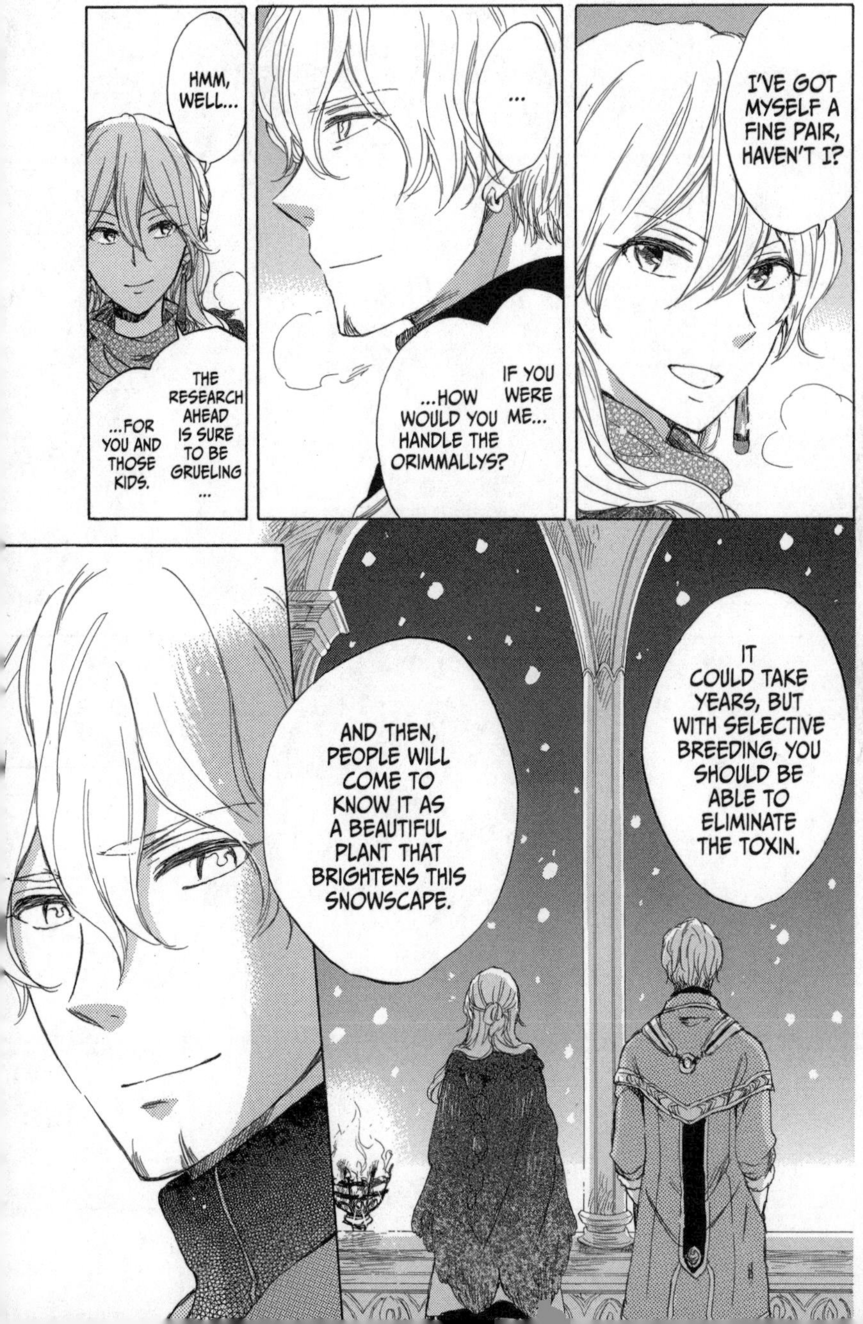
I'VE GOT MYSELF A FINE PAIR, HAVEN'T I?
...
IF YOU WERE ME...
...HOW WOULD YOU HANDLE THE ORIMMALLYS?
HMM, WELL...
THE RESEARCH AHEAD IS SURE TO BE GRUELING...
...FOR YOU AND THOSE KIDS.
IT COULD TAKE YEARS, BUT WITH SELECTIVE BREEDING, YOU SHOULD BE ABLE TO ELIMINATE THE TOXIN.
AND THEN, PEOPLE WILL COME TO KNOW IT AS A BEAUTIFUL PLANT THAT BRIGHTENS THIS SNOWSCAPE.

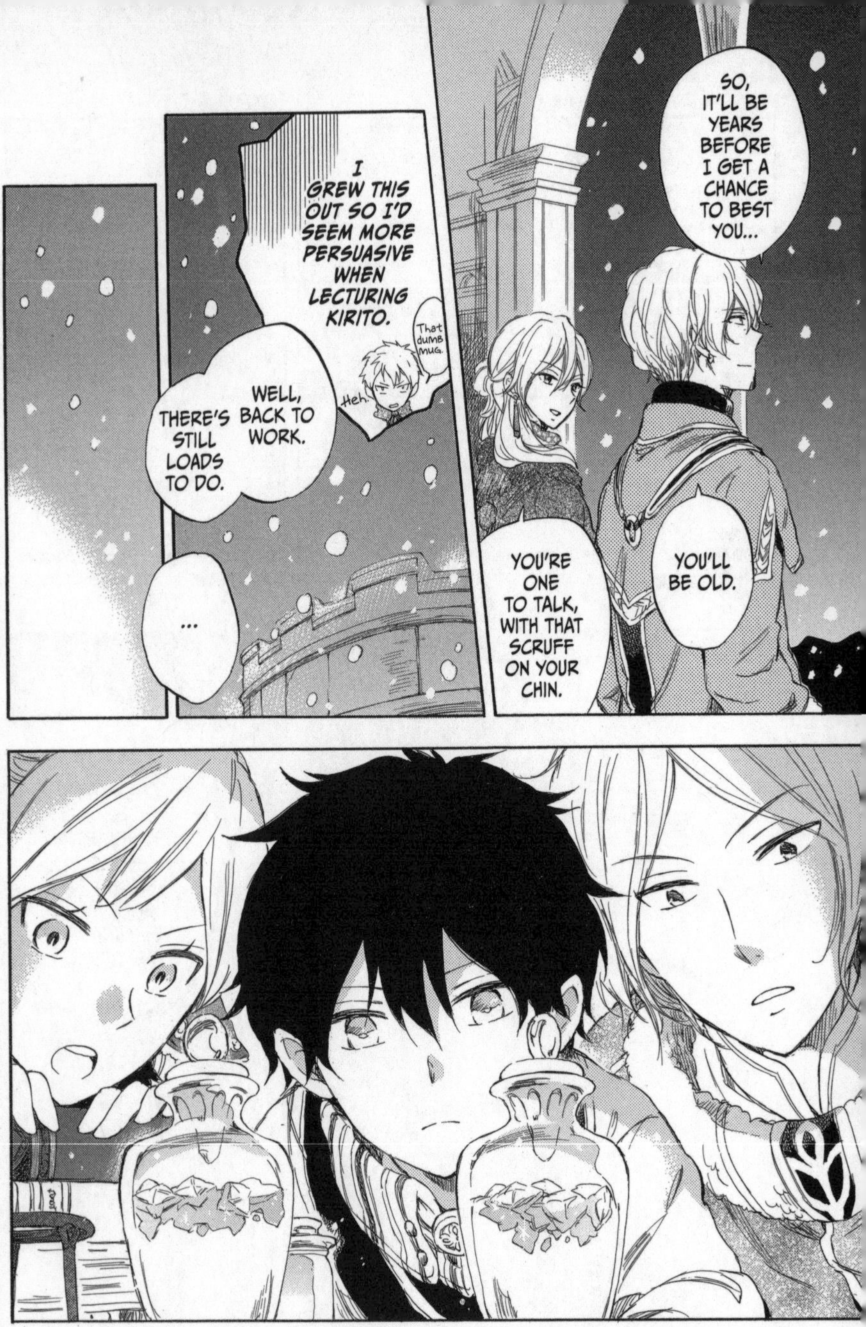
SO, IT'LL BE YEARS BEFORE I GET A CHANCE TO BEST YOU...
YOU'LL BE OLD.
YOU'RE ONE TO TALK, WITH THAT SCRUFF ON YOUR CHIN.
I GREW THIS OUT SO I'D SEEM MORE PERSUASIVE WHEN LECTURING KIRITO.
That dumb mug.
Heh.
WELL, BACK TO WORK. THERE'S STILL LOADS TO DO.
...

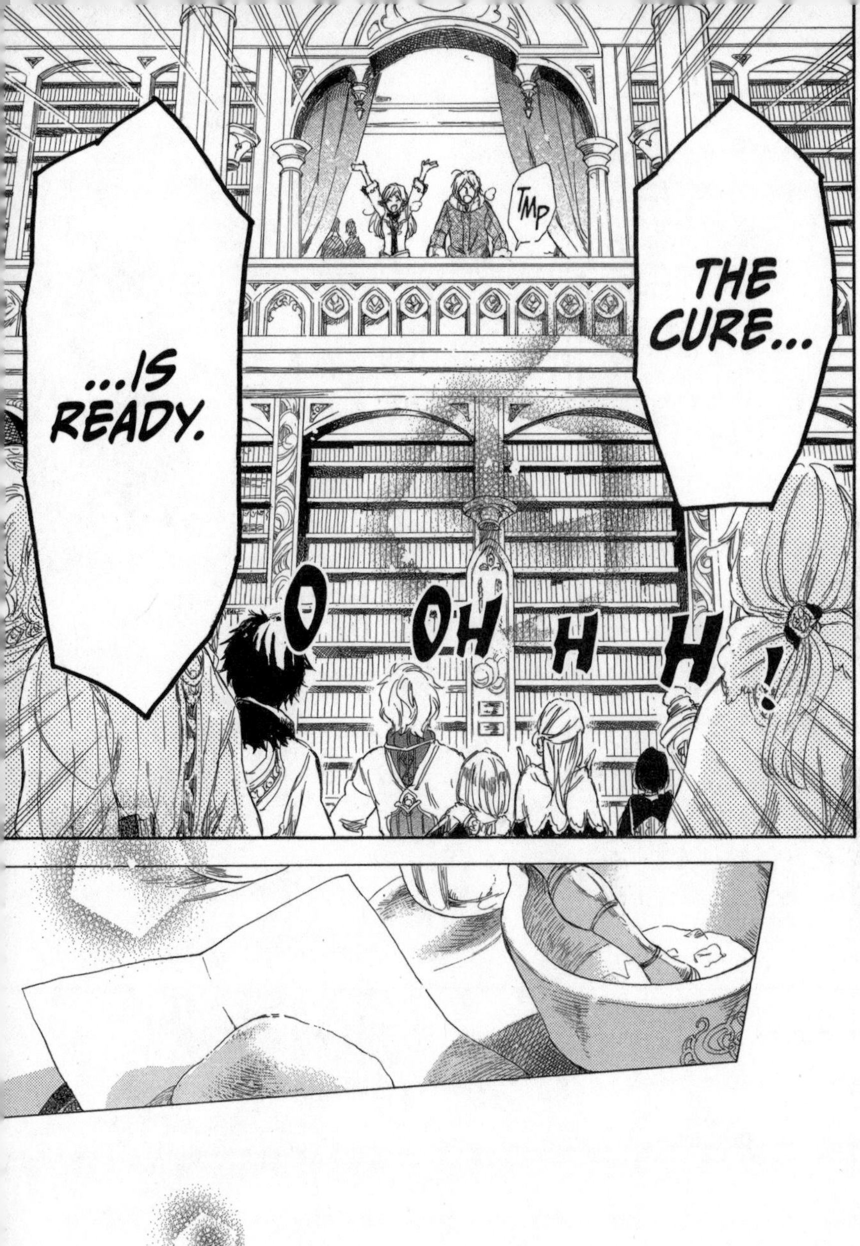
THE CURE...
TMP
...IS READY.
OOHHHH!

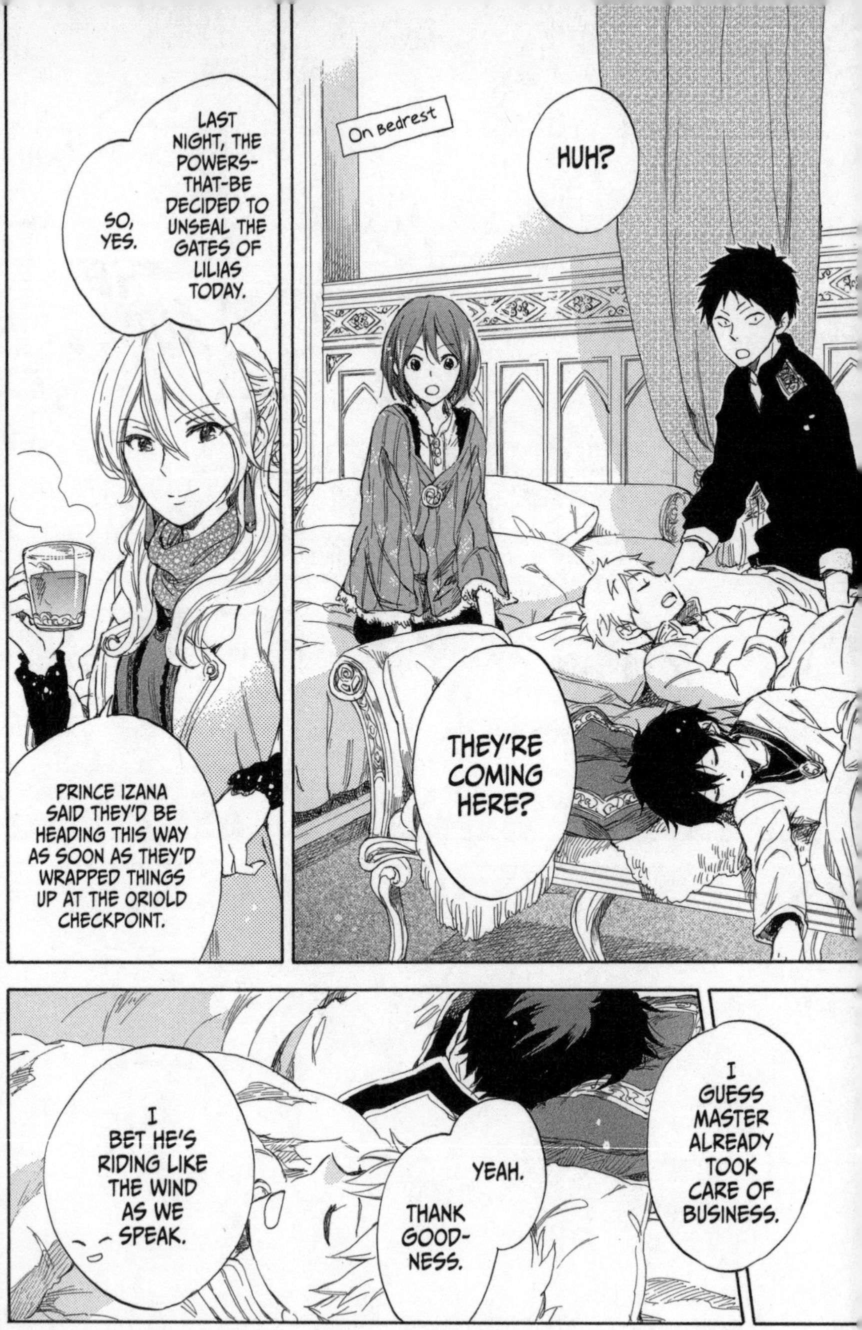
HUH?
On bedrest
THEY'RE COMING HERE?
LAST NIGHT, THE POWERS-THAT-BE DECIDED TO UNSEAL THE GATES OF LILIAS TODAY.
SO, YES.
PRINCE IZANA SAID THEY'D BE HEADING THIS WAY AS SOON AS THEY'D WRAPPED THINGS UP AT THE ORIOLD CHECKPOINT.
I GUESS MASTER ALREADY TOOK CARE OF BUSINESS.
YEAH.
THANK GOOD-NESS.
I BET HE'S RIDING LIKE THE WIND AS WE SPEAK.

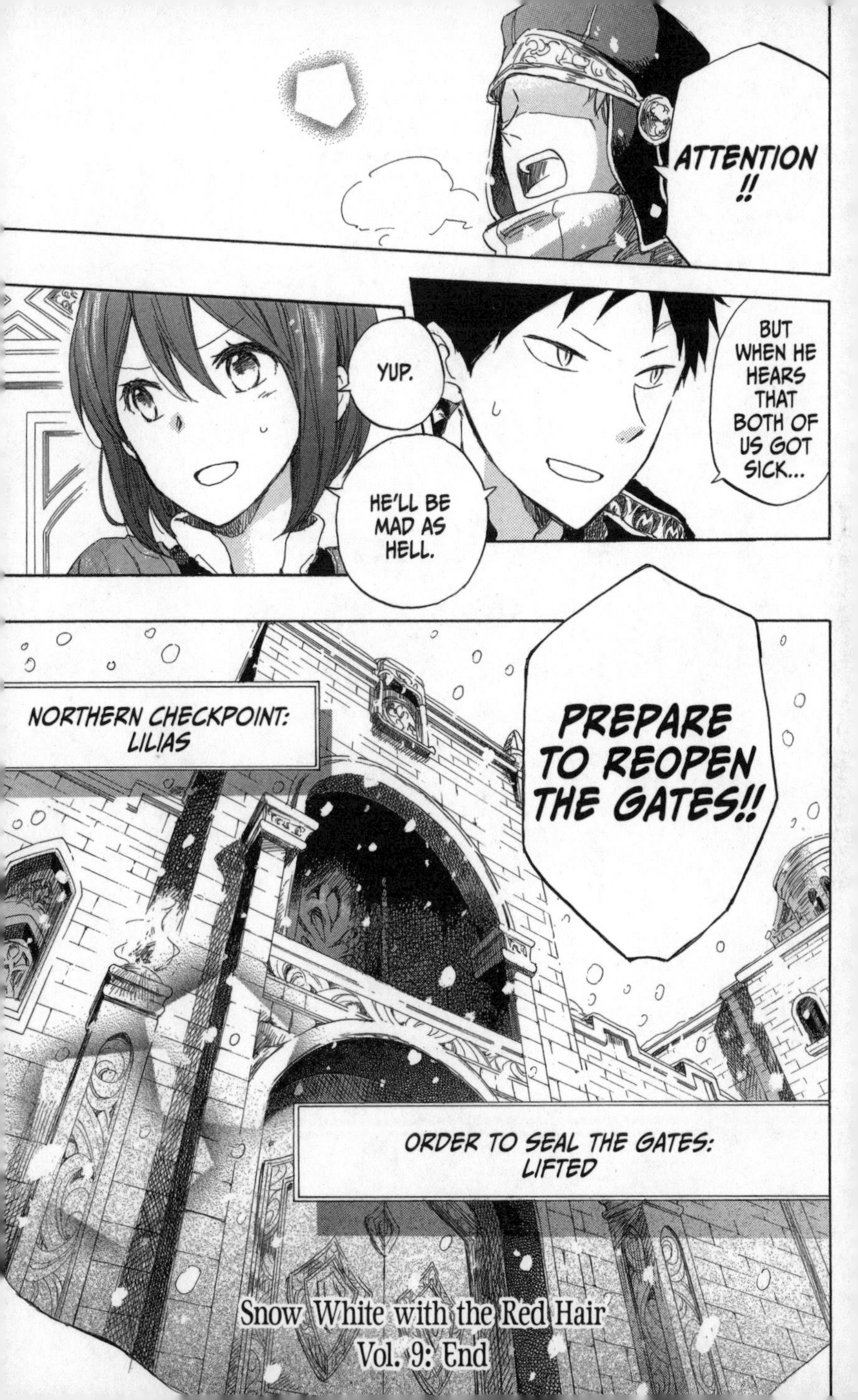
ATTENTION!!
BUT WHEN HE HEARS THAT BOTH OF US GOT SICK...
YUP.
HE'LL BE MAD AS HELL.
PREPARE TO REOPEN THE GATES!!
NORTHERN CHECKPOINT: LILIAS
ORDER TO SEAL THE GATES: LIFTED
Snow White with the Red Hair
Vol. 9: End

More Talk About Bathing Scenes

Haa.

Sure is cold up here in the north.

Finally, the time has come, my good Mitsuhide...

Well, get on in there.

Into the bath.

The bath? Why?

"Why?" he asks.

Don't you remember when we all stayed at that inn?

Everyone got a chance to bathe except for you.

I did bathe.

But we didn't get to see it!

Why would anyone have seen it? I went in alone.

Just Friends

There's something I've been wondering about.
Why do you always say, "I'm single" when you introduce yourself, Suzu?
Because that extra little detail might earn me a marriage proposal one day. It's my way of asking...
"Well? Like what you see?"
...
Has it ever worked?
Not even once.
How about you?
Like what you see?
Real smooth, Suzu.

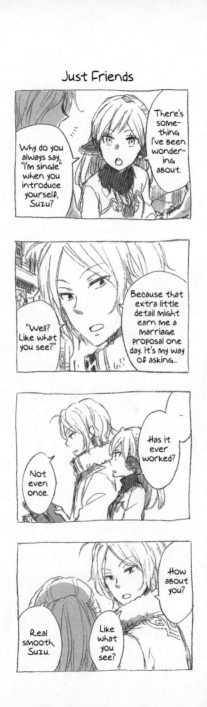

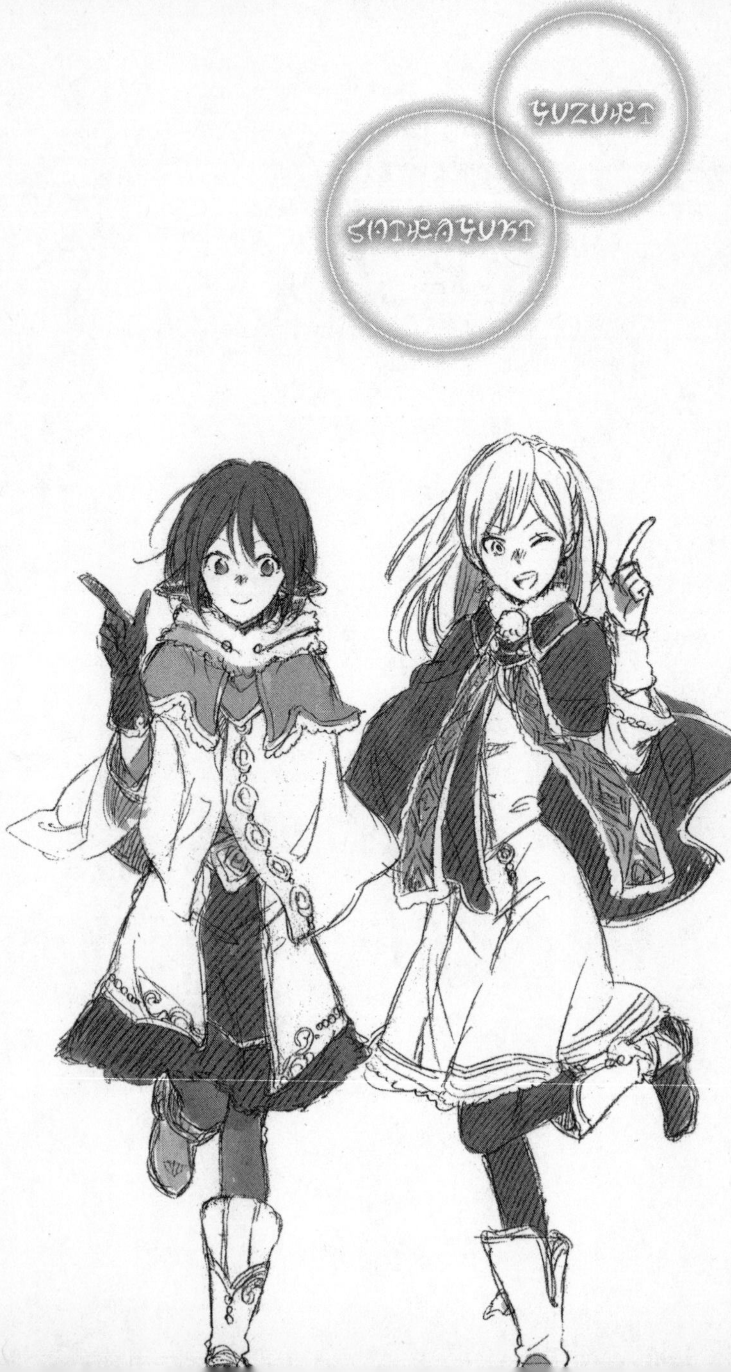

Earmuffs

Your earmuffs are super cute, Yuzuri.
Y'think so? I bought 'em here in Lilias!
Hey. Ryu.
You just got muffed!
?!
Ah ha ha ha ha ha ha!
What a cutie!
A new discovery—the rare ice elf!
...
Oh, me, me. Let me try next.
...
You look like some sorta were-fox.

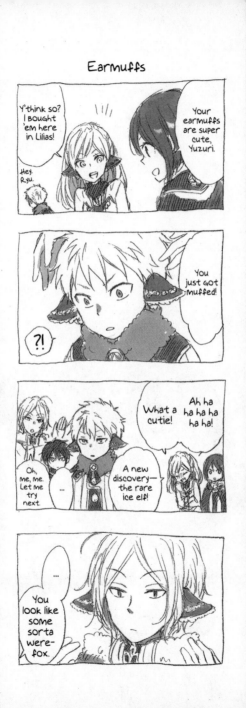

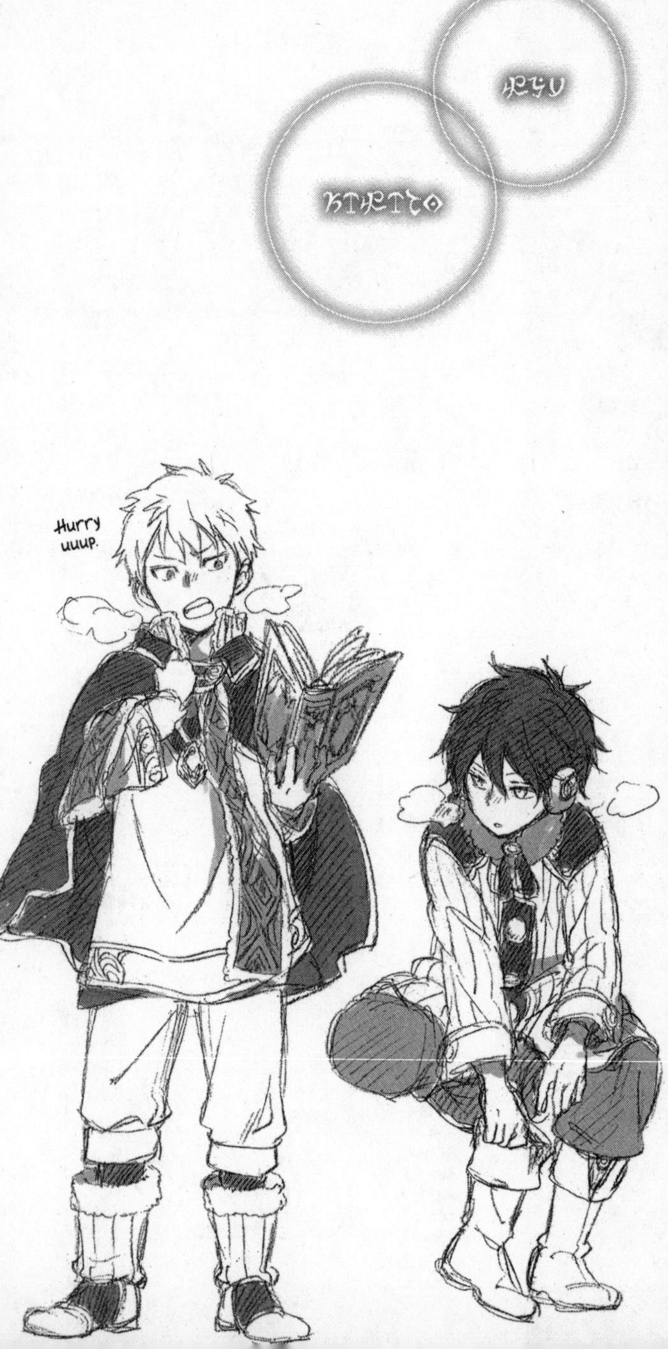
Hurry uuup.

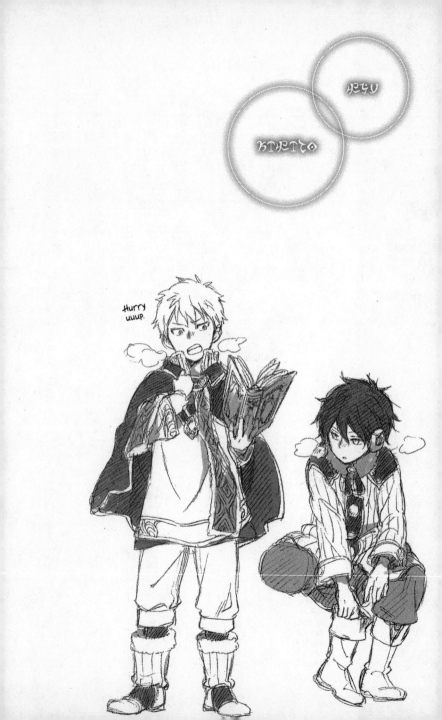

Prince Louen

Hey, you! You ever meet real royals?
Like the prince?
What's he like?
Um...
What's he like?
...
Erm.
I can tell you about Louen, I guess?
Who?
The tall man who came with us.
Oh.
Dun care.
I barely noticed the guy.
...
W-what's with that look?
Was I s'posed to notice him?

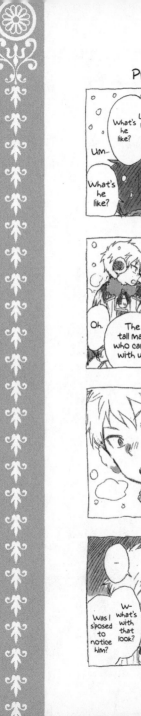

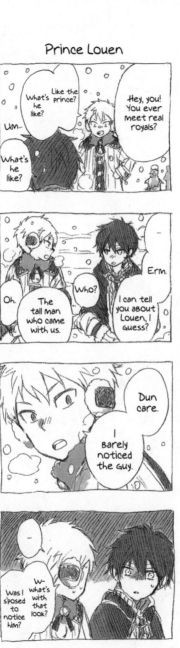

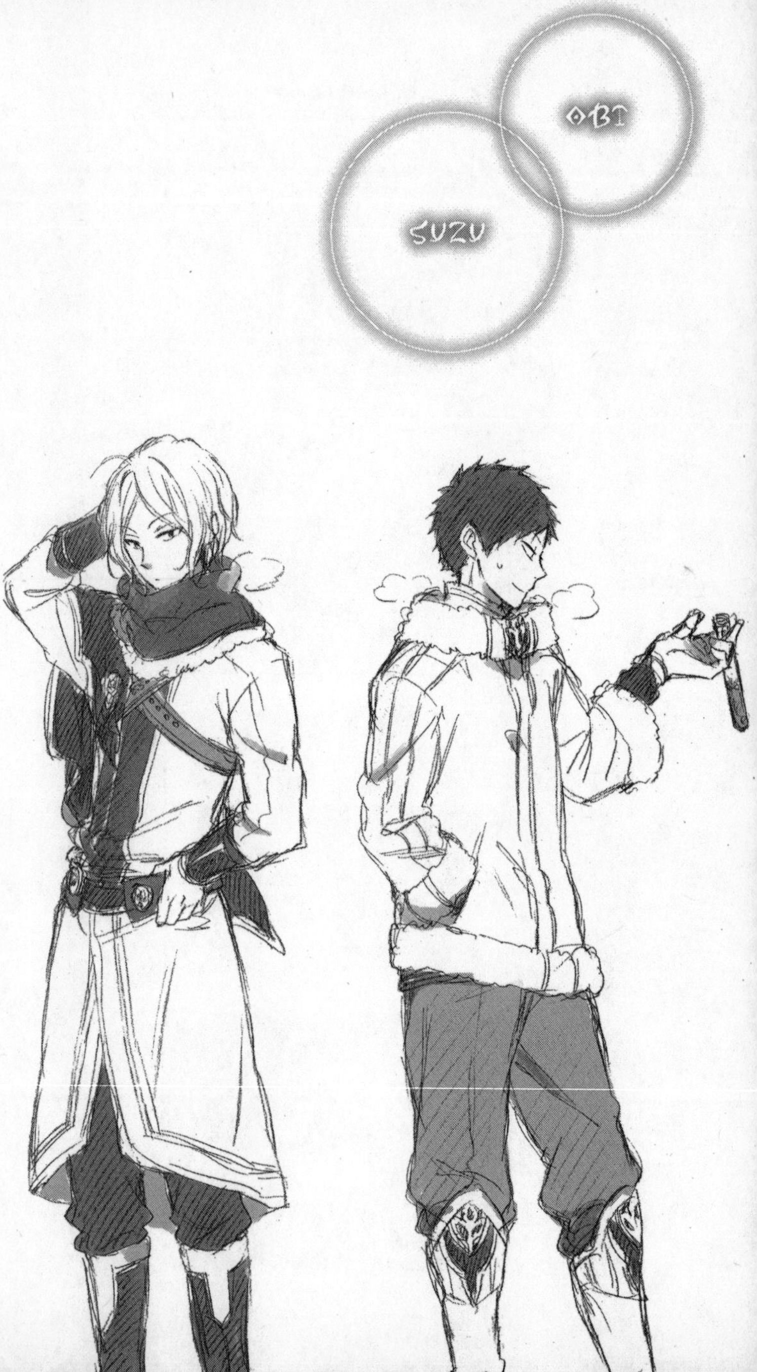
OBI
SUZU

Polar Opposite

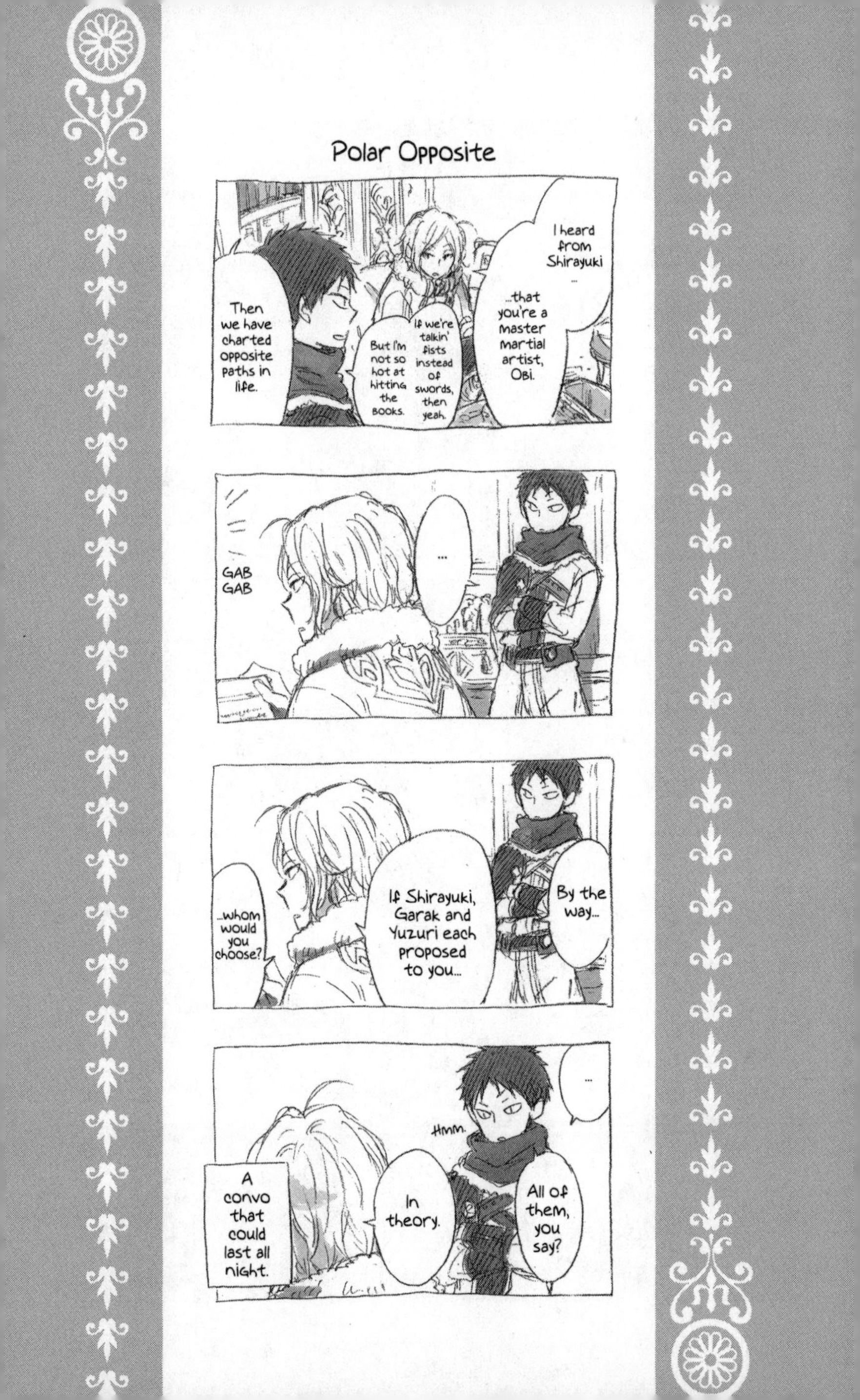
I heard from Shirayuki...
...that you're a master martial artist, Obi.
If we're talkin' fists instead of swords, then yeah.
But I'm not so hot at hitting the books.
Then we have charted opposite paths in life.
...
GAB GAB
By the way...
If Shirayuki, Garak and Yuzuri each proposed to you...
...whom would you choose?
...
Hmm.
All of them, you say?
In theory.
A convo that could last all night.

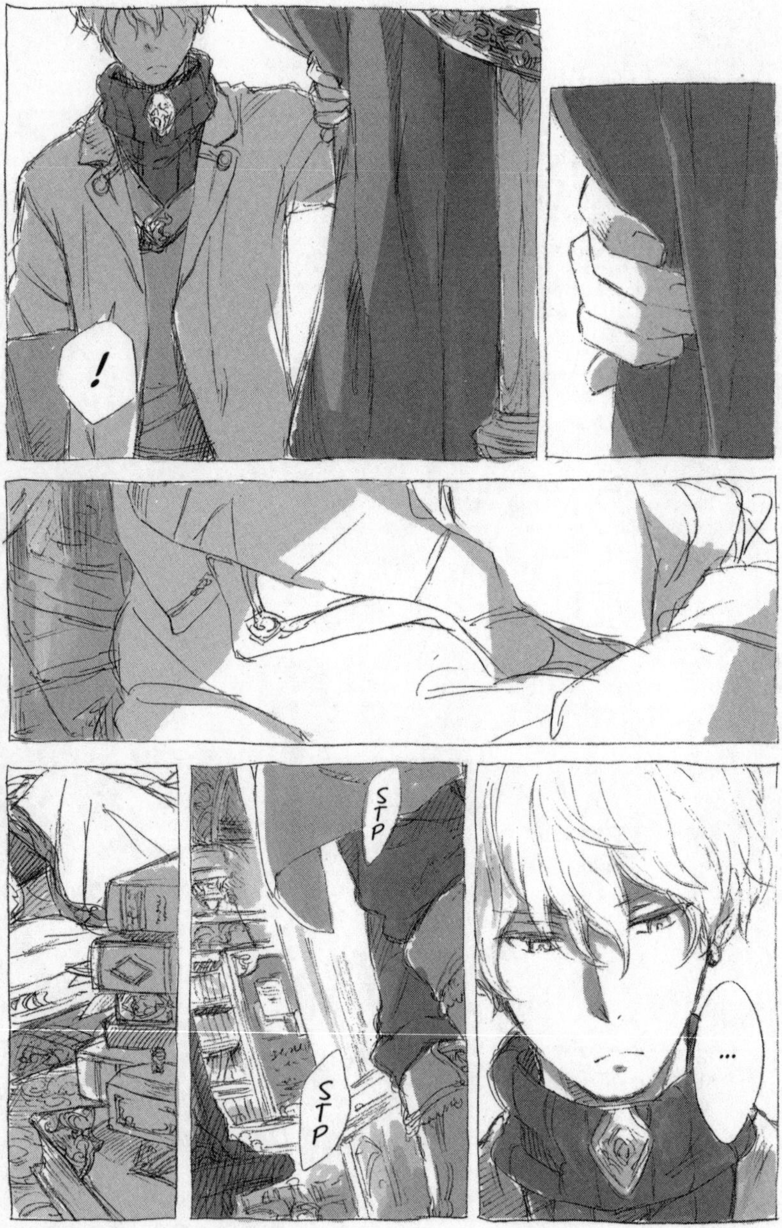
!
...
STP
STP

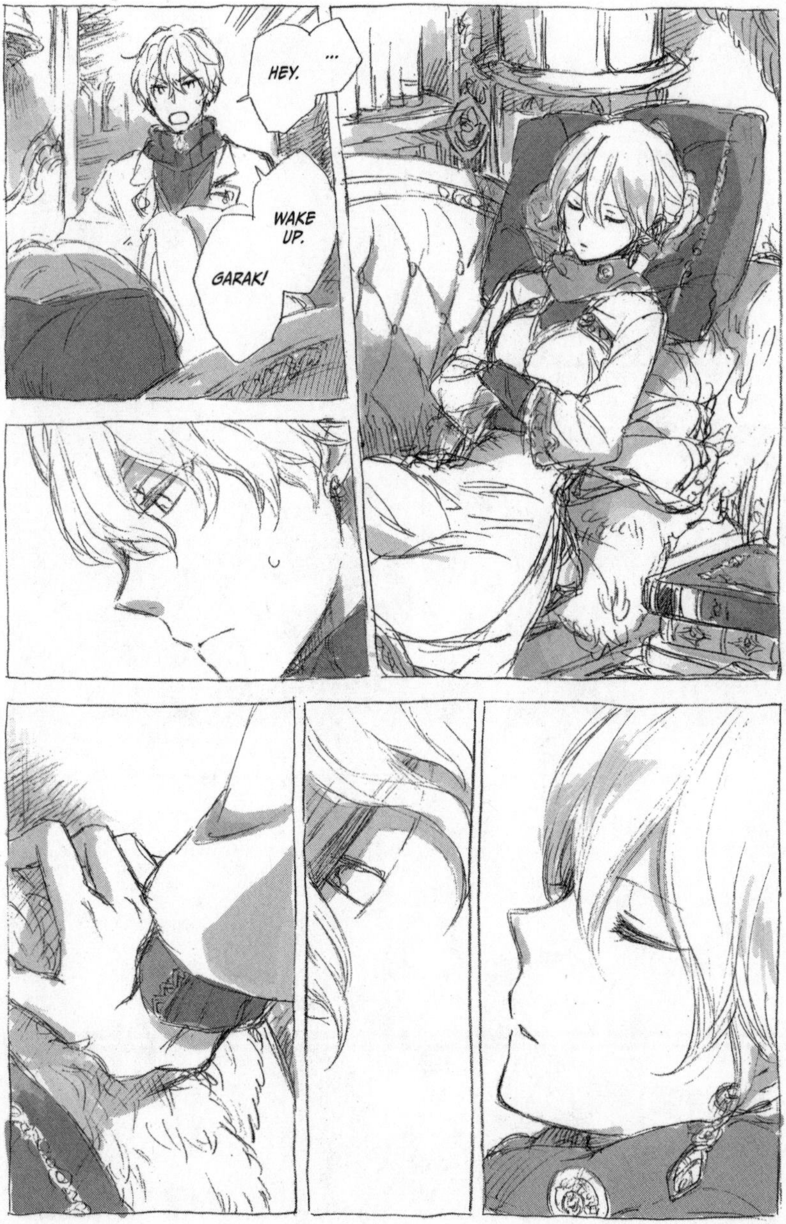

... HEY.
WAKE UP.
GARAK!

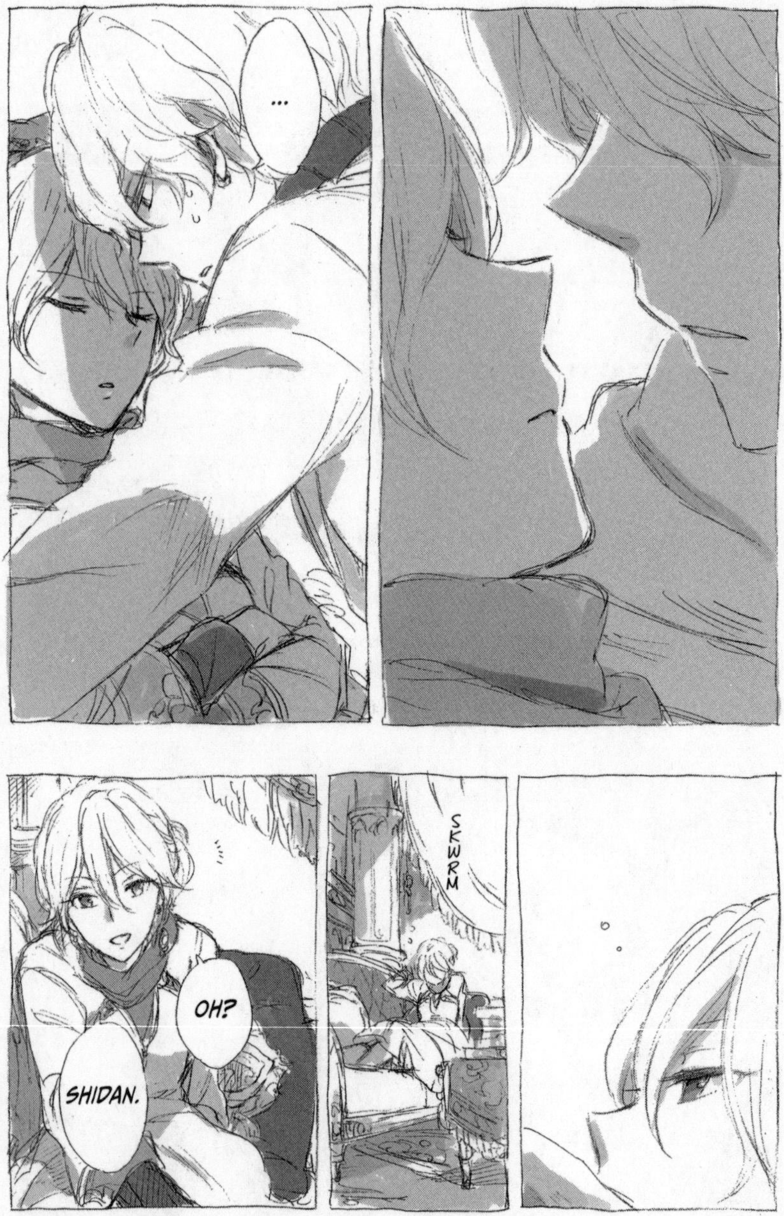
...
SKWRM
OH?
SHIDAN.

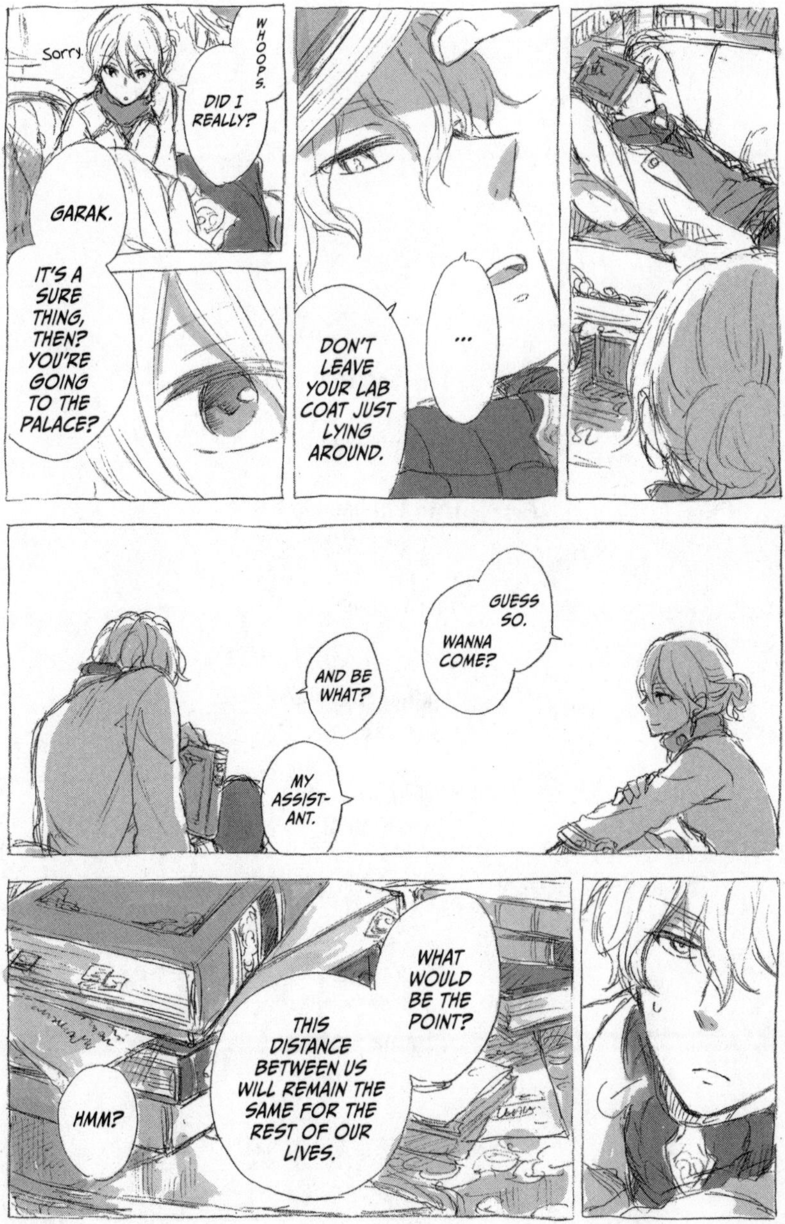
...
DON'T LEAVE YOUR LAB COAT JUST LYING AROUND.
WHOOPS. DID I REALLY?
Sorry.
GARAK.
IT'S A SURE THING, THEN? YOU'RE GOING TO THE PALACE?
GUESS SO. WANNA COME?
AND BE WHAT?
MY ASSIST-ANT.
WHAT WOULD BE THE POINT?
THIS DISTANCE BETWEEN US WILL REMAIN THE SAME FOR THE REST OF OUR LIVES.
HMM?

Big Thanks To:

-My editor

-The editorial staff at *LaLa*

-Yamashita-sama

-Everyone in Publishing/Sales

-Noro-sama

-My mother, big sister
and father

-Everyone who sends
in fan mail!

AND YOU!!

-Sorata Akiduki

Sorata Akiduki was born on March 21 and is an accomplished shojo manga author. She made her debut in January 2002 with a one-shot titled "Utopia." Her previous works include *Vahlia no Hanamuko* (Vahlia's Bridegroom), *Seishun Kouryakubon* (Youth Strategy Guide) and *Natsu Yasumi Zero Zero Nichime* (00 Days of Summer Vacation). *Snow White with the Red Hair* began serialization in August 2006 in *LaLa DX* in Japan and has since moved to *LaLa*.

Snow White
with the Red Hair

9

SHOJO BEAT EDITION

STORY AND ART BY
Sorata Akiduki

TRANSLATION **Caleb Cook**
TOUCH-UP ART & LETTERING **Brandon Bovia**
DESIGN **Francesca Truman**
EDITOR **Karla Clark**

Akagami no Shirayukihime by Sorata Akiduki
© Sorata Akiduki 2013
All rights reserved.
First published in Japan in 2013 by HAKUSENSHA, Inc., Tokyo.
English language translation rights arranged with HAKUSENSHA, Inc., Tokyo.

The stories, characters and incidents mentioned
in this publication are entirely fictional.

Published by VIZ Media, LLC
P.O. Box 77010
San Francisco, CA 94107

10 9 8 7 6 5 4 3 2 1
First printing, September 2020

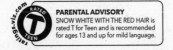

MEDIA
viz.com

shojobeat.com

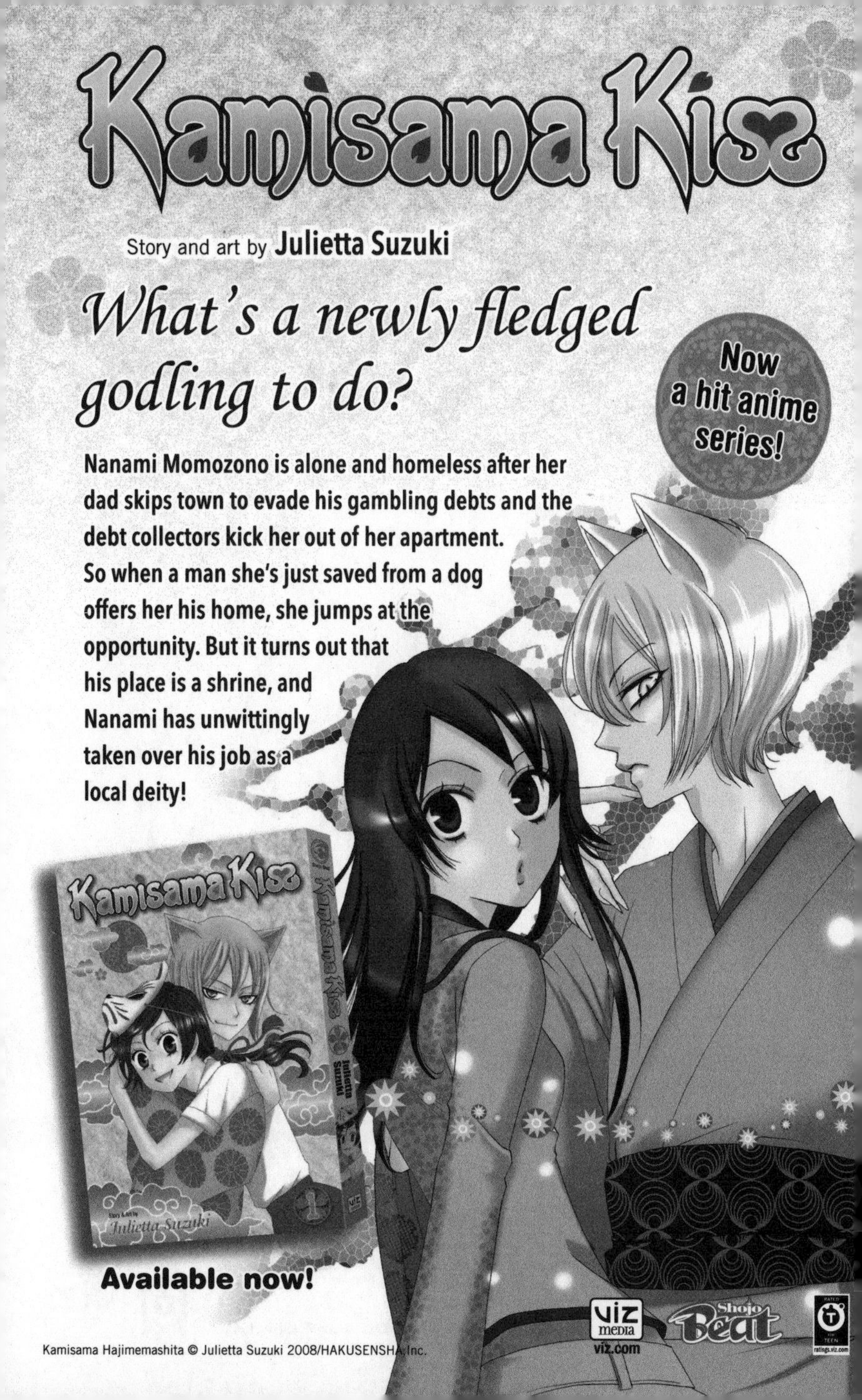
Kamisama Kiss
Story and art by Julietta Suzuki
What's a newly fledged godling to do?
Now a hit anime series!
Nanami Momozono is alone and homeless after her dad skips town to evade his gambling debts and the debt collectors kick her out of her apartment. So when a man she's just saved from a dog offers her his home, she jumps at the opportunity. But it turns out that his place is a shrine, and Nanami has unwittingly taken over his job as a local deity!
Kamisama Kiss
Story & Art by
Julietta Suzuki
Available now!
Kamisama Hajimemashita © Julietta Suzuki 2008/HAKUSENSHA, Inc.
viz media
viz.com
Shojo Beat

IDOL dreams

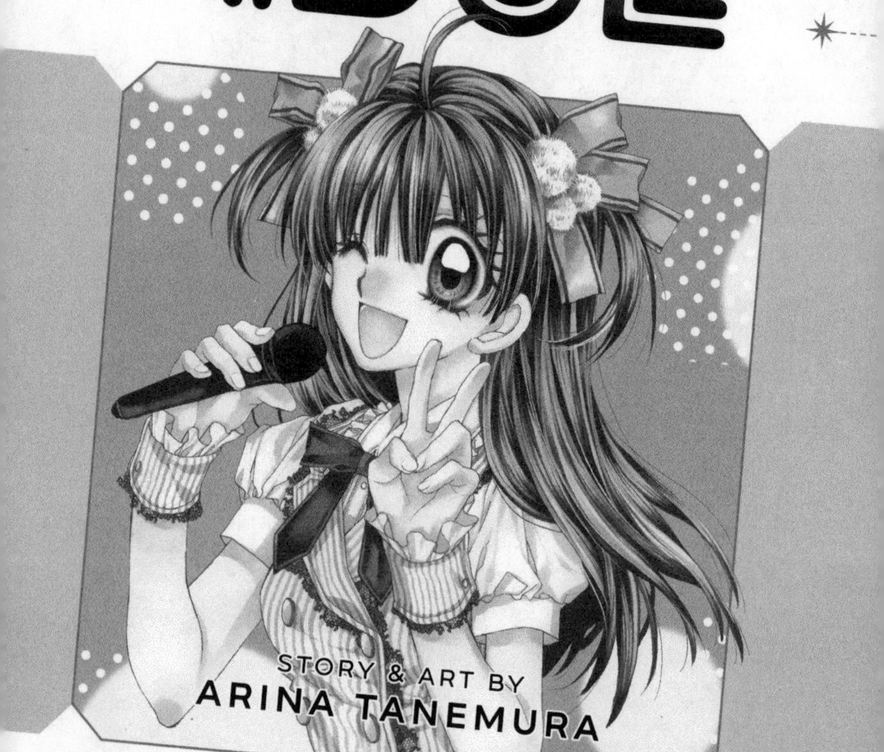

STORY & ART BY
ARINA TANEMURA

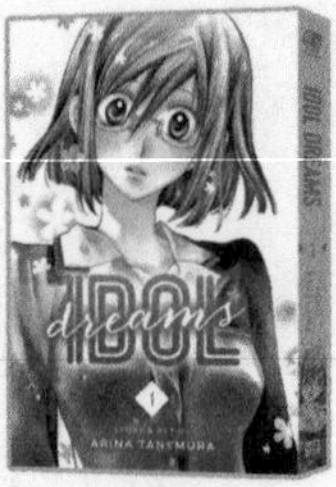
IDOL DREAMS
IDOL
dreams
1
ARINA TANEMURA

At age 31, office worker Chikage Deguchi feels she missed her chances at love and success. When word gets out that she's a virgin, Chikage is humiliated and wishes she could turn back time to when she was still young and popular. She takes an experimental drug that changes her appearance back to when she was 15. Now Chikage is determined to pursue everything she missed out on all those years ago—including becoming a star!

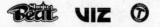

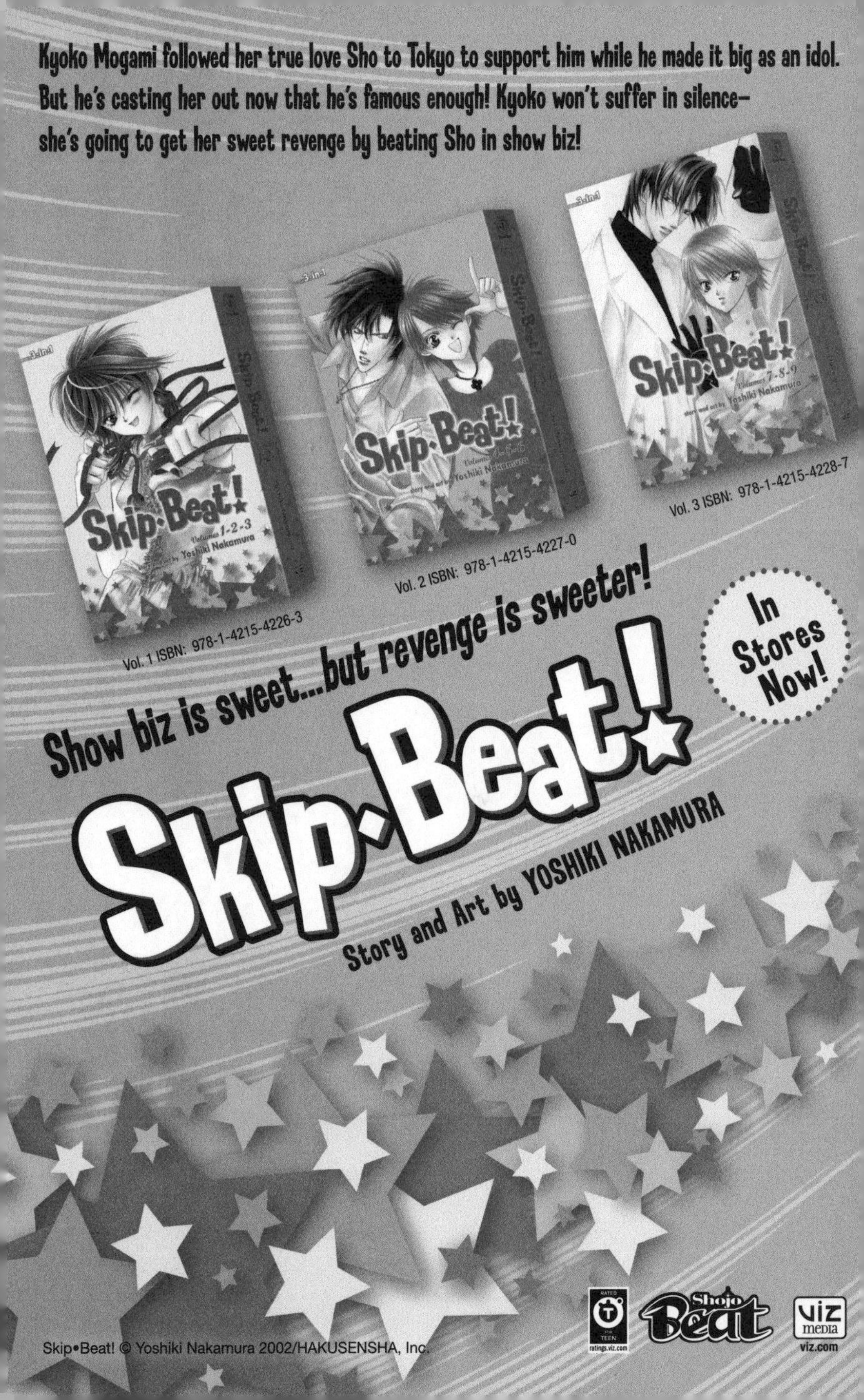
Kyoko Mogami followed her true love Sho to Tokyo to support him while he made it big as an idol. But he's casting her out now that he's famous enough! Kyoko won't suffer in silence—she's going to get her sweet revenge by beating Sho in show biz!
Skip·Beat!
Volumes 1-2-3
Yoshiki Nakamura
Vol. 1 ISBN: 978-1-4215-4226-3
Skip·Beat!
Vol. 2 ISBN: 978-1-4215-4227-0
Skip·Beat!
Volumes 7-8-9
Yoshiki Nakamura
Vol. 3 ISBN: 978-1-4215-4228-7
Show biz is sweet...but revenge is sweeter!
In Stores Now!
Skip·Beat!
Story and Art by YOSHIKI NAKAMURA
Skip•Beat! © Yoshiki Nakamura 2002/HAKUSENSHA, Inc.
RATED T FOR TEEN
ratings.viz.com
Shojo Beat
viz media
viz.com

YOU'RE READING THE WRONG WAY!

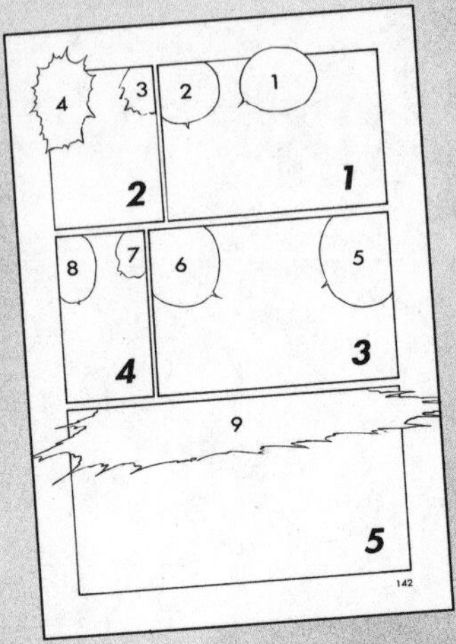

1
2
3
4
1
2
5
6
7
8
3
4
9
5
142

Snow White with the Red Hair reads from right to left, starting in the upper-right corner. Japanese is read from right to left, meaning that action, sound effects and word-balloon order are completely reversed from English order.

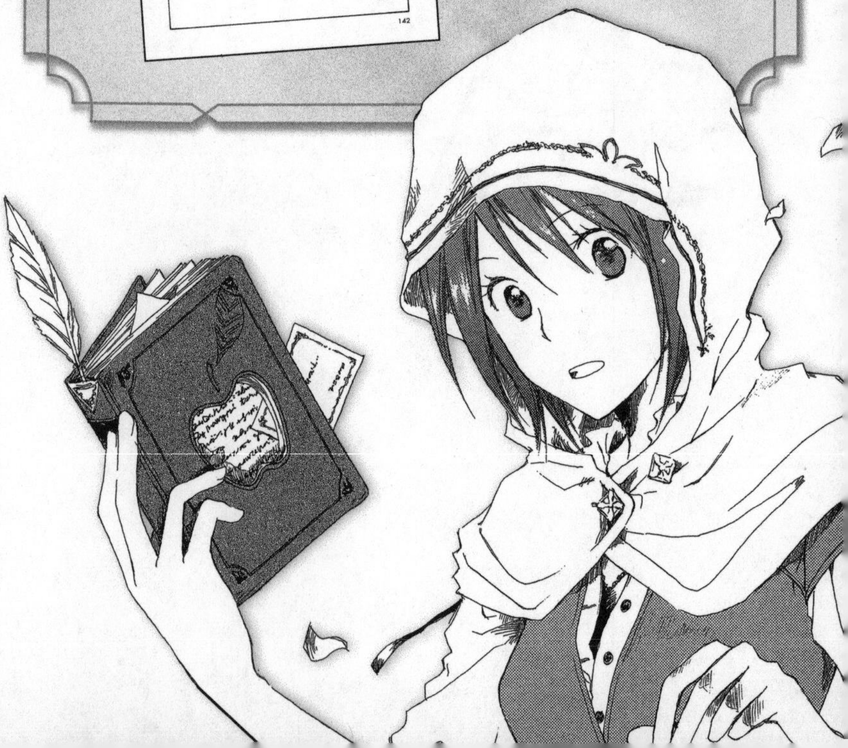